Spring, 2006

BAPTIST ROOTS

BAPTIST ROOTS

**A Reader in the Theology
of a Christian People**

Curtis W. Freeman
James Wm. McClendon, Jr.
C. Rosalee Velloso Ewell

Judson Press
Valley Forge

Baptist Roots: A Reader in the Theology of a Christian People
© 1999 by Judson Press, Valley Forge, PA 19482-0851
All rights reserved.

Bible quotations in the volume are from *The Holy Bible,* King James Version unless indicated otherwise.

Cover art: "Baptism in Big Stranger Creek" by John Steuart Curry. Used with permission of the Billy Graham Center Museum, Wheaton College, Wheaton, Illinois.

Library of Congress Cataloging-in-Publication Data

Freeman, Curtis W.
Baptist roots : a reader in the theology of a Christian people /
   Curtis W. Freeman, James Wm. McClendon, Jr., C. Rosalee Velloso
   da Silva.
      p.   cm.
   Includes bibliographical references and index.
   ISBN 0-8170-1281-8 (pbk. : alk. paper)
   1. Baptist – Doctrines – History – Sources.
I. McClendon, James William.   II. Velloso da Silva, C. Rosalee.
BX6331.2.B27   1999
230'.6'09 – DC21   98-54393

Printed in the U.S.A.
06   05   04   03   02
  6   5   4   3   2

Contents

Part Five
TO BE A RIGHTEOUS CHURCH
The Twentieth Century

Preface

This book grew out of an attempt to answer a single question. Do Baptists have a theological heritage? Puzzling over this quandary we turned for help to others who had studied the matter, rediscovering the marvelous collection *A Baptist Treasury* by Sydnor Stealey and the important volume *Shapers of Baptist Thought* by James Tull. We are indebted to both. Yet our students, who included women, people of color, and non-Westerners, reminded us what was missing from these earlier works. Part of our concern then became a broadening of the theological conversation so as to encourage the practice of listening to voices that have been ignored or marginalized. We also wanted to provide a sense of the significant theological activity of Baptists beyond North America as well as the connectedness with the larger free church tradition, described so well by Donald Durnbaugh in *The Believers' Church*. We have attempted to account for this wider vision by distinguishing Baptists as an extended denominational family from other baptists as spiritual and theological kindred.

We also wanted to make primary source material more available. William Brackney's *Baptist Life and Thought* and Leon McBeth's *A Sourcebook for Baptist Heritage* provide excellent resources for students of Baptist history. William Lumpkin's *Baptist Confessions of Faith* and Howard Loewen's *One Lord, One Church, One Hope, and One God* contain important confessional statements from Baptist and Mennonite communities. Our readings extend these anthologies with selections from theological texts. Two recent volumes guided our choice of materials: *Baptist Theologians*, edited by Timothy George and David Dockery, and *Essays in Anabaptist Theology*, edited by Wayne Pipkin. Without their efforts our task would have been considerably harder. As our volume of texts grew, an answer to our question began to emerge. Baptist theology is not in the first place an academic discipline that reduces faith to a set of ideas in order to make it intelligible. It is rather a particular standpoint from which to reflect on the convictions and practices that comprise the living out of the shared life in Christ. What must we do to be saved? Why don't we baptize babies? What is the path of spiritual growth? How do we preach the gospel, lift the fallen, welcome the stranger, stand for righteousness, or reach the nations? These texts remind us that the vital matters of faith for baptists are not necessarily dependent on the problems raised by skeptics in the eighteenth century, historians in the nineteenth century, or scientists in the twentieth century. The pressing theological task is both to think out and live out the faith by keeping alive the questions that pertain to the being and well-being of our common life.

We owe special gratitude to the librarians of the libraries at Houston Baptist University, Fuller Theological Seminary, and the Divinity School of Duke University, who assisted us in securing copies of books, articles, and unpublished manuscripts. Terry Larm undertook the tedious job of scanning the photocopied material and converting it to an electronic version for which we are most appreciative. We also want to thank our students at Houston Baptist University and Fuller Theological Seminary who read earlier versions of the book and helped us to see how to shape it so as to speak to their concerns and perspectives. Mike Broadway, Jay Givens, Barry Harvey, Jon Lemmond, Philip Thompson, and Murray Wagner offered helpful advice and criticism along the way. Even more are we grateful to the thinkers whose writings are in these pages. They worked out in the first place the material we have attempted to work with. We are especially thankful to Nancey Murphy, who first suggested the idea for this book, and to Sam Ewell and Debra Freeman, whose incentive enabled us to complete it. To the many others who encouraged us in this project and to the future generations who will be enriched by studying theology from the standpoint of the baptist vision we dedicate this collection.

CURTIS W. FREEMAN
JAMES WM. McCLENDON, JR.
C. ROSALEE VELLOSO EWELL

Introduction

Baptist Theology in the Third Millennium

The dawn of the new century — and the new millennium — is an exciting time for Baptist theology. Past generations of Baptists have faced obstacles not of their own choosing. For centuries their style of church life and their deepest religious convictions were forbidden by law, and even when, after the Enlightenment (which began in the early 1700s), these laws were gradually revoked — so that it became possible, for example, for Virginia Baptists to preach without risk of being jailed as punishment, or possible for British Baptists to earn degrees at Cambridge and Oxford, their own national universities — strong social pressures upon Baptists and other convinced Christians demanded conformity to the dominant society and its ways.

One good consequence of the new pluralism of common life in the West is that these pressures diminish. Baptists among others are freer than they were to ask themselves which aspects of the current social order deserve their participation and which do not. Furthermore, the end of five hundred years of European colonization around the globe, a withdrawal almost complete at this writing, has liberated all kinds of baptists (note the small *b* — a spelling we will sometimes use because not all those who side theologically with Baptists are called by that name, just as not all catholics are labeled Catholic) in these countries to enculturate their convictions within the various national host communities.

What Baptist (and more broadly, baptist) theology is to be in the millennium now dawning is still to appear. Baptists do not want to lose the treasured past. Likewise, as missionaries to the future, they do not mean to discard the new opportunities the times afford. The wise kingdom scribe brings out of the kingdom's storehouse things new and old (Matthew 13:52).

The Baptist Stream

Theology has always to look backward to its past as well as forward to its future. Surprising to some, Christian history, whether Baptist or

1

other, is not a straight line drawn from one agreed theological standpoint to the next (e.g., Paul to Augustine to Calvin to A. H. Strong). In
fact, Baptist thinking is a melange of data of mixed or unknown value,
so that an important part of the theologian's task is to discover the community's formative convictions before trying to interpret them and then
to restate them for the future. (An explanation of this threefold theological task appears in McClendon, *Ethics: Systematic Theology, Volume I*,
chap. 1.) The present editors have tried to find in every century representative theological writings that display well the main convictions of
baptist Christians in that century. In doing this, we have had to make a
theological selection, and serious readers must share our task by retriev-
ing what they will from the testimonies provided here. Doing this work
serves to make present baptist convictions intelligible and thus make future convictions in this heritage possible. Only as we see where we have
been do we see where we are going.

The discovery that the Christian gospel in history has never been
limited to one universal (or as some say, "catholic") community of followers, but has truly appeared in multiple branches or streams, may
distress even the open-minded adherent of any one such stream. Of these
several streams of Christian life, the baptist stream is only one. So the
question arises concerning this stream as it should for all the others:
Why pitch our tents alongside this particular stream of Christian life
and thought? What about the others? Various answers appear.

One common but defective solution to the variety of Christianities is
to see the various denominations or communions as so many branches
growing from a common trunk: call it the "tree" model of church history. This model has the advantage of reminding us of the biblical
"roots" of all Christian existence — a metaphor that we have deliberately retained in our title. Regrettably, though, this tree-and-branches
solution makes baptists at best latecomers (who can without severe exaggeration recall only six centuries or so of continuous history), and of
necessity it makes baptists seem mainly ignorers of church history and
deviants from its central stem. That is not a fair account of the way
baptist Christians actually think. The "tree" account also falsifies earliest Christianity, where (as Walter Bauer showed in 1934 in *Orthodoxy
and Heresy in Earliest Christianity* and James D. G. Dunn more recently
in *Unity and Diversity in the New Testament*) there were already multiple streams in place well before a Catholic dominance suppressed most
of the others. Still, some baptists have embraced the "tree" model. One
(Baptist) example (other denominations have their own "tree" versions
of Christian history) that has enjoyed some popularity is the "Trail of
Blood" history represented in this volume by the J. M. Carroll selection.

A better model than the tree is the streams or rivers model. From time
to time in Christian history, rivulets well up to the surface. Some of these

become great streams, and some flow together and flow on while others eventually dry up. On this view, all Christian history matters. We cannot deny that other streams, even those now run dry, were God-given servants in their generation and have instructive similarities to our own. As for the varied, living streams, some of them may someday converge in ways we cannot now foresee — a possibility that the "tree" model cannot display. In any case, this book explores one often-neglected theological current, that of the Baptists, who are in turn part of a wider stream that (following the custom of many scholars) we label baptist. Our task is to explore this wide stream and especially its Baptist component and to locate its course on the theological map of the kingdom of God.

This cautious way of putting matters will show our careful reader that we are well aware that others (including some other Baptists) do not see matters just as we do. The challenge from those to our right, who regard true Baptists as the only true Christians, has just been mentioned. At the opposite extreme, and equally inclined to disagree with us, are Christians who reject the role of any sort of organized Christianity. They believe that the kingdom of God or the church (terms they usually cannot define very clearly, but whose very vagueness sometimes works to their advantage in argument) is not usefully divided into branches or streams at all. "Away with all that," they say; "let us simply identify with all true Christians (or, in one version, truly religious folk), past, present, and future, without respect to labels of any sort."

Surely there is something right about this vague inclusiveness. We, too, acknowledge "evangelicals" or "believers" who follow Jesus without regard to name brands. Yet there is a difficulty in their viewpoint, for Christianity by its very nature involves morals and doctrine. Early Christians were called "the Way" even before they were called Christians, and Christian teaching began with the great Teacher himself. This being the case, conflicts about the way and disputes about the content of teaching will certainly arise. Broad labels such as "protestant," "catholic," and "baptist" have arisen to acknowledge these disagreements, and we favor using such distinguishing labels, without prejudice against those who reject all of them, until the need for such description is past. Narrower identifications have also been created. These "denominations" (literally, "names") have arisen to identify Christian groupings that associate for ministry or mission in particular times and in given ways, and these concrete groupings give us labels such as "American Baptist" or "Church of England" or "Roman Catholic." Here we are going to pay relatively little attention to these narrower labels (concretely, we are not going to invest energy in distinguishing English from Scottish Baptists, or in sorting out the significant differences between Disciples of Christ and Churches of Christ). We do mean to sort out baptist from catholic and protestant styles of Christian thought, even while insisting that these have more in common than what distinguishes them from one another. Our way of doing this will be to provide actual samples of baptist thought from fifteenth- and sixteenth-century beginnings in continuity to the present day.

One thing we do have in common with our challengers from both sides, those who insist theirs is the only Christian way and those who insist that the divisions we acknowledge are not worth the bother: we all agree that in the end Christian unity is the goal of God's biblical people. Where we disagree, perhaps, is in what is to be done in light of this goal. Those interested in the background theory behind our approach may want to read Anglican Bishop Stephen Sykes' *The Identity of Christianity*, where he points out that basic human thinking involves "essentially contested concepts," examples being concepts such as "justice," or "democracy," or (the case in point) "Christian identity" (Sykes, *The Identity of Christianity*, 251ff.; Sykes draws heavily on the work of philosopher W. B. Gallie). Until we acknowledge the contest over such essentials, our own thought and speech may be essentially confused! Application of this insight to (essentially contested) concepts such as "baptist" and "catholic" and "protestant" identity are found in a key article by present editor McClendon, writing with John Howard Yoder ("Christian Identity in Ecumenical Perspective"). Such discussions make clear that our standpoint in this book is only one side of a many-sided argument. We acknowledge this and ask that our opponents also acknowledge it.

The Baptist Vision

Baptists today do well to remember that the things that unite them with all Christians are often more important than the things that divide them. At times in the past, however, they lost sight of their connection to the other streams and began to think of themselves as just another branch or as only one — sometimes as the one only — denomination. Yet there were some who never lost sight of this connection. Petr Chelčický, Balthasar Hubmaier, Thomas Grantham, William Carey, Alexander Campbell, and Robert Walton (each with selections in this book) were among those who endeavored to keep the catholic vision in full view. They called for baptists to recognize the universal faith that unites all Christians from the days of the apostles to the present (diachronic catholicity) and which is shared in common by believers throughout the whole earth (synchronic catholicity).

In 1806 William Carey wrote a letter to Andrew Fuller, then the secretary of the Baptist Missionary Society:

> Would it not be possible to have a general association of all denominations of Christians, from the four quarters of the world? ...I earnestly recommend this plan...[and] have no doubt but it would be attended with very important effects; we could understand one another better, and more entirely enter into one another's views by two hours conversation than by two or three years of epistolary correspondence. (In McBeth, *The Baptist Heritage*, 518–19)

To some of the faithful back in England this was just "another of brother Carey's pleasant dreams," but his hope was guided by a catholic vision of the church. Yet as important as the catholicity of the faith was for baptists, they sought also to distinguish themselves from other Christians, their churches from other churches. From the fifteenth to the twentieth centuries, baptism, obedience, freedom, apostolicity, and righteousness have been divisive issues that distinguish the baptist vision of the church from other views. What is distinctive about Baptist (and more broadly, baptist) theology?

One way of answering this question is to search for distinguishing features of baptist theology in their *doctrines*. John Quincy Adams *(Baptists, The Only Thorough Reformers)* and Timothy George *(Baptist Theologians,* 13–25) are two exponents of the doctrinal distinctiveness approach. They suggest that what separates Baptists from all other Christians is displayed in their teachings. George and Adams call attention to the similarity of Baptist doctrines with Reformed theology on such themes as the authority of the Scriptures, the Trinity, the person and work of Christ, and the kingdom of God, but they maintain that Baptists carried forward the reform of the church, which the Reformation only began. We agree that doctrines are necessary because they declare what the church must teach in order to be a faithful and radically reforming church.

Another method seeks to capture Baptist distinctives in summarizing *principles* or self-evident *axioms*. Jeremiah B. Jeter (with presidents and professors from Crozer, Newton, Rochester, Southern, and Chicago seminaries) in *Baptist Principles Reset* and Francis Wayland (of Brown University) in *Notes on the Principles and Practices of Baptist Churches* represent the former and E. Y. Mullins (of Southern Seminary) in *The Axioms of Religion* exemplifies the latter. Here Baptist identity is thought to be expressed in the basic ideas to which they were committed: regenerate church membership, believers baptism, religious liberty, soul competency. No doubt these "ideas" witness to what Baptists hold important.

We recommend a different strategy of defining the baptist perspective by naming its identifying *marks*, or better, its characteristic *practices.* Among the practices of the believers church listed by Donald Durnbaugh are voluntary membership, covenant discipleship, Christian works, faithful admonition, benevolent giving, and biblical authority (*The Believers' Church,* 32–33). James McClendon notes the marks of the baptist vision as biblicism, mission, liberty, discipleship, and community (*Ethics,* 28). The attention to marks and practices has the advantage of not stating baptist distinctives in an implicitly superior fashion (i.e., we are the *most* "reformed" or *truly* "rational" church). One recent attempt to identify the distinctive practices of the baptist vision has been made in a document signed by all three present authors and other contemporary baptist theologians. The statement affirms Bible study in reading communities; following Jesus as a call to shared discipleship; free common life in Christ in gathered reforming communities; baptism, preaching, and the Lord's Table as powerful signs; and freedom as a distinct people under God. (See Freeman, "Can Baptist Theology Be Revisioned?" 273–310. The "Baptifesto," as it is affectionately called, appears on pp. 303–10 of Freeman's article.)

But can the distinctive perspective of baptists be stated still more simply? In his 1943 presidential address to the American Society of Church History, Harold Bender delivered his now classic account of "the Anabaptist vision." Bender's presentation was far from the "horse and buggy" image of Anabaptists that many still held. What was distinctive about the Anabaptists was that they envisioned Christianity as discipleship, the church as a brotherhood, and the Christian ethic as love and nonresistance (*The Anabaptist Vision,* 20).

As Bender suggests, this radical perspective is attained by converting, not merely convincing. Stated simply, it was "a way of seeing." McClendon has attempted to summarize the baptist vision yet more simply as a basic stance or hermeneutical perspective in which "the church now *is* the primitive church; *we* are Jesus' followers; the commands are addressed directly to *us*" (*Ethics,* 33). The baptist vision may be further defined as

> the way the Bible is read by those who (1) accept the plain sense of Scripture as its dominant sense and recognize their continuity with the story it tells, and who (2) acknowledge that finding the point of that story leads them to its application, and who also (3) see past and present and future linked by a "this is that" and "then is now" vision, a trope of mystical identity binding the story now to the story then, and the story then and now to God's future yet to come (McClendon, *Doctrine,* 45).

Perhaps this vision can be illustrated better than it can be stated. In 1787 William Carey addressed the Ministers Fraternal of the Northampton (England) Association. He asked those gathered to ponder "whether the command given the apostles to teach all nations was not binding on all succeeding ministers to the end of the world." Dr. John Ryland Sr., a hyper-Calvinist and respected Baptist leader, is reported to have called Carey an enthusiast and told him to sit down. Carey may have sat down, but he did not stop asking the question until he had convinced a group of fellow Baptists (including Andrew Fuller, John Sutcliff, John Ryland Jr., John Fawcett, and Robert Hall Jr.) that the Great Commission was addressed directly to *them*. They were Jesus' disciples. This is that. Then is now. In 1792 the baptist vision launched a modern missionary effort that sent Carey as its first missionary to India. The same year Carey published his classic missionary tract, *An Enquiry into the Obligation of Christians to Use Means for the Conversion of the Heathen,* which presented the question to a wider audience.

This hermeneutical stance was shared by Anabaptists who came to believe that in the Sermon on the Mount Jesus spoke directly to them; by Anne Hutchinson who knew that God addressed her in Scripture by immediate revelation; by Nat Turner who followed God's word to "slay utterly old and young, both maids, and little children, and women"; by William Bishop Johnson who connected the forty years after emancipation with the forty years of wilderness wandering and God's scourge of Israel with the suffering of the Negro people. The hermeneutical perspective of the baptist vision is not just a set of ideas or doctrines. It is a way of living: God's people with an open Bible, ready to follow. Yet the practices that enact this vision require doctrines to teach believers how to live them out and from time to time demand ideas to display and defend them. Above all else, the baptist vision and its practices must be focused on its central exemplar, Jesus the Christ. Thus, some "performances" of it are more faithful than others. So focused, this perspective most simply defines the distinctive standpoint of baptist theology.

The Baptist Voice(s)

Carol Gilligan describes how young women wanting to "make it" in society learn to be silent. Yet she observes that their empowerment comes only by the recovery of speech (*In a Different Voice.*) In her study of torture, Elaine Scarry has shown that totalitarian regimes do not seek "information" but instead attempt to dismantle "selves" through the destruction of language. The antidote to pain is speech (*The Body in Pain*). Rebecca Chopp has provided a biblical and theological account whereby women may be brought to speech in a world that has devalued and effaced them (*The Power to Speak*). What these very different books share is the insight that speech is a decisive and political act. Those who speak are empowered, and those who have no voice are disenfranchised and marginalized. If this is so, who may speak about God (*theo-logia*)?

A standard answer is that any Christian may speak of God. In the baptist understanding of the church, all believers are priests and so may pray for others, comfort the afflicted, or proclaim the gospel. But when it comes to speaking about God, this conviction has too often lacked a practice to sustain it. Baptist theology would appear (at least by some accounts) to be the exclusive privilege of Anglo men in North America. We hope to show that such an account is only possible when other baptist voices have been silenced, distorted, or ignored. Baptists, not being immune from the ideological biases or cultural assumptions of the societies in which they live, have been witting (and unwitting) participants in the marginalization of women, people of color, and non-Westerners. Even the language of Zion has sometimes been turned to the advantage of the dominant culture by endorsing its reigning assumptions: "Let your women keep silence in the churches" (1 Corinthians 14:34); "Servants, be subject to your masters with all fear" (1 Peter 2:18). Other voices in the baptist family, repeatedly silenced, persistently demand to be brought to speech along with the dominant and traditional ones lest distinctions of ethnicity, class, and gender continue to belie the oneness that Christ established (Galatians 3:28). As the conventional patterns of certitude, privilege, and power engendered by modernity are now coming to an end, it becomes possible to look differently at the past, raise new questions, and allow other voices to speak.

As we began to search for writings from those on the margins, we were happily surprised by what we found. In every century there were important voices who as yet have not received a wide hearing: theological writings from women, African Americans, and Christians from the postcolonial two-thirds world which have been largely ignored or suppressed by the wider baptist community. Their perspective, which Bonhoeffer called a "view from below," is essential in the practice of faithful and vital theological reflection. Alongside such familiar names as John Smyth, Isaac Backus, John Dagg, and Augustus Strong appear unfamiliar ones like Hannah Corbin, Rufus Perry, Helen Montgomery, and Osadolor Imasogie. By including representative selections from these little-known writings with the better-known ones, our hope is to invite a rich and robust conversation. How might such a discussion commence? A model from the baptist heritage is instructive.

For sixteenth-century baptist groups there was no Vincentian Canon to define what they had believed "in all times" and "in all places" and therefore to rule which voices were true and which were false. The direction of the gospel and the leading of the Spirit were discerned within communal conversation. These baptists (and many later Baptists too) practiced their polity, not according to Robert's Rules, but the Rule of Christ (Matthew 18:15–20) and the Rule of Paul (1 Corinthians 14:26–29). The first describes a process aimed toward discipleship and reconciliation. The second guides conversational practice in the power of the Spirit. Everyone has the opportunity to speak, not based on some vague egalitarian or democratic principles, but because everyone has been gifted and therefore has something to bring to the conversation.

John Howard Yoder calls this conversational practice "the hermeneutics of peoplehood" (*The Priestly Kingdom*, 28–34). Yoder outlines the procedure for an orderly but open (and no doubt lively) conversation that contains prophetic, didactic, historical, and political voices. Each is to be heard and weighed, and none is to be silenced or privileged. In this process the Spirit moves the conversation in the direction of the gospel. Such a practice allows for diversity while seeking unity. It encourages dissent but desires consensus. It does not permit one voice to silence the speech of others or to ventriloquize them by making them speak words not of their own uttering. Its goal is to display the mind of Christ and to speak the common language of the Spirit.

Our critics may worry that such a discussion would quickly devolve into the strife of interests: one more multicultural cacophony, a theological Babel. To be sure, bringing voices from the margins to speech could prove critical or even subversive because they may call into question the prevailing consensus and established orders of theological discourse — conservative, moderate, and liberal. Speech is a radical and counter-cultural force. But some readers may wonder if our deliberate inclusion of *other* voices is not at the expense of those that previous generations have already recognized as significant. We simply ask those who raise this point to consider that the fifty selections in this book (surely of some numerological significance — Jubilee? Pentecost?) include previously excluded voices without neglecting already acknowledged ones. Other critics may suggest that our selections do not incorporate enough of the broader baptist vision. To this charge we plead guilty, and we solicit their help in bringing these voices to speech as well. Still others may doubt whether, in the crisis occasioned by the modern-becoming-postmodern world, baptist theology can be revisioned so as to be still faithful to its heritage, responsive to the present issues, and prepared for future developments. We are hopeful that by listening to baptist voices other than our own, the vision can be revisioned. Our aim is to practice a hermeneutics of peoplehood that reaches out to *all* people, especially to those at the margins, without privileging any voice from the outset. And if the Spirit is in our conversation, it is yet possible that from the many voices there will emerge, not a Babel, but a symphony, a theological Pentecost.

In organizing the selections by centuries and themes within each century, we have attempted to let the polyphonic sounds come forth without forcing them into a contrived harmony. Readers may wonder on what basis these fifty voices were chosen. Our plan was to include baptists who were no longer living (or whose life work was complete) and who had made a lasting contribution to theology in or since their day. We propose these readings as representative with no claim that they are exhaustive. Finally, some may ask "Has our theology changed?" (see Basden, ed., *Has Our Theology Changed?*). That is surely one of the questions that the following chapters set out to clarify. Part of the difficulty in answering it is determining who is signified by the "our" in the question. It is easier to detect change when fewer voices are included in the conversation. All living things change: trees send out new branches, and rivers cut new courses. Readers are invited to stand with us on Jordan's stormy banks, where we cast a wistful eye — to the waters of that glad river whose tide flows on to the throne of God and to the Lamb.

Part One

TO BE A BAPTIZING CHURCH

The Fifteenth and Sixteenth Centuries

Introduction

The Fifteenth and Sixteenth Centuries

Contrary to what many school children in recent generations have been taught, the Middle Ages were richly productive times in European history. Besides the amazing artwork represented in present-day museums of fine art and the magnificent cathedrals and other public buildings on European city skylines, this period saw the birth of modern commerce and politics, the rise of what we know as science, and (most important for present purposes) produced theological riches that today still guide the faith of hundreds of millions of Christians worldwide. This is not to say that all this was good or desirable; from the standpoint of the theologians whose work is collected in this book, much of that theology was not. Yet today's baptist theologians must not carelessly trash medieval culture, for in doing so they may desecrate the unmarked graves of their own spiritual ancestors. To show that this is so is the task of Part One.

Particularly toward the end of the Middle Ages, particularly among the rising middle class who had a freedom for reflection and travel their ancestors had not had, and particularly in the cities, where commerce flourished and ideas fermented, new kinds of Christianity began to appear. (Church authorities of the time called this ferment not Christianity but heresy, and persecuted it vociferously and violently.) Nevertheless, awakened by the Renaissance recovery of their own European past — Rome and Greece with their art and literature — and stirred by spiritual hungers that the received traditional religion no longer satisfied, these restless European Christians began movements that developed into new communions. Those who followed the signals that came from Wittenberg or Geneva became today's Protestants — a word whose root meaning was not "I reject" but rather "I affirm." These believers affirmed a continuing bond to church and state but called forth a new loyalty to Scripture, to preaching, and to individual, personal faith. In response to this Protestant revolt, the old church's Catholics did indeed urgently set out to reform the church, and in a great ecumenical Council at Trent (1545–63), its bishops clarified its doctrine and set the shape of modern Roman Catholic faith and life.

Yet numerous fifteenth- and sixteenth-century Christians were dissatisfied with both the magisterial (that is, government-approved) Protestants and the tradition-bound (and likewise government-approved) Roman Catholic religious structures. These left-out Christians were the baptists, whose communities have in recent times been called free church or believers church, and who are characterized by historians as radical or left-wing reformers. In their own day, these Christians were excoriated as "Anabaptists," because in their attempt to find a faith that was lived out as well as thought out, most of them administered baptism only to the converted, thereby rejecting (or as their critics said, illegitimately "repeating") the infant baptism that had become standard in Christendom. This recovery of "believers baptism" was the most visible feature of the radicals as well as one of their convinced practices, yet their movement involved much else. Like Catholicism it sought a single, universal Christianity in solidarity with the ancient apostles. Like Protestantism it emphasized Scripture and individual response to the gospel by each believer. Unlike either it usually found itself unable to secure the support of the local prince; more often, it refused to seek it, since such "principalities and powers" of government were bound up with the world's evil. Thus, there emerged in the fifteenth and sixteenth centuries a kind of Christianity rarely seen since the fourth. The radicals rarely or never constituted themselves a state church like the Catholic churches of southern Europe or the new Protestant state churches of northern Europe.

What, then, was their theology — or had they any theology? They often seemed to have none, at least in the ordinary sense. For one thing, many baptists had no quarrel with the received Catholic theology where it agreed with Scripture, as much of it did, so they seemed to have nothing theological to say. Most baptists, for example, embraced a trinitarian doctrine of God and all made faith in Christ central in their doctrine of salvation. They wrote hymns to educate believers in the narrative content of this received Christian faith (some of these pedagogical hymns' words are available in the German-language *Ausbund,* the old, still printed, Swiss baptist hymn collection, others in other sources). Although they were neither Catholics or Protestants (a point their Catholic and Protestant persecutors accepted, even emphasized), baptists as a class did not deny the historic Christian creeds. Admittedly some took up positions on disputed issues (e.g., the Lord's Supper) that brought further persecution upon them. Yet such disputes were common in medieval Europe and were the hallmark of contemporary Protestants as well. The real distinctive of baptist theology was that it came not from university theologians or subtle disputants in monasteries but from the everyday needs of members. It was first-order theology, the theology that churches had to teach in order to function as churches, rather than second-order theology of the hair-splitting sort universities sponsored. Much baptist theology was therefore overlooked or dismissed as not really theology. In our own day considerable work has been done to correct this mistake, showing that the radicals produced genuine theology, but that was not recognized for centuries by Catholic or Protestant scholars.

From the sixteenth century until today, self-styled orthodox religious historians, whether Catholic or Protestant, sought to discount their baptist fellow Christians as damnable heretics. In many cases, these condemnations of the "Anabaptists" are preserved in confessions of faith not corrected even today by the communions that created them. In addition, Heinrich Bullinger (1504–75), the successor of Zwingli in Zurich, wrote a defamatory account of the ("Anabaptist") Swiss Brethren, who had diverged from Zwingli's reformation. Sadly, Bullinger's historical distortions became the model for church historians down to the present. "Anabaptists" were defamed (even the name their opponents gave them was defamatory by baptist lights); they were held to be dangerous to society, their neighbors, and one another; their deep convictions were twisted and denied. This defamation was then taken for granted as standard fare in Christian church history lectures to the present, including lectures given in some baptist seminaries, long after the controversies that had produced these slurs were otherwise forgotten.

Again and again these historical errors were corrected by competent scholars: by Gottfried Arnold in 1699; again by the scientific church historians of nineteenth-century Netherlands and Germany; still again in the United States in the twentieth century by Baptist historian A. H. Newman and later by Mennonite historian Harold Bender. Yet there is still corrective work to do, as shown by the lively pages of current journals (see, for example, *Mennonite Quarterly Review*). In the past quarter-century a sociologically oriented school of sixteenth-century historians has discovered, for example, that there were tighter links between the Anabaptists and the Peasants' Revolt than was previously believed, and thus that not all Anabaptists were committed to nonviolence. It was also discovered that not all their number sprang from the same roots in Zurich, Switzerland: Anabaptists, these new revisionists found, had arisen in a "polygenesis" rather than a "monogenesis," to use their technical terms. A useful selection of current research is found in H. Wayne Pipkin's *Essays in Anabaptist Theology;* C. Arnold Snyder provides an up-to-date overall history of the period in *Anabaptist History and Theology;* while a brief resumé of recent historical work is Walter Klaassen's article, "Anabaptism," in *Mennonite Encyclopedia* (vol. 5). In general, today's scholarship has once again corrected the old misconceptions created by Bullinger and company. Yet these corrections are still neglected by many Christian scholars, and one of the purposes of the present volume is to present the fifteenth- and sixteenth-century radicals as they were, rather than as they have been caricatured.

We think the best way to do this is to show what these baptists wrote, and in the selections that follow in Part One readers can sample representative excerpts. Our selection of theologians may not satisfy everyone, but we believe it is a good start. Once again, recall that these fifteenth- and sixteenth-century writers were first-order theologians, many of them martyrs, who were shaping baptist teaching by what they did, rather than second-order critics or gossamer academic theorists. Consequently, looking at their work gives some sense of actual church life among the radicals.

So far little has been said about the radical Christians of still earlier centuries. It seems suitable to say less here, for some earlier reforming radicals, such as scholarly priest John Wyclif (c. 1328–84) and his Lollard followers who set out to reconstruct British church life along New Testament lines, or even earlier, rich Lyonnaise merchant Peter Valdes or Waldo (c. 1140–c. 1218), who with his Waldensian followers applied the standards of poverty and discipleship not just to members of monastic orders but to themselves and all Christians, are fairly well recognized in church history. In any case, their writings are not included in this volume. Yet it seemed needful to provide a token of these earlier manifestations of baptist-style Christian life, so we have chosen a paraphrased (rather than strictly translated) selection from Czech theologian and church leader Petr Chelčický, a representative of the movement in Bohemia that stemmed from John Hus (c. 1373–1415) and the variety of reform movements that sprang up in Hus's wake. If we do not provide still more selections from these earlier reformers before the Reformation, it is not because we think their thought irrelevant but because they are so numerous and so varied as to require a separate volume.

In this book's introduction we singled out some of the distinctives of this enduring theological movement — elements that identify this Christian strand by distinguishing it from other strands. Most or all of these baptist distinctives can be found in one or another of the writings in this present chapter. Without repeating these distinctives, we point out some further, special features of these late medieval and renaissance baptist theologians, ways in which they differ from the radicals who preceded and followed them. One difference is that all our fifteenth- and sixteenth-century witnesses lived and died in continental Europe. Though we know that some went farther in their missionary work, the surviving theological documents reflect those who remained within the borders of "Christendom," and not all of Christendom: British radicals in these centuries, for example, have left few documentary traces.

The other noteworthy feature of this period is its concentration on costly martyrdom. The union of church and state both north and south meant that it was everywhere — not least in sturdy Switzerland, which in later centuries so prided itself on its peoples' freedom — illegal to practice Christian faith as a baptist. Consequently, those who bore open witness to their faith were repeatedly hauled into court, imprisoned, fined, and in many cases put to death, perhaps by burning at the stake. One early document, the Schleitheim agreement of 1527, is so conscious of this constant danger that it makes provision for succession in leadership whenever one of the shepherds is removed by the powers that be. As Balthasar Hubmaier would say, recognizing that most of the truth-bearers were destined to die soon, *Die Wahrheit ist untödlich:* "nevertheless, they can't kill the truth."

– 1 –

Petr Chelčický

As noted above, the Christian reformer John Hus of Bohemia, now the Czech Republic, led Catholic Christianity in his region to undergo extensive changes. Historian Franklin Littell thinks it appropriate to date the modern believers church idea from Hussite beginnings (cited in Durnbaugh, The Believers' Church). This "beginning" is worthy of note, yet it is important to see that the baptist movement had no founder in the sense that John Wesley was the founder of Methodism or Martin Luther was the founder of the German evangelical movement we call Lutheranism. Instead, there were at different times and places remarkably similar yet independent attempts to realize afresh the Christian idea and to practice obedience to Jesus. Among martyr John Hus's numerous successors many groups were determined to compel their own version of Christian faith in Bohemia by force of arms. Others, however, sought a more clearly biblical way of restoring primitive Christianity. Among these one leader eventually emerged, Petr Chelčický (1390?–1460?). Born in rural Bohemia, Chelčický (pronounced something like Hell´chitsky), though lacking formal education, debated other leaders in Prague, arguing that Christians could not achieve reform by warfare. In time he returned to his namesake village, still preaching the law of love, a free church, the abolition of class distinctions — all on New Testament grounds. The community he gathered is thus for baptists a more important precedent than Hus's own heroic reform, even though Chelčický did not rediscover believers baptism. His best-known theological work, The Net of Faith (c. 1440), is here described and paraphrased from the Czech original by historian Murray Wagner. As Wagner writes, Chelčický's overriding conviction is that "true Christians [must] withdraw from the world not to fuse into mystic union with the Godhead but to form a concrete community made historically visible as the faithful seek perfection in the imitation of Christ" (Petr Chelčický, p. 147). In other words, faithful Christians were to stand together in a faithful church. In this conviction, the radical reformation as we know it today had begun.

The Net of Faith

The text is the sermon for the Fifth Sunday after Trinity. Luke 5:1–11: the call of the disciples. Christ's command to Peter to cast his net into the deep, followed by the catch of a great shoal of fish, gave Chelčický the biblical metaphor for his treatise. The net of faith is the law of God, bound together in the faithfulness of those believers loyal to the disciplined life of the early church. Out of the sea of the world, the net hauls in God's elect. But the net has taken in more than ordinary fish. Its binding in the law of God has been ripped through by two huge predators, the pope and the emperor....

The two vicious intruders have thrashed around in the net, venting hostility toward God's ordinances. The net of faith is now so mangled that there remain only the barely visible shreds of the apostles' original net, the primitive church. Not only have the two killer whales twisted and torn the net beyond recognition, they have spawned a vicious school of "factions" that have "claimed for themselves pagan and secular rule, holding to it with all their strength because each wants to rule."

The argument that dominates the entire work is Chelčický's sectarian insistence on total separation of ecclesiastical order and civil functions. The first part of the book, comprising two-thirds of the writing, expounds the same doctrinal themes of separatist Christianity that determine all of [his] previous writings. In *Net of Faith,* however, Chelčický came closest to a comprehensive, though by no means systematic, statement of his religious beliefs. The extensive treatment gives each of separatist Christianity's most distinctive testimonies a proportionate amount of consideration as fundamental elements in a whole confession. The work also represents the reflections of a mature thinker who develops the consistent convictions of an entire lifetime. The second part of the book turns to Chelčický's acerbic prose in attacks upon the secular and ecclesiastical power groups, which in his judgment were given illegitimate birth by the "whoremongering" of pope and emperor.

Chelčický devoted a major portion of the first part to his understanding of the apostolic community. He appealed to an ideal pattern of faith and order: namely, that of the primitive church, of those who gathered as voluntary confessors and who lived the faith without state privilege and protection. The true church was a persecuted, despised, and rejected fellowship of suffering. The secular powers, always dead unto God's commandments and impervious to the wisdom of the cross, spilled the blood of the innocent for the 320 years prior to Constantine's ascension to power. Chelčický was certain that all who would be true Christians will always be reviled, rebuked, and despised by those who seek an earthly kingdom. The world will always be scandalized by the folly of the cross. He repeated his denial of credibility to the medieval church's claim that since the conversion of Emperor Constantine, the church and state had been joined in divine harmony. The scholastics had admitted that Christians were indeed persecuted during an age when pagan rulers were hostile to the church, but argued that once the whole of society took the name Christian, then the church should become the willing and faithful partner of the state and embrace its order. Chelčický's retort was again a categorical refutation of the Constantinian premise. The ritual baptism of a Roman emperor could not possibly transform the world into *corpus christianum*. The world will remain the world and no power on earth can make it Christian. It is a depraved and decadent order, forever corrupted by the urge to kill and to revel in the flesh. The true church in pursuit of perfection can have no formal liaison with the profane without polluting its life. Petr was sure that Christians who enjoy the world's favor and privilege have necessarily abandoned the law of God.

While Chelčický repeated his utter lack of confidence in human progress, he held high hope for new life within the fellowship of believers. The church must be a community of saints whose members, though imperfect, still strive to duplicate in their lives what they confess to be true in the example of Christ. Such aspirations cannot be compromised by a world that lusts after power and dominion. If the law of love is to be fulfilled, Christians must be of an entirely different order. Only then can the faithful begin to realize what is evident from the witness of the early church:... "the apostles introduced in these people an equality so that they might not be indebted to each other, only that they love one another, serving one another as a body of many members works together with Christ as the head."

Christians living in such fellowship, acting in love, not out of coercion, have no need of public "executioners, jurymen, neither judges and princes with pagan offices" to enforce church discipline.... "According to the ordinances of Christ, the wicked shall not be coerced in any way, neither shall any kind of vengeance be practiced against them, but they shall be improved only through brotherly good [will] and be led to penitence." Those members of the fellowship who lapse from the rule of love must never be returned to discipline by magisterial coercion. Disciplinary action shall be taken by the fellowship itself through measures "far removed from the pagan and secular ordinances."

Chelčický's assertion that the church and the world are of separate orders and live by two distinct rules of conduct constantly tempted him to divide reality into good and evil. His philosophical disposition was to deny any ontological principle that would unite the profane world of matter and the sacred life of the spirit. Chelčický, however, did not leave the world beyond the pale of God's providence.... He resolved the question only by suggesting that whatever the fate of Cain's generation, it is God's affair alone. Only God knows why he has chosen to exclude the reprobate from the congregation of the elect. Nonetheless, Chelčický held to the notion that the fallen are not to be abandoned to their own devices. In his exposition of Romans 13, Chelčický conceded that God ordained the authority of the magistrates to restrain the outrages of the world and set it under threat of the sword. The secular state, despite its paganism, serves God's purposes by punishing the sins of society so that temporal life can survive with some semblance of order. Toward what end it survives is not at all apparent to him. He sought to avoid the dualist's *faux pas* by insisting that secular rulers have no power in and of themselves. He declared that there could be no authority, neither good nor evil, which rules of its own volition, for there can be no force that God does not will and empower.

Though Chelčický affirmed that God has appointed the secular sword to hold secular sinners in check, he declared that instruments of coercion must be wielded by sinners, not by Christians. The truly obedient Christian must abstain from public "offices and administration that are in such opposition to his King [Christ] and his people." While the masters of Prague and the prelates of *corpus christianum* assume that "among Christians, the best Christian would have to be the king," unaware that true Christians would never venture "to commit things so contrary to Christ," it was inconceivable to Chelčický that a true Christian could render the services required of a secular ruler. He recognized that magistrates and princes cannot rule without recourse to violence. Suppression and murder are simply the inevitable affairs of secular rulers. The very definition of public offices makes the idea of Christian royalty impossible. There is no way a king can turn his people to God's love. He cannot improve upon the wicked; he can only hang them. The only way a king can bring souls to repentance is to resign the office, become a priest, and preach the gospel that converts without coercion.

Chelčický then turned to argue the case for a secular authority that is unimpeded by religious sanctions. He contended that the wisdom of the gospel is so much in contradiction to the requirements of secular power that its practical application would completely ruin the function of public officers. If the civil authorities were bound to the law of love in administering justice, the thievery and murder of the world would run rampant. To Chelčický, it was impossible to believe that secular society should be regulated by Christian discipline. Secular authorities must employ coercion, threat, and punishment to fulfill the responsibilities of their office. Though the true church is obliged to forswear ultimate allegiance to the state and to refuse public service to a world that remains without the hope of ever being Christianized, Christians are nonetheless subject to secular authority.

As the early church rendered obedience unto Caesar, so too must the faithful of all ages be subordinate to the magistrates. Petr argued that since Christians live under the civil government's sphere of influence, enjoying the benefits of homes, property, and other material advantages, they must consider it their duty to regard its rule with due respect and pay their taxes. He tried to assure the faithful that such compliance will not compromise good conscience. His advice was a cautious warning not to give the authorities a pretext for persecuting the church. True Christians will suffer enough harassment without foolishly provoking unnecessary penalties. As a people separate from the world, leading peculiar lives under allegiance to another Lord, Christians will always be hated by the heathen. Therefore, the faithful must take care not to incite deliberately the wrath of the princes and the powers.

Obedience to secular power has definite limits. In matters contrary to the law of God, the Christian is obliged to refuse obedience to the magistrate's order. In such case, the faithful must willingly suffer whatever penalties the state imposes. Directives such as those to wield the sword, to swear an oath, or to enter a public court to settle a dispute, must be disobeyed in the spirit of nonresistance. Chelčický admitted that few have ever been able to summon the courage to passively resist the authorities. Such is not the way of the frivolous and the foolish. Again Petr flayed away at the hypocrisy of imperial Christianity. The ancient church, whose Roman bishops from Peter to Sylvester suffered persecution and even death at the hands of secular officials, was no longer the ideal of official Christendom. At the Council of Basel, Palomar of Barcelona [had] scoffed at the primitive church as a fellowship of the "stupid and the gloomy." Chelčický wrote that apostolic Christianity "stinks to the Roman Church like an abominable heresy." Now popes who claim apostolic succession ... parade through the streets of Rome to the amazement of the world. Children cry "Papa, papa! What is that? Look, the emperor has saddled a horse and put up the priest and is riding around the city with him."

Chelčický reiterated his charge that the papal alliance with emperors whose predecessors persecuted the early church had "opened the wound for all the blood that has been spilt among Christians to this day, as well as all that which will be spilt until the end of time." The church's fourth-century baptism of the social order joined ecclesiastical discipline with civil law, mixing into the faith ordinances that were originally pagan, "and Christians confused these deviances with discipleship." The corruption has been extended and expanded by every generation until today "we, the latest ones to be sitting under the shadow of these laws, only faintly speak of divine laws and ordinances, for the darkness of these laws has veiled our eyes."

The amalgamation of the two orders has made possible the conspiring and plotting of two "fat and gluttonous Baals," namely, the secular nobility and the priestly orders. They represent the church of imperial Christianity at its worst. "These two Baals together devour the land and drink the bloody sweat of the third estate, who then drenched with sweat must satisfy the gluttony of the two Baals." Their betrayal of the faith and their contempt for the people aroused Chelčický's angry attack on the vanity of the nobility and the indolence of the clergy in part two of *Net of Faith*. . . .

Chelčický saw his time foreshadowed by the Apocalypse, the world controlled by the hosts of Antichrist; and he named them legion: the nobility, the new class of urbanites, the monastic orders, the university masters, and the parish priests. Though they were divided into factions feuding among themselves, they were, nonetheless, allied in their hostility toward Christ and his elect. They had invaded and seized all corners of the earth, controlling all offices of both church and state, holding all fortresses, castles, cities, cloisters, and parishes. Christ and his elect were everywhere excluded. His law of love was so violated and his gospel so suppressed that it could be no less than miraculous when someone escaped the satanic grip of Christendom. Yet there were those who resisted Antichrist and his hordes. They made up the true church that Chelčický described in the final chapters of *Net of Faith*. . . . "The Holy Spirit makes this communion or fellowship among the saints, that is, the union of the members with each other and to Christ's spiritual body. . . . "

Apparent from the outset of Chelčický's commentaries on church and society is an ecclesiology that holds in paradox several diverse, even contradictory notions of the church. By logical definition, an exclusivist polity of a disciplined minority based on a separatist understanding of the primitive church stands in contradiction to Wyclif's doctrine of magisterial inclusivism as expressed in a pragmatic ecclesiology of Christian dominion. Theoretically, the classic definition of the church as the invisible congregation of the elect precludes the positive identity of either the chosen or the reprobate by any finite standard. Yet, for the ideological and practical purposes of national reformations in England and Bohemia, Wyclif's ecclesiology objectified the invisible church in a visible political community. Church and commonwealth, religion and realm were one and the same and thus Constantinian in character. . . .

Chelčický issued a protest against every attempt to reconcile the ideal of the church with the reality of the world. He could only recognize the radical contradictions between Christ and Antichrist, divine law and human law, the church and the state — all of which becomes a crisis of conscience for Christians obligated by the conflicting loyalties of heaven and earth. Chelčický's definition of Christian life has its point of reference in a transcendent order of the spirit set in a sectarian form of revelational positivism that resides beyond material corruptions.

Certainly, such rarefied notions remain pure abstractions unless they are converted into an empirical reality. Unless it is to remain a simple ideology of immaterialism, the spiritual fellowship must be attributed with some form of corporeality. At this turn in his thought, Chelčický reified the invisible congregation of the elect as a separatist community modeled on his primitive myth of the apostolic church. The idea became flesh neither in clerical offices nor in territorial commonwealths but in a historical fellowship of believers who gather to duplicate what they understand of the New Testament church in a highly visible life of discipleship.

While Wyclif's idea of the invisible congregation of the elect took form in a nationalist expression of church polity in both England and Bohemia, Chelčický's use of the same concept served his notion of separatist Christianity. He succeeded in logically combining the Augustinian doctrine of the invisible church mediated through Wyclif's theological realism with the concept of the church as a voluntary association of believers. Never under the influence of any pre-Enlightenment notion of free decisions by liberated individuals, Petr simply assumed that the true church would make its elect visible by calling its membership into a fellowship of restituted apostolic Christianity.

[Reprinted by permission of Herald Press, Scottdale, Pennsylvania, from *Petr Chelčický: A Radical Separatist in Hussite Bohemia* by Murray L. Wagner.]

– 2 –

Conrad Grebel

The label "Anabaptist," as we have seen, was a term of contempt applied to continental reforming Christians. It was also applied, again disparagingly, to English Christians who would call themselves Baptist. In every case "Anabaptist" was an epithet, an emotive label of reproach equivalent to today's "sect" or "cult." The fault imputed to both the Continental radicals and the English Baptists was the same: when they administered baptism to confessing, converted believers, they were illicitly repeating (Greek ana, *again) the proper church-and-state rite that had long admitted European infants to civil society and to Christ's church. This repetition was a crime punishable by death in the Holy Roman Empire; in any case it was considered a blasphemous practice that had to be stamped out. Today scholars use "Anabaptist," without prejudice, of any sixteenth-century Christians who practiced believers baptism rather than infant baptism. (Some present-day Christians also apply this old epithet to themselves to affirm their continuity with the sixteenth-century radicals; others prefer other terms.) In the historian's sense, though, the word first refers to those sixteenth-century Christians who called themselves (Swiss) Brethren. The converted scholar,* bon vivant, *and humanist who led this little band of Bible readers to initiate a radical baptist movement was Conrad Grebel (c. 1498–1526). In a tense but awesome Zurich prayer meeting in 1525, he had initiated the baptisms that marked its beginning. Arrested, imprisoned, escaped, and laboring as an evangelist in the Swiss mountains, Grebel succumbed to the plague. The present letter, speaking for these Brethren, was drafted by Grebel and addressed to Thomas Münzer, a radical closer to the Lutheran reformers. It displays the intense and lively mood of the Zurich movement. (Readers will note that numbers 1, 8, and 12 were not indicated in Grebel's original text.) Characteristically, it also shows itself willing to be corrected by others who want to go to the root of the matters it addresses (see Matthew 18:15ff., often called the Rule of Christ). For further study of Grebel and the early Swiss radical movement, see Leland Harder,* The Sources of Swiss Anabaptism.

Letter from Conrad Grebel to Thomas Münzer

> May peace, grace, and mercy from God, our Father,
> and Jesus Christ, our Lord, be with us all. Amen.

Dear Brother Thomas:

For God's sake do not marvel that we address thee without title, and request thee like a brother to communicate with us by writing, and that we have ventured, unasked and unknown to thee, to open up intercourse between us. God's Son, Jesus Christ, who offers himself as the one master and head of all who would be saved, and bids us be brethren by the one common word given to all brethren and believers, has moved us and compelled us to make friendship and brotherhood and to bring the following points to thy attention. Thy writing of two tracts on Fictitious Faith *[von dem erdichten glauben]* has also caused us to do so. Therefore we ask that thou wilt take it kindly for the sake of Christ our Savior. If God wills, it shall serve and work to our good. Amen.

Just as our forebears fell away from the true God and the knowledge of Jesus Christ and of the right faith in him, and from the one true, common, divine word, from the divine institutions, from Christian love and life, and lived without God's law and gospel in human, useless, un-Christian customs and ceremonies, and expected to attain salvation therein, yet fell far short of it, as the evangelical preachers have declared, and to some extent are still declaring; so today, too, every man wants to be saved by superficial faith, without fruits of faith, without baptism of test and probation, without love and hope, without right Christian practices, and wants to persist in all the old fashion of personal vices, and in the common ritualistic and anti-Christian customs of baptism and of the Lord's Supper, in disrespect for the divine word and in respect for the word of the pope and of the anti-papal preachers, which yet is not equal to the divine word nor in harmony with it. In respecting persons and in manifold seduction there is grosser and more pernicious error now than ever has been since the beginning of the world. In the same error we, too, lingered as long as we heard and read only the evangelical preachers who are to blame for all this, in punishment for our sins. But after we took the Scriptures in hand, too, and consulted it on many points, we have been instructed somewhat and have discovered the great and hurtful error of the shepherds, of ours too, namely, that we do not daily beseech God earnestly with constant groaning to be brought out of this destruction of all godly life and out of human abominations, and to attain to true faith and divine institutions. The cause of all this is the [policy of] false caution, the hiding of the divine word, and the mixing of it with the human. Aye, we say it harms all and frustrates all things divine. There is no need of specifying and reciting.

While we were marking and deploring these facts, thy book against false faith and baptism was brought to us, and we were more fully informed and confirmed, and it rejoiced us wonderfully that we found one who was of the same Christian mind with us and dared to show the evangelical preachers their lack, how that in all the chief points they are acting with a false caution and set their own opinions, and even those of anti-Christ, above God and against God, as befits not the ambassadors of God to act and preach. Therefore we beg and admonish thee as a brother by the name, the power, the word, the spirit, and the salvation, which has come to all Christians through Jesus Christ our Master and Savior, that thou wilt take earnest heed to preach only the divine word without fear, to set up and guard only divine institutions, to esteem as good and right only what may be found in pure and clear Scripture, to reject, hate, and curse all devices, words, customs, and opinions of men, including thine own.

We understand and have seen that thou hast translated the mass into German and hast introduced new German hymns. That cannot be well, for we find nothing taught in the New Testament about singing, no example of it. Paul scolds the learned Corinthians more than he praises them, because they mumbled in meeting as if they sang, just as the Jews and the Italians chant their words song-fashion. Secondly, since singing in Latin grew up without divine instruction and apostolic example and custom, without producing good or edifying, it will still less edify in German and will create a faith consisting in mere outward seeming. Thirdly, Paul even clearly forbids singing in Ephesians 5 and Colossians 3, since he says and teaches that they are to speak to one another and teach one another with psalms and spiritual songs, and if anyone would sing, he should sing and give thanks in his heart. Fourthly, whatever we are not taught by clear passages or examples must be regarded as forbidden, just as if it were written: "This do not; sing not." Fifthly, Christ in the Old and especially in the New Testament bids his messengers simply proclaim the word. Paul, too, says that the word of Christ profits us, not the song. Whoever sings poorly gets vexation by it; whoever can sing well gets conceit. Sixthly, we must not follow our notions; we must add nothing to the word and take nothing from it. Seventhly, if you want to abolish the mass, it must not be done by supplanting it with German singing, which perhaps is thy device, or comes from Luther. It must be rooted up by the word and command of Christ. 9. For it is not planted by God. 10. The supper of fellowship Christ did institute and plant. 11. The words found in Matthew 26, Mark 14, Luke 22, and 1 Corinthians 11 alone are to be used, no more, no less. [12.] He who serves [as leader] from among the church shall pronounce them from one of the evangelists or from Paul. 13. They are the words of the instituted meal of fellowship, not words of consecration. 14. Ordinary bread shall be used, without idols and additions. 15. For [the latter] creates an external reverence and veneration of the bread, and a turning away from the internal. An ordinary drinking-vessel, too, shall be used. 16. This would do away with the adoration and bring true understanding and appreciation of the Supper, since the bread is naught but bread, by faith the body of Christ and the becoming one body with Christ and the brethren; only it must be eaten and drunk in spirit and love, as John shows in chapter 6 and the other passages, Paul in 1 Corinthians 10 and 11, and as is clearly learned in Acts 2. 17. Although it is simply bread, yet if faith and brotherly love precede it, it is to be received with joy, since, when it is used in the church, it is to show us that we are truly one bread and one body, and that we are and wish to be true brethren with one another, etc. 18. But if one is found who will not live the brotherly life, he eats unto condemnation, since he eats it without discerning, like any other meal, and dishonors love, which is the inner bond, and the bread, which is the outer bond. 19. Since also it does not call to his mind Christ's body and blood of the covenant of the cross, so that for the sake of Christ and the brethren, of the head and the members, he may be willing to live and suffer. 20. Neither is it to be ministered by thee [i.e., ritually, as in the mass]. That was the beginning of the mass — that only a few partook. Whereas the Supper is an expression of fellowship, not a mass and sacrament. Therefore none is to receive it alone, neither on his deathbed nor otherwise. Neither is the bread to be locked away, etc., for the use of a single person, since no one shall take for himself alone the bread that belongs to those in fellowship; unless he is out of fellowship with himself, and no one is so, etc. 21. Neither is it to be used in temples according to all Scripture and example, since that creates a false reverence. 22. It is to be used much and often. 23. It is not to be used without the rule of Christ in Matthew 18; otherwise it is not the Lord's Supper; for without that rule every man will run after the externals; the inner matter, love, will be passed by, if brethren and false brethren approach or eat it. 24. If ever thou wouldst serve it, we wish it would be done without priestly garment and vestment of the mass, without singing, without addition. 25. As for the time, we know that Christ gave it to the apostles at the Supper and that the Corinthians had the same usage. We fix no definite time with us, etc.

[Let this suffice], since thou art much better instructed about the Lord's Supper, and we only state things as we understand them. If we are not in the right, teach us better, and do thou drop singing and the mass [or chanted liturgies], and act in all things only according to the word, and bring forth and establish by the word the usages of the apostles. If that cannot be done, it would be better if all things remained in Latin and without changing and accommodating. If the right cannot be established, then neither do thou minister according to a usage of thine own or the priestly usage of the Anti-Christ, and at least teach how it ought to be, as Christ does in John 6, and teaches how we are to eat and drink his flesh and blood, and has no regard for the apostasy and the anti-Christian caution, of which the most learned and foremost evangelical preachers have made a regular idol and have propagated it in all the world. It is much more desirable that a few be rightly taught through the word of God, believing and walking aright in virtues and customs, than that many believe falsely and hypocritically through adulterated doctrine. Though we admonish and beseech thee, we are in hopes that thou wilt do it of thine own accord; and we admonish the more willingly, because thou hast so kindly listened to our brother and confessed that thou too hast given way too much, and because thou and Carlstadt are esteemed by us the purest proclaimers and preachers of the purest word of God; and if you two rebuke, and justly, those who mingle the words and customs of men with those of God, you must by rights cut yourselves loose and be completely purged of the benefices of the priesthood and all new and ancient customs, and of your own and ancient notions. If your benefices, as with us, are supported by interest and tithes, which are both true usury, and if you do not get your support from an entire church, we beg that you will give up your benefices. Ye know well how a shepherd should be supported.

We have good hopes of Jacob Strauss and a few others, who are little esteemed by the slothful scholars and doctors at Wittenberg. We, too, are thus rejected by our learned shepherds. All men follow them, because they preach a sinful sweet Christ, and they lack clear discernment, as thou hast set forth in thy tracts, which have taught and strengthened beyond measure us who are poor in spirit. And so we are in harmony in all points, except that we have learned with sorrow that thou hast set up tablets, for which we find no text nor example in the New Testament. In the Old it [the Law] was to be written outwardly, but now in the New it is to be written on the fleshly tablets of the heart, as the comparison of both Testaments proves, as we are taught by Paul, 2 Corinthians 3, Jeremiah 31, Hebrews 8, Ezekiel 36. Unless we are mistaken, which we do not think and believe, do thou abolish the tablets again. The matter has grown out of thine own notions, a futile expense [of effort?], which will increase and become quite idolatrous, and spread into all the world, just as happened with the idolatrous images. It would also create the idea that something external always had to stand and be set up in place of the idols, whereby the unlearned might learn, while in fact only the external word is to be so used according to all example and commandment of Scripture, as is declared especially, 1 Corinthians 14 and Colossians 3. It is true that this learning from the one Word might in time lag, [the connection is not clear] but even if it [the setting up of the tablets] would never do any harm, yet I would never want to invent and

set up anything new and to follow and imitate the slothful and mislead-
ing scholars with their false caution, and from my own opinion invent,
teach, and establish a single thing.

Go forward with the word and establish a Christian church with the
help of Christ and his rule, as we find it instituted in Matthew 18 and
applied in the epistles. Use determination and common prayer and decision according to faith and love, without command or compulsion, then
God will help thee and thy little flock to all sincerity, and the singing and
the tablets will cease. There is more than enough of wisdom and counsel
in the Scripture, how all classes and all men may be taught, governed,
instructed, and turned to piety. Whoever will not amend and believe, but
resists the word and doings of God and thus persists, such a man, after
Christ and his word and rule have been declared to him and he has been
admonished in the presence of the three witnesses and the church, such
a man, we say, taught by God's word, shall not be killed, but regarded
as a heathen and publican and let alone.

Moreover, the gospel and its adherents are not to be protected by
the sword, nor are they thus to protect themselves, which, as we learn
from our brother, is thy opinion and practice. True Christian believers
are sheep among wolves, sheep for the slaughter; they must be baptized
in anguish and affliction, tribulation, persecution, suffering, and death;
they must be tried with fire, and must reach the fatherland of eternal
rest, not by killing their bodily, but by mortifying their spiritual enemies. Neither do they use worldly sword or war, since all killing has
ceased with them; unless, indeed, we are still of the old law; and even
there (much as we consider it) war was a misfortune after they had once
conquered the Promised Land. [Neither the text nor the meaning of the
last sentence is quite certain.] No more of this.

On the matter of baptism thy book pleases us well, and we desire to
be further instructed by thee. We understand that even an adult person
is not to be baptized without Christ's rule of binding and loosing. The
Scripture describes baptism thus, that it signifies the washing away of
sins by faith and the blood of Christ (to him that is baptized, changes
his mind and believes before and after it); that it signifies that a man
is dead and ought to be dead to sin and walks in newness of life and
spirit, and that he shall certainly be saved if by the inner baptism he
lives his faith according to this significance; so that the water does not
confirm or increase faith, as the scholars at Wittenberg say, and how
it gives very great comfort and is the final refuge on the deathbed. Also
that it does not save, as Augustine, Tertullian, Theophylact, and Cyprian
have taught, dishonoring faith and the suffering of Christ in the case of
the old and adult, and dishonoring the suffering of Christ in the case
of the unbaptized infants. We hold according to the following passages,
Genesis 8, Deuteronomy 1, 30, 31, and 1 Corinthians 14, Wisdom 12,

1 Peter 2, Romans 1, 2, 7, 10, Matthew 18, 19, Mark 9, 10, Luke 18, etc., that all children who have not yet come to discernment of the knowledge of good and evil, and have not yet eaten of the tree of knowledge, that they are surely saved by the suffering of Christ the new Adam, who has restored their vitiated life, because they would have been subject to death and condemnation only if Christ had not suffered, but have not yet grown up to the infirmity of our broken nature, unless, indeed, it can be proved that Christ did not suffer for the children. But as to the objection that faith is demanded of all who are to be saved, we exclude children from this and hold that they are saved without faith, and we do not believe from the above passages [that children must be baptized], and we conclude from the description of baptism and from the accounts of it (according to which no child was baptized), also from the above passages (which alone apply to the question of children, and all other Scriptures do not refer to children) that infant baptism is a senseless, blasphemous abomination, contrary to all Scripture, contrary even to the papacy; since we find that for many years after the apostolic times believers and unbelievers were baptized together by Cyprian and Augustine, for six hundred years, etc. Since thou knowest this ten times better and hast published thy protests against infant baptism, we hope that thou art not acting against the eternal word, wisdom, and commandment of God, according to which only believers are to be baptized, and art not baptizing children. If thou or Carlstadt will not write sufficiently against infant baptism with all that applies, as to how and why we should baptize, etc., I (Conrad Grebel) will try my hand....

Whatever we have not understood correctly, inform and instruct us.

[September 5, 1524]

["Letter to Thomas Münzer by Conrad Grebel," trans. Walter Rauschenbusch, *The American Journal of Theology* 9 (1905): 91–99.]

– 3 –

Balthasar Hubmaier

More than most of the Anabaptists, Balthasar Hubmaier (c. 1480–1528) was highly educated and richly equipped with the debating skills that medieval universities prized. Born in Friedberg near Augsburg, Germany, he studied for the priesthood and eventually earned a doctorate at Ingolstadt — he was the only Anabaptist leader so equipped. His doktorvater, *mentor John Eck, was later the great opponent of Luther. After his baptist conversion, Hubmaier's churchly ministry was undergirded by a deep sense of the sacraments of medieval Christianity, and especially of baptism, the Lord's Supper, and confession — each of which he sought to reshape into powerful signs of Christian life within the radical movement. The debate, with several participating, reported here took place in August 1525, in the Basel home of theologian Oecolampadius (1482–1531), who sided with Zwingli's magisterial Reformation. Hubmaier had by this time become a major actor in the swirling baptist revolution. On the eve of Easter, 1525, he with sixty of his congregants had been baptized in his Waldshut parish church. In the course of the Easter week that followed, "Hubmaier led Waldshut to a more thoroughgoing reform than had been realized anywhere in Europe," write Pipkin and Yoder in the book from which the present extract is taken (p. 81). He provided a restructuring of baptismal and eucharistic practice, each when possible validated by the civil authorities — a validation the Zurich Anabaptists had at first wished for but having been denied it had then renounced. Though he attempted civil discussion of his standpoint (such as the present dialogue), soon after this debate Hubmaier was put to flight by Catholics and then by Protestants; he was imprisoned in Protestant Zurich, passed as a refugee through Constance and Augsburg, found for a time a safe haven in Nikolsburg, Moravia, but was eventually summoned by state and church authorities to Hapsburg Catholic Vienna, examined, and burned at the stake (March 10, 1528) for his refusal to retract his convictions. His wife, for her like loyalty, was drowned in the Danube.*

32

On Infant Baptism against Oecolampad

Oecolampad: Let us begin in the name of the Lord. The rebaptizers have boasted here and there as to how in the recent dialogue between us held in the parsonage at Saint Martin at Basel, they were honorably victorious and silenced us. Therefore I want to point out in writing what both sides at that time presented so that their glory is further praised and proclaimed, and so that everybody may see of what kind of spirit these skillful fellows are, and where they are hurting.

Balthasar: It is quite right, my Oecolampad, that you now want to bring forth the rebaptizers into the light. However, do such with bright and clear Scripture, or you will truly come to shame in the matter, however scholarly you are. For truth is immortal. It can be overcome neither through the respect of persons, nor with high-blown rhetoric or flowery speech, although it can be spoken in all simplicity by Balaam's donkey, Tobith's dog, or David's mule.

Oecolampad: What I have said, preached, and written I would henceforth also do and prayerfully command others also to do, for your teaching is a wholly new fantasy, begun here and elsewhere in the past two years. Therefore it is suspect.

Balthasar: I beseech you for the sake of God, my Oecolampad, let these devious arguments be stuck under the bench and deal with clear Scripture. For you know that the teaching of Christ always suffered this blow on the cheeks, i.e., that it was called a new teaching, Mark 1:27. And to Paul it was said: "What does this slanderer want? He is a proclaimer of new devils. May we also learn what kind of new teaching it is which is preached by you. You put new teaching in our ears," Acts 17:18. We have not invented it, but Christ has thus commanded it, and the apostles practiced it. Therefore we have wanted to present ourselves against you and everyone before the judgment chair of Holy Scripture. If we are right in this and other articles, why are we beaten? If, however, we are not wrong, then give witness with the Scripture concerning the evil and then punish us afterward in life and limb.

Oecolampad: If this teaching is tested it will be found that it is directly against true love.

Balthasar: If in the testing of the Scriptures it is found that water baptism was instituted for the instructed and believers and not for cradle babies, then it is the truth. But Paul writes that love rejoices in the truth, 1 Cor. 13:6. How now is truth against love? But you speak perhaps of worldly love, which cannot suffer the divine truth, for its works are evil. Therefore it hates the light, John 3:20.

Oecolampad: It is also disgraceful to the Christian community that we should have erred so long.

Balthasar: That is a light-headed argument. The godless also make it. It is certainly necessary that you defend yourself, that you have drawn this straw-sword with which, if it were sharp, the papists would have stabbed you to death long ago.

Oecolampad: This teaching, however, is directed toward separation and sectarianism, which cannot be of the Spirit of God.

Balthasar: Are you amazed? Christ himself is a sign that will be spoken against, Luke 2:34. He sent a sword and not peace, Matt. 10:34. Five in a house will be contentious, the father against the son and the son against the father, the mother against the daughter and the daughter against the mother, Luke 12:52f. Oh, that is a blessed sectarianism and separation, says Chrysostom. And if Paul had been well pleasing to the world he would not have been a servant of Christ, Gal. 1:10. However, that the truth gives birth to rebellion is not its fault but the fault of our wickedness, as the murderer Herod, not the newborn Christ, was guilty of the grim murder of the innocent children.

Oecolampad: Tell me, who has thus taught till now, or when has one kept such a custom?

Balthasar: Christ so taught us when he instituted water baptism in the church, Matt. 28:19; Mark 16:16. And the apostles have written and practiced thus, 1 Pet. 3:21; Heb. 6:2; 10:22; Acts 2:38; 8:12, 37f.; 9:18; 10:47–48; 11:16; 16:15, 33; 18:8; 19:5; 22:16. Examine the Scripture rightly, then you will explicitly find that in seven years no argument has come into the way that is more clearly expressed than that Christ instituted his water baptism for believers and not for unknowing children.

Oecolampad: I know enough of the histories that children's baptism has never been forbidden from the time of the apostles until now.

Balthasar: But it was before the time of the apostles. Search the Scripture, says Christ, not the histories.

Oecolampad: It has also been the custom of the mothers in the church to baptize children.

Balthasar: Yes, of the papist but not of the Christian mothers in the church, nor of their Father, who is in heaven. He would have instituted it otherwise through his Son Christ Jesus, whom he also commanded us to hear, Matt. 15:10; 17:5. He, not custom, is the way, truth, and life, John 14:6.

Oecolampad: Infant baptism was also treated in the Council of Milevis over which Saint Augustine presided.

Balthasar: Let Augustine or a council say what they may, Augustine greatly erred in his canon *Firmissime*, De Con., dist. 4 [Canon "Most Firmly," "On Consecration," Distinction 4]. If he had written *Impijssime* [Most impiously] for that he would have been better off. If you can justify Augustine, I will praise you.

Oecolampad: Oh, it would have been a good support for the Pelagians if they had been able to invent the idea that infant baptism was forbidden by the apostles.

Balthasar: What is not commanded in Scripture is already forbidden in those matters concerning the honor of God and the salvation of our souls. For Christ does not say: "What God my heavenly Father has forbidden must be rooted out." Rather, he says "All plants which God my heavenly Father has not planted must be rooted out," Matt. 15:13. Paul calls all teachings which are not contained in the Holy Gospel a curse, even if an angel were to bring them down from heaven, Gal. 1:8f. Peter calls them false teachings of the lying masters, 2 Pet. 2:1. So Christ earnestly commands that we should teach all things which he has commanded us to teach, Matt. 28:20. Or the apocalyptic plagues will come over us, Rev. 22:18. Do you see, Oecolampad? Either you must point out with a clear Scripture where God has instituted infant baptism or it must be rooted out. One of these must be or God will not remain God. How does this Scotistic argument please you?

Oecolampad: Now the Pelagians were also highly learned in the Scripture. Likewise, Cyprian and the Council of Carthage have not been able to reject infant baptism.

Balthasar: I will trust Cyprian, councils, and other teachings just as far as they use the Holy Scripture, and not more. They themselves also desire nothing more than that from me. With this I let it lie.

Oecolampad: Origen was approximately fifty years before Cyprian. He points out clearly in the epistle to the Romans that such a custom came from the apostles. Origen is also in no way to be judged that he might have failed in this matter, although otherwise he certainly erred badly in much.

Balthasar: You should look at Origen more carefully on the word of Paul "to the ignorant" in Romans, also on Luke 3 and Homily 8 on Exodus 8, page 43. There you will find much that is different. And although Origen wrote such, since he erred badly in many other things, then he could also have erred in that.

Oecolampad: Now you do not want to consider the many hundreds of thousands who up till now have been baptized in childhood as Christian brothers. How can you make Christ's kingdom so narrow?

Balthasar: Now you will not consider as Christian brothers the many hundreds of thousands who up till now have honored and worshiped the bread and wine in the mass for the flesh and blood of Christ. How can you make Christ's kingdom so narrow?

Oecolampad: If you are only introducing a new sect, then you are grafting yourself to the devil.

Balthasar: Blasphemy. Give testimony with the Scripture, Scripture, Scripture, that baptizing according to the indisputable order of Christ is grafting oneself to the devil. If you look to the only master in the heavens and to truth itself with a gentle and eager-to-learn heart, then you will avoid such scolding and shameful words. But you have spoken out of anger and evil. May God, who thereby gives us to recognize that you can also fall like a human being, forgive you this.

Oecolampad: I know and want not to teach such schism. I must teach faith and love.

Balthasar: Whoever rightly teaches baptism and the Supper rightly teaches faith and love. On this matter I appeal to the baptismal vow and pledge of love. If you teach faith, then you teach that all works that do not flow out of faith are sin, Rom. 14:23. Now, however, infant baptism is a work without faith, or prove it with the Word from which faith flows, Rom. 10:17. There the hare is caught again in the hedge.

Oecolampad: Papal abuses and infant baptism are two different things. The abuses are against the Scripture, and they have never been accepted everywhere.

Balthasar: Infant baptism is against the Scripture, for what is not with the Scripture is against the Scripture. Or point out where the Scripture commands baptizing children. Then the Word of Christ is also such a teaching which is contradicted everywhere, Acts 28:22.

Oecolampad: Here, however, in the case of infant baptism it is another matter deliberately to overthrow a practice which is not forbidden in Scripture.

Balthasar: To overthrow a practice which is not instituted in Scripture is not an abuse but a command of Christ, Matt. 15:13. The Spirit of God speaks also through Isaiah: "Woe to you, children, who leave me, who take counsel, but not from me," Isa. 30:1. Here you yourself write concerning these words: "Whoever makes something from out of himself although God has not forbidden the same with a particular command, the same does what is forbidden by God, for he does something not out of God."

Oecolampad: I do not want to occupy myself with strange ceremonies such as exorcising devils, salting, burning candles, spittle, breathing on, and others, for I myself have no praise for them, etc.

Balthasar: If you want to praise the one, you must glorify the other. One Satan came in with the other.

Oecolampad: If the apostles baptized whole households, then presumably among these numbers there were also children.

Balthasar: Explain the term *whole households* correctly according to the way of Scripture, or you must confess that also unbelieving men were baptized with the believing women and fools. Thinking, having opinions, and imagining do not count in Scripture; knowing counts. Also, you have not believed all your life long that any young child was baptized. Show me one in Scripture; then I will be defeated.

Oecolampad: You have the burden of proof that infant baptism is forbidden.

Balthasar: The burden of proof lies with you that God has instituted infant baptism, for the need to prove stands with the affirming and not with the denying. Or it will become a self-chosen worship, that is, a church law created out of human will and fantasy.

Oecolampad: I want to do it.

Balthasar: *Ad kalendas grecas* [at the Greek calends, i.e., never].

Thomas [Geyerfalk, an Augustinian novice master in Basel]: Where, however, is a woman mentioned by name who was baptized?

Balthasar: *Bene veneritis* [You may have arrived at something], dear teacher of the Augustinians. Have you never heard read at the table the 8th and 16th chapters of the Acts of the Apostles (16:14–15) of the Samarian women and Lydia, the seller of purple? In fact you are a teacher in name only. Pfui, be ashamed in your heart that you are said to be a preacher, teacher, and knowledgeable person in Christian discussions and have never read so much in Scripture whether the apostles also have baptized women, and moreover you yourself let such mockery go out in public print. Who has so entirely bewitched you that you do not look to the truth? . . .

•

Immelen [another Basel preacher, favoring infant baptism]: We have it that God loves children and that they have the promise. Why then should one not baptize them?

Balthasar: Well then, let God love the children, still you have not proved that one should baptize them. For baptismal Scriptures do not apply to them but to those who now believe and confess their faith orally. On this confession Christ built his church, Matt. 16:18. And this is the order: (1) Christ, (2) word, (3) faith, (4) confession, (5) water baptism, (6) church. If you understand that, then you should be satisfied. When you say, however, that the children have the promise, you imply that they also have their own faith. For promises are given in vain to those who are without faith. What need then do the children have of the alien faith of their fathers, mothers, godparents, or the church, as you argue, wholly without any basis in the Scriptures.

Immelen: It is written in Mark 10:14 that "of these is the kingdom of heaven."

Balthasar: Immelen, I love you from the heart but love the truth more. Therefore I must instruct you better in the Scripture. Show me where you have ever read in Scripture that Christ has said to the children: "Of these is the kingdom of heaven." You do violence and injustice to Christ and the Scripture. It is written "of such" and not "of these." Now "of such" and "of these" are so far from one another as heaven and earth. But the false baptism book of Zurich has seduced you. Look at the Scriptures yourself, Matt. 19:14, Mark 10:14, Luke 18:16, then you will find it.

Immelen: What should then hinder our taking them into the Christian church and society with baptism?

Balthasar: This hinders, that they do not yet themselves believe. Christ says: "Whoever believes and is baptized." Not for vicarious faith; for if I believe for another, then I should also be baptized for him, for faith is always more than baptism. Although some highly boast here of an infused faith, there is no basis for that in Scripture.

Immelen: Peter says: "Who may then deny water that these be baptized who have received the Holy Spirit even as we also?"

Balthasar: Paul uses this saying for the believing Cornelius and his household, Acts 10:47. You misuse it then for those who have not reason. That is called torturing the Scripture.

The Second Part

Oecolampad: There are two kinds of baptism: of adults and of the children of believers.

Balthasar: That is rightly said. For the first is based in Scripture, the second not at all; therefore there are indeed two kinds.

Oecolampad: I want to point it out from the book of Exodus and ask first of all whether the children of the Jews also belonged to the people or not.

Balthasar: Water baptism is a ceremony of the New Testament. Therefore I demand from you a clear word out of the New Testament with which you bring to us this infant baptism. The word, the word, the word belongs to the species of the night owl and hates the light; it will not come forth into the sun. But you prove infant baptism from Exodus just as Zwingli his "Est" for "Significat" from Genesis.

Oecolampad: Whoever is inwardly baptized cannot be condemned, for God would have to condemn himself in them.

Balthasar: Those who are inwardly baptized will let themselves truly be also outwardly baptized, and they do not despise the command of Christ, where they otherwise are able to have baptizer and water. The three thousand people, Acts 2:41; the treasurer, Acts 8:36f.; Paul, Acts 9:18; Cornelius, Acts 10–11; Lydia and the jailer, Acts 16:15, 33, testify to that — also the twelve Ephesians, Acts 19:5. With this argument then, as it appears, you want to throw over and pour out Christ's water baptism entirely.

Oecolampad: There are many who are baptized who do not have faith and deceive us Christians regarding the water.

Balthasar: We are discussing how it ought to be and not how it is. Without doubt many also sit down at the Supper of Christ who have never examined themselves. Nevertheless, the truth of the Word remains: the person should examine himself, 1 Cor. 11:28.

Oecolampad: The fact is, baptism is for the sake of the person.

Balthasar: *Deo gratias* [Thanks be to God]. Therefore the believing person will recognize the obligation of water baptism by virtue of the command of Christ, and not dispute further.

Oecolampad: Yes, the parents see also with joy that their children are killed in the name of Christ.

Balthasar: My Ecolampad. What kind of death do the children die in water baptism? If physical death, then drown the baby. If you are speaking of spiritual death, which is the death of the old Adam, then I hear you saying that cradle children can also sin and resist sin, which is against the clear Word of God, Deut. 1:39. O God, where does the truth force you to go?

Oecolampad: What need is there for schism for the sake of water?

Balthasar: It is not for the sake of water, but for the sake of the high command and the baptism of Christ. Water is not baptism. . . .

[Oecolampad continues to raise objections: the practice of the Anabaptists is inconsistent with the nature of baptism itself; Hubmaier replies point by point for another nine exchanges and the debate ends.]

[Reprinted by permission of Herald Press, Scottdale, Pennsylvania, from *Balthasar Hubmaier: Theologian of Anabaptism*, translated and edited by H. Wayne Pipkin and John H. Yoder.]

– 4 –

Michael Sattler

Another Roman Catholic who embraced radical Christianity was Michael Sattler (c. 1490–1527). He had risen to the rank of prior (second only to the abbot) in a Benedictine abbey located northeast of Freiburg in Germany's Black Forest. There, influenced by the Protestant reformers, Sattler had left the abbey, married, and then joined Zurich's new Anabaptist movement. He labored in Zurich and in South Germany for this cause, establishing churches and deepening the faith of believers, until the events reflected in the present documents. These sprang from a meeting or conference of radical leaders at Schleitheim, near the Swiss-German border, in 1527. Would it be possible, as many early leaders hoped, for the radical movement to transform existing church life from within, or must the pressure of the times force them to organize as separate congregations bound together by an understanding or agreement (Vereinigung). (Compare this with the earlier Chelčický developments.) The Schleitheimers' answer was spelled out in these two circular letters, which Sattler recorded and quite likely himself drafted. They were meant to maintain the basic ideas that distinguished the Schleitheim participants and their allies from the established churches of the time. As such they had to be hidden from the authorities of church and state, but were later adopted by many baptists as definitive. Combating antinomianism within their ranks and facing persecution from without, the first document demands integrity in facing a hostile and persecuting world, while the second document requires inward structure, shaping a pattern of common life and shared worship that could sustain such a witness. Shortly after this meeting, Sattler was arrested at Horb in the Black Forest, where he led a congregation, and was jailed in the town tower at nearby Binsdorf. Horb's city council refusing the honor, Michael Sattler was tried in Rottenburg on the Neckar. Accused, he did not say, "Here I stand"; instead, he asked to consult with the brothers and sisters. Given this permission, he did so and then made faithful answer, was condemned, tortured, and burned to death as a practicing heretic. See further John H. Yoder, translator and editor, The Legacy of Michael Sattler.

The Schleitheim Confession

Brotherly Union of a Number of Children of God Concerning Seven Articles

May joy, peace and mercy from our Father through the atonement of the blood of Christ Jesus, together with the gifts of the Spirit — who is sent from the Father to all believers for their strength and comfort and for their perseverance in all tribulation until the end, Amen — be to all those who love God, who are the children of light, and who are scattered everywhere as it has been ordained of God our Father, where they are with one mind assembled together in one God and Father of us all: Grace and peace of heart be with you all, Amen.

Beloved brethren and sisters in the Lord: First and supremely we are always concerned for your consolation and the assurance of your conscience (which was previously misled) so that you may not always remain foreigners to us and by right almost completely excluded, but that you may turn again to the true implanted members of Christ, who have been armed through patience and knowledge of themselves, and have therefore again been united with us in the strength of a godly Christian spirit and zeal for God.

It is also apparent with what cunning the devil has turned us aside, so that he might destroy and bring to an end the work of God which in mercy and grace has been partly begun in us. But Christ, the true Shepherd of our souls, who has begun this in us, will certainly direct the same and teach [us] to his honor and our salvation, Amen.

Dear brethren and sisters, we who have been assembled in the Lord at Schleitheim on the Border, make known in points and articles to all who love God that as concerns us we are of one mind to abide in the Lord as God's obedient children, sons and daughters, we who have been and shall be separated from the world in everything, [and] completely at peace. To God alone be praise and glory without the contradiction of any brethren. In this we have perceived the oneness of the Spirit of our Father and of our common Christ with us. For the Lord is the Lord of peace and not of quarreling, as Paul points out. That you may understand in what article this has been formulated you should observe and note [the following].

A very great offense has been introduced by certain false brethren among us, so that some have turned aside from the faith, in the way they intend to practice and observe the freedom of the Spirit and of Christ. But such have missed the truth, and to their condemnation are given over to the lasciviousness and self-indulgence of the flesh. They think faith and love may do and permit everything, and nothing will harm them nor condemn them, since they are believers.

Observe, you who are God's members in Christ Jesus, that faith in the Heavenly Father through Jesus Christ does not take such form. It does not produce and result in such things as these false brethren and sisters do and teach. Guard yourselves and be warned of such people, for they do not serve our Father, but their father, the devil.

But you are not that way. For they that are Christ's have crucified the flesh with its passions and lusts. You understand me well and [know] the brethren whom we mean. Separate yourselves from them for they are perverted. Petition the Lord that they may have the knowledge which leads to repentance, and [pray] for us that we may have constancy to persevere in the way which we have espoused, for the honor of God and of Christ, His Son, Amen.

The articles which we discussed and on which we were of one mind are these 1. Baptism; 2. The Ban [excommunication]; 3. Breaking of Bread; 4. Separation from the Abomination; 5. Pastors in the Church; 6. The Sword; and 7. The Oath.

First. Observe concerning baptism: Baptism shall be given to all those who have learned repentance and amendment of life, and who believe truly that their sins are taken away by Christ, and to all those who walk in the resurrection of Jesus Christ, and wish to be buried with him in death, so that they may be resurrected with him, and to all those who with this significance request it [baptism] of us and demand it for themselves. This excludes all infant baptism, the highest and chief abominations of the pope. In this you have the foundation and testimony of the apostles. Mt. 28, Mk. 16, Acts 2, 8, 16, 19. This we wish to hold simply, yet firmly and with assurance.

Second. We agree as follows on the ban: The ban shall be employed with all those who have given themselves to the Lord, to walk in his commandments, and with all those who have been baptized into the one body of Christ and who are called brethren and sisters, and yet who slip sometimes and fall into error and sin, being inadvertently overtaken. The same shall be admonished twice in secret and the third time openly disciplined or banned according to the command of Christ. Mt. 18. But this shall be done according to the regulation of the Spirit (Mt. 5) before the breaking of bread, so that we may break and eat one bread, with one mind and in one love, and may drink of one cup.

Third. In the breaking of bread we are of one mind and are agreed [as follows]: All those who wish to break one bread in remembrance of the broken body of Christ, and all who wish to drink of one drink as a remembrance of the shed blood of Christ, shall be united beforehand by baptism in one body of Christ which is the church of God and whose head is Christ. For as Paul points out we cannot at the same time be partakers of the Lord's table and the table of devils; we cannot at the same time drink the cup of the Lord and the cup of the devil. That is, all those who have fellowship with the dead works of darkness have no part in the light. Therefore all who follow the devil and the world have no part with those who are called unto God out of the world. All who lie in the evil have no part in the good.

Therefore it is and must be [thus]: Whoever has not been called by one God to one faith, to one baptism, to one Spirit, to one body, with all the children of God's church, cannot be made [into] one bread with them, as indeed must be done if one is truly to break bread according to the command of Christ.

Fourth. We are agreed [as follows] on separation: A separation shall be made from the evil and from the wickedness which the devil planted in the world; in this manner, simply that we shall not have fellowship with them [the wicked] and not run with them in the multitude of their abominations. This is the way it is: Since all who do not walk in the obedience of faith, and have not united themselves with God so that they wish to do his will, are a great abomination before God, it is not possible for anything to grow or issue from them except abominable things. For truly all creatures are in but two classes, good and bad, believing and unbelieving, darkness and light, the world and those who [have come] out of the world, God's temple and idols, Christ and Belial; and none can have part with the other.

To us then the command of the Lord is clear when he calls upon us to be separate from the evil and thus he will be our God and we shall be his sons and daughters.

He further admonishes us to withdraw from Babylon and the earthly Egypt that we may not be partakers of the pain and suffering which the Lord will bring upon them.

From all this we should learn that everything which is not united with our God and Christ cannot be other than an abomination which we should shun and flee from. By this is meant all popish and antipopish works and church services, meetings and church attendance, drinking houses, civic affairs, the commitments [made in] unbelief and other things of that kind, which are highly regarded by the world and yet are carried on in flat contradiction to the command of God, in accordance with all the unrighteousness which is in the world. From all these things we shall be separated and have no part with them for they are nothing but an abomination, and they are the cause of our being hated before our Christ Jesus, who has set us free from the slavery of the flesh and fitted us for the service of God through the Spirit whom he has given us.

Therefore there will also unquestionably fall from us the unchristian, devilish weapons of force — such as sword, armor and the like, and all their use [either] for friends or against one's enemies — by virtue of the word of Christ, Resist not [him that is] evil.

Fifth. We are agreed as follows on pastors in the church of God: The pastor in the church of God shall, as Paul has prescribed, be one who out-and-out has a good report of those who are outside the faith. This office shall be to read, to admonish and teach, to warn, to discipline, to ban in the church, to lead out in prayer for the advancement of all the brethren and sisters, to lift up the bread when it is to be broken, and in all things to see to the care of the body of Christ, in order that it may be built up and developed, and the mouth of the slanderer be stopped.

This one moreover shall be supported of the church which has chosen him, wherein he may be in need, so that he who serves the gospel may live of the gospel as the Lord has ordained. But if a pastor should do something requiring discipline, he shall not be dealt with except [on the testimony of] two or three witnesses. And when they sin they shall be disciplined before all in order that the others may fear.

But should it happen that through the cross this pastor should be banished or led to the Lord [through martyrdom] another shall be ordained in his place in the same hour so that God's little flock and people may not be destroyed.

Sixth. We are agreed as follows concerning the sword: The sword is ordained of God outside the perfection of Christ. It punishes and puts to death the wicked, and guards and protects the good. In the law the sword was ordained for the punishment of the wicked and for their death, and the same [sword] is [now] ordained to be used by the worldly magistrates.

In the perfection of Christ, however, only the ban is used for a warning and for the excommunication of the one who has sinned, without putting the flesh to death, — simply the warning and the command to sin no more.

Now it will be asked by many who do not recognize [this as] the will of Christ for us, whether a Christian may or should employ the sword against the wicked for the defense and protection of the good, or for the sake of love.

Our reply is unanimously as follows: Christ teaches and commends us to learn of him, for he is meek and lowly in heart and so shall we find rest to our souls. Also Christ says to the heathenish woman who was taken in adultery, not that one should stone her according to the law of his Father (and yet he says, As the Father has commanded me, thus I do), but in mercy and forgiveness and warning, to sin no more. Such [an attitude] we also ought to take completely according to the rule of the ban.

Secondly, it will be asked concerning the sword, whether a Christian shall pass sentence in worldly dispute and strife such as unbelievers have with one another. This is our united answer: Christ did not wish to decide or pass judgment between brother and brother in the case of the inheritance, but refused to do so. Therefore we should do likewise.

Thirdly, it will be asked concerning the sword, Shall one be a magistrate if one should be chosen as such? The answer is as follows: They wished to make Christ king, but he fled and did not view it as the arrangement of his Father. Thus shall we do as he did, and follow him, and so shall we not walk in darkness. For he himself says, He who wishes to come after me, let him deny himself and take up his cross and follow me. Also, he himself forbids [the employment of] the force of the sword saying, The worldly princes lord it over them, etc., but not so shall it be with you. Further, Paul says, Whom God did foreknow he also did predestinate to be conformed to the image of his Son, etc. Also Peter says, Christ has suffered (not ruled) and left us an example, that ye should follow his steps.

Finally, it will be observed that it is not appropriate for a Christian to serve as a magistrate because of these points: The government magistracy is according to the flesh, but the Christians' is according to the Spirit; their houses and dwelling remain in this world, but the Christians' citizenship is in heaven; the weapons of their conflict and war are carnal and against the flesh only, but the Christians' weapons are spiritual, against the fornication of the devil. The worldlings are armed with steel and iron, but the Christians are armed with the armor of God, with truth, righteousness, peace, faith, salvation and the Word of God. In brief, as is the mind of Christ toward us, so shall the mind of the members of the body of Christ be through him in all things, that there may be no schism in the body through which it would be destroyed. For every kingdom divided against itself will be destroyed. Now since Christ is as it is written of him, his members must also be the same, that his body may remain complete and united to its own advancement and upbuilding.

Seventh. We are agreed as follows concerning the oath: The oath is a confirmation among those who are quarreling or making promises. In the law it is commanded to be performed in God's name, but only in truth, not falsely. Christ, who teaches the perfection of the Law, prohibits all swearing to his [followers], whether true or false, — neither by heaven, nor by the earth, nor by Jerusalem, nor by our head, — and that for the reason which he shortly thereafter gives, For you are not able to make one hair white or black. So you see it is for this reason that all swearing is forbidden: we cannot fulfill that which we promise when we swear, for we cannot change [even] the very least thing on us.

Now there are some who do not give credence to the simple command of God, but object with this question: Well now, did not God swear to Abraham by himself (since he was God) when he promised him that he would be with him and that he would be his God if he would keep his commandments, — why then should I not also swear when I promise to someone? Answer: hear what the Scripture says: God, since he wished more abundantly to show unto the heirs the immutability of his counsel, inserted an oath, that by two immutable things (in which it is impossible for God to lie) we might have a strong consolation. Observe the meaning of this Scripture: What God forbids you to do, he has power to do, for everything is possible for him. God swore an oath to Abraham, says the Scripture, so that he might show that his counsel is immutable. That is, no one can withstand nor thwart his will; therefore he can keep his oath. But we can do nothing, as is said above by Christ, to keep or perform [our oaths]: therefore we shall not swear at all [*nichts schweren*].

Then others further say as follows: It is not forbidden of God to swear in the New Testament, when it is actually commanded in the Old, but it is forbidden to swear by heaven, earth, Jerusalem and our head. Answer: hear the Scripture, he who swears by heaven swears by God's throne and by him who sitteth thereon. Observe: It is forbidden to swear by heaven, which is only the throne of God: how much more is it forbidden [to swear] by God himself! Ye fools and blind, which is greater, the throne or him that sitteth thereon?

Further some say, Because evil is now [in the world, and] because man needs God for [the establishment of] the truth, so did the apostles Peter and Paul also swear. Answer: Peter and Paul only testify of that which God promised to Abraham with the oath. They themselves promise nothing, as the example indicates clearly. Testifying and swearing are two different things. For when a person swears he is in the first place promising future things, as Christ was promised to Abraham whom we a long time afterwards received. But when a person bears testimony he is testifying about the present, whether it is good or evil, as Simeon spoke to Mary about Christ and testified, Behold this (child) is set for the fall and rising of many in Israel, and for a sign which shall be spoken against.

Christ also taught us along the same line when he said, Let your communication be Yea, yea; Nay, nay; for whatsoever is more than these cometh of evil. He says, Your speech or word shall be yea and nay. (However) when one does not wish to understand, he remains closed to the meaning. Christ is simply Yea and Nay, and all those who seek him simply will understand his word. Amen.

•

Dear brethren and sisters in the Lord: These are the articles of certain brethren who had heretofore been in error and who had failed to agree in the true understanding, so that many weaker consciences were perplexed, causing the Name of God to be greatly slandered. Therefore there has been a great need for us to become of one mind in the Lord, which has come to pass. To God be praise and glory!

Now since you have so well understood the will of God which has been made known by us, it will be necessary for you to achieve perseveringly, without interruption, the known will of God. For you know well what the servant who sinned knowingly heard as his recompense.

Everything which you have unwittingly done and confessed as evil doing is forgiven you through the believing prayer which is offered by us in our meeting for all our shortcomings and guilt. [This state is yours] through the gracious forgiveness of God and through the blood of Jesus Christ. Amen.

Keep watch on all who do not walk according to the simplicity of the divine truth which is stated in this letter from [the decisions of] our meeting, so that everyone among us will be governed by the rule of the ban and henceforth the entry of false brethren and sisters among us may be prevented.

Eliminate from you that which is evil and the Lord will be your God and you will be his sons and daughters.

Dear brethren, keep in mind what Paul admonishes Timothy when he says, The grace of God that bringeth salvation hath appeared to all men, teaching us that, denying ungodliness and worldly lusts, we should live soberly, righteously, and godly, in this present world; looking for that blessed hope, and the glorious appearing of the great God and our Saviour Jesus Christ; who gave himself for us, that he might redeem us from all iniquity, and purify unto himself a people of his own, zealous of good works. Think on this and exercise yourselves therein and the God of peace will be with you.

May the Name of God be hallowed eternally and highly praised, Amen. May the Lord give you his peace, Amen.

The Acts of Schleitheim on the Border [Canton Schaffhausen, Switzerland], on Matthias' [Day], Anno MDXXVII.

[*Baptist Confessions of Faith*, ed. William L. Lumpkin (Valley Forge, Pa.: Judson, 1969).]

Congregational Order

Since the almighty eternal and merciful God has made his wonderful light break forth in this world and [in this] most dangerous time, we recognize the mystery of the divine will, that the word is preached to us according to the proper ordering of the Lord, whereby we have been called into his fellowship. Therefore, according to the command of the Lord and the teachings of his apostles, in Christian order, we should observe the new commandment in love one toward another, so that love and unity may be maintained, which all brothers and sisters of the entire congregation should agree to hold to as follows:

1. The brothers and sisters should meet at least three or four times a week, to exercise themselves in the teaching of Christ and his apostles and heartily to exhort one another to remain faithful to the Lord as they have pledged.

2. When the brothers and sisters are together, they shall take up something to read together. The one to whom God has given the best understanding shall explain it, the others should be still and listen, so that there are not two or three carrying on a private conversation, bothering the others. The Psalter shall be read daily at home.

3. Let none be frivolous in the church of God, neither in words nor in actions. Good conduct shall be maintained by them all also before the heathen.

4. When a brother sees his brother erring, he shall warn him according to the command of Christ, and shall admonish him in a Christian and brotherly way, as everyone is bound and obliged to do out of love.

5. Of all the brothers and sisters of this congregation none shall have anything of his own, but rather, as the Christians in the time of the apostles held all in common, and especially stored up a common fund, from which aid can be given to the poor, according as each will have need, and as in the apostles' time permit no brother to be in need.

6. All gluttony shall be avoided among the brothers who are gathered in the congregation; serve a soup or a minimum of vegetable and meat, for eating and drinking are not the kingdom of heaven.

7. The Lord's Supper shall be held, as often as the brothers are together, thereby proclaiming the death of the Lord, and thereby warning each one to commemorate, how Christ gave his life for us, and shed his blood for us, that we might also be willing to give our body and life for Christ's sake, which means for the sake of all the brothers.

[Reprinted by permission of Herald Press, Scottdale, Pennsylvania, from *The Legacy of Michael Sattler*, translated and edited by John Howard Yoder.]

– 5 –

Menno Simons

The historians' recovery of the polygenesis or multiple origins of sixteenth-century radicalism permits a fresh look at the powerful originality of North German and Dutch Anabaptism. One need not suppose that Dutch Anabaptism simply repeated Swiss Anabaptism, or developed from it in a straight line. North German and Dutch Anabaptism has its own distinctive qualities. Doubtless the best known of the Dutch Doopsgesinden, *or baptism-minded, folk in sixteenth-century Holland, given that the movement adopted his name as its own, was Menno Simons (c. 1496–1561). Systematizer, pastor, denominational organizer, and strong witness, Menno gave such firm shape to a previously not-always-pacifist movement that after his day its pacifism (and pragmatically speaking, its survival) was assured. Like others, Menno began his career as a Catholic priest, was attracted to Lutheran thought, but turned away, first from Lutheranism, and in time from the militant Anabaptism of Münster as well. His numerous writings include the orderly* Foundation-Book *(1537), available today in* The Complete Writings of Menno Simons c. 1496–1561. *Anabaptism, as the notes in that book point out (see its index under "tau") had its mystical side. "Tau," the final letter of the Hebrew alphabet, had been regarded by the violent Münster radicals as the sign of the last day, affixed to the foreheads of the sword-bearing saints. Menno corrects this by showing the character of the true sheep of Christ's fold. This selection, drawn from his booklet on church discipline, gives a hint of this sign-mysticism, as well as of Menno's eloquence — still another important factor in his success.*

The Sign of Tau

If this good and perfect gift of the new birth be given us of the Father of light, by grace, then we become the chosen children of God, Jn. 1; Eph. 1; then we are the true sisters and brethren of Christ, Luke 8; then we are conformed unto Christ, Rom. 8; then we are created after the image of God, Col. 3; Eph. 4; then we have the sign Tau on our fore-heads; then the kingdom of God is ours, Luke 18; then we are the bride of Christ, Jn. 3, the church of Christ, Eph. 6, the body of Christ, 1 Cor. 12; Eph. 1. Col. 1; then Christ dwells in our hearts, Eph. 3; then we are led by the Holy Ghost, Rom. 8; we are the chosen generation, the royal priesthood, the holy, begotten people, which is God's own, 1 Pet. 2; then we are the temple of the Lord, 1 Cor. 3; 6; 2 Cor. 6; the spiritual Mount Zion, the new heavenly Jerusalem, Heb. 12; the spiritual Israel of God, Gal. 6; we are of divine mind and nature; we are delivered from the sentence of the law, Isa. 9; Gal. 6; 1 Tim. 3; yea from hell, sin, devil, and eternal death, Eph. 2; then we have Christ Jesus forever blessed; his word, life, flesh, blood, cross, suffering, bitter death, burial, resurrection, ascension, kingdom and eternal joy, with him, received as a gift from God the Father, Rom. 8. But in case we be not born again (understand, — those of understanding age), then we have not such promises.

Therefore, sincerely beloved brethren, partakers of the heavenly calling through Christ Jesus; "Humble yourselves therefore under the mighty hand of God," 1 Pet. 5:6, and sincerely deny yourselves. Fear God in all your thoughts, words and works, love and serve God and your neighbor; love God above all things created, and your neighbor as yourselves, Matt. 22. Let all your meditations be in the law of the Lord, Ps. 1. Keep God's word; I repeat it, brethren, keep the word of God which has been so often taught you in love, both verbally and in writing.

Let your ardent prayer at all times go up to God, for all men; for emperors, kings, lords, princes, judges, and for all those that are placed in authority, that God may so direct their hearts that we, if it be his blessed will, may lead a peaceable and godly life, 1 Tim. 2:2.

Be not envious in your hearts and not inconsiderate in your talking about others, whether he be a slanderer, traitor, persecutor, priest or monk, no matter who he be; for they shall receive their reward from God. But ever remember the longsuffering of our beloved Lord Jesus Christ, as also, that we were all foolish and unbelieving, erring, serving divers lusts and desires; we were also naturally, children of the wrath, the same as they are. Willingly obey all human ordinances if they be not against the ordinances of God, 1 Pet. 2. Be liberal in rendering assistance to all the children of God. Receive each other without murmuring, 1 Pet. 4. Let each one work with his own hands, and eat his own bread, if possible, 2 Thess. 3. Shun all manner of idleness and worldly pomp. Take faithful care of each other by admonitions, Heb. 10, as I have verbally admonished you to do before, and now again in this epistle.

Wash the feet of your beloved brethren and sisters who are come to you from a distance, tired. Be not ashamed to do the work of the Lord, but humble yourselves with Christ, before your brethren's feet, that all humility, according to the divine nature, may be found in you, Jn. 13; 1 Tim. 5.

Above all pray for your poor humble servant, whose life is sought with all diligence, that God the gracious Father, may strengthen him with his Holy Spirit, and save him from the hands of those who so unjustly seek his life, if it be his fatherly will, and if it be not his will, that he may then give him in all tribulation, torture, oppression and death, such heart, mind, wisdom and strength, that he may steadily fulfill the glorious work of God, which is begun in us, by the Holy Ghost, to the praise of the Lord.

O, beloved brethren, fulfill my desire, and finish, as obedient children of God that which I have faithfully taught, admonished and written unto you from the word of God, to your eternal salvation, that you may also be partakers of the glorious crown, hope and joy, in the day of the coming of Christ, 1 Thess. 2. "Not slothful in business; fervent in spirit," Rom. 12:11. Bless God in all his works toward us, and pray him to guide your way, and let all your counsel be in him, Tob. 4. Walk fearlessly in the commandments of the Lord. Go not in any manner beyond the gospel of Christ, Gal. 1. Be firm in the way of the Lord. Overcome the world, the flesh, and the devil by the most holy faith which is in you, 1 Jn. 5. Joyfully serve each other, "In patience possess ye your souls," Luke 21:10. "Be patient in tribulation," Rom. 12:12. Prepare your hearts for the cross of Christ, so that when it comes you may not be terrified with the cowardly.

No more at present, but watch closely all the days of your lives, the unexpected coming of our beloved Lord Jesus Christ, who has made us such dear creatures, bought us with his precious blood, graciously called, enlightened and regenerated us, and who will crown us with the crown of glory, array us in the garment of unblamableness, and give us the gift of eternal life. To him be eternal praise and glory, now and forever, Amen.

Ponder, holy brethren, upon every word which I have written unto you; read it attentively; reflect upon it diligently, understand it rightly, judge spiritually, and live up to it divinely. O, brethren, then my admonition and writing, and your perusal and hearing shall be fruitful.

I pray you with holy Paul, by the grace of God, not to suppress this admonition, nor to lay it away, but to read it to all faithful brethren and sisters in the Lord; as also to all the apostates who are not entirely given up, that they may be won back. Yea, not alone to these, but to all men in or out of the church, who may desire to hear it. The grace of our beloved Lord Jesus Christ be with all true brethren and sisters, Amen.

Again, pray for me and for all your servants in the Lord.

Beware of all doctrine and works which are not conformable to the gospel of Christ. Beware.

May grace and peace remain with all the true children of God, and fellow-laborers of the promise, in the kingdom of Christ.

[*The Complete Works of Menno Simon* (*sic*) (Elkhart, Ind.: John F. Funk and Brother, 1871), 448–49.]

– 6 –

Claesken Gaeledochter

Fifteenth- and sixteenth-century radicals could cope with the decimation of their number in terrible persecutions only by a theology of martyrdom that made some sense of their dreadful suffering. Ethelbert Stauffer, in an important essay, claims that this understanding of what it meant to be a martyr was the central Anabaptist doctrine. See Stauffer's essay in Wayne Pipkin, ed., Essays in Anabaptist Theology *(pp. 211–44). Such convictions led to collections of martyr stories by these radical Christians, the chief one being the volume today known as* Martyrs Mirror, *which first appeared in 1660 but included martyr stories from New Testament days to its own time. Still in print, it remains a standard volume on the shelves of today's baptists. One of its brief martyr stories tells of Claesken Gaeledochter (15??–1559), a Dutch woman who, having been baptized contrary to the laws of both church and state, suffered arrest, imprisonment, and death by drowning. A skilled Bible reader and eloquent witness to her shared faith, Claesken's letters and testimony found their way into the martyrology. Women martyrs and witnesses — and women who were first-order theologians as well — were by no means the exception in sixteenth-century baptist life, as one can see by turning the pages of* Martyrs Mirror.

If We Suffer with Him

Questions and answers between the inquisitor and Claesken:

Inquisitor. "Why did you have yourself baptized?" *Claesken.* "The Scriptures speak of a new life. John first calls to repentance, Christ himself also, and afterwards the apostles; they taught the people to repent and reform, and then to be baptized. Thus did I repent and reform, and was baptized." Against this he did not say much. *Inq.* "Why did you not have your children baptized?"

Cl. "I cannot find in the Scriptures that this ought to be." *Inq.* "David says: 'I was shapen in iniquity, and in sin did my mother conceive me.' Ps. 51:5. Since children are born with original sin, they must be baptized, if they are to be saved." *Cl.* "If a man can be saved by an external sign, then Christ has died in vain." *Inq.* "It is written, John 3:5, that we must be born again, of water and of the Spirit; hence, children must be baptized." *Cl.* "Christ does not say this to children, but to the adult; therefore did I become regenerated. We know that the children are in the hands of the Lord. The Lord said: 'Suffer little children to come unto me; for of such is the kingdom of heaven.'" Matthew 19:14. *Inq.* "The household of Stephanas was baptized, which probably also included children." 1 Cor. 1:16. *Cl.* "We do not depend on probabilities; we have the certain assurance." He did not say much against this either. *Inq.* "What do you think of the holy church?" *Cl.* "I think much of it." *Inq.* "Why then do you not go to church?" *Cl.* "I think nothing of your churchgoing." *Inq.* "Do you believe that God is Almighty?" *Cl.* "Yes, I believe this." *Inq.* "Do you then also believe that Christ consecrates himself and is present in the bread? Paul says: 'The bread which we break, is it not the communion of the body of Christ? And the cup which we bless, is it not the communion of the blood of Christ?'" 1 Cor. 10:16. *Cl.* "I well know what Paul says, and believe it, too." *Inq.* "Christ said: 'Take, eat; this is my body'; and Paul likewise." Matt. 26:26; 1 Cor. 11:24. *Cl.* "I well know what Christ and Paul say, and thus I believe." *Inq.* "Do you believe that Christ consecrates himself, and is present in the bread?" *Cl.* "Christ sitteth at the right hand of His Father; He does not come under men's teeth." *Inq.* "If you continue in this belief, you will have to go into the abyss of hell forever. It is what all heretics say. Jelis of Aix-la-Chapelle has deceived you; he himself has renounced his belief, because he saw that he had erred." *Cl.* "I do not depend on Jelis, or any other man, but only on Christ; he is our foundation, upon whom we have built ourselves, even as Christ teaches us in his Gospel: 'Whosoever heareth my words, and doeth them, I will liken him unto a wise man, who built his house upon a rock; and though storms come, and beat against the house, yet it will not fall.' Matt. 7:24. These now are the storms that beat against our house; but Christ is our stronghold, and He will preserve us." *Inq.* "You do not understand it; there are many other writings, of which you know nothing." *Cl.* "We need no other writings than the holy Gospel, which Christ himself, with his blessed mouth, has spoken to us, and sealed with his blood; if we can observe that, we shall be saved." *Inq.* 'You should suffer yourself to be instructed; the holy fathers instituted churching fifteen hundred years ago." *Cl.* "The holy fathers did not have this holiness; these are human commandments and institutions. Neither did the apostles practice this holiness; I never read it." *Inq.* "Are you wiser than the holy church?" *Cl.* "I do not wish to do anything against the holy church; I have yielded myself to the obedience of the holy church." *Inq.* "You should think: Do I know better than the holy fathers fifteen hundred years ago? You should think that you are simple." *Cl.* "Though I am simple before men, I am not simple in the knowledge of the Lord. Do you not know that the Lord thanked his Father, that he had hid these things from the wise and prudent, and had revealed them to the simple and unto babes?" Matt. 11:25.

At one time there were also two monks with him, who were to instruct me. They had but little to say, only that we were people of corrupt minds, reprobate concerning the faith, ever learning, and never able to come to the knowledge of the truth. 1 Tim. 6:5; 2 Tim. 3:7, 8. I replied: "When the day of the Lord will come, you will find it to be otherwise; take heed lest you then be of those who will say: 'These are they whom we had in derision; behold, how they are now numbered among the children of God, and their lot is among the saints.' " Wisd. 5:3, 5. Then they said: "Behold, she judges us." I replied: "I do not judge you; but I tell you to take heed unto yourselves. Now our life is accounted madness, and our end to be without honor; but when the day of the Lord comes, it will be found quite different." The sum of the matter was, that I had a devil, and was deceived. I said: "Is Christ then a deceiver?" He replied: "No, Christ is no deceiver." I said: "Then I am not deceived; I neither seek nor desire anything else than to fear the Lord with all my heart, and (knowingly) not to transgress one tittle of his commandments." After he had talked to me still further, he said: "I can tell you nothing else; you may consider the matter." I replied: "I need not consider it otherwise; I know full well that I hold the truth."

When I came before him again, he said: "Claesken, to what conclusion have you come?" *Cl.* "I have concluded to adhere to that to which the Lord has called me." Matt. 20:1. *Inq.* "The devil has called you, who transforms himself into an angel of light in you people."

When he examined me the sixth time, he asked me: "When Christ held his supper with his apostles, did he not give them his flesh to eat, and his blood to drink?" *Cl.* "He gave them bread and wine, and he gave them his body for redemption." *Inq.* "Christ certainly clearly says: 'Take, eat; this is my flesh'; you certainly cannot contradict this." *Cl.* "Paul says: 'I have received of the Lord that which also I delivered unto you, That the Lord Jesus, the same night in which he was betrayed, took bread, and when he had given thanks, he brake it, and gave it to his apostles, and said, Take, eat; this is my body, which is broken for you; this do in remembrance of me. After the same manner also he took the cup, when he had supped, saying, This cup is the new testament in my blood: this do ye, as oft as ye drink it, in remembrance of me. For as often as ye eat this bread, and drink this cup, ye do show the Lord's death till he come.' 1 Cor. 11:23–26. Thus Christ left us his supper, that we should remember his death by it, that he gave his body and shed his blood for us. This supper I want to hold with the people of God, and no other."

He held to his twaddle: that we must eat Christ's flesh, and drink his blood, since these were clearly implied by the words of Christ and of Paul.

Cl. "Since the words are so plain, I can well understand them, but it is as Paul says: that those who do not turn to the Lord, have a veil before their hearts; but those who turn to the Lord, from their hearts the veil is taken away. 2 Cor. 3:14–16. We have turned to the Lord; nothing is hid to us." *Inq.* "In the 6th chapter of John (verse 53) Christ also clearly says that we must eat his flesh, and drink his blood." *Cl.* "It is also written there: 'Then the Jews murmured, and said: How can this man give us his flesh to eat? Then Christ said: Except ye eat the flesh of the Son of man, ye have no life in you.' Again, he says: 'Whoso eateth my flesh, and drinketh my blood, hath eternal life': he also said: 'Flesh and blood profit nothing: the words that I speak unto you, they are spirit, and they are life.' Those who believe in God, and walk in all righteousness, they are temples of God, in whom God will dwell and walk, as Paul testifies." 2 Cor. 6:16.

When he examined me the seventh time, he said: "Do you not believe that the apostles ate the flesh of Christ?" *Cl.* "Christ took the bread, gave thanks, brake it, and gave it to his disciples, and his body he gave for their redemption." *Inq.* "Do you not believe otherwise?" *Cl.* "I do not believe otherwise than Christ has spoken." *Inq.* "Then I declare unto you, that I am clear of your blood; your blood be upon your own head." *Cl.* "I am well satisfied with this." *Inq.* "Herewith I commit you to the Lord."

He afterwards examined me once more, and asked me: "Do you not yet believe that the apostles ate the flesh of Christ?" *Cl.* "I have told you." *Inq.* "Tell it now." *Cl.* "I will not tell it again." *Inq.* "Do you still persist in your views respecting baptism?" *Cl.* "You certainly well know that the penitent ought to be baptized." *Inq.* "This is true enough, if for instance a Jew comes, who is not baptized yet. Are you still of the same opinion in regard to infant baptism?" *Cl.* "Yes." *Inq.* "Do you not believe otherwise?" *Cl.* "I do not believe otherwise than Christ has commanded." *Inq.* "Then I declare unto you, that you will be tormented forever in the abyss of hell." *Cl.* "How dare you judge me so awfully, seeing judgment belongs to the Lord alone? Acts 17:31. I am not terrified by this; I know better, when the day of the Lord comes, it will be found different."

I then asked him: "What does my husband say?" *Inq.* "Your husband also still persists in his views; may the Lord enlighten you." *Cl.* "We are already enlightened, the Lord be praised."

Concerning my baptism he did not say much, nor about infant baptism, but the whole of his talk was that we must eat the flesh of Christ, and drink his blood, and that this had been instituted fifteen hundred years ago, and that I was simple and had hardly once read the Testament through. I said: "Do you think that we run on uncertainties? We are not ignorant of the contents of the New Testament. We forsake our dear children, whom I would not forsake for the whole world, and we stake upon it all that we have — should we run on uncertainties yet? We seek nothing but our salvation; you certainly cannot prove to us by the Scriptures, that we practice and believe one tittle against the Word of the Lord." But he only said that we had all from the devil, and that we were possessed of the devil of pride. I said: "We know that the proud are cast down from their seats." Luke 1:52. He talked so long, that he sometimes already fancied that I would heed him; hence I had to speak now and then, because I did not want him to think this; I could not bear to hear him speak so awfully against the truth.

*A letter by Claesken to her friends according to the
flesh, and also according to the spirit, written in
prison, the 14th of March, A.D. 1559, at
which time, or thereabouts, she, her dear
husband, and her brother Jacques, were
put to death for the testimony of Jesus*

My dearly beloved friends, lay it to heart, for it is done out of sincere, ardent love, which I have for your souls, because I am certain and assured, that there is no other way by which we can be saved; hence I warn you out of a pure heart, and it will never be found otherwise. Therefore, though, some have much to talk or say, they do this because they do not want to take upon them the cross of Christ, and be persecuted for it, as Paul says (Gal. 6:12), but [let us] take for an example, that we are to follow Christ's steps, and that all the Scriptures constrain us, to submit ourselves to and prepare for suffering, even as also Paul says: "If we suffer with him, we shall also rejoice with him"; and as the sufferings of Christ abound in us, so our consolation also aboundeth by Christ; and we also read that all the holy men of God were tried by many tribulations and sufferings (Judith 8:25), and how that they would joyfully receive sufferings; yea, that they greatly rejoiced that they were counted worthy to suffer for the name of God; but those who do not truly love the Lord want to be exempt from suffering, and love this temporal life more than their Lord and God, although Christ says: "Whosoever shall seek to save his life shall lose it; but whosoever shall lose his life for my sake and the gospel's, the same shall save it forever." Mark 8:35. Not that we must all die for the word of the Lord; but the mind must be in such a state, that we would rather die, than once knowingly and willingly transgress one of the Lord's commandments; hence Christ says: "he that loveth aught more than me is not worthy of me." Matt. 10:37.

Therefore, my dearest friends, whom I love with all my heart, do not regard what men say, but look only to Christ Jesus, how he went before us in tribulation and suffering. Love the Lord your God with all your heart, and with all your power and strength; yea, though the whole world should rise up against and assail you, no one can harm you, if you have God for your Father, and if you have true love to God and his saints, for love can do all things (1 Cor. 13:7); but where there is no true love, there will soon be confusion, when persecution and distress come (Matt. 13:21), but for him that commits himself to the Lord and is possessed of love, nothing is difficult; had I not experienced this myself, it were impossible for me to know that it is so easy. Hence Christ says: "My yoke is easy, and my burden is light." Matt. 11:30. Yes, dear friends, thus I am still minded, and I so love my Lord and God, that if I could save my life by a thought, and would know that it did not please the Lord, I would rather die than think such thought. Not that I am boasting, the Lord well knows how vile I have shown myself before him; but it is through the great grace and mercy and love shown us that we are elected to his heavenly kingdom. Eph. 2:7. Now only do I feel within me the inexpressible grace and mercy of God, and his love, and how we therefore ought to love him in return (1 John 4:19); yea, this grace and love are so great before my eyes, that my sorrow is turned into joy.

I must further relate to you something of the sorrow which I had before I was apprehended. Now I remember the words of the apostle, that I have had godly sorrow, and that godly sorrow worketh repentance to salvation. 2 Cor. 7:1. Yea, I had such sorrow at times, that I did not know whither to turn, and sometimes cried to the Lord with a loud voice saying: "O Lord, crush my old heart, and give me a new heart and mind, that I may be found upright before thine eyes." Ezek. 36:26. I said to my dear husband: "When I apply the rule of the Scriptures to my life, it seems to me as though I must perish." Well may I say with David: "Mine iniquities are gone over mine head: as a heavy burden they are too heavy for me." Ps. 38:4. I said: "My dear husband, pray the Lord for me; I am so harassed — the more I direct my thoughts to the Lord, the more the tempter assails me with other thoughts." I Pet. 5:8. Thus I cried to the Lord, and said: "O Lord, thou surely knowest that I desire nothing but to fear Thee." My husband would comfort me sometimes; it seemed to him that I did nothing but what could stand in the sight of the Lord. I said: "I have not my first love (Rev. 2:4); therefore I grieve, so that I cannot sleep. There is no hope to die unto sin, I apprehend to live a long time yet; though I strive never so much to reform, yet I remain as vile as ever: 'O wretched man that I am, whither shall I go?' " Rom. 7:24.

I should have written more to you, but the messenger came and informed me that we were to go [die]. My dearly beloved friends, such was the joyful sentence my husband and I, and our brother heard: we showed each other such love, and had such a glad heart. I thanked the Lord so greatly, that the lords all heard it. They bade me keep silence, but I spoke fearlessly. When we had heard our sentence, all three of us spoke, and said that they had condemned righteous blood, and other words. My dear husband spoke so friendly, and said so often with a glad countenance, that all the people beheld it: "Yes we thank the Lord!"

Herewith I commend you to the Lord. Hasten to come to us, and that we may live with each other in eternity.

[*The Bloody Theater or Martyrs Mirror of the Defenseless Christians*, ed. Thieleman J. van Braght (Scottdale, Pa.: Herald, 1990), 611–16. Our extract is from the 3d ed. of 1886.]

– 7 –

Dirk (Dietrich) Philips

*Dirk (in German, Dietrich) Philips (1504–68) was himself the illegiti-
mate son of a Dutch priest, for a time served as a Franciscan monk, but
in 1533 joined the Northern wing of the Anabaptist movement. Living
in a dangerous era, he was a stern man whose firmness is well displayed
in the following selection from the* Handbook *(1564) composed of his
collected writings. These, together with Dirk's personal witness, made
him the leading theologian among the North German and Dutch Anabaptists of his day. He was later revered by Amish leaders in America
because of his unyielding stance on the ban. Two features may strike the
reader of this excerpt from his collection: one is how strongly the baptist movement emphasized actual practice: faith without deeds is indeed
no faith. The other is that these practices are significant only to the extent that they are shaped by the convictions of those who practice them.
(1) Scripture (with its true ministers), (2) signs of salvation (baptism and
Lord's Supper), (3) ritual washing of feet, (4) separation from sin (the
ban), (5) shared communal love, (6) commandment-keeping, and (7) enduring martyrdom are all seven "ordinances," that is, constitutive of a
God-given way of life that is at once action and conviction, practice and
persevering faith.*

On the Seven Ordinances of the Church of God

The Father, Son, and Holy Ghost, then, is the only true and living God
and Lord (Isa. 40:28; 42:5), beside whom there is no other God and
Lord, neither in heaven nor upon earth; the first and the last, the only,
eternal, wise and just God, Redeemer and Savior (Rev. 1:17; 22:13).
And this knowledge of God must exist in connection with the new
birth, in a good conscience with true faith in the word of God (John
3:36), comprehended by the enlightenment of the Holy Spirit, of which
we have written at more length at another place. Of such regenerated
people and new creatures Jesus Christ has gathered his church, and for
them he has established a number of rules or ordinances, and given them

a command that they must keep them, and thereby be known as his church.

The first rule of order is that the church above all other things maintain the pure and unadulterated doctrine of the word of God (Matt. 28:19, 20) and along with this have true ministers who are properly called and chosen by the Lord and the church.

[Here follows an explanation of the first rule, followed by the second, which is the right use or practice of baptism and the Lord's Supper.]

The third [rule or] ordinance is the washing of feet of the saints, which Jesus Christ commanded his disciples to observe (John 13:17), and this for two reasons. First, he would have us know that he himself must cleanse us after the inner man, and that we must allow him to wash away the sins which beset us (Heb. 12:1) and all filthiness of the flesh and the spirit (Ezek. 36:25; 2 Cor. 7:1), that we may become purer from day to day, as it is written: He that is righteous, let him become more righteous; and he that is holy (or pure), let him become more holy (or purer) (Rev. 22:11). And this is necessary, yea, it must be done, if we would be saved; therefore Christ says to Peter: "If I wash thee not, thou hast no part with me" (John 13:8). Then Peter answered: "Lord, not my feet only, but also my hands and my head." To this Jesus replied: He that is washed needeth not save to wash his feet, and is clean every whit" (John 13:10).

By this Christ makes it evident that the washing of feet (wherewith Christ washes us) is very necessary, and what it signifies, inasmuch as those whom he does not wash shall have no part with him, and that those who have been washed by him need no more than that their feet are washed, and they are clean every whit or wholly clean, for it is Christ who must cleanse us from our sins with his blood, and he that is sprinkled and washed therewith needs have no more than that the earthly members, the evil lusts and desires of the flesh, be put to death or mortified and overcome for him, and by grace he is wholly clean and no sin is imputed to him (Rom. 3:24; Eph. 1:4–7; Col. 3:5; 1 John 1:7; Rev. 1:5; Rom. 8:13).

The second reason why Jesus instituted the ordinance of footwashing is that we shall humble ourselves among one another — (Rom. 12:10; Phil. 2:3; 1 Peter 5:5; James 4:10, 11), and that we hold our fellow-believers in the highest respect, for the reason that they are the saints of God and members of the body of Jesus Christ, and that the Holy Ghost dwells in them (Rom. 12:10; Col. 3:13; 1 Cor. 3:16), which Jesus teaches us in these words: "Ye call me Master and Lord: and ye say well; for so I am. If I then, your Lord and Master, have washed your feet; ye also ought to wash one another's feet. For I have given you an example, that ye should do as I have done to you, Verily, verily, I say unto you,

The servant is not greater than his lord; neither he that is sent greater than he that sent him. If ye know these things, happy [or blessed — Gr. trans.] are ye if ye do them" (John 13:13–17).

Now, if they are happy or blessed who know and do this, how void of blessing those remain who profess to be apostles or messengers of the Lord and do not know these things; or, if they know, do not do them nor teach others to do them. But their heart is altogether too proud and puffed up, so that they will not humble themselves according to the command and example of Christ. They are either ashamed to do so, or else it appears like folly to them (exactly as the wisdom of God has always been looked upon by the world as foolishness, 1 Cor. 1:18–21; 2:14). But they greatly prefer to have the honor of men; they love to be called Doctors, Masters and Sirs (John 5:11); for the honor that comes from God, and which is obtained by genuine faith and a holy life they do not aspire to, yet they want to be the church of Church [church of God?] and be so known, yea, held exclusively as such. But God, who resisteth the proud and giveth grace to the humble (1 Peter 5:5; James 4:10), knows them well, and will at the last day make it evident what kind of a church (or one might more properly say sect) they have been.

The fourth rule or ordinance is evangelical separation, without which the church of God cannot stand or be maintained. For if the unfruitful branches of the vine are not pruned away they will injure the good and fruitful branches (John 15:2–6). If offending members are not cut off, the whole body must perish (Matt. 5:30; 18:7–9); that is, if open sinners, transgressors and disobedient are not excluded, the whole body must perish (1 Cor. 5:9–13; 1 Thess. 5:14), and if false brethren are retained in the church we become partakers of their sins. Of this we have many examples and evidences in the Scripture (1 John 1:10; 2 John 10).

In the book of Joshua we have the terrible example of Achan, who had stolen some of the condemned or accursed goods in Jericho and hidden them in his tent (Josh. 7:1). Because of this the Lord's anger was stirred against Israel, so that he permitted a number in Israel to be slain in battle and among other things he said to Joshua: "The children of Israel could not stand before their enemies, but turned their backs before their enemies, because they were accursed: neither will I be with you any more, except ye destroy the accursed from among you" (Josh. 7:12). Therefore Achan and all that belonged to him were destroyed and rooted out of Israel, Joshua saying to him: "Why hast thou troubled us? The Lord shall trouble thee this day" (Josh. 7:25). And all Israel stoned him with stones.

We have likewise in the book of Numbers a notable example in Dathan, Abiram and Korah, who set themselves up against Moses and

Aaron, and many of the most prominent or righteous in Israel took their part. But Moses said to the congregation of the Lord: "Depart, I pray you, from the tents of these wicked men, and touch nothing of theirs, lest ye be consumed in all their sins" (Num. 16:26).

From such and like historical incidents and examples given in holy writ it may be easily observed and understood that no church or congregation can be maintained before God that does not properly and earnestly exercise the ban, or separation according to the command of Christ and the teaching and example of the apostles, but that they will fare according to the old proverb that "a little leaven leaveneth the whole lump," and that "one black (or scabbed) sheep will mar the whole flock" (1 Cor. 5:6); yea, "like people, like priest" (Hosea 4:9).

Separation or exclusion must also be practiced for the reason that thereby the offender may be mortified in the flesh and be made ashamed, and so may repent that he may be saved in the day of the Lord Jesus (1 Cor. 5:5), which is the highest love, and the best remedy for his poor soul, as may be observed in the case of the Corinthian fornicator. Moreover necessity demands that there be a separation from apostates and wicked persons, that the name of God, the gospel of Jesus Christ and the church of the Lord be not on their account put to shame (Psa. 50:21; Ezek. 36:20–24: Rom. 2:24).

Now, what those sins are which must be punished with the ban are shown us by the evangelists and apostles in express words (Matt. 18:13–17; Rom. 16:17; 1 Cor. 5:10; 1 Thess. 5:14; 1 Tim 3:1–7; Tit. 3:10; 2 John 10) and we have also in our confession regarding the evangelical ban carefully explained it. And what the church of the Lord thus passes judgment upon by the word of God, the same is judged before God, for Christ gave his church the keys of the kingdom of heaven (Matt. 16:19) that they might punish, exclude and put away the wicked and receive the penitent and believing. What the church thus binds upon earth shall be bound in heaven, and, on the other hand, what she looses on earth shall be loosed in heaven. This must not be understood as meaning that men have power to forgive sins or to retain them (John 20:23), as some imagine, and therefore deal with the confessional and absolution as with merchandise. No minister of Christ is to do this, neither is the church of the Lord to admit any Simonites (Acts 8:9, 13, 18), for no prophet or apostle on earth has presumed to forgive sin, to hear confession and to grant absolution to the people, although Christ said to his disciples: "Receive ye the Holy Ghost: whose soever sins ye remit, they are remitted unto them; and whose soever sins ye retain, they are retained" (John 20:22, 23). The holy men of God did not assume divine honor, but were perfectly conscious of the fact, through the indwelling of the Holy Ghost, that God alone forgives and can forgive sin, as the scripture unanimously testifies. But the church has received the Holy Ghost and the gospel from Jesus Christ (Matt. 9:6; Psa. 51:4) in which is proclaimed and promised forgiveness of sins, reconciliation with God, and eternal life to all who truly repent and believe in Jesus Christ; on the other hand, disfavor, wrath and damnation are threatened and promised toward all unbelievers, disobedient and perverted ones. These words, together with the Holy Spirit, are the judge in the church against all false brethren (Rom. 16:17, 18; 1 Cor. 5:3–5; 2 Tim. 2:3; Tit. 3:10), against all heretics and all disorderly and disobedient persons who after sufficient admonition do not repent; and on the judgment day no other sentence will be pronounced as the Lord himself says; and this word the church has received from God, by which, in the name of Jesus Christ and in the power of the Holy Spirit she testifies, judges, receives and expels, and what she thus binds or looses on earth with the word and Spirit of the Lord, is bound or loosed in heaven.

The fifth ordinance is the command of love which Christ gave his disciples, saying: "A new commandment I give unto you, That ye love one another; as I have loved you that ye also love one another. By this shall all men know that ye are my disciples, if ye have love one to another" (John 13:34, 35; 15:12, 17). From this it is easy to understand that pure brotherly love is a sure sign of genuine faith and true Christianity. But this is true brotherly love, that our chief desire is one another's salvation, by our fervent prayers to God, by scriptural instruction, admonition and rebuke, that thereby we may instruct him who is overtaken in a fault, in order to win his soul, and all this with Christian patience (Gal. 6:3; 2 Thess. 1:11; James 5:19; 1 John 5:16), and thus having forbearance toward the weak and not simply pleasing ourselves.

Then again brotherly love is shown in this, that among one another we cheerfully bear one another's burdens, not only in spiritual matters, but also with temporal gifts, which we have received from the Lord, that we minister to the necessity of the saints (Rom. 12:13), and give liberally according to our ability; yea, that it be done among us as it was done in the Israel of old, namely, he that gathered much manna had nothing over, and he that gathered little had no lack (Ex. 16:18; 2 Cor. 8:15). So then the rich, who have received many temporal possessions from the Lord, are to minister to the poor therewith (Rom. 15:27; 1 Cor. 8:10) and supply their lack, or minister to their needs, so that the poor in turn serve them as they may have need of their services. Therefore Christ says in the gospel: "Make to yourselves friends of the mammon of unrighteousness; that, when ye fail, they may receive you into everlasting habitations" (Luke 16:9). And Paul writes to Timothy: "Charge them that are rich in this world; that they be not highminded, nor trust in uncertain riches, but in the living God, who giveth us richly all things to enjoy; that they do good, that they be rich in good works, ready to distribute, willing to communicate; laying up in store for themselves a good foundation against the time to come, that they may lay hold on eternal life" (1 Tim. 6:17–19). And John writes in his epistle: "Hereby perceive we the love of God, because he laid down his life for us: and we ought to lay down our lives for the brethren. But whoso hath this world's goods, and seeth his brother have need, and shutteth up his bowels of compassion from him, how dwelleth the love of God in him? My little children, let us not love in word, neither in tongue; but in deed and in truth" (1 John 3:16–18).

How necessary love is, the apostles show us everywhere in all their writings, especially Paul to the Corinthians, when he writes: "Though I speak with the tongues of men and of angels, and have not charity, I am become as sounding brass, or a tinkling cymbal. And though I have the gift of prophecy, and understand all mysteries, and all knowledge; and though I have all faith, so that I could remove mountains, and have not charity; I am nothing. And though I bestow all my goods to feed the poor, and though I give my body to be burned, and have not charity, it profiteth me nothing" (1 Cor. 13:1–4).

From this it may be easily understood how widely those differ from the genuine faith and Christianity who do not love one another, who do not show their love toward one another by their works, but allow their poor to suffer want and openly beg for bread, against the command of the Lord (Deut. 15:4; Rom. 12:13; 2 Cor. 8:14; Gal. 6:8), contrary to all Christian nature and contrary to brotherly love and fidelity. And, what is worse, they quarrel, hate, envy, backbite, scold, blaspheme, persecute, throttle and kill one another, as is plainly seen before our eyes and their deeds show; and although they do this, nevertheless they want to be called Christians and the church of God. But if they do not repent they will find out, on that day when they appear before the judgment seat of Christ, what fine [?] Christians they have been; for where love is not, God is not (1 John 4:8), seeing that God is love, as John says: "He that dwelleth in love dwelleth in God, and God in him" (1 John 4:16). But he that dwells not in love "is in darkness, and walketh in darkness, and knoweth not whither he goeth, because that darkness hath blinded his eyes" (1 John 2:11).

[There follow discussions of the Sixth Ordinance (keeping all Christ's commandments) and the Seventh (all Christians must be persecuted, but must themselves persecute no one).]

I have now briefly pointed out and discussed what the church of God is, how and by what means it is built up, what ordinances and rules are included, by what symbols it is portrayed, how it may be recognized, and how distinguished from all sects: for in all false and antichristian churches these things are not found, namely, no real new birth, no real distinction between law and gospel, that brings forth fruit, and by which people truly repent and are converted from unrighteousness unto God (Matt. 3:8; Luke 3:8), no true knowledge of the only and eternal God, who is life eternal, the fullness of wisdom and of righteousness, that is manifested by the keeping of the commandments of Christ (John 17:3; Wis. of Sol. 15:3), no true knowledge of the pure, holy, and spotless humanity of Jesus Christ, no faith that produces fruits, no scriptural baptism or Lord's Supper, no Christian washing of the feet of saints (John 13:5–17) in the quietness of true humility, no key to the kingdom of heaven, no evangelical ban or separation, no shunning of the temples of idolatry and of false worship, no undissimulated brotherly love, no godfearing life, no keeping of the commands of Christ, no persecution for righteousness' sake. All these ordinances and evidences of true Christianity are found in no antichristian churches in true form and condition, but everywhere the reverse, as may be clearly seen in these days, if so be that a man has eyes to see, ears to hear, and a heart to understand (Matt. 13:9; Rev. 2:7; 3:6).

[Dietrich Philips, *Enchiridion or Handbook of the Christian Doctrine and Religion*, trans. A. B. Kolb (Elkhart, Ind.: Mennonite Publishing Co., 1910), 383–400.]

A Parting Hymn

If now parting it must be
May God's grace accompany thee.
   Go now to thine own place
   To make of it a space
   That echoes with the grace
Of God's true Word possessing.

Since this life is filled with cares,
Let us turn from dull affairs.
   The end approaches fast;
   We see God's kingdom vast
   That frees us from the past
With tribulations pressing.

In this crisis, we've one mind:
Leaving every sin behind,
   Forsake the way of wrath;
   God's watchful servant hath
   To take the righteous path
That shall receive his blessing.

Attributed to Michael Sattler
(d. 1527), *Ausbund* #136

Part Two

TO BE AN OBEDIENT CHURCH

The Seventeenth Century

Introduction

The Seventeenth Century

The seventeenth century was a turbulent time in which the world was turned upside down — socially, politically, and theologically. The century began hopefully just after the signing of the Edict of Nantes in 1598. In this document, which granted freedom of worship to French Protestants (Huguenots), King Henry IV (a newly converted Catholic) officially ended a period of bloody conflict between Protestants and Catholics. Yet hostilities continued intermittently until King Louis XIV revoked the Edict of Nantes in 1685, making Protestantism once again illegal in France (a period known by French Protestants as "the Desert") and producing a Huguenot migration to England, the Netherlands, and North America.

Elsewhere in Europe, the Peace of Augsburg (1555) failed to settle the disagreement between Lutherans and Catholics. Beginning in 1618 a series of horrific conflicts known as the Thirty Years War continued until the Peace of Westphalia in 1648, which extended terms of peace to Lutherans, Catholics, and Calvinists — the state-established churches. The privileges of peace, however, did not apply to the free churches of Europe. The old Mennonite *Martyrs Mirror* tells how baptist Christians continued to be thrown out of their homes and into the prisons even after they ceased to be thrown into the rivers and fires (see Thieleman J. van Braght, *The Martyrs Mirror*, 1122–41).

England similarly experienced social and political upheaval during the reign of Charles I (1625–49), who continued the authoritarian policies of his father, James I (1603–25). These Stuart kings attempted to return the Church of England to a theological position close to Catholicism. Civil War broke out in 1642. The Parliamentary Army led by Oliver Cromwell and supported by Protestants finally defeated Royalist forces, and in 1649 Parliament executed the king. For a brief time Cromwell ruled as Lord Protector of England (1653–58).

To be sure, these so-called "wars of religion" were about far more than "religion." Power, politics, class, and wealth were decisive factors too, although the competing theological visions of various Protestants and Catholics undoubtedly fueled the conflicts. Yet Protestantism in the seventeenth century was not homogenous. The broad contours of the Lutheran, Reformed, Radical, and Anglican movements were still visible, but these divisions became further fragmented.

Several Protestant factions emerged in seventeenth-century England. One branch became known as Puritans because of their insistence that the Church of England be purified by returning to biblical authority and by purging the latent Catholicism in the theology and liturgy of the church. They hoped to reform the Anglican Church as John Knox (1513–72) had done in the Church of Scotland. English Puritans, however, were not agreed on how to implement this reform. The more moderate saw no need to change the existing episcopalian polity. Others urged the adoption of a presbyterian form of church government ruled by elders. The more radical advocated the independence of each congregation. Like their predecessor John Foxe (1516–87), whose *Book of Martyrs* told the story of the Marian persecutions, these Puritans were committed to England as the elect nation and the Church of England as God's chosen instrument.

Not satisfied simply to be leaven in the lump of the Anglican Church, a second group began to form congregations separated from the Church of England and so became known as Separatists. Robert Browne (1550–1633), who urged "reformation without tarrying for any," established an independent congregation in 1581. When King James I (1603–25) ascended to the English throne, Puritans thought he might favor a Protestant reform of the state church. Instead, he expelled Puritan clergy from their parishes and declared that there was no more in common between the monarchy and the presbytery than between God and the devil. Puritans understandably preferred the Geneva Bible (1560) to the King James Version (1611). Disheartened, many Puritans became Separatists, and some fled to the Netherlands, following the lead of Francis Johnson (c. 1562–c. 1617), whose congregation had gone to Amsterdam in 1593.

Among the Jacobean exiles in the Netherlands were the Scrooby Manor congregation led by John Smyth (1570?–1612) and the Gainsborough church under the leadership of John Robinson (1572–1625). In Holland the separatism of the Smyth congregation radicalized, leading them to reject infant baptism and practice believers baptism. Robinson's views moderated toward the center of Puritanism, and in 1620 a portion of his congregation set sail for the new world on the *Mayflower*. They were followed by a larger migration of Congregationalists to New England between 1630 and 1642.

The theological fault line of seventeenth-century Protestantism ran between Calvinism and Arminianism. Professor Jacobus Arminius (1560–1609) of the University of Leyden and his supporters issued in 1610 a document (or Remonstrance) summarizing their views of Reformed faith in five articles: the predestination of believers, the universality of the atonement, the capability for good, the resistibility of grace, and the possibility of apostasy. Meeting at the Synod of Dort (1618–19), an assembly of mostly Dutch Reformed church leaders drafted a counterstatement along strict Calvinist lines, affirming total depravity, unconditional election, limited atonement, irresistible grace, and perseverance of the saints. The five points of Dort (known by students of theology under the acronym TULIP) became, along with the Westminster Confession (1647), the standard of later Calvinist orthodoxy.

After John Smyth arrived in Amsterdam, he composed a *Short Declaration of Faith* (1609), which asserted that "God has created and redeemed the human race to his own image, and has ordained all men (no one being reprobated) to life" (article 2). Although similar to all five points of Arminianism, Smyth's theology seems to have been influenced by his contacts with Waterlander Mennonites, whose theological standpoint was close to Arminianism. Smyth presented the statement with his application for admission to the Waterlanders. Thomas Helwys (1550?–1615?), though differing sharply with Smyth on other matters, continued to share Smyth's view of a general atonement. After Helwys and a small group broke fellowship with Smyth, they returned to England in 1611 and established a congregation near London. This was the beginning of the General Baptists.

The history of the Particular Baptists is somewhat more complex. When Henry Jacob returned in 1616 to England from Amsterdam, he founded a church of Congregationalist Separatists in London. Jacob, who emigrated to Virginia, was succeeded in 1624 by John Lathrop, and Lathrop by Henry Jessey in 1637. The JLJ church (after the abbreviation of its first three pastors) split into several congregations. One group led by Samuel Eaton and Richard Blunt withdrew in 1633, having received a "further baptism." This vague reference may indicate they had begun to practice believers baptism. In 1638 another faction, who were of the same mind (apparently about baptism) as the Eaton party, left the JLJ church. They joined a group led by John Spilsbury. Several more schisms in the JLJ church occurred over the issue of true baptism, but eventually Jessey himself was convinced and baptized by Hanserd Knollys in 1645. Particular Baptists undoubtedly had much in common with Mennonites and General Baptists when it came to the practice of believers baptism, but Particular Baptists were otherwise Reformed in theology. Their writings and confessions indicate that they shared many of the same convictions as the Westminster theologians.

Baptists did their best to mitigate their radical image as dissenting Christians. Thomas Grantham (1634–92) and the *Orthodox Creed* (1679) attempted to bring General Baptists closer to Calvinism. The signers of the *First London Confession* of Particular Baptists (1646) attached a concluding statement addressed to Parliament. They expressed hope that their confession might prove them to be "a conscionable, quiet, and harmless people." Despite their mainstream convictions, Baptists in England and the colonies were held in suspicion by the established churches. The confusion was due in part to the proliferation of disestablished religious groups, many of which were subversive. Tumultuous times gave rise to radical religion: Levelers wanting democracy and equality, Diggers advocating economic equality, Ranters seeking to abolish priests and sin. Membership in any "sect" risked being politicized by authorities of church and state. After the restoration of the monarchy in England, Parliament passed a series of legislative acts known as the Clarendon Code and aimed at suppressing religious groups that did not conform to the Church of England. Quakers were particularly affected, as an estimated twelve thousand of them were imprisoned in England between 1661 and 1689. But John Bunyan, who spent almost one-third of his life in jail, took heart in the fact that "God's people are...looked upon to be a turbulent, seditious and factious people."

Yet at the center of this turbulence was a rock solid conviction that God's call was to gospel obedience. What does the church need to practice and teach in order to be an obedient church? Baptists in the seventeenth century were deeply convinced that the established churches — Roman Catholic, Reformed Protestant, Anglican, and New England Congregationalist — were not obedient churches. The following readings come from the theological literature of General Baptists, Particular Baptists, and Independent Congregationalists in England and America. Regrettably, the larger baptist vision is underrepresented in these selections from the seventeenth century. Still there emerges a beginning list of practices necessary for gospel obedience: conversion (Bunyan), believers baptism (Smyth and Helwys), regular observance of the Lord's Table (Grantham), and liberty of conscience (Milton, Williams, and Hutchinson). The section concludes with John Bunyan's hymn, "Who Would True Valour See," which originally appeared in *Pilgrim's Progress,* Part 2. Addressing Christiana and Mr. Greatheart, Mr. Valiant-for-Truth explains, "I believed and therefore came out, got into the way, fought all that set themselves against me, and by believing am come to this place." As Bunyan well understood, obedience is a journey.

– 8 –

John Smyth

Among the Jacobean exiles living in the Netherlands was a small Separatist congregation led by John Smyth (1570?–1612). In 1593 Smyth received the M.A. degree from Christ's College Cambridge. By 1606 he was living in Gainsborough in Lincolnshire, where he became the pastor of a congregation that joined themselves together by covenant "as the Lord's free people." With funds provided by a wealthy member named Thomas Helwys (1550?–1615?), the congregation journeyed in 1607 to Amsterdam where they renounced infant baptism and baptized themselves as believers in 1609. This little band became the first church of the General Baptists, so called because like Mennonites and Arminians, they believed that Christ died for all humankind, not just the elect. Later the same year Smyth published his views in The Character of the Beast, *in which he argued "that infants are not to be baptized" and "that anti-Christians converted are to be admitted into the true church by baptism" (*The Complete Works of John Smyth, *ed. W. T. Whitley, 2:574). Throughout this piece Smyth treats the Separatist congregations led by his old Cambridge tutor Francis Johnson (1562?–1617?) and his former ministerial colleague John Robinson (1572–1625) as misguided but true because they were constituted freely by covenant. However, in the preface (which follows), written later than the text, Smyth rejected these other Separatist congregations as false churches because they were constituted upon infant baptism. Smyth refers by name to Richard Clifton, who upon arriving in Holland was briefly associated with the Smyth congregation but who quickly joined Robinson and his Ancient Church. As Smyth began to have reservations about his self-baptism, he entered into conversation with the Dutch Mennonites. Helwys and a small faction who did not share Smyth's changing views soon returned to England. Three years after Smyth died, his followers merged with a congregation of Waterlander Mennonites. James Coggins observes that the basic difference between the Smyth community and other Separatists was their conviction that "the elect and holy nation" was not England or the Netherlands but rather "the congregation of saints ultimately committed and loyal to God and each other" (*John Smyth's Congregation, 159).*

The Character of the Beast

It may be thought most strong that a man should oft times change his religion, and it cannot be accounted a commendable quality in any man to make many alterations and changes in such weighty matters as are the cases of conscience, but if constancy be commendable in anything, it is most commendable in the best things which is religion, and if inconstancy be worthy reproof in matters of inferior estimation, it is much more blamable in matters of salvation. In respect whereof the wisest and most religious men have been always most constant in their profession and faith and inconstant persons cannot escape the deserved imputation of folly or weakness of judgment therein.

This must needs be true (and we confess it) if one condition be admitted, that the religion which a man changeth be the truth, for otherwise to change a false religion is commendable, and to retain a false religion is damnable. For a man of a Turk to become a Jew, of a Jew to become a Papist, of a Papist to become a Protestant are all commendable changes though they all of them befall one and the same person in one year, nay, if it were in one month. So that not to change religion is evil simply and therefore that we should fall from the profession of Puritanism to Brownism, and from Brownism to true Christian baptism, is not simply evil or reprovable in itself, except it be proved that we have fallen from true religion. If we therefore being formerly deceived in the way of pedobaptistry, now do embrace the truth in the true Christian Apostolic baptism, then let no man impute this as a fault unto us. This therefore is the question: whether the baptism of infants be lawful, yea or nay, and whether persons baptized being infants must not renounce that false baptism and assume the true baptism of Christ which is to be administered upon persons confessing their faith and their sins. This being the controversy now betwixt us, and the separation commonly called Brownists. For the glory of God, the manifesting of the truth to our own nation and the destruction of the man of sin we have thought good to publish this present treatise wherein the whole cause is handled. Let the indifferent reader judge of the whole and give sentence without partiality, and I doubt not but he shall be constrained to give glory to God in acknowledging the error of baptizing infants to have been a chief point of antichristianism and the very essence and constitution of the false Church as is clearly discovered in this treatise.

Now happily some man will wish that the controversy had been with the rabbis of the separation and not with Mr. Clifton whom they calumniate to be a weak man unable to deal in so great a controversy. Well, let the reader take notice that although it be Mr. Clifton's pen yet it is not only Mr. Clifton's cause and defense, but his allegations and reasons are the best plea of the greatest rabbis themselves, and if they think that they can say better, they may now speak, for by publishing answer to their reasons we do challenge all the separation in special to the combat. Be it known therefore to all the separation that we account them in respect of their constitution to be as very a harlot as either her mother England or her grandmother Rome is out of whose loins she came, and although once in our ignorance we have acknowledged her a true Church yet now being better informed we revoke that our erroneous judgment and protest against her as well for her false constitution as for her false ministry, worship, and government.

The true constitution of the Church is of a new creature baptized into the Father, the Son, and the Holy Ghost. The false constitution is of infants baptized. We profess therefore that all those Churches that baptize infants are of the same false constitution, and all those Churches that baptize the new creature, those that are made disciples by teaching men confessing their faith and their sins, are of one true constitution. And therefore the Church of the Separation being of the same constitution with England and Rome is a most unnatural daughter to her mother England and her grandmother Rome, who being of the self same genealogy and generation, (that of the prophet being true of her as is the mother so is the daughter) she dare notwithstanding most impudently wipe her own mouth and call her mother and grandmother adulteresses. Herein therefore we do acknowledge our error that we retaining the baptism of England which gave us our constitution did call our mother England a harlot and upon a false ground made our separation from her. For although it be necessary that we separate from England, yet no man can separate from England as from a false Church except he also do separate from the baptism of England which giveth England her constitution, and whosoever doth retain the baptism of England doth withal retain the constitution of England and cannot without sin call England a harlot as we have done, and this we desire may be well minded of all that separate from England. For if they retain the baptism of England, viz. the baptism of infants as true baptism, they cannot separate from England as from a false Church though they may separate for corruptions, and whosoever doth separate from England as from a false Church must needs separate from the baptism of England as from false baptism. For the baptism of England cannot be true and to be retained and the Church of England false and to be rejected. Neither can the Church of England possibly be false except the baptism be false unless a true constitution could be in a false Church which is as impossible as for light to have fellowship with darkness. It is impossible that contraries or contradictions should be both true, and so it is impossible that a false Church should have a true constitution or a true baptism to say thus:

England hath a false constitution.
England hath a true baptism is as much as to say thus.
England hath a false constitution.
England hath a true constitution which is to contradict.

But the separation they say England hath a false constitution and is a false Church and to be separated from, and yet they say also England hath a true baptism (that is a true constitution) which is not to be separated from. For a true constitution and true baptism are one and the same, so is a false constitution and a false baptism. So that the speeches and actions of the separation are contradictory in this particular. Finally, they that defend the baptism of infants cannot with any truth or good conscience separate from England as from a false Church though they may separate for corruptions, and they that do separate from England as from a false Church must of necessity separate from the baptism of England and account the baptism of England false and so account the baptism of infants false baptism. Therefore the separation must either go back to England or go forward to true baptism, and all that shall in time to come separate from England must separate from the baptism of England, and if they will not separate from the baptism of England there is no reason why they should separate from England as from a false Church, and this is more at large proved in the second question of this discourse whither the reader is to be referred.

Now concerning this point of baptizing infants we do profess before the Lord and before all men in sincerity and truth that it seemeth unto us the most unreasonable heresy of all antichristianism, for considering what baptism is, an infant is no more capable of baptism than is any unreasonable or insensible creature. For baptism is not washing with water, but it is the baptism of the Spirit, the confession of the mouth, and the washing with water. How then can any man without great folly wash with water which is the least and last of baptism one that is not baptized with the Spirit and cannot confess with the mouth or how is it baptism if one be so washed? Now that an infant cannot be baptized with the Spirit is plain, 1 Peter 3:21 where the Apostle saith that the baptism of the Spirit is the question of a good conscience into God, and Hebrews 10:22 where the baptism which is inward is called the sprinkling of the heart from an evil conscience. Seeing therefore infants neither have an evil conscience, nor the question of a good conscience, nor the purging of the heart, for all these are proper to actual sinners, hence it followeth that infant baptism is folly and nothing. Again, John's baptism was the baptism of repentance. Infants have not repentance and therefore cannot have the baptism of repentance. That infants cannot have repentance is evident, seeing repentance is knowledge of sin by the law, sorrow for sin by the gospel, mortification of sin and new obedience, all which are as much in the basin of water, as in the infant baptized.

Now I confess the pedobaptists have many shows of reason for the maintenance of their heresy, and one man shapeth them into one form, another man into an other, as every man's wit and learning teacheth him, but indeed they are all built upon the self same sandy foundations, the wresting of some places of Scripture, all which (in a manner) are discovered in some measure in this treatise, whereby the reader may perceive the manifest perverting of the scriptures from their true sense. Now because men call for antiquity, and except they see antiquity they will not believe though the Scriptures be the most ancient. I have thought good therefore to propound two pregnant testimonies of antiquity against baptism of infants that men may know that this truth also hath her footsteps among the Fathers.

Tertullianus *lib. de baptismo adversus Quintillam* hath these words than which nothing is more plain:

> Therefore, to defer and not to hasten baptism is more profitable for the condition, disposition, and age of every person, but especially as concerning young children. For what necessity is there to bring sureties into danger for the baptizing of infants if there be no such necessity of hastening the baptizing of infants. Seeing the sureties ofttimes are disabled to perform their promise both by reason of mortality, and of the evil disposition of some children when they come to years, for whom they promised in baptism. Indeed the Lord saith, forbid them not to come unto me. Therefore, let them come to Christ but let them come when they are grown, when they learn, and when they are taught to what they come. Let them by baptism be made Christians when they can know Christ by instruction. Why doth the innocent age hasten to the remission of sins? We deal more safely in worldly matters. Shall we commit heavenly things to young children unto whom we dare not commit our earthly substance? Let the first know how to ask salvation that so we may seem to give to him that asketh (Euseb. *Ecclesi. Hist. Lib.* 10. *Chap.* 15).

Athanasius's baptizing of children in sport that answered according to the custom of the *Catechumeni* is approved by Bishop Alexander of Alexandria and his clerks whence it is to be noted that these children baptized by Athanasius were unbaptized and yet knew the manner of baptism as being children borne in the Church. So that by this place and all other places of the *Ecclesi. Hist.* where like mention is made of the children of Christians first catechized and then baptized, it may easily be discerned that baptism of infants was not yet universally received but by little and little prevailed as other antichristian heresies have done in respect whereof Origen, Augustine, Cyprian, and all the Papists with one consent acknowledge it a tradition of the Church.

And thus much for the testimonies of antiquity which hereafter shall be produced more plentifully upon further occasion offered. If the separation or any other dare adventure the trial of the matter out of antiquity, but there is one, and indeed but one argument which the separation principally stands upon, and that is the covenant which say they if it be answered they must needs yield unto the truth now although this argument be answered in this writing even to the satisfaction of every indifferently minded man that loveth and seeketh the knowledge of the truth more then the defense and justification of error. Yet seeing many things are variably alleged concerning the covenants made with Abraham and his seeds and concerning Abraham's fatherhood and concerning circumcision which is called a scale of the righteousness of faith. I have thought good to refer these particulars to a more full discourse entertained upon occasion with another of the masters of the separation, not doubting but very shortly through God's goodness that treatise also shall be published, wherein the reader shall find larger instruction and satisfaction concerning the forsaid particulars of the covenants or test and other matters thereto appertaining.

In the meantime I desire the reader to make use of this writing, and to read without prejudice or partiality, and I doubt not but that through God's mercy much light of truth shall shine in his heart even by this present discourse and for the separation who are the stiffest and most obstinate adversaries of this truth of the Lord I could wish as the tyrant wished concerning the people of Rome that all their heads were joined into one and all their strength comprised into one writing, that with the sword of the Spirit it might be smitten off at once that so we might have an end of this controversy and that we might not be troubled and charged with the writing and printing of many books. Howsoever it be, we profess our readiness to employ our time and cost for the manifestation of the truth, and we desire the separation that they will not in craftiness withdraw from the combat as hitherto they have done in the matter of the translation, worship, and the Presbytery, but we require them in the fear of the Lord that seeing they have suffered so much for so much truth as they profess they would not now subtly (being guilty in their consciences of their disability to defend their errors) draw back, and pretend excuses as they do, but we require them, nay we charge them, yea we challenge them to the defense of their errors.

Lo we protest against them to be a false Church falsely constituted in the baptism of infants, and their own unbaptized estate, we protest against them to have a false worship of reading books. We protest against them to have a false government of a triformed Presbytery. We protest against them to have a false ministry of doctors or teachers. Finally, we protest against them that seeing their constitution is false, therefore there is no one ordinance of the Lord true among them. These things we have published, and of these things we require answer. For we proclaim against them as they proclaim against their own mother England that the separation, the youngest and the fairest daughter of Rome, is a harlot. For as is the mother so is the daughter. Now furthermore we desire the separation and all men that they would not impute unto us untruths and condemn the innocent without cause. For we disclaim the errors commonly, but most slanderously imputed unto us. We are indeed traduced by the world as atheists by denying the Old Testament and the Lord's day, as traitors to magistrates in denying magistracy, and as heretics in denying the humanity of Christ.

Be it known therefore to all men, first that we deny not the Scriptures of the Old Testament, but with the Apostles acknowledge them to be inspired of God, and that we have a sure word of the prophets whereunto we ought to attend as unto a light shining in a dark place, and that whatsoever is written aforetime is written for our instruction that we through patience and comfort of the Scriptures might have hope, and that we ought as Christ counseleth to search the Scriptures of the Old Testament as the men of Beræa did because that in them we may find everlasting life, and that they do testify of Christ. This we believe according to these Scriptures (John 5:39, Acts 17:11, Romans 15:4, 2 Timothy 3:16, 2 Peter 1:19). Yet nevertheless we affirm all the ordinances of the Old Testament, viz. the Church, ministry, worship, and government of the Old Testament to be abolished all which were types and shadows of God's things to come but the body is in Christ (Colossians 2:14–17, 20).

Secondly, we acknowledge that according to the president of Christian disciples and the primitive Churches, the saints ought upon the first day of the week which is called the Lord's day (Revelation 1:10) to assemble together to pray, prophesy, praise God, and break bread, and perform other parts of spiritual communion for the worship of God, their own mutual edification, and the preservation of true religion and piety in the Church, and that we might be better enabled to the foresaid duties we ought to separate ourselves from the labors of our callings which might hinder us thereto, and that according to these Scriptures (John 20:19, Acts 2:1, 41–42 and 20:7, 1 Corinthians 16:1).

Thirdly, concerning magistrates, we acknowledge them to be the ordinance of the Lord that every soul ought to be subject unto them that they are the ministers of God for our wealth, that we ought to be subject unto them for conscience sake, that they are the ministers of God to take vengeance on them that do evil, that we ought to pray for them that are in authority, that we ought not to speak evil of them that are in dignity nor to despise government but to pay tribute, toll, custom, and that according to these Scriptures (Romans 13:1-7, 1 Timothy 2:2, 1 Peter 2:13-15, 2 Peter 2:10, Jude 8). But of magistrates converted to the faith and admitted into the Church by baptism there may many questions be made, which to answer neither will we if we could, neither can we if we would, when such things fall out, the Lord we doubt not will direct us into the truth concerning that matter. In the meantime we are assured according to the Scripture that the kings of the earth shall at the length bring their glory and honor to the visible Church (Revelation 21:24).

Finally, concerning the flesh of Christ we do believe that Christ is the seed of Abraham, Isaac, and Jacob, and of David according to the prophecies of the Scriptures, and that he is the son of Mary his mother, made of her substance, the Holy Ghost overshadowing her. So have other children their bodily substance from their parents also that Christ is one person in two distinct natures, the Godhead and manhood, and we detest the contrary errors. Our grounds of Scripture are these (Genesis 22:18, 26:4, 28:14, Psalms 132:11, compared with Acts 2:30, Romans 1:3-4, Hebrews 1:8-10, 2:11, 14:16).

Briefly to conclude let the separation be advertised that whereas they do so confidently through their self love and self conceit fill their mouths with heresy and heretics as if thereby they would fear babes that herein they tread in the steps of all the antichristians their predecessors. Do not the Papists call the Protestants heretics and call for fire and fagot? Do not the Protestants proclaim the separation schismatics and heretics and judge them worthy the gibbet? Not the affirmation of men without proof but the evidence of willful obstinacy in error maketh men heretics. And let them take heed that they notwithstanding their sirens songs prove not cages full of most ugly and deformed antichristian heretics. Thus desiring the separation not to be wise in their own eyes through pride, but to become fools that they may be made wise through humility, and desiring the forwardest preachers and professors of the English nation well to weigh what is the true constitution of the Church, and what is the subject of true Christian baptism, and accordingly to measure a true and a false Church, I cease, wishing the light and love of the truth to every one that readeth.

[*The Works of John Smyth*, ed. W. T. Whitley (Cambridge: The University Press, 1915), 2:752-60.]

– 9 –

Thomas Helwys

Although he led the group that founded the first Baptist congregation on English soil, Thomas Helwys (1550?–1615?) was never ordained. A wealthy merchant from Nottinghamshire, Helwys financed the voyage of the Smyth congregation to Amsterdam, leaving his family (safely he thought) behind. Irritated by Helwys' escape, the English authorities imprisoned his wife. As Smyth continued to move toward union with the Mennonites, Helwys published his own Declaration of Faith *in 1611, which denied baptismal successionism (Smyth accepted this doctrine) and affirmed oaths, the sword, and magistrates (some Mennonites rejected participation in all three). Still committed to English nationalism, Helwys and a fellowship of about ten others returned and established a General Baptist congregation in Spitalfield, just outside London. The church was basically Arminian in theology. Shortly afterward Helwys wrote an apocalyptic tract entitled* The Mystery of Iniquity *(1612). Here he identified the first beast of Revelation 13 with the Roman Catholic Church and the second beast, which imitated the first, with the Church of England. Helwys pleaded with his readers to come out of Babylon — the established church. Even the Separatist congregations were false churches because they simply mimicked the bishops and presbyters. Thus, the covenants that constituted their congregations were made with children of the flesh. Helwys argued that God only enters into covenant with those who believe and are baptized. These are the true heirs of Abraham. Apparently Helwys attempted to present a copy of his book to King James I (1603–25). When he was unable to do so, Helwys wrote a personal note in the flyleaf, which stated that as an earthly monarch James had power over the bodies of his citizens but no authority over their souls. James responded by throwing Helwys into Newgate Prison, where he died.*

The Mystery of Iniquity

The Inscription

Hear, O king, and despise not ye counsel of ye poor, and let their complaints come before thee. The king is a mortal man, and not God therefore hath not power over ye immortal souls of his subjects, to make laws and ordinances for them, and to set spiritual lords over them. If the king have authority to make spiritual lords and laws, then he is an immortal God, and not a mortal man. O king, be not seduced by deceivers to sin so against God, whom thou oughtest to obey, nor against thy poor subjects who ought and will obey thee in all things with body life and goods, or else let their lives be taken from ye earth.

To the Reader

The fear of the Almighty (through the work of his grace) having now at last over weighed in us the fear of men, we have thus far by the direction of God's word and Spirit stretched out our hearts and hands with boldness to confess the name of Christ before men and to declare to prince and people plainly their transgressions, that all might hear and see their fearful estate and standing, and repent and turn unto the Lord before the decree come forth, and before the day of their visitation be past, and that the things that belong to their peace be altogether hid from their eyes. And whereas in this writing we have with all humble boldness spoken unto our lord the king, our defense for this is that we are taught of God especially to make supplications, prayers, intercessions, and give thanks for our lord the king. And we are taught that the gracious God of heaven (by whom the king reigns) would that the king should be saved and come to the knowledge of the truth, and therefore we the king's servants are bound especially by all the godly endeavors of our souls and bodies to seek the salvation of the king although it were with the danger of our lives. For if we saw our lord the king's person in danger either by privy conspiracy or open assault we were bound to seek the king's preservation and deliverance, though it were with the laying down of our lives, which if we did not, we should readily and most worthily be condemned for traitors. How much more are we bound to seek the preservation and deliverance of the soul and body of our lord the king seeing we see him in much great spiritual danger as we do. And if any shall be offended at us for so doing they therein love not the king, and if our lord the king should be offended at us his servants for so doing the king therein loves not himself, and if all men and the king should for this be offended with us (which God forbid) yet herein we are sure our God will be well pleased with us, in that we have with our best strength and faithfulness obeyed him who commands and teaches us to admonish all men every where to repent, and this is our sure warrant and our assured hope and comfort.

Now as we have (according as we hold ourselves bound) thus far confessed Christ's name before men by writing, so we shall (the Lord assisting us) be ready as we hold ourselves bound to confess Christ before men by word of mouth, not fearing (through God's grace) them that kill the body and after that are not able to do any more. In this duty to God and his people we must needs confess we have hitherto greatly failed, but we will now be ready the Lord strengthening us rather to be sacrificed for the publishing of the Gospel of Jesus Christ and for the service of your faith then to fail as we have done both in our duties to God and you. This we readily vow to God and promise to you and to will to do this good is present with us, but we find no means in us to perform this duty and service, and we have a law in our flesh strongly rebelling against the law of our minds, but our assured wist and confidence is that God's grace alone is sufficient for us to make ye every way unto these things unto the which of our selves we are no way able, yet we will say with the holy Apostle Paul: "If God be on our side who can prevail against us and who shall separate us from the love of Christ? Shall tribulation, or anguish, or persecution, or famine, or nakedness, or peril, or sword? No the Lord we trust in these things will make us conquerors." And though our outward man should perish, or suffer many afflictions (which we were most foolish if we should not wait for) yet let the people of God look unto the truth we witness and consider with holy and wise hearts whether we have not good warrant, yea direct commandment to do that we do, though we be unfit and unworthy for such a service.

Shall we hear the Lord say, "Come out of her my people" and shall the Spirit of God command him, that heareth say "Come" and shall not we say "Come"? Shall the word of the Lord command to call up archers against Babel and all that bend the bow to besiege it round about and let none escape and to recompense her the double (Jer. 50:29; Rev. 18)? And shall we spare our arrows though they be weak? And shall the Spirit of God say, "All ye that are mindful of the Lord keep not silence" (Isa. 62:16)? And shall we hold our peace because we are not eloquent? No, no, we have too long neglected our duties herein, and now through God's grace we dare no longer do so and therefore do we thus cry unto you the people of God, saying, "Babylon is fallen, she is fallen. Come out of her. Come out of her. For if you still partake with her in her sins you shall certainly be partakers of her plagues." And therefore also we say, "Let him that is a thirst come, and let whosoever will take of the water of life freely." And we call unto all valiant archers that bend the bow to come to the siege against this great city, and we pray all that are mindful of the Lord not to keep silence nor to give the Lord rest till he repair and until he set up Jerusalem the praise of the world. And our continual prayers unto the Lord are and shall be that the Lord will enlighten your understandings and raise up all the affections of your souls and spirits that you may apply yourselves unto these things so far as his word and spirit doth direct you, and that you may no longer be deceived and seduced by those false prophets who prophesy peace unto you when war and destruction is at the door, which the Lord give both you and them to see, that you may all fly unto the Lord for your deliverance and salvation. Amen.

Children of the Flesh and Children of the Promise

And now let the covenant of the Lord stand firm and good against all the adversaries thereof, which covenant is, they which believe and are baptized shall be saved. The words whereof being spoken by him that made it, do with authority convince to the consciences of all that will hear them, that this covenant is made only with them that believe and are baptized, which is with them that [are] of the faith of Abraham and not they that are of the flesh of Abraham (Rom. 4:12–16). There are, saith the apostle, children of the flesh and children of the promise, but the children of the promise are counted for the seed (Rom. 9:8). How ignorant and obstinate are men become, whom no word of God can persuade, but they will have the children of the flesh to be the children of the promise and the seed. For they will have the seed of the faithful, that is, all the children begotten of their bodies, to be the children of the promise and the seed with whom the covenant is made, saying: the covenant is made with the faithful and their seed, meaning all the children begotten of the flesh. Yet the apostle saith, the children of the flesh are not the seed, but the apostle's testimony will not serve the turn. The pope saith it is not so, and the bishops and presbytery (having learned it of the pope) say it is not so. And the Brownists (having learned it of the bishops) say it is not so. There are many witnesses, and they have long and ancient custom, and the script is fair to look upon, and pleasant to the eye and mind, that infants are begotten and borne Christians. The most wicked and profane parents that are like this way, that they may be accounted to beget Christians and that their children may be made members of the body of Christ when they are new borne. The best men like this way, and the worst like it [this] way. This pleaseth all flesh in these parts of the world.

There was never any one doctrine of Christ nor of the apostles that ever was so acceptable to all men. It must needs be acceptable, because so good a thing is so easily come by. What a grievous thing would it be if one might not be a Christian, and member of Christ's body, before they had learned Christ and to believe in him. This would trouble children if they should be forced to learn to know Christ before they could be admitted to be his disciples and to be baptized, and this would be a great trouble to parents that their children should not be baptized before they had carefully brought them up in the instruction and information of the Lord, and this would be a great burden to bishops and priests if they should have none admitted members of their church, until by their diligent and faithful preaching of the gospel they were brought to knowledge, faith, and repentance, and to amend their lives and be baptized. If these old doctrines of Christ and his apostles should now be put in practice it would trouble and offend all the world, being so contrary to all custom, and counsels, and affections of men.

O crooked and foolish generation, how long shall the Lord bear with you? How long shall he suffer you? Will you make the way broad and wide which he hath made straight and narrow? Will you still walk in the traditions of men after the lusts of your own hearts and tread his statutes under your feet? Shall the long evil custom and false testimony of men agreeable to your own affections overthrow the divine and true witness of our Lord Christ and his Apostles? Doth our Savior Christ say that those with whom he hath made the new covenant are they in whose minds and hearts he hath written his Law, whom he declares to be those that believe and are baptized? And will you add unto the covenant of the Lord and say it is made with the faithful and their seed before they can believe? And doth the apostle say that the seed to whom the promise is made are they which are of the faith of Abraham not they that are of the flesh of Abraham, and will you say that they that are of the flesh of the faithful are the seed with whom the covenant is made? Can you devise in your hearts more directly to oppose the Lord and falsify his truth than you do herein? Will you thus contend against the Lord and despise the Spirit of grace and trample under foot the blood of the New Testament and think that you shall escape much more punishment then they that despised Moses law? Deceive not yourselves, and do not think that God careth not for these things and that he regardeth not the breach of his holy ordinances because he seems to hold his peace in that he strikes you not with bodily judgments. But except you repent he will reprove you and set all these things in order before you and tear you in pieces when there shall be none that can deliver you. Oh consider this and forget not God. What shall it profit you to have your infants washed with water and a few words whereby the name of the Lord is blasphemed, and you perish for so profaning his ordinance? The infant is never the better, it shall not be saved thereby, and there is no such obedience required at your hands. Let the word of the Lord be your guide in these things, and not the word of man nor long custom, although it be in a thing that is most pleasing to your carnal minds.

[Thomas Helwys, *A Short Declaration of the Mystery of Iniquity*, 1612 (London: n.p., 1612; reprint Macon, Ga.: Mercer University Press, 1998), 1–2; 179–82.]

Thomas Grantham

Pastor, evangelist, and theologian, Thomas Grantham (1634–92) was one of the most important seventeenth-century General Baptist leaders in England. He described himself as belonging to the "poor kindred" of the "ancient family of the Granthams" (The Epistle Dedicatory to Christianismus Primitivus). *At age nineteen he made his profession of faith in baptism and united with a small congregation at Halton-Holegate, in Lincolnshire. Three years later (1656) the church called him as their pastor, having recognized that young Grantham "obtained favour of the Lord, to know his will, and to make the same known unto others" (Thomas Crosby,* The History of the English Baptists, *3:76). In 1666 Grantham was ordained as a messenger, which he regarded as a continuation of apostleship in the primitive church and whose function it was "to preach the gospel where it is not known; to plant churches where there is none; to ordain elders in churches remote, and to assist in dispensing the holy mysteries" (Christianismus Primitivus, IV/V, 167). Although he was self-educated, Grantham's writings reflect an encyclopedic knowledge of the texts and traditions of Christian Scripture, church fathers, medieval schoolmen, and Protestant reformers. In his magisterial work,* Christianismus Primitivus, *Grantham contended that the faith and practice of "the baptized churches" (i.e., Baptist) and primitive Christianity are the same. Yet his account of ancient religion is catholic and sacramental. Grantham's theology resonates with the language of* The Orthodox Creed *(1678) of the General Baptists, which states that as Israel "had the manna to nourish them in the wilderness to Canaan; so have we the sacraments, to nourish us in the church, and in our wilderness-condition" (Article XIX). In the following selection, Grantham argues that the reform of the church according to the primitive pattern is carried out by practicing, not neglecting, "the form of godliness" (e.g., believers baptism, the laying on of hands, and the Lord's Table).*

The Primitive Christian Religion

Of the True Way of Gathering Persons into the Church of Christ

As the internal part of Christian religion is carefully to be preserved, even so a necessity lieth upon the servants of God to preserve and maintain (as instruments in his hand) the external part of the Christian religion also, lest at any time they be deceived by a specious pretence to the power, the better to subvert the form of godliness, or the form of doctrine which was delivered to the primitive churches (Rom. 6; Heb. 6). For certain it is, that where the true power of godliness dwells, there will not be wanting a due zeal for the form of godliness also "I praise you brethren, that you remember me in all things, and keep the ordinances, as I delivered them to you" (1 Cor. 11:2) and this zeal will be so much the more, as by how much the ways of truth are opposed by evil men. "It is time for thee, Lord, to work, for men have made void thy law: therefore I love thy commandments above gold, yea above fine gold: therefore I esteem all thy precepts concerning all things to be right, and I hate every false way" (Ps. 119:126–28).

And verily where the form of godliness is neglected, religion will in a little time either vanish, or become an unknown conceit, every man being at liberty to follow what he supposes to be the motions of the Spirit of God, in which there is so great a probability of being mistaken, as in nothing more; for man's ignorance being very great, and Satan very subtle, and the way of the Lord neglected, men lie open to every fancy which pleaseth best, or which hath the greatest shew of "voluntary humility" or will worship, in "neglecting the body not in any honour to the satisfying of the flesh" (Col. 2:18, 23).

To avoid all which dangerous mistakes in religion, we shall endeavour plainly to set down the practical way of God's worship, as settled in the Christian Church by Christ our Lord, and his holy Apostles. And because we know no way so effectual to accomplish this work, as by clear description of the Church of the living God, in which only can be found the undoubted worship of God, we shall therefore do what we may briefly shew this house or Church of God to the children of men, and let them measure the pattern, and consider all ordinances thereof, and the forms thereof, that they may keep all the ordinances, and the forms thereof, and do them, always remembering that the whole circuit of this house is most holy, that being the end of the Lord in all things, which he requires his people to observe. Yea, holiness becomes his house forever (Ez. 43; Ps. 93:5).

For the definition of the Christian Church, we shall not much vary from that which hath therein been done by the ancient or modern writers. Lactantius gives this brief definition of the Church, "It is only the catholic Church which hath the true worship and service of God" *(Sola Catholica Ecclesia).* Our modern Protestants usually define the Church thus, "where the word of God is sincerely taught, and the sacraments rightly administered, there is the true Church." Dr. Wollebius gives it thus, "The visible Church is a visible society of men, called to the state of grace, by the word and sacraments."

Again, the definition of Christ's Church may be taken out of the word *kahal* or *ecclesia,* [that is], *evocare,* to call, or *evocatus per evangelium,* to call, or called out by the gospel. Then the Church is defined, "a company of men called out of the world by the voice or doctrine of Christ, to worship one true God according to his will." But if the definition be made of the thing itself according to the larger consideration, then it may be this, "the whole number of the saved ones, from the beginning of the world to the end thereof." This is that body whereof Christ is said to be the Saviour (Eph. 5:23) called the "general assembly or Church of the first-born who are written in heaven," which in respect of all the individuals is not known in this world by men, "God only knowing who are his."

Yet thus much we may say in general, that such as only fell in Adam and have no personal guilt of their own together with all such in every age and nation as fear the God of heaven and work righteousness are rationally supposed to be within the verge of this vast body and may by the grace of God be heirs of salvation. Because Christ is the Lamb slain from the beginning to take away the sin of the world, or original sin, in the condemning power of it, also to abolish death the effect thereof. So justifying the whole world who were found guilty by that Law freely by his grace "through the redemption which is in Christ Jesus, whom God hath set forth to be a propitiation through faith in his blood, for the remission of sins that are past through the forbearance of God" (Rom. 3:25).

But the Church or body of Christ thus considered, as containing the whole number of the saved, is not the immediate subject of our discourse, and therefore we shall intermit what might be said further in that case, bending our state to set forth the Church of Christ as now obliged by gospel rules, to worship God according to his will, declared in the Holy Scriptures which are strictly to be observed, for "a testament is of force after men are dead" (Heb. 9:17). "And if it be but a man's covenant, yet when it is confirmed, no man disannulleth or addeth ought thereto" (Gal. 3:15). Nor shall we incumber the reader with the distinctions made by some learned men in this manner, as that of those the Church of Christ some are only *numero,* some *numero* and *merito,* and some *numero, merito,* and *electio.*

For though it be very true that some do only fill up the number of visible professors, and of these some more deserving than others, and yet at last but a few that shall be chosen, as our Saviour teacheth. Yet since we are not judges in these cases, but must leave secrets to God, we shall only concern ourselves with the true or orderly state of Christ's Church in the profession of the gospel, meddling little with the state of the Church of God before Christ's incarnation, but as occasion shall require it, for the order, state, or economy of the Church of God hath varied greatly, both, in respect of the subjects and usages thereof. But howsoever God hath spoken in time past to the fathers, it is all to be so improved, as to serve to the furtherance of the gospel, that Christ as a Son over his own house or Church, may have the preeminence, as being that Messiah which indeed was to teach us all things, and whole house are we, if we hold fast the confidence, and the rejoicing of the hope firm unto the end (Heb. 3:6)....

Of the Divine Use of the Lord's Table

To set forth Christ and him crucified, is the great design of the gospel, and made the reason of the present ordinance by the apostle: "For as often as ye eat this bread...ye shew forth the Lord's death..." (1 Cor. 11:26). It was our Saviour's design by this holy rite, to keep himself the better in the remembrance of his chosen disciples. And if they that had seen him had need of such an ordinance, how should we not accept it with great thankfulness "who having not seen him" yet by this we see great cause to "love him" while he is hereby "evidently set forth" crucified and to come again (1 Pet. 1:7–8). Holy Peter was careful that the Christians should have these things always in remembrance by which he had made known the power and coming of the Lord. And indeed upon this depends our life and all happiness, for if in this life only we have hope in Christ, we are of all men most miserable. Now Christ is our hope, our life, and when he shall appear, we shall appear with him in glory. The due understanding of the Lord's Table is of great advantage in many ways.

1. It provides against all future offerings for sin, there being no other propitiatory sacrifice since the dying of the Lord Christ either required by God or performable by man. For by one offering he hath perfected forever them that are sanctified. And again, where remission of sin is, there is no more offering for sin, and whoso denies cleansing by this death of the Lamb of God will find there is no more sacrifice for sin.

2. This ordinance representeth Christ as having really died for us, his body really put to death by the wicked hands of the Jews, and not as our late enthusiasts do speak, when they tell men Christ lieth dead in them, because unregenerate. When in truth he is not in such men

at all. Otherwise then as his kingdom ruleth over all, however, he is not dead in them for he died but once. Death hath no more dominion over him, and now he ever liveth to make intercession to God for us. How certain it is that the body of Christ was broken and his blood shed as the breaking of the bread doth plainly shew, so it is most carefully asserted and delivered with such solemnity as it is not at all to be doubted or transferred to a mystery. For thus saith the Scripture, "But one of the soldiers pierced his side, and forthwith came there out blood and water. And he that saw it bare record, and his record is true; and he knoweth that he saith true, that ye might believe" (John 19:34–35).

3. This ordinance plainly sheweth that the blood of Christ shed for remission of sins was really seen with mortal eyes contrary to that dangerous saying of the Quakers which I have in writing from them "that the blood of Christ which cleanseth from sin was never seen with mortal eyes." And further asserting most falsely "that nothing which was mortal was called Christ." It is no marvel therefore that those false spirits do reject this ordinance which standeth as a constant witness against their delusions and by it we are admonished to beware of their great mistakes.

Again, the second coming of our Lord in person or in that body which died for us is hereby evidently held forth as the great expectation of all that believe on him, which is not to be understood of his appearing to his disciples soon after his resurrection nor yet his giving them the plentiful fruits of the Spirit on the day of Pentecost next after he rose from the dead, but is plainly declared by the angels of God to be coming so or in like manner as they saw him "ascend up into heaven" when "a cloud received him out of their sight" (Acts 1:9). And as plainly is this truth delivered by the apostle [Peter]: "God shall send Jesus who before was preached unto you, whom the heavens shall retain until the time of the restitution of all things" (Acts 3:21). And Paul teacheth the Thessalonian saints to "look for the Son of God from heaven, even Jesus which delivered us from wrath to come" (1 Thess. 1:10). In the mean time this holy ordinance serves to manifest the Lord Jesus to the children of God and seems to be made use of by himself to that end after he was risen from the dead: "And it came to pass as he sat at meat with them, he took bread and blessed it, and brake and gave to them, and their eyes were opened and they knew him" (Luke 24:30–31). Certain it is many of the ancient Christians understood this place of the breaking of bread according to Christ's institution (Luke 22). And perhaps herein we might fulfill what he then said concerning his drinking the fruit of the vine new with his disciples in the kingdom of God, he having now overcome death and become King of Kings and Lord of Lords and the power of the kingdom of God being now also advanced by virtue of all power both in heaven and in earth. And that which adds further strength to this is the report which these disciples make to the eleven, how that Christ "was known in the breaking of bread" (Luke 24:35).

The Lord's Table Teaches Humility and Brotherly Love

[The Lord's Table] teacheth humility because it setteth forth Christ in the greatest of his self-abasement, yea the depth of his humility shewed forth in his bearing the revilings, contradictions, and murder of his enemies when he could have prevented them by destroying them all. "He humbled himself and became obedient unto death, even the death of the cross" (Phil. 2:8). When they hear Christ saying, "the cup that my heavenly Father hath appointed me to drink, shall I not drink it?" (John 18:11), which our Saviour expounds of his death and bitter passion, and all this excellently commemorated in the Table of the Lord, how teachable must it needs be to the pious Christian? Sure this is no less efficacious to teach this duty of humility than the word preached, "for consider him that endured such contradiction of sinners against himself, lest ye be weary and faint in your minds" (Heb. 12:1–3).

Paul was a zealous Christian for this ordinance (Acts 20; 1 Cor. 11) and we find him well instructed in the doctrine of it, being desirous to "know Christ, the fellowship of his sufferings, and the power of his resurrection, being made conformable to his death" (Phil. 3:10). Let no man strive therefore against this gospel precept, because as they are pleased to speak, it is a low ministration since what may rightly be said of its final beauty in the judgment of men doth argue the necessity and true usefulness of it being therein made to set forth Christ in his humiliation and consequently the conformity of the Church to Christ in his abasement which she must learn during the time her Lord exercises her under the word of his patience. Nevertheless this ordinance, as all other gospel services, hath also a clear evidence of the glory of Christ in it, as it directeth us to the manifestation of the Son of God, "when he shall come to be glorified in his saints, and to be admired in all them that believe" (2 Thess. 1:10).

We may justly conclude that such as reject Christ as held forth in this ordinance do therein declare themselves averse to the true steps of humility, notwithstanding great and voluntary pretences that way (Col. 2), pretending, but very falsely, to know Christ after a more excellent way, than he is held forth in this ordinance, else doubtless they would follow him therein. Yea they tell us this is to know Christ after the flesh as if Christ taught no spiritual matter in this ordinance, or as if the doctrine of his cross and our conformity to him therein were not as necessary as any thing to demonstrate the spirituality of a Christian while the Church is militant, or as if it were not the best conquest to have every thought brought in to the obedience of Christ who is the great commander in this service as well as the rest of his holy precepts.

Again, this holy service teacheth Christian love as effectually as any part of Christ's doctrine because it holds forth the love of Christ to his [own], even to the end (John 13:1f.) and was the highest sign of his love to sinners in general as it beareth forth the witness of his dying for them and hence Christians ought to infer from these fair premises that if Christ so loved them they ought also "to love one another" (1 John 4:11). If Christ loved them when they were enemies to him by wicked works, they ought to love their enemies, and above all it teacheth love to God the Father [and] to Christ his beloved Son. For what pious Christian can behold the things set forth under these considerations of the Father giving the beloved of his soul to be an offering for the sin of the world and the Son of God crying out upon the cross under the burden of their iniquities and not be moved with very great affection towards this gracious God and our Lord Jesus Christ?

Oh how ingrateful are those men that condemn this precept wherein we so evidently see the "love of our Lord Jesus Christ, who though he was rich, yet for our sakes he became poor, that we through his poverty should be made rich" (2 Cor. 8:9). Do we not here see him deserted of friends, divested of raiment, degraded of honour, being numbered with transgressors and which was above all forsaken of God in some sense, and all this in pure love to our souls that we might be clothed with his righteousness and honoured with the friendship of heaven itself? May not men as well condemn any part of the gospel as this precept? Is any part of greater evidence of God's love than this? Nay do they not in effect condemn the whole that condemn a part, especially such a part? Ingrateful men! Doth Christ require this to be done in remembrance of him, and will you scorn to remember him therein? Surely had he commanded some great thing you ought to have done it (on this account at least) how much more when he saith, "Do this in remembrance of me"? Sure in this ordinance we have a real offer made of the flesh and blood of Christ for us to feed upon by faith as in any other part of the gospel of God.

The Lord's Table Teaches Unity

Nor is the Table of the Lord inferior to any doctrine in the gospel tending to preserve unity in the Church of God. Hence it is expressly called the communion of the body and blood of Christ: "The bread which we break is it not the communion of the body of Christ? The cup which we bless is it not the communion of the blood of Christ?" (1 Cor. 10:16). And again, "We being many are one body and one bread, even as we are all partakers of that one bread" (1 Cor. 10:17). Can anything be more effectually spoken to unite the members of Christ or will any man say these things are not spoken of this ordinance? If so he may see his folly by reading 1 Corinthians 11 throughout where the apostle plainly refers to the institution of Christ and affirms that he delivered that to them which he received of the Lord and plainly calls that bread and cup "the bread and cup of the Lord" (1 Cor. 11:27). Yea here Christ gathers his people together at his own Table as one family. And it is that Table to which all saints are to approach with such preparation as may render them fit for communion in that mystical body, the Church, which is also called Christ because of that unity they have in him and one another in him: "For as the body is one and hath many members, so also is Christ (that is, the Church). For by one Spirit are we all baptized into one body, and have been all made to drink into one Spirit" (1 Cor. 12:12–13). [This] is true not only for that this one body hath one Spirit, but also for that it hath one faith, one baptism, and one holy Table of the Lord wherein the members communicate together by the operation of that one Spirit.

What shall we say? Doth not our cheerful joining together in prayer demonstrate our union? How then should not our sincere communicating in this holy manducation be as great an evidence of Christian unity? Doubtless when our Saviour enjoined all that sat with him "to eat this bread and to drink all of that cup" his design was therein to engage them in the unity of himself and one another, especially the faithful. For as for Judas and all hypocrites as Christ himself is to them the savour of death unto death, so also is this ordinance, yea and every truth of the gospel. And here our blessed Saviour, after he had given those whom he had chosen this precept, prays for them several times that they might be in love and unity together. Let us therefore keep this feast with the unleavened bread of sincerity and truth for that is the scope of all religious performances, to teach us to love God and one another as he in Christ hath loved us.

The Lord's Table Is Conducive to the Stability of Christians in Faith

This Table of the Lord rightly understood is of great validity to establish Christians in the true faith. For when our Saviour saith, "This cup is the new testament in my blood," he shews the nature of this ordinance is to assure the saints as by a pledge or token that the new testament is ratified and confirmed by the death of the testator, so that whether we regard the certainty or sufficiency of the gospel, both declared in this ordinance as much as any other. For all the offices of Christ do meet and shew forth themselves in this service.

1. His kingly office, in that he makes a new law for his Church and abrogates the old, "for in that he saith a new covenant, he hath made the first old: now that which decayeth and waxeth old is ready to vanish away" (Heb. 8:13). But in this ordinance he expressly declares the establishment of the new testament or covenant in his blood and therefore doth here also shew the abrogation of the old.

2. His priestly office is most perspicuous in this service, the great sacrifice of the flesh and blood of Christ being the main thing to be always commemorated in the Church by this ordinance, "for as often as ye eat this bread and drink this cup, ye do shew forth the Lord's death" (1 Cor. 11:26).

3. His prophetical office. Here he teacheth that the law could not give life, for as the apostle saith, then "Christ had died in vain" (Gal. 2:21) and righteousness should have been by the law, but now remission of sin is herein set forth by the blood of the new testament, there being none other that could purge the conscience from dead works to serve the living God. In this ordinance Christ shewed beforehand who should betray him and foretells the kingdom of glory at his second coming and the kingdom of grace which should presently be established in his death and resurrection wherein all things are made new: "Therefore if any man be in Christ, he is a new creature. Old things are passed away, behold all things are become new" (2 Cor. 5:17). No ordinance (no not preaching of the word) is of greater use to establish God's people in the faith than this, for here we see with the eye and by it the judgment is informed as we hear with the ear and so receive instruction. And doubtless where Christ is known and believed in according to what this ordinance declares of him, there the impieties of antichrist cannot enter whose design is to deny Christ to be come in the flesh. Yet so mysteriously as that did he not oppose the ordinances of Christ which were appointed to set him forth as come in the flesh, it were much more hard to discover him then now it is.

For being pressed by the evidence given on that account by baptism and the Table of the Lord where the reality of Christ's humanity, his death, burial, resurrection, and second coming are so evidently displayed that the adversary hath no way but boldly to shake off these precepts as favouring too much of a fleshly Christ (as he is pleased to speak) when doubtless it is the most spiritual attainment in this life to know and walk with Christ as he is held forth in these two ordinances which comprehend briefly what is said of him in respect of his kingly, priestly, and prophetical office as before is shewed as also what concerns the Christian man in new birth, new life, self examination, mortification of the old man, the putting on of Christ, the feeding upon him as meat and drink indeed, and finally the resurrection of the dead and eternal life is undeniably set forth in the right use of these ordinances which therefore are of great advantage to establish through God's blessing and Spirit going along with them all such as love Christ and wait for his appearing.

[Thomas Grantham, *Christianismus Primitivus: or The Ancient Christian Religion*, II/I/1 and II/II/3–6 (London: Francis Smith, 1678), 1–3, 85–90.]

– II –

John Bunyan

John Bunyan (1628–88) described himself as an "unlettered and simple man," yet his stirring classic Pilgrim's Progress *is, next to the Bible, perhaps the world's all time best-selling book. After some schooling in the Bedfordshire village of his birth, Bunyan learned the tinker's trade. From 1644 to 1647 he served in the Parliamentary Army. Returning home he experienced a wrenching conversion recounted in* Grace Abounding *(1666). Upon his profession of faith and baptism in 1655 Bunyan was received into the Bedford congregation and soon became (unordained) the pastor. Agents of the restored monarchy arrested him in 1660 for unlicensed preaching. He spent the next twelve years in prison. During his several imprisonments, Bunyan studied the Bible and Foxe's* Book of Martyrs. *Also from jail he wrote books, including* Grace Abounding *and* Pilgrim's Progress. *That Bunyan is claimed by both Congregationalists and Baptists is understandable. Lines of demarcation between religious groups in seventeenth-century England were vague. Baptists and Congregationalists were often lumped together with Quakers, Levelers, Diggers, Ranters, Muggletonians, and Fifth Monarchists (See Christopher Hill,* A Turbulent, Seditious, and Factious People*). The boundaries between Congregationalists and Baptists were also permeable. The Bedford congregation was Independent, meaning that they practiced but did not require believers baptism for membership and they openly accepted all Christians for communion. In* Differences in Judgment about Water Baptism *(1673), Bunyan declared that "the Church of Christ hath no warrant to keep out of the communion the Christian that is discovered to be a visible saint of the word." In the selection from* Pilgrim's Progress, *when Christian arrives at Palace Beautiful (the church) he witnesses to his faith before Prudence, Piety, and Charity. Satisfied that he is truly converted, though there is no mention of baptism, they invite him to join them for supper (the Lord's Table). Bunyan's passionate account of the Christian life makes him one of the great lights, not only for Baptists, but for the communion of saints.*

The Palace Beautiful

So I saw in my dream, that he made haste, and went forward, that if possible he might get lodging there. Now before he had gone far, he entered into a very narrow passage, which was about a furlong off the Porter's lodge: and looking very narrowly before him as he went, he espied two lions in the way. Now, thought he, I see the dangers that Mistrust and Timorous were driven back by. (The lions were chained, but he saw not the chains.) Then he was afraid, and thought also himself to go back after them; for he thought nothing but death was before him. But the Porter at the lodge, whose name is Watchful, perceiving that Christian made a halt, as if he would go back, cried unto him, saying, Is thy strength so small? Fear not the lions, for they are chained, and are placed there for trial of faith where it is, and for discovery of those that have none: keep in the midst of the path, and no hurt shall come unto thee.

Then I saw that he went on, trembling for fear of the lions; but taking good heed to the directions of the Porter, he heard them roar, but they did him no harm. Then he clapped his hands, and went on till he came and stood before the gate where the Porter was. Then said Christian to the Porter, Sir, what house is this? and may I lodge here to-night? The Porter answered, This house was built by the Lord of the hill, and He built it for the relief and security of pilgrims. The Porter also asked whence he was, and whither he was going.

Chr. I am come from the City of Destruction, and am going to Mount Zion; but because the sun is now set, I desire, if I may, to lodge here to-night.

Port. What is your name?

Chr. My name is now Christian, but my name at the first was Graceless: I came of the race of Japheth, whom God will persuade to dwell in the tents of Shem.

Port. But how doth it happen you come so late? The sun is set.

Chr. I had been here sooner, but that, wretched man that I am, I slept in the arbour that stands on the hill side! Nay, I had, notwithstanding that, been here much sooner, but that in my sleep I lost my evidence, and came without it to the brow of the hill; and then feeling for it, and finding it not, I was forced with sorrow of heart to go back to the place where I slept my sleep, where I found it; and now I am come.

Port. Well, I will call out one of the virgins of this place, who will, if she likes your talk, bring you in to the rest of the family, according to the rules of the house. So Watchful the Porter rang a bell, at the sound of which came out of the door of the house a grave and beautiful damsel, named Discretion, and asked why she was called.

The Porter answered, This man is in a journey from the City of Destruction to Mount Zion; but being weary and benighted, he asked me if he might lodge here to-night: so I told him I would call for thee, who, after discourse had with him, mayest do as seemeth thee good, even according to the law of the house.

Then she asked him whence he was, and whither he was going; and he told her. She asked him also how he got into the way; and he told her. Then she asked him what he had seen and met with in the way; and he told her. And last she asked his name. So he said, It is Christian; and I have so much the more a desire to lodge here to-night, because, by what I perceive, this place was built by the Lord of the hill for the relief and security of pilgrims. So she smiled, but the water stood in her eyes; and after a little pause she said, I will call forth two or three more of my family. So she ran to the door, and called out Prudence, Piety, and Charity, who, after a little more discourse with him, had him in to the family; and many of them meeting him at the threshold of the house, said, Come in, thou blessed of the Lord; this house was built by the Lord of the hill, on purpose to entertain such pilgrims in. Then he bowed his head, and followed them into the house. So when he was come in and sat down, they gave him something to drink, and consented together that, until supper was ready, some of them should have some particular discourse with Christian, for the best improvement of time; and they appointed Piety, Prudence, and Charity to discourse with him; and thus they began.

Piety. Come, good Christian, since we have been so loving to you to receive you in to our house this night, let us, if perhaps we may better ourselves thereby, talk with you of all things that have happened to you in your pilgrimage.

Chr. With a very good will; and I am glad that you are so well disposed.

Piety. What moved you at first to betake yourself to a pilgrim's life?

Chr. I was driven out of my native country by a dreadful sound that was in mine ears; to wit, that unavoidable destruction did attend me, if I abode in that place where I was.

Piety. But how did it happen that you came out of your country this way?

Chr. It was as God would have it; for when I was under the fears of destruction, I did not know whither to go; but by chance there came a man, even to me, as I was trembling and weeping, whose name is Evangelist, and he directed me to the Wicket-gate, which else I should never have found, and so set me into the way that hath led me directly to this house.

Piety. But did you not come by the house of the Interpreter?

Chr. Yes, and did see such things there, the remembrance of which will stick by me as long as I live, especially three things; to wit, how Christ, in despite of Satan, maintains His work of grace in the heart;

how the man had sinned himself quite out of hopes of God's mercy; and also the dream of him that thought in his sleep the day of judgment was come.

Piety. Why, did you hear him tell his dream?

Chr. Yes, and a dreadful one it was, I thought; it made my heart ache as he was telling of it; but yet I am glad I heard it.

Piety. Was that all you saw at the house of the Interpreter?

Chr. No; he took me, and had me where he showed me a stately palace, and how the people were clad in gold that were in it; and how there came a venturous man, and cut his way through the armed men that stood in the door to keep him out; and how he was bid to come in, and win eternal glory. Methought those things did ravish my heart. I would have stayed at that good man's house a twelvemonth, but that I knew I had farther to go.

Piety. And what saw ye else in the way?

Chr. Saw? Why, I went but a little farther, and I saw one, as I thought in my mind, hang bleeding upon the tree; and the very sight of Him made my burden fall off my back; for I groaned under a very heavy burden, but then it fell down from off me. 'Twas a strange thing to me, for I never saw such a thing before: yea, and while I stood looking up (for then I could not forbear looking), three Shining Ones came to me. One of them testified that my sins were forgiven me; another stripped me of my rags, and gave me this broidered coat which you see; and the third set the mark which you see in my forehead, and gave me this sealed roll (and with that he plucked it out of his bosom).

Piety. But you saw more than this, did you not?

Chr. The things that I have told you were the best; yet some other matter I saw, as namely, I saw three men, Simple, Sloth, and Presumption, lie asleep, a little out of the way as I came, with irons upon their heels; but do you think I could awake them? I also saw Formality and Hypocrisy come tumbling over the wall, to go, as they pretended, to Zion; but they were quickly lost, even as myself did tell them, but they would not believe. But, above all, I found it hard work to get up this hill, and as hard to come by the lions' mouth; and truly, if it had not been for the good man the Porter, that stands at the gate, I do not know but that, after all, I might have gone back again; but now I thank God I am here, and I thank you for receiving of me.

Then Prudence thought good to ask him a few questions, and desired his answer to them.

Pr. Do you not think sometimes of the country from whence you came?

Chr. Yes; but with much shame and detestation. Truly, if I had been mindful of that country from whence I came out, I might have had opportunity to have returned; but now I desire a better country, that is, an heavenly.

Pr. Do you not yet bear away with you some of the things that then you were conversant withal?

Chr. Yes, but greatly against my will; especially my inward and carnal cogitations, with which all my countrymen, as well as myself, were delighted. But, now, all those things are my grief; and might I but choose mine own things, I would choose never to think of those things more; but when I would be adoing of that which is best, that which is worst is with me.

Pr. Do you not find sometimes as if those things were vanquished, which at other times are your perplexity?

Chr. Yes, but that is but seldom; but they are to me golden hours in which such things happen to me.

Pr. Can you remember by what means you find your annoyances at times as if they were vanquished?

Chr. Yes; when I think what I saw at the cross, that will do it; and when I look upon my broidered coat, that will do it; and when I look into the roll that I carry in my bosom, that will do it; and when my thoughts wax warm about whither I am going, that will do it.

Pr. And what is it that makes you so desirous to go to Mount Zion?

Chr. Why, there I hope to see Him alive that did hang dead on the cross; and there I hope to be rid of all those things that to this day are in me an annoyance to me: there they say there is no death, and there I shall dwell with such company as I like best. For, to tell you truth, I love Him because I was by Him eased of my burden; and I am weary of my inward sickness. I would fain be where I shall die no more, and with the company that shall continually cry, Holy, holy, holy.

Then said Charity to Christian, Have you a family? Are you a married man?

Chr. I have a wife and four small children.

Char. And why did you not bring them along with you?

Chr. Then Christian wept, and said, Oh, how willingly would I have done it! But they were all of them utterly averse to my going on pilgrimage.

Char. But you should have talked to them, and have endeavoured to have shown them the danger of being behind.

Chr. So I did; and told them also what God had showed to me of the destruction of our city; but I seemed to them as one that mocked, and they believed me not.

Char. And did you pray to God that He would bless your counsel to them?

Chr. Yes, and that with much affection; for you must think that my wife and poor children were very dear unto me.

Char. But did you tell them of your own sorrow, and fear of destruction? For I suppose that destruction was visible enough to you.

Chr. Yes, over, and over, and over. They might also see my fears in my countenance, in my tears, and also in my trembling under the apprehension of the judgment that did hang over our heads; but all was not sufficient to prevail with them to come with me.

Char. But what could they say for themselves why they came not?

Chr. Why, my wife was afraid of losing this world, and my children were given to the foolish delights of youth; so, what by one thing, and what by another, they left me to wander in this manner alone.

Char. But did you not with your vain life damp all that you, by words, used by way of persuasion to bring them away with you?

Chr. Indeed I cannot commend my life, for I am conscious to myself of many failings therein. I know also, that a man, by his conversation, may soon overthrow what by argument or persuasion he doth labour to fasten upon others for their good. Yet this I can say, I was very wary of giving them occasion, by any unseemly action, to make them averse to going on pilgrimage. Yea, for this very thing, they would tell me I was too precise, and that I denied myself of things (for their sakes) in which they saw no evil. Nay, I think I may say, that if what they saw in me did hinder them, it was my great tenderness in sinning against God, or of doing any wrong to my neighbour.

Char. Indeed, Cain hated his brother, because his own works were evil, and his brother's righteous; and if thy wife and children have been offended with thee for this, they thereby show themselves to be implacable to good; and thou hast delivered thy soul from their blood.

Now I saw in my dream, that thus they sat talking together until supper was ready. So when they had made ready, they sat down to meat. Now the table was furnished with fat things, and with wine that was well refined; and all their talk at the table was about the LORD of the hill; as, namely, about that HE had done, and whereof HE did what HE did, and why HE had builded that house; and by what they said, I perceived that HE had been a great warrior, and had fought with and slain him that had the power of death, but not without great danger to Himself, which made me love Him the more.

For, as they said, and as I believe, said Christian, He did it with the loss of much blood. But that which put glory of grace into all He did, was, that He did it out of pure love to his country. And besides, there were some of them of the household that said they had been and spoke with Him since He did die on the cross; and they have attested, that they had it from His own lips, that He is such a lover of poor pilgrims, that the like is not to be found from the east to the west. They, moreover, gave an instance of what they affirmed; and that was, He had stripped Himself of His glory that He might do this for the poor; and that they heard Him say and affirm, that He would not dwell in the mountain of Zion alone. They said, moreover, that He had made many pilgrims princes, though by nature they were beggars born, and their original had been the dunghill.

Thus they discoursed together till late at night; and after they had committed themselves to their Lord for protection, they betook themselves to rest. The pilgrim they laid in a large upper chamber, whose window opened towards the sun-rising. The name of the chamber was Peace, where he slept till break of day, and then he awoke and sang,

> Where am I now? Is this the love and care
> Of Jesus, for the men that pilgrims are,
> Thus to provide! that I should be forgiven,
> And dwell already the next door to heaven!

So in the morning they all got up; and, after some more discourse, they told him that he should not depart till they had showed him the rarities of that place. And first they had him into the study, where they showed him the records of the greatest antiquity; in which, as I remember my dream, they showed him first the pedigree of the Lord of the hill, that He was the Son of the Ancient of Days, and came by that eternal generation. Here also was more fully recorded the acts that He had done, and the names of many hundreds that He had taken into His service; and how He had placed them in such habitations, that could neither by length of days, nor decays of nature, be dissolved.

Then they read to him some of the worthy acts that some of His servants had done; as how they had subdued kingdoms, wrought righteousness, obtained promises, stopped the mouths of lions, quenched the violence of fire, escaped the edge of the sword, out of weakness were made strong, waxed valiant in fight, and turned to flight the armies of the aliens.

Then they read again in another part of the records of the house, where it was showed how willing their Lord was to receive into His favour any, even any, though they in time past had offered great affronts to His person and proceedings. Here also were several other histories of many other famous things, of all which Christian had a view; as of things both ancient and modern, together with prophecies and predictions of things that have their certain accomplishment, both to the dread and amazement of enemies, and the comfort and solace of pilgrims.

The next day they took him, and had him into the armoury, where they showed him all manner of furniture which their Lord had provided for pilgrims, a sword, shield, helmet, breastplate, all-prayer, and shoes that would not wear out. And there was here enough of this to harness out as many men for the service of their Lord, as there be stars in the heaven for multitude.

They also showed him some of the engines with which some of His servants had done wonderful things. They showed him Moses's rod; the hammer and nail with which Jael slew Sisera; the pitchers, trumpets, and lamps too, with which Gideon put to flight the armies of Midian. Then they showed him the ox's goad, wherewith Shamgar slew six hundred men. They showed him also the jawbone with which Samson did such mighty feats. They showed him moreover the sling and stone with which David slew Goliath of Gath, and the sword also with which their Lord will kill the man of sin, in the day that He shall rise up to the prey. They showed him besides many excellent things, with which Christian was much delighted. This done, they went to their rest again.

Then I saw in my dream, that on the morrow he got up to go forwards, but they desired him to stay till the next day also; and then, said they, we will, if the day be clear, show you the Delectable Mountains; which, they said, would yet further add to his comfort, because they were nearer the desired haven than the place where at present he was; so he consented and stayed. When the morning was up, they had him to the top of the house, and bid him look south. So he did, and behold at a great distance, he saw a most pleasant, mountainous country, beautified with woods, vineyards, fruits of all sorts, flowers also, with springs and fountains, very delectable to behold. Then he asked the name of the country. They said it was Immanuel's Land; and it is as common, said they, as this hill is, to and for all the pilgrims. And when thou comest there, from thence, said they, thou mayest see to the gate of the Celestial City, as the shepherds that live there will make appear.

Now he bethought himself of setting forward, and they were willing he should. But first, said they, let us go again into the armoury. So they did, and when he came there, they harnessed him from head to foot with what was of proof, lest perhaps he should meet with assaults in the way. He being therefore thus accoutred, walked out with his friends to the gate, and there he asked the Porter if he saw any pilgrims pass by. Then the Porter answered, Yes.

Chr. Pray did you know him? said he.

Port. I asked his name, and he told me it was Faithful.

Chr. Oh, said Christian, I know him; he is my townsman, my near neighbour, he comes from the place where I was born. How far do you think he may be before?

Port. He is got by this time below the hill.

Chr. Well, said Christian, good Porter, the Lord be with thee, and add to all thy blessings much increase of the kindness that thou hast showed to me.

Then he began to go forward; but Discretion, Piety, Charity and Prudence would accompany him down to the foot of the hill. So they went on together, reiterating their former discourses, till they came to go down the hill. Then said Christian, As it was difficult coming up, so, so far as I can see, it is dangerous going down. Yes, said Prudence, so it is; for it is an hard matter for a man to go down into the Valley of Humiliation, as thou art now, and to catch no slip by the way; therefore, said they, are we come out to accompany thee down the hill. So he began to go down, but very warily; yet he caught a slip or two.

[John Bunyan, *The Pilgrim's Progress,* The Puritan Edition (New York: Revell, 1903), 53–64.]

– 12 –

John Milton

Although John Milton (1608–74) is widely regarded as the greatest English poet after Shakespeare, his contribution to the advancement of baptist theology is little noted. He was born in London and educated at Christ's College, Cambridge. At first he intended to become a clergyman, but his growing disenchantment with the Anglican Church led him to poetry. When civil war broke out in the 1640s between the Parliamentary Army (loyal to the Protestants and led by Oliver Cromwell) and the Royalist forces (faithful to Charles I and the High Church episcopacy), Milton began writing tracts in support of the Protestant cause. He published The Reason of Church Government Urged against Prelatry *(1641–42), which attacked the institution of bishops, and* Areopagitica *(1644), which defended the freedom of the press. His break with the Presbyterians was final by 1646 when he penned* On the New Forcers of Conscience under the Long Parliament, *which concluded with the line* "New Presbyter *is but* Old Priest *writ Large." Once Milton parted company with the Presbyterians, his theological views tended toward the Independents. Historian Christopher Hill observes that "if we look for analogies with Milton's ideas among the radicals we shall easily find them" (*Milton and the English Revolution, *99). The company he kept included prominent Baptists Roger Williams (1603–83) and Hanserd Knollys (1599–1691). His support for Anabaptists is enshrined in a sonnet that memorialized the persecution of the Waldensians. Here Milton intoned,*

> *Avenge O Lord, thy slaughter'd saints, whose bones*
> *Lie scatter'd in the Alpine mountains cold.*

The selection from Milton's masterpiece, Paradise Lost *(1667), contains several speeches of the Seraph Abdiel before Satan. This faithful angel contends that "few sometimes may know, when thousands err," which is a reminder that the truth may most often lie in the voice of dissent.*

Paradise Lost
Book 5

    Thus far his bold discourse without control
Had audience, when among the Seraphim
Abdiel, than whom none with more zeal ador'd   805
The Deity, and divine commands obey'd,
Stood up, and in a flame of zeal severe
The current of his fury thus oppos'd.
    O argument blasphemous, false and proud!
Words which no ear ever to hear in Heav'n   810
Expected, least of all from thee, ingrate,
In place thyself so high above thy Peers.
Canst thou with impious obloquy condemn
The just Decree of God, pronounc't and sworn,
That to his only Son by right endu'd   815
With Regal Sceptre, every Soul in Heav'n
Shall bend the knee, and in that honor due
Confess him rightful King? unjust thou say'st
Flatly unjust, to bind with Laws the free,
And equal over equals to let Reign,   820
One over all with unsucceeded power.
Shalt thou give Law to God, shalt thou dispute
With him the points of liberty, who made
Thee what thou art, and form'd the Pow'rs of Heav'n
Such as he pleas'd, and circumscrib'd thir being?   825
Yet by experience taught we know how good,
And of our good, and of our dignity
How provident he is, how far from thought
To make us less, bent rather to exalt
Our happy state under one Head more near   830
United. But to grant it thee unjust,
That equal over equals Monarch Reign:
Thyself though great and glorious dost thou count,
Or all Angelic Nature join'd in one,
Equal to him begotten Son, by whom   835
As by his Word the mighty Father made
All things, ev'n thee, and all the Spirits of Heav'n
By him created in thir bright degrees,
Crown'd them with Glory, and to thir Glory nam'd
Thrones, Dominations, Princedoms, Virtues, Powers,   840
Essential Powers, nor by his Reign obscur'd,
But more illustrious made, since he the Head
One of our number thus reduc't becomes,

His Laws our Laws, all honor to him done
Returns our own. Cease then this impious rage,   845
And tempt not these; but hast'n to appease
Th' incensed Father, and th' incensed Son,
While Pardon may be found in time besought.
  So spake the fervent Angel, but his zeal
None seconded, as out of season judg'd,   850
Or singular and rash, whereat rejoic'd
Th' Apostate, and more haughty thus repli'd.
  That we were form'd then say'st thou? and the work
Of secondary hands, by task transferr'd
From Father to his Son? strange point and new!   855
Doctrine which we would know whence learnt: who saw
When this creation was? remember's thou
Thy making, while the Maker gave thee being?
We know no time when we were not as now;
Know none before us, self-begot, self-rais'd   860
By our own quick'ning power, when fatal course
Had circl'd his full Orb, the birth mature
Of this our native Heav'n, Ethereal Sons.
Our puissance is our own, our own right hand
Shall teach us highest deeds, by proof to try   865
Who is our equal: then thou shalt behold
Whether by supplication we intend
Address, and to begirt th' Almighty Throne
Beseeching or besieging. This report,
These tidings carry to th' anointed King;   870
And fly, ere evil intercept thy flight.
  He said, and as the sound of waters deep
Hoarse murmur echo'd to his words applause
Through the infinite Host, nor less for that
The flaming Seraph fearless, though alone   875
Encompass'd round with foes, thus answer'd bold.
  O alienate from God, O Spirit accurst,
Forsak'n of all good; I see thy fall
Determin'd, and thy hapless crew involv'd
In this perfidious fraud, contagion spread   880
Both of thy crime and punishment: henceforth
No more be troubl'd how to quit the yoke
Of God's *Messiah:* those indulgent Laws
Will not be now voutsaf'd, other Decrees
Against thee are gone forth without recall;   885
That Golden Sceptre which thou didst reject
Is now an Iron Rod to bruise and break

Thy disobedience. Well thou didst advise,
Yet not for thy advice or threats I fly
These wicked Tents devoted, lest the wrath   890
Impendent, raging into sudden flame
Distinguish not: for soon expect to feel
His Thunder on thy head, devouring fire.
Then who created thee lamenting learn,
When who can uncreate thee thou shalt know.   895
   So spake the Seraph *Abdiel* faithful found,
Among the faithless, faithful only hee;
Among innumerable false, unmov'd,
Unshak'n, unseduc'd, unterrifi'd
His Loyalty he kept, his Love, his Zeal;   900
Nor number, nor example with him wrought
To swerve from truth, or change his constant mind
Though single. From amidst them forth he pass'd,
Long way through hostile scorn, which he sustain'd
Superior, nor of violence fear'd aught;   905
And with retorted scorn his back he turn'd
On those proud Tow'rs to swift destruction doom'd.

Paradise Lost
Book 6

Satan with vast and haughty strides advanc'd,
Came tow'ring, arm'd in Adamant and Gold;   110
Abdiel that sight endur'd not, where he stood
Among the mightiest, bent on highest deeds,
And thus his own undaunted heart explores.
   O Heav'n! that such resemblance of the Highest
Should yet remain, where faith and realty   115
Remain not; wherefore should not strength and might
There fail where Virtue fails, or weakest prove
Where boldest; though to sight unconquerable?
His puissance, trusting in th' Almighty's aid,
I mean to try, whose Reason I have tri'd   120
Unsound and false; nor is it aught but just,
That he who in debate of Truth hath won,
Should Will in Arms, in both disputes alike
Victor; though brutish that contest and foul,
When Reason hath to deal with force, yet so   125
Most reason is that Reason overcome.
   So pondering, and from his armed Peers

Forth stepping opposite, half way he met
His daring foe, at this prevention more
Incenst, and thus securely him defi'd.   130
   Proud, art thou met? thy hope was to have reacht
The highth of thy aspiring unoppos'd,
The Throne of Clod unguarded and his side
Abandon'd at the terror of thy Power
Or potent tongue; fool, not to think how vain   135
Against th' Omnipotent to rise in Arms;
Who out of smallest things could without end
Have rais'd incessant Armies to defeat
Thy folly; or with solitary hand
Reaching beyond all limit, at one blow   140
Unaided could have finisht thee, and whelm'd
Thy Legions under darkness; but thou seest
All are not of thy Train; there be who Faith
Prefer, and Piety to God, though then
To thee not visible, when I alone   145
Seem'd in thy World erroneous to dissent
From all: my Sect thou seest, now learn too late
How few sometimes may know, when thousands err.
   Whom the grand Foe with scornful eye askance
Thus answer'd. Ill for thee, but in wisht hour   150
Of my revenge, first sought for thou return'st
From flight, seditious Angel, to receive
Thy merited reward, the first assay
Of this right hand provok'd, since first that tongue
Inspir'd with contradiction durst oppose   155
A third part of the Gods, in Synod met
Thir Deities to assert, who while they feel
Vigor Divine within them, can allow
Omnipotence to none. But well thou com'st
Before thy fellows, ambitious to win   160
From me some Plume, that thy success may show
Destruction to the rest: this pause between
(Unanswer'd lest thou boast) to let thee know;
At first I thought that Liberty and Heav'n
To heav'nly Souls had been all one; but now   165
I see that most through sloth had rather serve,
Minist'ring Spirits, train'd up in Feast and Song;
Such hast thou arm'd, the Minstrels of Heav'n,
Servility with freedom to contend,
As both thir deeds compar'd this day shall prove.   170
   To whom in brief thus *Abdiel* stern repli'd.

Apostate, still thou err'st, nor end wilt find
Of erring, from the path of truth remote:
Unjustly thou deprav'st it with the name
Of Servitude to serve whom God ordains,   175
Or Nature; God and Nature bid the Same,
When he who rules is worthiest, and excels
Them whom he governs. This is servitude,
To serve th' unwise, or him who hath rebell'd
Against his worthier, as shine now serve thee,   180
Thyself not free, but to thyself enthrall'd;
Yet lewdly dar'st our minist'ring upbraid.
Reign thou in Hell thy Kingdom, let mee serve
In Heav'n God ever blest, and his Divine
Behests obey, worthiest to be obey'd;   185
Yet Chains in Hell, not Realms expect: meanwhile
From mee return'd, as erst thou said'st, from flight,
This greeting on thy impious Crest receive.

[*Paradise Lost* (London: B. White and Son, 1793).]

– 13 –

Roger Williams

Roger Williams (1603–83) was a trailblazer for Baptists in North America. Although he was educated at Pembroke College, Cambridge (1623–29), Williams never embraced Anglican convictions. In 1631 he joined a growing Puritan population in New England who hoped to escape the repressive policies of Charles I (1625–49). Upon arrival Williams was offered a position as a teacher in the church of Boston, but he declined to "officiate to an unseparated people." As he moved to Salem, Plymouth, and Salem again, Williams also moved in the direction of Separatism, which brought him under the suspicion of Puritan authorities, especially the irascible Boston cleric John Cotton (1584–1652). Williams was banished by the General Court in 1635 for teaching "new and dangerous opinions." He fled Salem in January of 1636, taking refuge with his Indian friends. Williams would later write in his first book, A Key to the Language of America *(1643):*

> *If nature's sons both wild and tame*
> *Humane and courteous be,*
> *How ill becomes it sons of God*
> *To want humanity?*

In Christenings Make Not Christians, *Williams argued that forced conversion of the Indians would substitute Christendom for Christianity. This, as he saw it, was the error of the state churches. In the spring of 1636 Williams founded the colony of Rhode Island with the guarantee of the liberty of conscience for all citizens. In his famous "Ship of State" letter, written in reply to Rhode Islanders critical of his overbearing civic policies, Williams made clear that he was no libertarian pamphleteer, as later interpreters would argue. Liberty of conscience was simply freedom from* forced *religion and freedom to* uncoerced *religion. The ties of Williams to Baptists were brief. Rebaptized in March of 1639, he established the First Baptist Church of Providence, but three months later he became a Seeker. Yet from the perspective of the Baptists, history has vindicated him as "America's theologian" (see Gaustad,* Liberty of Conscience: Roger Williams in America, *193–219).*

Christenings Make Not Christians

I shall first be humbly bold to inquire into the name *heathen*, which the English give them, and the Dutch approve and practice in their name *heydenen*, signifying heathen or nations. How oft have I heard both the English and Dutch (not only the civil, but the most debauched and profane) say, "These heathen dogs, better kill a thousand of them than that we Christians should be endangered or troubled with them. Better they were all cut off, and then we shall be no more troubled with them. They have spilt our Christian blood. The best way to make riddance of them is to cut them all off and so make way for Christians."

I shall therefore humbly entreat my countrymen of all sorts to consider that although men have used to apply this word *heathen* to the Indians that go naked and have not heard of that one God, yet this word *heathen* is most improperly, sinfully, and unchristianly so used in this sense. The word *heathen* signifieth no more than *nations* or *gentiles*. So do our translations from the Hebrew גוים and the Greek ἔθνη in the Old and New Testaments promiscuously render these words *gentiles, nations, heathens*. Why nations? Because the Jews being the only people and nation of God, esteemed (and that rightly) all other People — not only those that went naked, but the famous Babylonians, Caldeans, Medes, and Persians, Greeks, and Romans, their stately cities and citizens — inferior themselves and not partakers of their glorious privileges, but gentiles, heathen, or nations of the world.

Now then we must inquire who are the people of God, his holy nation, since the coming of the Lord Jesus, and the rejection of his first typical holy nation the Jews. It is confessed by all that the Christians the followers of Jesus are now the only people of God, his holy nation (1 Pet. 2:9). Who are then the nations, heathen, or gentiles in opposition to this people of God? I answer, all people, civilized as well as uncivilized, even the most famous states, cities, and the kingdoms of the world, for all must come within that distinction (1 Cor. 5) within or without. Within — the people of God, his church at Corinth. Without — the city of Corinth worshipping idols and so consequently all other people, heathens or nations, opposed to the people of God, the true Jews. And therefore now the natural Jews themselves, not being of this people, are heathens, nations or gentiles. Yea, this will by many hands be yielded, but what say you to the Christian world? What say you to Christendom? I answer, what do you think Peter or John, or Paul, or any of the first Messengers of the Lord Jesus would say to a Christian world? Yea if the Lord Jesus himself were here (as he will be shortly) and were to make answer, what would he say to Christendom? And otherwise then what he would speak, that is indeed what he hath spoken and will shortly speak, must no man speak that names himself a Christian.

Herdious in his map of his Christian world takes in all Asia, Europe, a vast part of Africa, and a great part also of America, so far as the Pope's christenings have reached to. This is the Christian world or Christendom in which respect men stand upon their terms of high opposition between the Christian and the Turk, the Christian shore and the Turkish shore, between the Christians of this Christian world and the Jew and the Christian and the heathen, that is the naked American. But since without is turned to be within, the world turned Christian, and a little flock of Jesus Christ hath marvelously increased in such wonderful conversions, let me be bold to ask what is Christ? What are the Christians? The Hebrew משיח and the Greek χριστός will tell us that Christ was and is the anointed of God, whom the prophets and Kings and priests of Israel in their *anointing* did prefigure and type out, whence his followers are called χριστιανοῖ Christians, that is, anointed also. So that indeed to be a Christian implies two things: first, to be a follower of that anointed one in all his offices; secondly, to partake of his anointing, for the anointing of the Lord Jesus (like to the anointing of Aaron to which none might make the like on pain of death) descends to the skirt of his garments.

To come nearer to this Christian world, (where the world becomes Christian holy, anointed, God's people) what saith John? What saith the angel? Yea, what saith Jesus Christ and his Father from whom the Revelation came (Rev. 1:1)? What say they unto the Beast and his worshippers (Rev. 13)? If that beast be not the Turk nor the Roman emperor (as the grossest interpret), but either the general councils, or the catholic church of Rome, or the Popes or Papacy (as the most refined interpret) why then all the world, ὅλη ἡ γῆ (Rev. 13), wonders after the beast, worships the beast, followeth the beast, and boasts of the beast, that there is none like him and all people, tongues, and nations, come under the power of this beast, and no man shall buy nor sell, nor live who hath not the mark of the beast in his forehead, or in his hand, or the number of his name.

If this world or earth then be not intended of the whole terrestrial globe: Europe, Asia, Africa, and America, which sense and experience denies, but of the Roman earth, or world, and the people, languages, and nations, of the Roman monarchy, transferred from the Roman emperor to the Roman Popes, and the Popish kingdoms, branches of that Roman root as all history and content or time make evident, then we know by this time what the Lord Jesus would say of the Christian world and of the Christian, indeed what he saith (Rev. 14). If any man worship the Beast or his picture, he shall drink even the dread fullest cup that the whole book of God ever held forth to sinners. Grant this, say some of Popish countries, that notwithstanding they make up Christendom, or Christian world, yet submitting to that Beast they are the earth or world and must drink of that most dreadful cup. But now for those nations that have withdrawn their necks from that beastly yoke (and protesting against him are not Papists, but Protestants) shall we — may we think of them that they or any of them may also be called in true Scripture sense heathens, that is nations or gentiles in opposition to the people of God, which is the only holy nation?

I answer, that all nations now called Protestants were at first part of that whole earth, or main (antichristian) continent, that wondered after and worshipped the Beast. This must then with holy fear and trembling be attended to because it concerns the kingdom of God and salvation. Whether such a departure from the Beast and coming out from antichristian abominations, from his marks in a false conversion, and a false constitution, or framing of national churches in false ministries and ministrations of baptism, Supper of the Lord, admonitions, excommunications as amounts to a true perfect hand, cut off from that earth which wondered after and worshipped the Beast: or whether, not being so cut off, they remain not peninsula or necks of land, contiguous and joined still unto his Christendom? If now the bodies of Protestant nations remain in an unrepentant, unregenerate, natural estate and so consequently far from hearing the admonitions of the Lord Jesus (Mt. 18), I say they must sadly consider and know (least their profession of the name of Jesus prove at last but an aggravation of condemnation) that Christ Jesus hath said they are but as heathens and publicans (Mt. 18:17). How might I therefore humbly beseech my countrymen to consider what deep cause they have to search their conversions from that Beast and his picture? And whether having no more of Christ than the name (beside the invented ways of worship derived from or drawn after Rome's pattern) their hearts and conversations will not evince them unconverted and unchristian Christians, and not yet knowing what it is to come by true regeneration within to the true spiritual Jew from without amongst the nations, that is heathens or gentiles.

How deeply and eternally this concerns each soul to search into. Yea, and much more deeply such is profess to be guides, leaders, and builders of the house of God. First, as they look to forms and frame of buildings, or churches. Secondly, as they attend to means and instruments. Thirdly, as they would lay sure foundations and lasting groundsills. Fourthly, as they account the cost and charge such buildings will amount unto. Fifthly, so they may not forget the true spiritual matter and materials of which a true house, city, kingdom, or nation of God now in the New Testament are to be composed or gathered.

Now secondly, for the hopes of conversion and turning the people of America, that is, the Indians, unto God. There is no respect of persons with him, for we are all the work of his hands, from the rising of the sun to the going down thereof, his name shall be great among the nations from the east and from the west. If we respect their sins, they are far short of European sinners. They neither abuse such corporal mercies for they have them not, nor sin they against the gospel light which shines not amongst them as the men of Europe do. And yet if they were greater sinners than they are, or greater sinners than the Europeans, they are not the further from the great ocean of mercy in that respect. Lastly, they are intelligent, many very ingenuous, plain-hearted, inquisitive and, as I said before, prepared with many convictions.

Now secondly, for the conversion of the Catholics: although I believe I may safely hope that God hath his in Rome and Spain, yet if Antichrist be their false head (as most true it is) the body, faith, baptism, hope are opposite to the true (Eph. 4) and all false also. Yea consequently their preachings, conversions, salvations (leaving secret things to God) must all be of the same false nature likewise. If the reports (yea some of their own historians) be true, what monstrous and most inhumane conversions have they made; baptizing thousands, yea ten thousands of the poor natives sometimes by wiles and subtle devices, sometimes by force compelling them to submit to that which they understood not, neither before nor after such their monstrous christening of them.

Thirdly, for our New England parts, I can speak uprightly and confidently. I know it to have been easy for my self long ere this to have brought many thousands of these natives, yea the whole country, to a far greater antichristian conversion than ever was yet heard of in America. I have reported something in the chapter of their religion, how readily I could have brought the whole country to have observed one day in seven, to have received a baptism (or washing) though it were in rivers (as the first Christians and the Lord Jesus himself did), to have come to a stated church meeting, maintained priests and forms of prayer, and a whole form of antichristian worship in life and death. Let none wonder at this, for plausible persuasions in the mouths of those whom natural men esteem and love, for the power of prevailing forces and armies hath done this in all the nations (as men speak) of Christendom. Yea what lamentable experience have we of the turnings and turnings of the body of this land in point of religion in few years?

When England was all Popish under Henry VII, how easy was conversion wrought to half-Papist half-Protestant under Henry VIII? From half-Protestantism half-Popery under Henry VIII, to absolute Protestantism under Edward VI: from absolute Protestation under Edward VI to absolute Popery under Queen Mary, and from absolute Popery under Queen Mary (just like the Weathercock, with the breath of every prince) to absolute Protestantism under Queen Elizabeth.

For all this, yet some may ask, why hath there been such a price in my hand not improved? Why have I not brought them to such a conversion as I speak of? I answer, woe be to me, if I call light darkness or darkness light; sweet bitter or bitter sweet. Woe be to me if I call that conversion unto God which is indeed subversion of the souls of millions in Christendom from one false worship to another and the profanation of the holy name of God, his holy Son and blessed ordinances. America (as Europe and all nations) lies dead in sin and trespasses. It is not a suit of crimson satin that will make a dead man live. Take it off and change his crimson into white, he is dead still. Off with that and shift him into cloth of gold, and from that to cloth of diamonds, he is but a dead man still. For it is not a form nor the change of one form into another (a fine, a finer, and yet more fine) that makes a man a convert. I mean such a convert as is acceptable to God in Jesus Christ, according to the visible rule of his last will and testament. I speak, not of hypocrites which may but glisten and be no solid gold as Simon Magus or Judas, but of a true external conversion. I say then, woe be to me if intending to catch men (as the Lord Jesus said to Peter) I should pretend conversion and the bringing of men as mystical fish into a church estate, that is a converted estate, and so build them up with ordinances as a converted Christian people, and yet afterward still pretend to catch them by an after conversion. I question not but that it hath pleased God in his infinite pity and patience to suffer this among us, yea and to convert thousands, whom all men, yea and the persons (in their personal estates converted) have esteemed themselves good converts before.

But I question whether this hath been so frequent in these late years when the times of ignorance which God pleaseth to pass by are over, and now a greater light concerning the church, ministry, and conversion, is arisen. I question whether if such rare talents which God hath betrusted many of his precious worthies with were laid out (as they shall be in the Lord's most holy season) according to the first pattern. I say, I question whether or no where there hath been one (in his personal estate converted) there have not been, and I hope in the Lord's time shall be, thousands truly converted from antichristian idols (both in person and worship) to serve the living and true God. And lastly, it is out of question to me, that I may not pretend a false conversion, and false state of worship, to the true Lord Jesus.

If any noble Berean shall make inquiry what is that true conversion I intend; I answer first negatively. First, it is not a conversion of a people from one false worship to another, as Nebuchadnezzer compelled all nations under his monarchy. Secondly, it is not to a mixture of the manner or worship of the true God, the God of Israel, with false gods and their worships, as the people were converted by the King of Assyria (2 Kings 17) in which worship for many generations did these Samaritans continue, having a form of many wholesome truths amongst them concerning God and the Messiah (Jn. 4). Thirdly, it is not from the true to a false, as Jeroboam turned the ten tribes to their wine and dispersion unto this day (1 Kings 12). Fourthly, it must not be a conversion to some external submission to God's ordinances upon earthly respects, as Jacob's sons converted the Shechemites (Gen. 34). Fifthly, it must not be (it is not possible it should be in truth) a conversion of people to the worship of the Lord Jesus, by force of arms and swords of steel. So indeed did Nebuchadnezzar deal with all the world (Dan. 3) so doth his antitype and successor the Beast deal with all the earth (Rev. 13).

But so did never the Lord Jesus bring any unto his most pure worship, for he abhors (as all men, yea the very Indians do) an unwilling spouse and to enter into a forced bed. The will in worship, if true, is like a free vote: *nec cogit, nec cogitur.* Jesus Christ compels by the mighty persuasions of his messengers to come in, but otherwise with earthly weapons he never did compel nor can be compelled. The not discerning of this truth hath let out the blood of thousands in civil combustion in all ages and made the whore drunk and the earth drunk with the blood of the saints and witnesses of Jesus. And it is yet like to be the destruction and dissolution of (that which is called) the Christian world unless the God of peace and pity look down upon it and satisfy the souls of men that he hath not so required. I should be far yet from unsecuring the peace of a city of a land, which I confess ought to be maintained by civil weapons and which I have so much cause to be earnest with God for. Nor would I leave a gap open to any mutinous hand or tongue, nor wish a weapon left in the hand of any known to be mutinous and peace-breakers. I know (lastly) the consciences of many are otherwise persuaded, both from Israel's state of old and other allegations. Yet I shall be humbly bold to say, I am able to present such considerations to the eyes of all who love the Prince of truth and peace, that shall discover the weakness of all such allegations, and answer all objections, that have been, or can be made in this point. So much negatively.

Secondly, affirmatively I answer in general. A true conversion, whether of Americans or Europeans, must be such as those conversions were of the first pattern, either of the Jews or the heathens. That rule is the golden mace wand in the hand of the angel or messenger (Rev. 11:1) beside which all other are leaden and crooked. In particular first, it must be by the free proclaiming or preaching of repentance and forgiveness of sins (Lk. 24) by such messengers as can prove their lawful sending and commission from the Lord Jesus to make disciples out of all nations, and so to baptize or wash them into the name (εἰς τὸ ὄνομα) or profession of the holy Trinity (Mt. 28:19, Rom. 10:14–15). Secondly, such a conversion so far as man's judgment can reach, which is fallible, as was the judgment of the first messengers as in Simon Magus, is a turning of the whole man from the power of Satan unto God (Acts 26). Such a change, as if an old man became a new baby (2 Jn. 3) yea, as amounts to God's new creation in the soul (Eph. 2:10).

Thirdly, visibly it is a turning from idols not only of conversation but of worship (whether Pagan, Turkish, Jewish, or antichristian) to the living and true God in the ways of his holy worship appointed by his Son (1 Thes. 1:9). I know objections use to be made against this, but the Golden Rule, if well attended to, will discover all crooked swerving and aberrations.

If any now say unto me, why then if this be conversion (and you have such a key of language, and such a core of opportunity, in the knowledge of the country and the inhabitants) why proceed you not to produce in America some patterns of such conversions as you speak of? I answer, first, it must be a great deal of practice and mighty pains and hardship undergone by my self or any that would proceed to such a further degree of the language, as to be able in propriety of speech to open matters of salvation to them. In matters of earth men will help to spell out each other, but in matters of heaven (to which the soul is naturally so averse) how far are the ears of man hedged up from listening to all improper language? Secondly, my desires and endeavors are constant (by the help of God) to attain a propriety of language. Thirdly, I confess to the honor of my worthy countrymen in the Bay of Massachusetts and elsewhere that I received not long since expressions of their holy desires and proffers of assistance in the work by the hand of my worthy friend Colonel Humphreys during his abode there. Yet fourthly, I answer if a man were as affectionate and zealous as David to build a house for God, and as wise and holy to advise and encourage as Nathan to attempt this work without a word, warrant and commission, for matter, and manner, from God himself, they must afterwards hear a voice (though accepting good desires, yet reproving want of commission). Did I ever speak a word saith the Lord (2 Sam. 7:7)?

The truth is, having not been without (through the mercy of God) abundant and constant thoughts about a true commission for such an embassy and ministry. I must ingenuously confess the restless unsatisfiedness of my soul in divers main particulars: As first whether (since the Law must go forth from Zion and the word of the Lord from Jerusalem) I say whether God's great business between Christ Jesus the holy Son of God and Antichrist the man of sin and son of perdition must not be first over, and Zion and Jerusalem be rebuilt and reestablished, before the Law and word of life be sent forth to the rest of the nations of the world, who have not heard of Christ. The prophets are deep concerning this. Secondly since there can be no preaching, according to the last will and testament of Christ Jesus, without a true sending (Rom. 14:15), where is the power and authority of sending and giving that commission (Mt. 28:8)? I say where that power now lies?

It is here unseasonable to number up all that lay claim to this power with their grounds for their pretences, either those of the Romish sort,

or those of the reforming or rebuilding sort, and the mighty controversies which are this day in all parts about it. In due place happily I
may present such sad queries to consideration that may occasion some
to cry with Daniel concerning Jerusalem's desolation (Dan. 9). Under
the whole heaven hath not been done as hath been done to Jerusalem
and with Jeremiah in the same respect (Lam. 2:12). Have you no respect all you that pass by? Behold and see if there were ever sorrow
like to my sorrow wherewith the Lord hath afflicted me in the day of
his fierce wrath. That may make us ashamed for all that we have done
(Ez. 43) and loath ourselves for that (in whorish worships) we have broken him with our whorish hearts (Ez. 9) to fall dead at the feet of Jesus
as John did (Rev. 1) and to weep much as he (Rev. 5) that so the Lamb
may please to open unto us that wonderful book and the seven sealed
mysteries thereof.

[*The Complete Works of Roger Williams* (New York: Russell and Russell, 1963),
7:31–41.]

– 14 –

Anne Hutchinson

Anne Hutchinson (1591–1643) is celebrated today as an emblem of liberty and equality. Yet to her Puritan contemporaries, her "opinions" were a "leprosy" that would "eat out the very bowels of religion." Her indomitable spirit was rooted in the baptist conviction that in the Bible God speaks directly to each Christian. (See McClendon on the baptist vision in Ethics, *33). But her story also serves as a warning that this standpoint is rightly viewed as subversive to powers who would speak with one voice by silencing all others — especially feminine ones. Anne Hutchinson began studying Scripture under the guidance of her clergyman father, once himself imprisoned for zealous preaching. Later she came under the influence of Puritan cleric John Cotton (1584–1652), whom, with her husband and eleven children, she followed from England to America in 1634. She began inviting women into her home for theological discussions. Her growing popularity threatened the authorities, who summoned her before the General Court in 1637. Hutchinson contended that church ministers taught a covenant of works, not grace. They charged Anne with antinomianism — denying the necessity of works as evidence of one's election. She countered that the proof of saving grace is inward witness not outward works. Banished by the Court, Hutchinson and her family moved to Rhode Island, then to New York, where tragically she was killed by Indians. Her emphasis on interiority was continued by subsequent generations of Baptists, Quakers, and even Jonathan Edwards (1703–58), the greatest of the Congregationalist theologians. Hutchinson also anticipated the expanding role of women in the church that accompanied the evangelical revivals of the eighteenth century. Susan Juster notes that baptist piety and polity offered "a slender reed upon which to build a more egalitarian vision of society," which, she adds, "unraveled in the revolutionary crisis of the late eighteenth century" as men alone assumed their place in the governing structures of the church and the new republic (*Disorderly Women, 12–13).

The Examination of Mrs. Anne Hutchinson

Mrs. Hutchinson. I am called here to answer before you but I hear no things laid to my charge.

Gov. I have told you some already and more I can tell you.

Mrs. H. Name one Sir.

Gov. Have I not named some already?

Mrs. H. What have I said or done?

Gov. Why for your doings, this you did harbour and countenance those that are parties in this faction that you have heard of.

Mrs. H. That's matter of conscience, Sir.

Gov. Your conscience you must keep or it must be kept for you.

Mrs. H. Must not I then entertain the saints because I must keep my conscience....

Gov. Why do you keep such a meeting at your house as you do every week upon a set day?

Mrs. H. It is lawful for me so to do, as it is all your practices and can you find a warrant for yourself and condemn me for the same thing? The ground of my taking it up was, when I first came to this land because I did not go to such meetings as those were, it was presently reported that I did not allow of such meetings but held them unlawful and therefore in that regard they said I was proud and did despise all ordinances, upon that a friend came unto me and told me of it, and I to prevent such aspersions took it up, but it was in practice before I came, therefore I was not the first.

Gov. For this, that you appeal to our practice you need no confutation. If your meeting had answered to the former it had not been offensive, but I will say that there was no meeting of women alone, but your meeting is of another sort for there are sometimes men among you.

Mrs. H. There was never any man with us.

Gov. Well, admit there was no man at your meeting and that you was sorry for it, there is no warrant for your doings, and by what warrant do you continue such a course?

Mrs. H. I conceive there lies a clear rule in Titus, that the elder women should instruct the younger and then I must have a time wherein I must do it.

Gov. All this I grant you, I grant you a time for it, but what is this to the purpose that you Mrs. Hutchinson must call a company together from their callings to come to be taught of you?

Mrs. H. Will it please you to answer me this and to give me a rule for then I will willingly submit to any truth. If any come to my house to be instructed in the ways of God what rule have I to put them away?

Gov. But suppose that a hundred men come unto you to be instructed will you forbear to instruct them?

Mrs. H. As far as I conceive I cross a rule in it.

Gov. Very well and do you not so here?

Mrs. H. No, sir, for my ground is they are men.

Gov. Men and women all is one for that, but suppose that a man should come and say, Mrs. Hutchinson, I hear that you are a woman that God hath given his grace unto and you have knowledge in the word of God. I pray instruct me a little. Ought you not to instruct this man?

Mrs. H. I think I may. Do you think it not lawful for me to teach women and why do you call me to teach the court?

Gov. We do not call you to teach the court but to lay open yourself.

Mrs. H. I desire you that you would then set me down a rule by which I may put them away that come unto me and so have peace in so doing. . . .

Dep. Gov. I would go a little higher with Mrs. Hutchinson. About three years ago we were all in peace. Mrs. Hutchinson from that time she came hath made a disturbance, and some that came over with her in the ship did inform me what she was as soon as she was landed. . . . Now if all these things have endangered us as from that foundation and if she in particular hath disparaged all our ministers in the land that they have preached a covenant of works, and only Mr. Cotton a covenant of grace, why this is not to be suffered, and therefore being driven to the foundation and it being found that Mrs. Hutchinson is she that hath depraved all the ministers and hath been the cause of what is fallen out, why we must take away the foundation and the building will fall.

Mrs. H. I pray, sir prove it that I said they preached nothing but a covenant of works.

Dep. Gov. Nothing but a covenant of works, why a Jesuit may preach truth sometimes.

Mrs. H. Did I ever say they preached a covenant of works then?

Dep. Gov. If they do not preach a covenant of grace clearly, then they preach a covenant of works.

Mrs. H. No, sir. One may preach a covenant of grace more clearly than another, so I said.

D. Gov. We are not upon that now but upon position.

Mrs. H. Prove this then, sir, that you say I said.

D. Gov. When they do preach a covenant of works, do they preach truth?

Mrs. H. Yes, sir. But when they preach a covenant of works for salvation, that is not truth.

D. Gov. I do but ask you this: when the ministers do preach a covenant of works, do they preach a way of salvation?

Mrs. H. I did not come hither to answer to questions of that sort.

D. Gov. Because you will deny the thing.

Mrs. H. Ey, but that is to be proved first.

D. Gov. I will make it plain that you did say that the ministers did preach a covenant of works.

Mrs. H. I deny that.

D. Gov. And that you said they were not able ministers of the new testament, but Mr. Cotton only.

Mrs. H. If ever I spake that, I proved it by God's word.

Court. Very well, very well.

Mrs. H. If one shall come unto me in private and desire me seriously to tell them what I thought of such an one, I must either speak false or true in my answer.

D. Gov. Likewise I will prove this that you said the gospel in the letter and words holds forth nothing but a covenant of works and that all that do not hold as you do are in a covenant of works.

Mrs. H. I deny this, for if I should so say, I should speak against my own judgment.

Mr. Endicot. I desire to speak seeing Mrs. Hutchinson seems to lay something against them that are to witness against her.

Gov. Only I would add this. It is well discerned to the court that Mrs. Hutchinson can tell when to speak and when to hold her tongue. Upon the answering of a question which we desire her to tell her thoughts of she desires to be pardoned.

Mrs. H. It is one thing for me to come before a public magistracy and there to speak what they would have me to speak and another when a man comes to me in a way of friendship privately there is difference in that....

Gov. What say you to this, though nothing be directly proved, yet you hear it may be.

Mrs. H. I acknowledge using the words of the apostle to the Corinthians unto him, that they that were ministers of the letter and not the spirit did preach a covenant of works. Upon his saying there was no such scripture, then I fetched the Bible and shewed him this place, 2 Cor. 3.6. He said that was the letter of the law. No, said I, it is the letter of the gospel.

Gov. You have spoken this more than once then.

Mrs. H. Then upon further discourse about proving a good estate and holding it out by the manifestation of the spirit he did acknowledge that to be the nearest way, but yet said he, will you not acknowledge that which we hold forth to be a way too wherein we may have hope; no, truly if that be a way, it is a way to hell.

Gov. Mrs. Hutchinson, the court you see hath laboured to bring you to acknowledge the error of your way that so you might be reduced, the time now grows late, we shall therefore give you a little more time to consider of it and therefore desire that you attend the court again in the morning....

Dep. Gov. They affirm that Mrs. Hutchinson did say they were not able ministers of the new testament.

Mr. Cotton. I do not remember it.

Mrs. H. If you please to give me leave I shall give you the ground of what I know to be true. Being much troubled to see the falseness of the constitution of the church of England, I had like to have turned separatist; whereupon I kept a day of solemn humiliation and pondering of the thing; this scripture was brought unto me — he that denies Jesus Christ to be come in the flesh is antichrist — This I considered of and in considering found that the papists did not deny him to be come in the flesh, nor we did not deny him — who then was antichrist? Was the Turk antichrist only? The Lord knows that I could not open scripture; he must by his prophetical office open it unto me. So after that being unsatisfied in the thing, the Lord was pleased to bring this scripture out of the Hebrews. He that denies the testament denies the testator, and in this did open unto me and give me to see that those which did not teach the new covenant had the spirit of antichrist, and upon this he did discover the ministry unto me and ever since. I bless the Lord, he hath let me see which was the clear ministry and which the wrong. Since that time I confess I have been more choice and he hath let me to distinguish between the voice of my beloved and the voice of Moses, the voice of John Baptist and the voice of antichrist, for all those voices are spoken of in scripture. Now if you do condemn me for speaking what in my conscience I know to be truth, I must commit myself unto the Lord.

Mr. Nowell. How do you know that that was the spirit?

Mrs. H. How did Abraham know that it was God that bid him offer his son, being a breach of the sixth commandment?

Dep. Gov. By an immediate voice.

Mrs. H. So to me by an immediate revelation.

Dep. Gov. How! an immediate revelation.

Mrs. H. By the voice of his own spirit to my soul. I will give you another scripture, Jer. 46.27, 28 — out of which the Lord shewed me what he would do for me and the rest of his servants. But after he was pleased to reveal himself to me, I did presently like Abraham run to Hagar. And after that he did let me see the atheism of my own heart, for which I begged of the Lord that it might not remain in my heart, and being thus, he did shew me this (a twelvemonth after), which I told you of before. Ever since that time I have been confident of what he hath revealed unto me.

[It says in] another place out of Daniel chap. 7 . . . wherein he shewed me the sitting of the judgment and the standing of all high and low before the Lord and how thrones and kingdoms were cast down before him. When our teacher came to New England it was a great trouble unto me, my brother Wheelwright being put by also. I was then much troubled concerning the ministry under which I lived, and then that place in the 30th of Isaiah was brought to my mind. Though the Lord give thee bread of adversity and water of affliction yet shall not thy teachers be removed into corners any more, but thine eyes shall see thy teachers. The Lord giving me this promise and they being gone there was none then left that I was able to hear, and I could not be at rest but I must come hither. Yet that place of Isaiah did much follow me, though the Lord give thee the bread of adversity and water of affliction. This place lying I say upon me then this place in Daniel was brought unto me and did shew me that though I should meet with affliction yet I am the same God that delivered Daniel out of the lion's den, I will also deliver thee. Therefore I desire you to look to it, for you see this scripture fulfilled this day and therefore I desire you that as you tender the Lord and the church and commonwealth to consider and look what you do. You have power over my body but the Lord Jesus hath power over my body and soul, and assure yourselves thus much, you do as much as in you lies to put the Lord Jesus Christ from you, and if you go on in this course you begin you will bring a curse upon you and your posterity, and the mouth of the Lord hath spoken it.

[Charles Francis Adams, ed., *Antinomianism in the Colony of Massachusetts Bay* (Boston: the Prince Society of Massachusetts, 1894).]

Who Would True Valour See

Who would true valour see
Let him come hither;
One here will constant be,
Come wind, come weather.
There's no discouragement,
Shall make him once relent,
His first avow'd intent,
To be a pilgrim.

Who so beset him round,
With dismal Storys,
Do but themselves confound;
His strength the more is.
No lyon can him fright,
He'l with a gyant fight,
But he will have a right,
To be a pilgrim.

Hobgoblin, nor foul fiend,
Can daunt his spirit:
He knows, he at the end,
Shall life inherit.
Then fancies fly away,
He'l fear not what men say,
He'l labour night and day,
To be a pilgrim.

John Bunyan (1684)

Part Three

TO BE A FREE CHURCH

The Eighteenth Century

Introduction

The Eighteenth Century

The dawn of a new century inaugurated an era of freedom from state persecution, but ironically with such freedom came also the decline of the Baptist churches. In England the accession of William III and his wife, Mary, and the Act of Toleration passed in 1689 signified that the dissenting churches could meet and worship openly. Though many Anglicans still despised the nonconformists, members of dissenting churches were now exempt from penalties for nonattendance in the Church of England and were allowed to build meeting houses, publish confessions of faith, and establish their own theological academies. Sadly, however, such toleration and material accumulation led only to spiritual apathy, theological lethargy, and ecclesiastical entropy. The strong convictions that had led many Baptists down the path of martyrdom in the previous century turned into petty church squabbles and flaccid idealizations of the past.

Various factors contributed to the decline of Baptists in England. Both General and Particular Baptists suffered from the influence of the Industrial Revolution and from a kind of intellectual revolution that swept through all of England. In addition, since Baptists had been barred from attending the major universities, pulpits were filled with untrained and uneducated pastors who were unable and unwilling to counteract the tendencies of the times. A. C. Underwood has explained that the religious questions that preoccupied England in the seventeenth century gave way to interests in commerce and science in the eighteenth *(A History of the English Baptists)*. Furthermore, the philosophies of Locke and Hume and the rise of deism led many Baptists, particularly those in the General Baptist group, to question the validity and truthfulness of the orthodox doctrines of the atonement and the Trinity.

The strong doctrine of free grace that was characteristic of General Baptists atrophied to a lukewarm and vague notion of inclusivism. Also influenced by the writings of such people as Matthew Caffyn (1628–1714) and Joseph Priestly (1733–1804), General Baptists regressed to Unitarianism and even Socinianism, thus denying the doctrine of the Trinity and the full divinity of Christ. Had it not been for the important

131

work of Dan Taylor (1738–1816), it is possible that the General Baptists eventually would have dwindled to extinction.

Taylor was the son of a coal miner from Yorkshire and was a convert from the Wesleyan revival movement. He had left the Methodists because he was unhappy with their "dictatorial" style of leadership and was persuaded by the Baptist practice of believers baptism. (For a more detailed study of the Wesleys and the revivals in England see Albert Outler, *John Wesley,* and Frank Whaling, *John and Charles Wesley.*) In 1763 Taylor joined the General Baptists but was soon frustrated and offended at the doctrinal heresies and inner church strife that plagued the congregations. At first Taylor set out to change and correct General Baptists in matters both ecclesial and doctrinal. His efforts, however, were in vain, so in 1770 Taylor and some friends pulled out of the fellowship of General Baptists and formed the New Connection of General Baptists.

In a brief statement of 1770 the New Connection affirmed that its purpose was "to revive Experimental Religion or Primitive Christianity in Faith and Practice." Taylor and his colleagues also signed a brief confession of faith that was by no means a comprehensive declaration of their beliefs, but rather an explanation of six points on which they differed from the Old Connection (this was the name given to the original General Baptists who did not follow Taylor). Of notable importance in the confession is the New Connection's affirmation of the divinity of Christ (article 3) and the necessity of believers baptism by immersion (article 6). By the end of his life, Taylor and the New Connection members had breathed evangelical life back into their remnant of the General Baptists. The churches that stayed with the Old Connection either became unitarian or simply dwindled and died. Those with the New Connection eventually entered conversations with the Particular Baptists regarding a merger of the two Baptist groups.

Particular Baptists in England also experienced decline during the eighteenth century due largely to individualism, hyper-Calvinism, and antinomianism. The spirit of the Industrial Revolution pervaded the middle-class culture with a sense of self-sufficiency. Particular Baptists held an unbending attitude toward local church autonomy to such an extent they were reluctant to cooperate with other congregations and thus made little national impact. Most destructive of all, however, was the sterility brought on by a rigorous Calvinistic orthodoxy. From non-Baptist writings such as those of Tobias Crisp (1600–1642) and later from the works of Baptist pastor and theologian John Gill (1696–1771), the Particular Baptist emphases on election and evangelism were twisted into extreme Calvinism and moral laxity. The doctrines of election and predestination were judged to be so utterly incompatible with an evangelical gospel that many Particular Baptist pastors refused even to preach to nonbelievers. Many hyper-Calvinists further exaggerated these doctrines to extend predestination beyond matters of salvation to personal actions. Some even went so far as to preach antinomianism — to argue that following a moral law was unnecessary for the predestined since those elect were already saved no matter what actions they took.

However, strict Calvinist orthodoxy did not have the final word. Similar to the influence of the New Connection among General Baptists in the 1770s, the latter half of the eighteenth century witnessed a revival among Particular Baptists. An important figure in the early revival of Particular Baptists was John Fawcett (1740–1817), who in 1764 was called to be a pastor of the Baptist chapel at Wainsgate. He had been influenced by the Wesleyan revival and especially by the preaching of George Whitefield (1714–70). In his own life and preaching, Fawcett embodied the spirit of moderate Calvinism and evangelistic fervor that was lacking among Particular Baptists.

In the 1770s John Ryland Jr. (1753–1825), Robert Hall (1728–91), John Sutcliff (1752–1814), and especially Andrew Fuller (1754–1815) came under the influence of Jonathan Edwards, the progressive Calvinist and revivalist preacher of the Great Awakening in America. Fuller's leadership in particular nurtured the missionary impulse that eventually led to the formation of the Baptist Missionary Society in 1792. It was this same society that sent William Carey (1761–1834) to India as its first missionary. The mission movement had a leavening effect among Particular Baptists. Without forcing a schism, a sterile orthodoxy was invigorated with an evangelical spirit.

While the eighteenth century witnessed the decline of Baptists in England, in America Baptists grew from a small and neglected minority of around 800 members in 1700 to become the largest denomination in America, with over 65,000 members by the end of the eighteenth century. Numerous factors contributed to the rise of Baptists in America, but perhaps most of all there was the impact of the Great Awakening upon Baptist life and thought.

Prior to the revival of the 1730s and 1740s, many American religious groups, including the Baptists, were caught in a trench of spiritual decline and ecclesial disorganization. The awakening led by Jonathan Edwards (1703–58) was characterized by fervent preaching and spiritual renewal (see Edwin Gaustad, *The Great Awakening in New England*). The movement was by no means accepted by all, and many Baptists initially either criticized or tried to ignore the revivalist meetings. However, one result of the Awakening was a division among Congregational churches into those that were prorevivalist and those that opposed the revivals. The churches in favor of the Awakening were called "New Lights." By the 1740s and 1750s many of these New Light churches found their religious, social, and political views to be much more akin to those of Baptists than to Congregationalists. Many New

Lights embraced believers baptism and were thus at odds with the rest of the Congregationalists. Eventually, a large portion of the New Light churches made the transition to Baptist affiliation, thus bringing into Baptist churches not only numbers but also new life and new evangelical fervor.

Along with the impact of the Great Awakening, Baptist emphases on religious liberty and separation of church and state found new sympathies in the political climate of eighteenth-century America. Baptists, who had been persecuted and despised in previous years, now found themselves at the forefront of the revolutionary movement. With strong leaders like Isaac Backus (1724–1806) and John Leland (1754–1841), Baptist preachers proclaimed liberty from the English crown and religious freedom in America.

Moreover, Enlightenment ideals of toleration and individualism contributed to the development and emphasis among Baptists of the believer's freedom from state or ecclesial constraints to respond to and worship God. Such views further contributed to Baptist involvement in and struggle for religious and political freedom. In addition, the growth in numbers among Baptists allowed them to form organized associations and establish academies, such as Rhode Island College (1764), in which Baptist beliefs and practices were taught to a new generation of leaders.

Though Baptists shared such common ideals as those listed above, they were not a uniform group. Like English Baptists, the Americans were divided along Calvinist-Arminian lines, and some were in favor of the revivals while others opposed them. The more Calvinistic and anti-revivalists came to be called Regular Baptists while the Arminian-pro-revivalists were called Separate Baptists. These groups, however, were not as distinct as their English counterparts. By the beginning of the nineteenth century, even in the Southern colonies where their differences were more pronounced, Regular and Separate Baptists merged into one organized and influential denomination. In addition to the Regular and Separate Baptists, there were smaller baptist groups such as Mennonites, Quakers, and Brethren continuously (and sometimes powerfully) active in this century. Though we have excerpted none of these here, their ongoing life and theological thought deserve fresh attention from baptist scholars.

The selections that follow are drawn from a variety of English and American Baptists, some of whom have been described briefly above. The documents contain primary theological discussions that indicate to some degree the difficulties and issues these writers of the eighteenth-century sought to overcome, and show how they proposed answers that might further help the Baptists continue to be the church.

– 15 –

John Gill

Often considered the most powerful voice among eighteenth century Particular Baptists, John Gill (1696–1771) is largely responsible for the hyper-Calvinism that so diminished English Baptists. Raised in Kettering, Northamptonshire, Gill was the son of a wool tradesman. By the age of eleven he had mastered Latin and Greek but was not allowed to continue his formal studies because of the headmaster's refusal to teach non-Anglican students. Gill continued to study on his own. Around the age of twelve he experienced Christian conversion after hearing a sermon on God's call to Adam (Genesis 3:9). He was baptized a few years later, in 1716. Soon after this, Gill began preaching and teaching in nearby villages until in 1719 he became pastor of Horsleydown Church, London. There he remained for over fifty years, preaching and publishing sermons and countless other works. For nearly thirty years Gill also gave weekly lectures that attracted listeners from all London. Gill's publishing career began in 1724 with the publication of a funeral sermon. Around 1728 he published a treatise defending baptism by immersion; it was widely circulated in England and America. Some of his other writings include The Doctrine of the Trinity Stated and Vindicated *(1731),* The Dissenter's Reasons for Separating from the Church of England *(1753), and most famously,* A Body of Doctrinal Divinity *(1769), from which the following selection is drawn. A product of the modern age, Gill argued that Scripture study was a science and that theology was to gather from Scripture the principles of evangelical truth. Strongly influenced by strict Calvinistic doctrines drawn largely from the Synod of Dort (1618–19), Gill's theology emphasized the absolute sovereignty of God and the doctrines of election and predestination. God chooses some individuals for eternal life and others for eternal damnation. This led him "to refuse to offer Christ to unregenerate sinners" (McBeth,* The Baptist Heritage, *176). Gill influenced many Particular Baptists in this direction, diminishing the evangelistic spirit among Particular Baptists — a diminution Baptists could ill afford, since without hereditary membership, evangelism was the arterial flow of their church life. His* Body of Doctrinal Divinity *covers the principal Christian themes and tries to counteract the rising deist and antitrinitarian movements in England.*

Election and Rejection

Of Election

The special decrees of God respecting rational creatures, commonly go under the name of predestination.... Predestination is usually considered as consisting of two parts, and including the two branches of election and reprobation, both with respect to angels and men; for each of these have place in both. Angels; some of them are called elect angels (1 Tim. 5:21), others are said to be "reserved in chains," in the chains of God's purposes and providence, "unto" the "judgment" of the great day (2 Pet. 2:4). Men; some of them are vessels of mercy, aforeprepared for glory; others vessels of wrath, fitted for destruction; some are the "election," or the elect persons, that obtain righteousness, life, and salvation; and others are the "rest" that are left in, and given up to blindness (Rom. 9:22–23, 11:7). Though sometimes predestination only respects that branch of it called election, and the predestinated signify only the elect; for who else are called, justified, and glorified, enjoy adoption and the heavenly inheritance? Not, surely, the non-elect (Rom. 8:29–30; Eph. 1:5, 11)....

Some are of the opinion that this doctrine of election, admitting it to be true, should not be published, neither preached from the pulpit, nor handled in schools and academies, nor treated of in the writings of men; the reasons they give are because it is a secret, and secret things belong to God; and because it tends to fill men's minds with doubts about their salvation, and to bring them into distress, and even into despair; and because some may make a bad use of it, to indulge themselves in a sinful course of life, and argue, that if they are elected they shall be saved, let them live as they may, and so it opens a door to all licentiousness: but these reasons are frivolous and groundless — the doctrine of election is no secret, it is clearly and fully revealed, and written as with a sunbeam in the sacred scriptures. It is true indeed, it cannot be said of particular persons, that such a man is elected, and such a man is reprobated; and especially when both appear to be in a state of unregeneracy; yet when men, in a judgment of charity, may be hoped to be called by grace, they may be concluded to be the elect of God, though it cannot be said with precision. And on the other hand, there may be black marks of reprobation on some men, or at least things have such a very dark aspect on them, that we are apt to say, when we hear a man cursing and swearing, and see him in all excess of wickedness with boldness and impudence, What a reprobate creature is this! Though indeed no man, be he ever so vile, is out of the reach of powerful and efficacious grace; and therefore it cannot be absolutely said that he is rejected of God: and whereas there may be only the appearance of grace, and not the truth of it, in such that profess to have it; it cannot be said with certainty that such a one is an elect person, yet in charity it may be so concluded. However, a truly gracious man may know for himself his "election of God," as the apostle affirms; and that in this way, "the gospel being come to him, not in word only, but in power, and in the Holy Ghost" (1 Thess. 1:4–5), who by means of it has begun, and will carry on and perform the work of grace in him. Wherefore such persons will not be filled with doubts and fears about their salvation, nor be led into distress and despair through the doctrine of election; nor need any be distressed about it that are inquiring the way of salvation, or have any knowledge of it; for the first question to be put to a man by himself, is not, am I elected; but, am I born again? Am I a new creature? Am I called by the grace of God, and truly converted? If a man can arrive to satisfaction in this matter, he can have no doubt about his election; that then is a clear case and out of all question....

The several properties of election, may be gathered from what has been said of it; as:

1. That it is eternal; it does not commence upon believing, and much less at perseverance in faith and holiness; but it was an act in God before the foundation of the world (Eph. 1:4).

2. It is free and sovereign; God was not obliged to choose any; and as it is, he chooses whom he will, and for no other reason excepting his own glory, but because he will; "what if God willing," etc. and the difference in choosing one and not another, is purely owing to his will (Rom. 9:18, 22–23).

3. It is absolute and unconditional; clear of all motives in man, or conditions to be performed by him; for it "stands not of works, but of him that calleth," the will of him that calls (Rom. 9:11).

4. It is complete and perfect; it is not begun in eternity and completed in time, nor takes its rise from the will of God, and is finished by the will of man; nor is made perfect by faith, holiness, obedience, and persevering in well-doing, but has its complete being in the will of God at once.

5. It is immutable and irrevocable; God never repents of, nor revokes the choice he has made; some choose their friends and favorites, and alter their minds and choose others; but God is in one mind, and never makes any alteration in the choice he has made; and hence their state is safe and secure.

6. It is special and particular; that is, those who are chosen are chosen to be a special people above all others, and are particular persons, whose names are written in the book of life; not in general, men of such and such characters, but persons well known to God, and distinctly fixed on by him.

7. Election may be known by the persons, the objects of it; partly by

the blessings flowing from it, and connected with it, before observed, bestowed upon them; for to whomsoever such blessings of grace are applied, they must be the elect of God (Rom. 8:30). They may know it from the efficacy of the Gospel upon them, in their vocation and conversion (1 Thess. 1:4–5) and by the Spirit of God testifying their adoption to them, to which they are predestinated (Rom. 8:15–16), and they may be able to make it known to others, by their holy lives and conversations; which is meant by making their calling and election sure, even by their good works, as some copies read (2 Pet. 1:10), since both calling and election are to be made sure, and therefore by some third thing: indeed no man can know his election of God until he is called; it would be presumption in him to claim this character, until he is born again; nor should any man conclude himself a reprobate because a sinner, since all men are sinners; even God's elect, who are by nature, and in no wise better than others, but children of wrath, even as others.

There are many things objected to this doctrine of election; but since it is so clear and plain from scripture, and is written as with a sunbeam in it, all objections to it must be mere cavil. It is urged, that God is said to be "good to all, and his tender mercies over all his works" (Ps. 145:9), which seems inconsistent with his choosing some and leaving others; but this is to be understood not of his special grace, but of his providential goodness, which extends to the elect and non-elect, the evil and the good, the just and the unjust (Matt. 5:45) and in this sense he is the savior, preserver, and bountiful benefactor of all men, but especially of them that believe (1 Tim. 4:10). It is observed that Christ says he was sent not to "condemn the world, but that the world through him might be saved," and therefore not some only but all; but to understand this of all the individuals in the world is not true, because all are not saved; and so this end of Christ's mission, so understood, is not answered; but by the world is meant the world of God's elect, whom he was reconciling in Christ, and for whom Christ gave his life, and became the propitiation for their sins, even for all the chosen throughout the whole world, and particularly among the Gentiles. Nor is 1 Tim. 2:4 any objection to this doctrine, "Who will have all men to be saved, and to come unto the knowledge of the truth," for all men are not eventually saved, nor do all come to the knowledge of the truth of the Gospel; nor indeed have all the means of that knowledge: but the sense is, either, that all that are saved, God wills to be saved; or, that it is his will that men of all sorts and of all nations, Jews and Gentiles, should be saved; which agrees with the context (vv. 1–2, 7). And when it is said of God, that he is "not willing that any should perish, but that all should come to repentance" (2 Pet. 3:9), this must be interpreted, not of all mankind, but of the elect, to whom this and the preceding epistle are inscribed, and who are in v. 8 styled "beloved," and in this verse, the "us" towards whom "God is long-suffering." Now it is the will and pleasure of God that none of those should perish, but all in due time be brought to faith in Christ, and to repentance towards God: but objections from hence, with others of the like kind, are not sufficient to overturn this truth, so abundantly established in the sacred scriptures.

Of Rejection

The moving, or impulsive cause of God's making such a decree, by which he has rejected some of the race of Adam from his favor, is not sin, but the good pleasure of his will: sin is the meritorious cause of eternal death, wrath, and damnation; wrath is revealed from heaven against all unrighteousness and ungodliness of men, and comes upon the children of disobedience, whom God leaves in it; the wages, or demerit of sin, is death; even death eternal. But then it is not the impulsive cause of the decree itself; not of preterition, because that, as election, was before good or evil were done, and irrespective of either; nor of pre-damnation, God, indeed, damns no man but for sin; nor did he decree to damn any but for sin; but yet, though sin is the cause of damnation and death, the thing decreed, it is not the cause of the decree itself: it is the cause of the thing willed, but not the moving cause of God's will; for nothing out of God can move his will; if it could, the will of God would be dependent on the will and actions of men; whereas, his purpose, whether with respect to election or rejection, stands not on the works end will of men, but on his own will and pleasure. Besides, if sin was the cause of the decree itself, or of God's will to reject men, then all would be rejected, since all fell in Adam; all are under sin, all have sinned, and come short of the glory of God; all are, by nature, children of wrath, and deserving of it. What then could move God to choose one and reject another but his sovereign goodwill and pleasure? That then is the sole moving and impulsive cause of such a decree; when we have searched the scriptures most thoroughly, and employed our reasoning powers to the highest pitch, and racked our invention to the uttermost; no other cause of God's procedure in this affair be assigned, but what Christ has expressed; "Even so, Father, for so it seemed good in thy sight" as to hide the things of his grace and gospel from some, and reveal them to others; so to decree and determine within himself, to act in this manner (Matt. 11:25–26).

The final cause, or end of this decree, is his own glory; this is the ultimate end of all his decrees and appointments, and so of this, appointing the wicked for the day of evil. It was for this purpose he raised up Pharaoh, and decreed all he did concerning him, that he might show his power in him, his sovereignty and dominion over him, and that his name and glory might be declared throughout all the earth. And the same view he has with respect to all the vessels of wrath, namely, to show his wrath, and to make his power known, in their destruction, which is of themselves. It is not the death and damnation of the sinner, in which he delights not that is his ultimate end; it is his own glory, the glory of his perfections, and particularly the glory of his justice and holiness (Prov. 16:4; Rom. 9:17, 22).

[John Gill, *A Body of Doctrinal Divinity* (London: n.p., 1769; reprint Atlanta: Turner Lasseter, 1950), books II/II, II/III, 176–78, 190–91, 197–98.]

Andrew Fuller

Born on a farm in Cambridgeshire, England, Andrew Fuller (1754–1815) was perhaps the most significant leader in the revival movement among Particular Baptists in the eighteenth century. His life and work inspired Particular Baptists with evangelical fervor, and he was the strong force behind the formation of the Baptist Missionary Society. Fuller grew up in a hyper-Calvinistic church strongly influenced by John Gill and John Brine (1703–65). At sixteen he was converted and baptized in the church. Less than a year later and with no formal training, Fuller was preaching and assisting the pastorate at Soham, Cambridgeshire. When he was twenty years old he was ordained at Soham. In 1783 Fuller was called to be a pastor at Kettering — the same church at which John Gill had begun his own ministry years earlier. Despite difficulties and conflicts with the congregation, Fuller served tirelessly at Kettering until his death in 1815. Fuller's move away from hyper-Calvinism began in 1775 when he read a pamphlet that recalled in him many doubts he had previously had regarding the teachings of Gill and Brine. After serious and deliberate study of the Scriptures, and in dialogue with close friends like William Carey and John Ryland Jr., Fuller became convinced that nowhere in the example of Jesus and the apostles was there a warrant for Christians not to preach the gospel to all, sinners and elect alike. In clearly written essays such as the famous Gospel Worthy of All Acceptation *(1785) excerpted below, Fuller argued against what he called the "system of False Calvinism." He proclaimed instead a moderate, evangelical Calvinism that affirmed the doctrines of election and predestination but that also called for preaching the Good News to all who would hear. In addition to writing major theological treatises, Fuller served as founder, leader, and fund-raiser for the Baptist Missionary Society.*

The Gospel Worthy of All Acceptation

Concluding Reflections

*First, Though faith be a duty, the requirement of it is not to be consid-
ered as a mere exercise of authority, but of infinite goodness, binding
us to pursue our best interest....* If faith in Christ be the duty of the
ungodly, it must of course follow that every sinner, whatever be his
character, is completely warranted to trust in the Lord Jesus Christ for
the salvation of his soul. In other words, he has every possible encour-
agement to relinquish his former attachment and confidences, and to
commit his soul into the hands of Jesus to be saved. If believing in Christ
be a privilege belonging only to the regenerate, and no sinner while unregenerate be warranted to exercise it, as Mr. Brine maintains, it will
follow either that a sinner may know himself to be regenerate before
he believes, or that the first exercise of faith is an act of presumption.
That the bias of the heart requires to be turned to God antecedently to
believing has been admitted, because the nature of believing is such that
it cannot be exercised while the soul is under the dominion of willful
blindness, hardness, and aversion. These dispositions are represented in
the Scriptures as a bar in the way of faith, as being inconsistent with it;
and which consequently require to be taken out of the way. But whatever necessity there may be for a change of heart in order to believe it
is neither necessary nor possible that the party should be conscious of it
till he has believed. It is necessary that the eyes of a blind man should be
opened before he can see; but it is neither necessary nor possible for him
to know that his eyes are open till he does see. It is only by surrounding
objects appearing to his view that he knows the obstructing film to be
removed. But if regeneration be necessary to warrant believing, and yet
it be impossible to obtain a consciousness of it till we have believed, it
follows that the first exercise of faith is without foundation; that is, it is
not faith, but presumption.

If believing be the duty of every sinner to whom the gospel is
preached, there can be no doubt as to a warrant for it, whatever be
his character; and to maintain the latter, without admitting the former, would be reducing it to a mere matter of discretion. It might be
inexpedient to reject the way of salvation, but it could not be unlawful.

*Secondly, Though believing in Christ is a compliance with a duty, yet
it is not as a duty, or by way of reward for a virtuous act, that we are
said to be justified by it.* It is true God does reward the services of his
people, as the Scriptures abundantly teach; but this follows upon justification. We must stand accepted in the Beloved, before our services can
be acceptable or rewardable. Moreover, if we were justified by faith as a
duty, justification by faith could not be, as it is, opposed to justification

by works: "To him that worketh is the reward not reckoned of grace, but of debt. But to him that worketh not, but believeth on him that justifieth the ungodly, his faith is counted for righteousness." The Scripture doctrine of justification by faith, in opposition to the works of the law, appears to me as follows: By believing in Jesus Christ, the sinner becomes vitally united to him, or, as the Scriptures express it, "joined to the Lord," and is of "one spirit with him"; and this union, according to the Divine constitution, as revealed in the gospel, is the ground of an interest in his righteousness. Agreeable to this is the following language: "There is now, therefore, no condemnation to them that are in Christ Jesus." — "Of him are ye in Christ Jesus, who of God is made unto us righteousness," etc. — "That I may be found in him, not having mine own righteousness which is of the law, but that which is through the faith of Christ." As the union which, in the order of nature; precedes a revealed interest in Christ's righteousness, is spoken of in allusion to that of marriage, the one may serve to illustrate the other. A rich and generous character, walking in the fields, espies a forlorn female infant, deserted by some unfeeling parent in the day that it was born, and left to perish. He sees its helpless condition, and resolves to save it. Under his kind patronage the child grows up to maturity. He now resolves to make her his wife; casts his skirt over her, and she becomes his. She is now, according to the public statutes of the realm, interested in all his possessions. Great is the transition! Ask her, in the height of her glory, how she became possessed of all this wealth; and, if she retain a proper spirit, she will answer in some such manner as this: It was not mine, but my deliverer's; his who rescued me from death. It is no reward of any good deeds on my part; it is by marriage; . . . it is "of grace."

It is easy to perceive, in this case, that it was necessary she should be voluntarily married to her husband, before she could, according to the public statutes of the realm, be interested in his possessions; and that she now enjoys those possessions by marriage: yet who would think of asserting that her consenting to be his wife was a meritorious act, and that all his possessions were given her as the reward of it?

Thirdly, From the foregoing view of things, we may perceive the alarming situation of unbelievers. By unbelievers, I mean not only avowed infidels, but all persons who hear, or have opportunity to hear the gospel, or to come at the knowledge of what is taught in the Holy Scriptures, and do not cordially embrace it. It is an alarming thought to be a sinner against the greatest and best of beings; but to be an unbelieving sinner is much more so. There is deliverance from "the curse of the law," through him who was "made a curse for us." But if, like the barren fig tree, we stand from year to year, under gospel culture, and bear no fruit, we may expect to fall under the curse of the Saviour; and who is to deliver us from this? "If the word spoken by angels was steadfast, and every transgression and disobedience received a just recompense of reward; how shall we escape if we neglect so great salvation?"

. We are in the habit of pitying heathens, who are enthralled by abominable superstition, and immersed in the immoralities which accompany it; but to live in the midst of gospel light, and reject it, or even disregard it, is abundantly more criminal, and will be followed with a heavier punishment. We feel for the condition of profligate characters; for swearers, and drunkards, and fornicators, and liars, and thieves, and murderers; but these crimes become tenfold more heinous in being committed under the light of revelation, and in contempt of all the warnings and gracious invitations of the gospel. The most profligate character, who never possessed these advantages, may be far less criminal, in the sight of God, than the most sober and decent who possesses and disregards them. It was on this principle that such a heavy woe was denounced against Chorazin and Bethsaida, and that their sin was represented as exceeding that of Sodom.

The gospel wears an aspect of mercy towards sinners; but towards unbelieving sinners the Scriptures deal wholly in the language of threatening. "I am come," saith our Saviour, "a light into the world, that whosoever believeth on me should not abide in darkness. If any man hear my words and believe not, I judge him not — (that is, not at present); for I came not to Judge the world, but to save the world. He that rejecteth me, and receiveth not my words, hath one that judgeth him: the word that I have spoken, the same shall judge him in the last day." It will be of but small account, in that day, that we have escaped a few of "the lusts of the flesh," if we have been led captive by those of the "mind." If the greatest gift of Heaven be set at nought by us, through the pride of science, or a vain conceit of our own righteousness, how shall we stand when he appeareth?

It will then be found that a price was in our hands to get wisdom, but that we had "no heart to it"; and that herein consists our sin, and hence proceeds our ruin. God called, and we would not hearken; he stretched out his hand, and no man regarded; therefore he will laugh at our calamity and mock when our fear cometh. It is intimated, both in the Old and New Testament, that the recollection of the means of salvation having been within our reach will be a bitter aggravation to our punishment. "They come unto thee," saith the Lord to Ezekiel, "as the people come, and they sit before thee as my people, and they hear my words, but they will not do them." — "And when this cometh to pass, (lo, it will come!) then shall they know that a prophet hath been among them." To the same purpose our Saviour speaks of them who should reject the doctrine of his apostles: "Into whatsoever city ye enter, and they receive you not, go your ways out of the streets of the same, and say, Even the very dust of your city, which cleaveth on us, we do wipe off against you: notwithstanding, be ye sure of this, that the kingdom of God is come nigh unto you."

Great as is the sin of unbelief, however, it is not unpardonable; it becomes such only by persisting in it till death. Saul of Tarsus was an unbeliever, yet he "obtained mercy"; and his being an unbeliever, rather than presumptuous opposer of Christ against conviction, placed him within the pale of forgiveness, and is, therefore, assigned as a reason of it (1 Tim. 1:13).

This consideration affords a hope even to unbelievers. O ye self-righteous despisers of a free salvation through a Mediator, be it known to you that there is no other name given under heaven, or among men, by which you can be saved. To him whom you have disregarded and despised you must either voluntarily or involuntarily submit. "To him every knee shall bow." You cannot go back into a state of non-existence, however desirable it might be to many of you; for God hath stamped immortality upon your natures. You cannot turn to the right hand, or to the left, with any advantage: whether you give a loose to your inclination, or put a force upon it by an assumed devotion, each will lead to the same issue. Neither can you stand still. Like a vessel in a tempestuous ocean, you must go this way or that; and go which way you will, if it be not to Jesus, as utterly unworthy, you are only heaping up wrath against the day of wrath. Whether you sing, or pray, or hear, or preach, or feed the poor, or till the soil, if self be your object, and Christ be disregarded, all is sin, and all will issue in disappointment: "the root is rottenness, and the blossom shall go up as the dust." Whither will you go? Jesus invites you to come to him. His servants beseech you, in his name, to be reconciled to God. The Spirit saith, Come: and the bride saith, Come; and "whosoever will, let him come, and take of the water of life freely." An eternal heaven is before you in one direction, and an eternal hell in the other. Your answer is required. Be one thing or another. Choose you, this day, whom ye will serve. For our parts, we will abide by our Lord and Saviour. If you continue to reject him, so it must be: "nevertheless, be ye sure of this, that the kingdom of God has come nigh unto you!"

Finally, From what has been advanced, we may form a judgment of our duty, as ministers of the word, in dealing with the unconverted. The work of the Christian ministry, it has been said, is to preach the gospel, or to hold up the free grace of God through Jesus Christ, as the only way of a sinner's salvation. This is, doubtless, true; and if this be not the leading theme of our ministrations, we had better be any thing than preachers. "Woe unto us, if we preach not the gospel!" The minister who, under a pretense of pressing the practice of religion, neglects its all-important principles, labors in the fire. He may enforce duty till duty freezes upon his lips; neither his auditors nor himself will greatly regard it. But, on the contrary, if by preaching the gospel be meant the insisting solely upon the blessings and privileges of religion, to the neglect of exhortations, calls, and warnings, it is sufficient to say that such was not the practice of Christ and his apostles. It will not be denied that they preached the gospel; yet they warned, admonished, and entreated sinners to "repent and believe"; to "believe while they had the light"; to "labor not for the meat that perisheth, but for that which endureth unto everlasting life"; to "repent, and be converted, that their sins might be blotted out"; to "come to the marriage supper, for that all things were ready"; in fine, to "be reconciled unto God."

If the inability of sinners to perform things spiritually good were natural, or such as existed independently of their present choice, it would be absurd and cruel to address them in such language. No one in his senses would think of calling the blind to look, the deaf to hear, or the dead to rise up and walk; and of threatening them with punishment in case of their refusal. But if the blindness arise from the love of darkness rather than light; if the deafness resemble that of the adder, which stoppeth her ear, and will not hear the voice of the charmer, charm he never so wisely; and if the death consist in alienation of heart from God, and the absence of all desire after him there is no absurdity or cruelty in such addresses.

But enforcing the duties of religion, either on sinners or saints, is by some called preaching the law. If it were so, it is enough for us that such was the preaching of Christ and his apostles. It is folly and presumption to affect to be more evangelical than they were. All practical preaching, however, is not preaching the law. That only, I apprehend, ought to be censured as preaching the law, in which our acceptance with God is, in some way or other, placed to the account of our obedience to its precepts. When eternal life is represented as the reward of repentance, faith, and sincere obedience, (as it too frequently is, and that under the complaisant form of being "through the merits of Christ,") this is preaching the law, and not the gospel. But the precepts of the law may be illustrated and enforced for evangelical purposes; as tending to vindicate the Divine character and government; to convince of sin; to show the necessity of a Saviour, with the freeness of salvation; to ascertain the nature of true religion; and to point out the rule of Christian conduct. Such a way of introducing the Divine law, in subservience to the gospel, is, properly speaking, preaching the gospel; for the end denominates the action.

If the foregoing principles be just, it is the duty of ministers not only to exhort their carnal auditors to believe in Jesus Christ for the salvation of their souls; but "it is at our peril to exhort them to any thing short of it, or which does not involve or imply it." I am aware that such an idea may startle many of my readers, and some who are engaged in the Christian ministry. We have sunk into such a compromising way of dealing with the unconverted as to have well nigh lost the spirit of the primitive preachers; and hence it is that sinners of every description can sit so quietly as they do, year after year, in our places of worship. It was not so with the hearers of Peter and Paul: They were either "pricked in the heart" in one way, or "cut to the heart" in another. Their preaching commended itself to "every man's conscience in the sight of God." How shall we account for this difference? Is there not some important error or defect in our ministrations? I have no reference to the preaching of those who disown the Divinity or atonement of Christ, on the one hand, whose sermons are little more than harangues on morality, nor to that of gross Antinomians on the other, whose chief business it is to feed the vanity and malignity of one part of their audience, and the sin-extenuating principles of the other. These are errors the folly of which is "manifest to all men" who pay any serious regard to the religion of the New Testament. I refer to those who are commonly reputed evangelical, and who approve of addresses to the unconverted. I hope no apology is necessary for an attempt to exhibit the Scriptural manner of preaching. If it affects the labors of some of my brethren, I cannot deny but that it may also affect my own. I conceive there is scarcely a minister amongst us whose preaching has not been more or less influenced by the lethargic systems of the age.

Christ and his apostles, without any hesitation, called on sinners to "repent, and believe the gospel"; but we, considering them as poor, impotent, and depraved creatures, have been disposed to drop this part of the Christian ministry. Some may have felt afraid of being accounted legal; others have really thought it inconsistent. Considering such things as beyond the power of their hearers, they seem to have contented themselves with pressing on them things which they could perform, still continuing the enemies of Christ; such as behaving decently in society, reading the scriptures, and attending the means of grace. Thus it is that hearers of this description sit at ease in our congregations. Having done their duty, the minister has nothing more to say to them; unless, indeed, it be to tell them occasionally that something more is necessary to salvation. But as this implies no guilt on their part, they sit unconcerned, conceiving that all that is required of them is "to lie in the way, and to wait the Lord's time." But is this the religion of the Scriptures? Where does it appear that the prophets or apostles ever treated that kind of inability which is merely the effect of reigning aversion as affording any excuse? And where have they descended, in their exhortations, to things which might be done, and the parties still continue the enemies of God? Instead of leaving out every thing of a spiritual nature, because their hearers could not find in their hearts to comply with it, it may safely be affirmed they exhorted to nothing else; treating such inability not only as of no account, with regard to the lessening of obligation, but as rendering the subjects of it worthy of the severest rebuke. "To whom shall I speak, and give warning, that they may hear? Behold, their ear is uncircumcised, and they cannot hearken: behold, the word of the Lord is unto them a reproach, and they have no delight in it." What then! Did the prophet desist from his work, and exhort them to something to which, in their present state of mind; they could hearken? Far from it. He delivers his message, whether they would hear, or whether they would forbear. "Thus saith the Lord, Stand ye in the ways, and see, and ask for the old paths, where is the good way, and walk therein, and ye shall find rest for your souls. But they said, We will not walk therein." And did this induce him to desist? No: he proceeds to read their doom and calls the world to witness its justice: "Hear, O earth! behold, I will bring evil upon this people, even the fruit of their thoughts, because they have not hearkened unto my words, nor to my law, but rejected it" (Jer. 6:10–19). Many of those who attended the ministry of Christ were of the same spirit. Their eyes were blinded, and their hearts hardened, so that they "could not believe"; yet, paying no manner of regard to this kind of inability, he exhorted them "to believe in the light while they had the light." And when they had heard and believed not, he proceeded, without hesitation, to declare, "He that rejecteth me, and receiveth not my words, hath one that judgeth him: the word that I have spoken, the same shall judge him in the last day."

Some years ago I met with a passage in Dr. Owen on this subject, which, at that time, sunk deep into my heart; and the more observation I have since made, the more just his remarks appear. "It is the duty of ministers," says he, "to plead with men about their sins; but always remember that it be done with that which is the proper end of law and gospel; that is, that they make use of the sin they speak against to the discovery of the state and condition wherein the sinner is, otherwise, haply, they may work men to formality and hypocrisy, but little of the true end of preaching the gospel will be brought about. It will not avail to beat a man off from his drunkenness into a sober formality. A skillful master of the assemblies lays his axe at the root, drives still at the heart. To inveigh against particular sins of ignorant, unregenerate persons, such as the land is full of, is a good work; but yet, though it may be done with great efficacy, vigor, and success, if this be all the effect of it, that they are set upon the most sedulous endeavors of mortifying their sins preached down, all that is done is but like the beating of an enemy in an open field, and driving him into an impregnable castle not to be prevailed against. Get you, at any time, a sinner at the advantage on the account of any one sin whatever; have you any thing to take hold of him by, bring it to his state and condition, drive it up to the head, and there deal with him. To break men off from particular sins, and not to break their hearts, is to deprive ourselves of advantages of dealing with them...." If we inculcate this doctrine, we need not fear exhorting sinners to holy exercises of heart, nor holding up the promises of mercy to all who thus return to God by Jesus Christ.

[John Ryland, ed., *The Works of the Rev. Andrew Fuller,* 8 vols. (London: B. J. Holdsworth, 1824), 1:160–89.]

– 17 –

William Carey

At a time when few Baptists interpreted the Great Commission as binding on present-day Christians, the powerful voice of William Carey (1761–1834) could be heard summoning all who believe in Jesus to share the Good News with the "heathen." A self-educated pastor, shoe cobbler, and schoolteacher from Paulersbury, Northamptonshire, Carey was raised in the Anglican tradition. Even as a child he expressed great interest in the lands outside England and was fascinated by stories of sailors and explorers. In 1779, four years after hearing his first Baptist sermon, Carey was converted, and in 1783 was baptized in the Nen River. Two years later he was ordained at the (Particular) Baptist church in Moulton. Carey was instrumental in the founding of the Baptist Missionary Society (1792). Encouraged by Andrew Fuller and others in the BMS, and acting on his strong conviction that God called all Christians to preach the gospel "to the ends of the earth," Carey, his wife, Dorothy, and their five children set out for India. Life in India was very difficult, and the Carey family struggled against famine, poverty, and illness. The circumstances proved too harsh for Dorothy and after years of suffering from fevers and depression, she died in Serampore, India. A very gifted man in languages, Carey continued his missionary work in India, preaching and translating Scripture into various Indian dialects and other Eastern languages, including Hindi and Chinese. His almost incredible efforts opened up Southeast Asia to Western gaze. The selection that follows is drawn from Carey's monumental work, An Enquiry into the Obligations of Christians to Use Means for the Conversion of the Heathens *(1792). The book was instrumental in the advancement of modern missions among all Baptists.*

An Enquiry

As our blessed Lord has required us to pray that his kingdom may come, and his will be done on earth as it is in heaven, it becomes us not only to express our desires of that event by words, but to use every lawful method to spread the knowledge of his name. In order to do this, it is necessary that we should become, in some measure acquainted with the religious state of the world; and as this is an object we should be prompted to pursue, not only by the gospel of our Redeemer, but even by the feelings of humanity, so an inclination to conscientious activity therein would form one of the strongest proofs that we are the subjects of grace, and partakers of that spirit of universal benevolence and genuine philanthropy, which appear so eminent in the character of God himself.

Sin was introduced amongst the children of men by the fall of Adam, and has ever since been spreading its baneful influence. By changing its appearance to suit the circumstances of the times, it has grown up in ten thousand forms, and constantly counteracted the will and designs of God. One would have supposed that the remembrance of the deluge would have been transmitted from father to son, and have perpetually deterred mankind from transgressing the will of their Maker; but so blinded were they, that in the time of Abraham, gross wickedness prevailed wherever colonies were planted, and the iniquity of the Amorites was great, though not yet full. After this, idolatry spread more and more, till the seven devoted nations were cut off with the most signal marks of divine displeasure. Still, however, the progress of evil was not stopped, but the Israelites themselves too often joined with the rest of mankind against the God of Israel. In one period the grossest ignorance and barbarism prevailed in the world; and afterwards, in a more enlightened age, the most daring infidelity, and contempt of God; so that the world which was once overrun with ignorance, now "by wisdom knew not God, but changed the glory of the incorruptible God" as much as in the most barbarous ages, "into an image made like to corruptible man, and to birds, and four-footed beasts, and creeping things." Nay, as they increased in science and politeness, they ran into more abundant and extravagant idolatries.

Yet God repeatedly made known his intention to prevail finally over all the power of the Devil, and to destroy all his works, and set up his own kingdom and interest among men, and extend it as universally as Satan had extended his. It was for this purpose that the Messiah came and died, that God might be just and the justifier of all that should believe in him. When he had laid down his life, and taken it up again, he sent forth his disciples to preach the good tidings to every creature, and to endeavor by all possible methods to bring over a lost world to God. They went forth according to their divine commission, and wonderful success attended their labors; the civilized Greeks, and uncivilized barbarians, each yielded to the cross of Christ, and embraced it as the only way of salvation. Since the apostolic age many other attempts to spread the gospel have been made, which have been considerably successful, notwithstanding which a very considerable part of mankind are still involved in all the darkness of heathenism. Some attempts are still making, but they are inconsiderable in comparison of what might be done if the whole body of Christians entered heartily into the spirit of the divine command on this subject. Some think little about it, others are unacquainted with the state of the world, and others love their wealth better than the souls of their fellow-creatures.

In order that the subject may be taken into more serious consideration, I shall inquire, whether the commission given by our Lord to his disciples be not still binding on us — take a short view of former undertakings — give some account of the present state of the world, consider the practicability of doing something more than is done — and the duty of Christians in general in this matter.

An Enquiry Whether the Commission Given by Our Lord to His Disciples Be Not Still Binding on Us

Our Lord Jesus Christ, a little before his departure, commissioned his apostles to "Go, and teach all nations"; or, as another evangelist expresses it, "Go into all the world, and preach the gospel to every creature." This commission was as extensive as possible, and laid them under obligation to disperse themselves into every country of the habitable globe, and preach to all the inhabitants, without exception, or limitation. They accordingly went forth in obedience to the command, and the power of God evidently wrought with them. Many attempts of the same kind have been made since their day, and which have been attended with various success; but the work has not been taken up, or prosecuted of late years (except by a few individuals) with that zeal and perseverance with which the primitive Christians went about it. It seems as if many thought the commission was sufficiently put in execution by what the apostles and others have done; that we have enough to do to attend to the salvation of our own countrymen; and that, if God intends the salvation of the heathen, he will some way or other bring them to the gospel, or the gospel to them. It is thus that multitudes sit at ease, and give themselves no concern about the far greater part of their fellow-sinners, who to this day, are lost in ignorance and idolatry. There seems also to be an opinion existing in the minds of some, that because the apostles were extraordinary officers and have no proper successors, and because many things which were right for them to do would be utterly unwarrantable for us, therefore it may not be immediately binding on us to execute the commission, though it was so upon them. To the consideration of such persons I would offer the following observations.

First, if the command of Christ to teach all nations be restricted to the apostles, of those under the immediate inspiration of the Holy

Ghost, then that of baptizing should be too; and every denomination of Christians, except the Quakers, do wrong in baptizing with water at all.

Secondly, if the command of Christ to teach all nations be confined to the apostles, then all such ordinary ministers who have endeavored to carry the gospel to the heathens, have acted without a warrant, and run before they were sent. Yea, and though God has promised the most glorious things to the heathen world by sending his gospel to them, yet whoever goes first, or indeed at all, with that message, unless he have a new and special commission from heaven, must go without any authority for so doing.

Thirdly, if the command of Christ to teach all nations extend only to the apostles, then, doubtless, the promise of the divine presence in this work must be so limited; but this is worded in such a manner as expressly precludes such an idea. "Lo, I am with you always, to the end of the world."

That there are cases in which even a divine command may cease to be binding is admitted — as for instance, if it be repealed, as the ceremonial commandments of the Jewish law; or if there be no subjects in the world for the commanded act to be exercised upon, as in the law of septennial release, which might be dispensed with when there should be no poor in the land to have their debts forgiven (Deut. 15:4), or if, in any particular instance, we can produce a counter-revelation, of equal authority with the original command, as when Paul and Silas were forbidden of the Holy Ghost to preach the word in Bithynia (Acts 16:6–7), or if, in any case, there be a natural impossibility of putting it in execution. It was not the duty of Paul to preach Christ to the inhabitants of Otaheite, because no such place was then discovered, nor had he any means of coming at them. But none of these things can be alleged by us in behalf of the neglect of the commission given by Christ. We cannot say that it is repealed, like the commands of the ceremonial law; nor can we plead that there are no objects for the command to be exercised upon. Alas! the far greater part of the world, as we shall see presently, are still covered with heathen darkness! Nor can we produce a counter-revelation, concerning any particular nation, like that to Paul and Silas, concerning Bithynia; and, if we could, it would not warrant our sitting still and neglecting all the other parts of the word; for Paul and Silas, when forbidden to preach to those heathens, went elsewhere, and preached to others. Neither can we allege a natural impossibility in the case. It has been said that we ought not to force our way, but to wait for the openings, and leading of Providence; but it might with equal propriety be answered in this case, neither ought we to neglect embracing those openings in providence which daily present themselves to us. What openings of providence do we wait for? We can neither expect to be transported into the heathen world without ordinary means, nor to be endowed with

the gift of tongues, etc. when we arrive there. These would not be providential interpositions, but miraculous ones. Where a command exists
nothing can be necessary to render it binding but a removal of those
obstacles which render obedience impossible, and these are removed already. Natural impossibility can never be pleaded so long as facts exist
to prove the contrary. Have not the popish missionaries surmounted all
those difficulties which we have generally thought to be insuperable?
Have not the missionaries of the *Unitas Fratrum,* or Moravian Brethren,
encountered the scorching heat of Abyssinia, and the frozen climes of
Greenland, and Labrador, their difficult languages, and savage manners?
Or have not English traders, for the sake of gain, surmounted all those
things which have generally been counted insurmountable obstacles in
the way of preaching the gospel? Witness the trade to Persia, the East-
Indies, China, and Greenland, yea even the accursed Slave-Trade on the
coasts of Africa. Men can insinuate themselves into the favor of the most
barbarous clans, and uncultivated tribes, for the sake of gain; and how
different so ever the circumstances of trading and preaching are, yet this
will prove the possibility of ministers being introduced there; and if this
is but thought a sufficient reason to make the experiment, my point is
gained.

It has been said that some learned divines have proved from Scripture that the time is not yet come that the heathen should be converted;
and that first the witnesses must be slain, and many other prophecies
fulfilled. But admitting this to be the case (which I much doubt) yet if
any objection is made from this against preaching to them immediately,
it must be founded on one of these things; either that the secret purpose
of God is the rule of our duty and then it must be as bad to pray for
them, as to preach to them; or else that none shall be converted in the
heathen world till the universal down-pouring of the Spirit in the last
days. But this objection comes too late; for the success of the gospel has
been very considerable in many places already.

It has been objected that there are multitudes in our own nation,
and within our immediate spheres of action, who are as ignorant as the
South-Sea savages, and that therefore we have work enough at home,
without going into other countries. That there are thousands in our own
land as far from God as possible, I readily grant, and that this ought to
excite us to ten-fold diligence in our work, and in attempts to spread
divine knowledge amongst them is a certain fact; but that it ought to
supersede all attempts to spread the gospel in foreign parts seems to
want proof. Our own countrymen have the means of grace, and may
attend on the word preached if they choose it. They have the means
of knowing the truth, and faithful ministers are placed in almost every
part of the land, whose spheres of action might be much extended if
their congregations were but more hearty and active in the cause: but

with them the case is widely different, who have no Bible, no written language, (which many of them have not,) no ministers, no good civil government, nor any of those advantages which we have. Pity therefore, humanity, and much more Christianity, call loudly for every possible exertion to introduce the gospel amongst them.

[William Carey, *An Enquiry into the Obligations of Christians to Use Means for the Conversion of the Heathens* (Leicester: n.p., 1792), 3–13.]

– 18 –

Isaac Backus

A native of colonial Connecticut, Isaac Backus (1724–1806) grew up in a Congregational church and experienced conversion in 1741 as a result of the great revival meetings that swept the colonies in the 1730s and 1740s. In 1746 Backus felt the call to become a pastor and gave his first sermon the following Sunday at the local New Light church. After a few troubled years as pastor of a small congregation in Titicut, Massachusetts, Backus started a new church in 1756 based on strict Baptist principles and served as its pastor till his death in 1806. By 1776 Backus had become one of the principal insurrectionist preachers in New England, preaching that in order for Christians to have a right relationship with God and keep their God-given covenant, they must be free from state and ecclesial coercion. Such liberty included freedom from British domination, which entailed revolution and the separation of church and state. In his arguments defending this Baptist view of liberty, Backus recalled Roger Williams and that early Baptist's struggle for religious liberty. Unlike Williams, however, Backus failed to proclaim the difference to Scripture interpretation made by the coming of Jesus Christ, a difference that entailed not the taking up of arms but the struggle and sacrifice for peace. The following selection highlights some of Backus's main interests, such as his emphasis on liberty of conscience for all people, his theory of two governments — the civil and the ecclesiastical — and the realms in which each functions, and the individualism inherent in the Enlightenment ideals he learned from the works of John Locke. Yet a robust theology of human depravity made Backus suspicious of fully integrating the philosophy of natural rights into the gospel. In addition to treatises on religious liberty such as An Appeal to the People of Massachusetts State against Arbitrary Power *(1780) and the one selected below, which was published in 1773, Backus also wrote a three-volume* History of Baptists in America *(1777–1796), which is one of the earliest known histories of a denomination in this country.*

An Appeal to the Public for Religious Liberty

Inasmuch as there appears to us a real need of such an appeal, we would previously offer a few thoughts concerning the general nature of liberty and government and then show wherein it appears to us that our religious rights are encroached upon in this land.

It is supposed by multitudes that in submitting to government we give up some part of our liberty because they imagine that there is something in their nature incompatible with each other. But the word of truth plainly shows, that man first lost his freedom by breaking over the rules of government and that those who now speak great swelling words about liberty, while they despise government, are themselves servants of corruption. What a dangerous error, yea, what a root of all evil then must it be, for men to imagine that there is anything in the nature of true government that interferes with true and full liberty! A grand cause of this evil is ignorance of what we are and where we are, for did we view things in their true light, it would appear to be as absurd and dangerous for us to aspire after anything beyond our capacity or out of the rule of our duty as it would for the frog to swell till he bursts himself in trying to get as big as the ox or for a beast or fowl to dive into the fish's element till they drown themselves. Godliness with contentment is great gain. But they that will take a contrary course "fall into temptation and a snare and into many foolish and hurtful lusts which drown men in destruction and perdition" (1 Tim. 6:6, 9).

The true liberty of man is to know, obey, and enjoy his Creator and to do all the good unto, and enjoy all the happiness with and in, his fellow creatures that he is capable of. In order to which the law of love was written in his heart which carries in its nature union and benevolence to Being in general and to each being in particular according to its relation and connection to and with the Supreme Being and ourselves. Each rational soul, as he is a part of the whole system of rational beings, so it was and is both his duty and his liberty to regard the good of the whole in all his actions. To love ourselves and truly to seek our own welfare, is both liberty and our indispensable duty. But the conceit that man could advance either his honor or happiness by disobedience instead of obedience was first injected by the father of lies, and all such conceits ever since are as false as he is.

Before man imagined that submission to government and acting strictly by rule was confinement and that breaking over those bounds would enlarge his knowledge and happiness, how clear were his ideas! (even so as to give proper names to every creature) and how great was his honor and pleasure. But no sooner did he transgress than instead of enjoying the boldness of innocency and the liberties of paradise he sneaks away to hide himself, and instead of clear and just ideas he adopted that master of all absurdities (which his children follow to this day) of thinking to hide from Omnisciency, and of trying to deceive Him who knows everything! Instead of good and happiness he felt evil, guilt and misery, and in the room of concord was wrangling both against his Creator and his fellow creatures even so that she who was before loved as his own flesh he now accuses to the great Judge. By which it appears that the notion of man's gaining any dignity or liberty by refusing an entire submission to government was so delusive that instead of its advancing him to be as Gods, it sunk him down into a way of acting like the beasts and like the Devil! The beasts are actuated by their senses and inclinations, and the Devil pursues his designs by deceit and violence. With malicious reflections upon God and flattering presences to man he drew him down to gratify his eyes and his taste with forbidden fruit: And he had no sooner revolted from the authority of Heaven than the beauty and order of his family was broken. He turns accuser against the wife of his bosom, his first son murders the next, and then lies to his Maker to conceal it, and that lying murderer's posterity were the first who broke over the order of marriage which God had instituted. And things proceeded from bad to worse till all flesh had corrupted his way, and the earth was filled with violence so that they could no longer be borne with, but by a just vengeance were all swept away, only one family.

Yet all this did not remove the dreadful distemper from man's nature, for the great Ruler of the universe directly after the flood gave this as one reason why he would not bring such another while the earth remains, namely, "For the imagination of man's heart is evil from his youth." So that if he was to drown them as often as they deserved it, one deluge must follow another continually. Observe well where the distemper lies; evil imaginations have usurped the place of reason and a well informed judgment and hold them in such bondage that instead of being governed by those noble faculties, they are put to the horrid drudgery of seeking out inventions for the gratification of fleshly lusts which war against the soul, and to guard against having these worst of all enemies detected and subdued. Enemies which are so far from being God's creatures that, strictly speaking, they have no being at all in themselves, only are the privation of his creatures' well-being. Therefore sin, with its offspring death, will, as to those who are saved, be swallowed up in victory. Sin is an enemy both to God and man which was begotten by Satan, and was conceived and brought forth by man, for lust when it is conceived bringeth forth sin, and sin when it is finished bringeth forth death.

Now how often have we been told that he is not a freeman but a slave whose person and goods are not at his own but another's disposal? And to have foreigners come and riot at our expense and in the fruit of our labors, has often been represented to be worse than death. And should the higher powers appear to deal with temporal oppressors according to their deserts, it would seem strange indeed if those who have suffered intolerably by them, should employ all their art and power to conceal them and so to prevent their being brought to justice! But how is our world filled with such madness concerning spiritual tyrants! How far have pride and infidelity, covetousness and luxury, yea, deceit and cruelty, those foreigners which came from Hell, carried their influence, and spread their baneful mischiefs in our world! Yet who is willing to own that he has been deceived and enslaved by them? Who is willing honestly to bring them forth to justice! All acknowledge that these enemies are among us, and many complain aloud of the mischiefs that they do, yet even those who lift their heads so high as to laugh at the atonement of Jesus and the powerful influences of the Spirit and slight public and private devotion are at the same time very unwilling to own that they harbor pride, infidelity, or any other of those dreadful tyrants. And nothing but the divine law referred to above, brought home with convincing light and power, can make them truly sensible of the soul-slavery that they are in. And 'tis only the power of the gospel that can set them free from sin so as to become the servants of righteousness, can deliver them from these enemies so as to serve God in holiness all their days. And those who do not thus know the truth and have not been made free thereby, yet have never been able in any country to subsist long without some sort of government. Neither could any of them ever make out to establish any proper government without calling in the help of the Deity. However absurd their notions have been, yet they have found human sight and power to be so short and weak, and able to do so little toward watching over the conduct and guarding the rights of individuals, that they have been forced to appeal to Heaven by oaths, and to invoke assistance from thence to avenge the cause of the injured upon the guilty. Hence it is so far from being necessary for any man to give up any part of his real liberty in order to submit to government that all nations have found it necessary to submit to some government in order to enjoy any liberty and security at all.

We are not insensible that the general notion of liberty is for each one to act or conduct as he pleases but that government obliges us to act toward others by law and rule which, in the imagination of many, interferes with such liberty. Though when we come to the light of truth what can possibly prevent its being the highest pleasure for every rational person to love God with all his heart and his neighbor as himself, but corruption and delusion which, as was before noted, are foreigners and not originally belonging to man. Therefore the divine argument to prove that those who promise liberty while they despise government are servants of corruption is this: "For of whom a man is overcome, of the same is he brought in bondage" (2 Pet. 2:18–19). He is so far from being free to act the man that he is a bond-slave to the worst of tyrants. And not a little of this tyranny is carried on by such an abuse of language as to call it liberty for men to yield themselves up to be so "foolish, disobedient and deceived as to serve divers lusts and pleasures" (Titus 3:3).

Having offered these few thoughts upon the general nature of government and liberty, it is needful to observe that God has appointed two kinds of government in the world which are distinct in their nature and ought never to be confounded together, one of which is called civil the other ecclesiastical government. And though we shall not attempt a full explanation of them yet some essential points of difference between them are necessary to be mentioned in order truly to open our grievances.

Section I
Some Essential Points of Difference between Civil and Ecclesiastical Government

1. The forming of the constitution and appointment of the particular orders and offices of civil government is left to human discretion, and our submission thereto is required under the name of their being the ordinances of men for the Lord's sake (1 Pet. 2:13–14). Whereas in ecclesiastical affairs we are most solemnly warned not to be "subject to ordinances after the doctrines and commandments of men" (Col. 2:20–22)....

2. That as the putting of any men into civil office is of men, of the people of the world, so officers have truly no more authority than the people give them. And how came the people of the world by any.

3. All acts of executive power in the civil state are to be performed in the name of the king or state they belong to, while all our religious acts are to be done in the name of the Lord Jesus and so are to be performed "heartily as to the Lord and not unto men." And it is but "lip service and vain worship if our fear toward him is taught by the precepts of men" (Col. 3:17, 23; Isa. 29:13; Matt. 15:9)....

4. In all civil governments some are appointed to judge for others and have power to compel others to submit to their judgment, but our Lord has most plainly forbidden us either to assume or submit to any such thing in religion (Matt. 23:1–9; Luke 22:25–27). He declares that the cause of his coming into the world was to bear witness unto the truth, and says he, "Everyone that is of the truth heareth my voice." This is the nature of his kingdom which he says is not of this world, and gives that as the reason why his servants should not fight or defend him with the sword (John 18:36–37). And it appears to us that

the true difference and exact limits between ecclesiastical and civil government is this, that the church is armed with light and truth to pull down the strongholds of iniquity and to gain souls to Christ and into his Church to be governed by his rules therein, and again to exclude such from their communion, who will not be so governed, while the state is armed with the sword to guard the peace and the civil rights of all persons and societies and to punish those who violate the same. And where these two kinds of government, and the weapons which belong to them are well distinguished and improved according to the true nature and end of their institution, the effects are happy, and they do not at all interfere with each other. But where they have been confounded together no tongue nor pen can fully describe the mischiefs that have ensued of which the Holy Ghost gave early and plain warnings. He gave notice to the church that the main of those anti-Christian confusions and abominations would be drawn by philosophy and deceit from the handwriting of ordinances that Christ had blotted out. And to avoid the same, he directs the saints to walk in Christ Jesus as they received him, rooted and built up in him, and established in the faith as they have been taught, viewing that they are "complete in him which is the head over all principality and power." Therefore he charges them not to be beguiled into a voluntary humility by such fleshly minds as do not hold this Head but would subject them to ordinances after the doctrines and commandments of man (Col. 2)....

Section II
A Brief View of How Civil and Ecclesiastical Affairs Are Blended Together among Us to the Depriving of Many of God's People of That Liberty of Conscience Which He Has Given Them

We are not insensible that an open appearance against any part of the conduct of men in power is commonly attended with difficulty and danger. And could we have found any way wherein with clearness we could have avoided the present attempt we would gladly have taken it. But our blessed Lord and only Redeemer has commanded us to stand fast in the liberty wherewith he has made us free. And things appear so to us at present that we cannot see how we can fully obey this command without refusing any active compliance with some laws about religious affairs that are laid upon us. And as those who are interested against us often accuse us of complaining unreasonably, we are brought under a necessity of laying open particular facts which otherwise we would gladly have concealed. And all must be sensible that there is a vast difference between exposing the faults, either of individuals or communities when the cause of truth and equity would suffer without it and the doing of it without any such occasion. We view it to be our incumbent duty to render unto Caesar the things that are his but also that it is of as much importance not to render unto him anything that belongs only to God, who is to be obeyed rather than any man. And as it is evident to us that God always claimed it as his sole prerogative to determine by his own laws what his worship shall be, who shall minister in it, and how they shall be supported, so it is evident that this prerogative has been, and still is, encroached upon in our land....

Another argument which these ministers often mention is the apostolic direction to us to pray for all that are in authority that we may lead a quiet and peaceable life in all godliness and honesty. But do they pray and act according to that direction? One while they cry up the great advantage of having religion established by law, and some have caused near as loud a clamor about it as the craftsmen did at Ephesus. But when it comes to be calmly represented that religion is a voluntary obedience unto God which therefore force cannot promote, how soon do they shift the scene and tell us that religious liberty is fully allowed to us only the state have in their wisdom thought fit to tax all the inhabitants to support an order of men for the good of civil society. A little while ago it was for religion, and many have declared that without it we should soon have no religion left among us, but now 'tis to maintain civility. Though, by the way, it is well known that no men in the land have done more to promote uncivil treatment of dissenters from themselves than some of these pretended ministers of civility have done. In 1644 the court at Boston passed an act to punish men with banishment if they opposed infant baptism or departed from any of their congregations when it was going to be administered. And after they had acted upon this law one of their chief magistrates observed, that such methods tended to make hypocrites. To which a noted minister replied, that if it did so, yet such were better than profane persons because, said he, "Hypocrites give God part of his due, the outward man, but the profane person giveth God neither outward nor inward man." By which it seems that in that day they were zealous to have the outward man, if no more, given to God. But now that conduct is condemned as persecution by their children who profess to allow us full liberty of conscience because they do not hinder our giving our inward man to God, only claim a power to seize our outward man to get money for themselves. And though many of us have expended ten or twenty times as much in setting up and supporting that worship which we believe to be right as it would have cost us to have continued in the fashionable way, yet we are often accused of being covetous for dissenting from that way and refusing to pay more money out of our little incomes to uphold men from whom we receive no benefit but rather abuse. How far is this from leading a peaceable life either of godliness or honesty!

Section III
A Brief Account of What the Baptists Have Suffered under This Constitution and of Their Reasons for Refusing Any Active Compliance with It

In civil states the power of the whole collective body is vested in a few hands that they may with better advantage defend themselves against injuries from abroad and correct abuses at home, for which end a few have a right to judge for the whole society. But in religion each one has an equal right to judge for himself, for we must all appear before the judgment seat of Christ, that every one may receive the things done in his body according to that "he hath done" — not what any earthly representative hath done for him (2 Cor. 5:10). And we freely confess that we can find no more warrant from divine truth for any people on earth to constitute any men their representatives to make laws, to impose religious taxes than they have to appoint Peter or the Virgin Mary to represent them before the throne above. We are therefore brought to a stop about paying so much regard to such laws as to give in annual certificates to the other denomination (i.e., the Congregational or Standing Churches) as we have formerly done.

1. Because the very nature of such a practice implies an acknowledgment that the civil power has a right to set one religious sect up above another, else why need we give certificates to them any more than they to us? It is a tacit allowance that they have a right to make laws about such things which we believe in our consciences they have not. For,

2. By the foregoing address to our legislature and their committee's report thereon it is evident that they claim a right to tax us from civil obligation as being the representatives of the people. But how came a civil community by any ecclesiastical power? How came the kingdoms of this world to have a right to govern in Christ's kingdom which is not of this world!

3. That constitution not only emboldens people to judge the liberty of other men's consciences and has carried them so far as to tell our General Assembly that they conceived it to be a duty they owed to God and their country not to be dispensed with, to lay before them the springs of their neighbors' actions, but it also requires something of the same nature from us. Their laws require us annually to certify to them what our belief is concerning the conscience of every person that assembles with us, as the condition of their being exempted from taxes to other's worship. And only because our brethren in Bellingham left that clause about the conscience out of their certificate last year a number of their society who live at Mendon were taxed, and lately suffered the spoiling of their goods to uphold pedobaptist worship.

4. The scheme we oppose evidently tends to destroy the purity and life of religion, for the inspired apostle assures us that the church is espoused as a chaste virgin to Christ and is obliged to be subject to him in everything as a true wife to her husband. Now the most chaste domestic obedience does not at all interfere with any lawful objection to civil authority. But for a woman to admit the highest ruler in a nation into her husband's place would be adultery or whoredom. And how often are men's inventions about worship so called in the sacred oracles? And does it not greatly concern us all earnestly to search out and put away such evils as we would desire to escape the awful judgments that such wickedness has brought on other nations! Especially if we consider that not only the purity but also the very life and being of religion among us is concerned therein, for 'tis evident that Christ has given as plain laws to determine what the duty of people is to his ministers as he has the duty of ministers to his people, and most certainly he is as able to enforce the one as the other. The common plea of our opponents is that people will not do their duty if rulers do not enforce it. But does not the whole book of God clearly show that ministers as often fail of doing their duty as the people do? And where is the care of rulers to punish ministers for their unfaithfulness? They often talk about equality in these affairs, but where does it appear! As Christ is the head of all principality and power, so the not holding the Head, from which all the body by joints and bands having nourishment ministered and knit together, increaseth with the increase of God," but bringing in an earthly power between Christ and his people has been the grand source of anti-Christian abominations and of settling men down in a form of godliness while they deny the power thereof. Has not this earthly scheme prevailed so far in our land as to cause many ministers, instead of taking heed to the ministry received from the Lord and instead of watching for souls as those who must give an account, rather to act as if they were not accountable to any higher power than that of the men who support them? And on the other hand, how do many people behave as if they were more afraid of the collector's warrant and of an earthly prison than of Him who sends his ministers to preach his gospel and says, "He that receiveth whomsoever I send, receiveth me," but declares that it shall be more tolerable in the day of judgment for Sodom than for those who receive them not? Yea, as if they were more afraid of an earthly power than of our great King and Judge who can this night require the soul of him that layeth up "treasure for himself and is not rich towards God," and will sentence all either to Heaven or Hell according as they have treated him well or ill in his ministers and members.

5. The custom which they want us to countenance is very hurtful to civil society, for by the law of Christ every man is not only allowed

but also required to judge for himself concerning the circumstantials as well as the essentials of religion and to act according to the "full persuasion of his own mind," and he contracts guilt to his soul if he does the contrary (Rom. 14:5, 23). What a temptation then does it lay for men to contract such guilt when temporal advantages are annexed to one persuasion and disadvantages laid upon another? I.e., in plain terms, how does it tend to hypocrisy and lying? Than which, what can be worse to human society! Not only so, but coercive measures about religion also tend to provoke emulation, wrath, and contention, and who can describe all the mischiefs of this nature that such measures have produced in our land! But where each person and each society (i.e., religious congregation) are equally protected from being injured by others, all enjoying equal liberty to attend and support the worship which they believe is right, having no more striving for mastery or superiority than little children (which we must all come to or not enter into the kingdom of Heaven) how happy are its effects in civil society? In the town of Boston they enjoy something of these blessings, and why may not the country have the same liberty? . . .

Conclusion

And now dear countrymen, we beseech you seriously to consider of these things. The great importance of a general union through this country in order to the preservation of our liberties has often been pleaded for with propriety, but how can such a union be expected so long as that dearest of all rights, equal liberty of conscience, is not allowed? Yea, how can any reasonably expect that He who has the hearts of kings in his hand will turn the heart of our earthly sovereign to hear the pleas for liberty of those who will not hear the cries of their fellow subjects under their oppressions? Has it not been plainly proved that so far as any man gratifies his own inclinations without regard to the universal law of equity so far he is in bondage? So that it is impossible for anyone to tyrannize over others without thereby becoming a miserable slave himself, a slave to raging lusts and a slave to guilty fears of what will be the consequence. . . .

Suffer us a little to expostulate with our fathers and brethren who inhabit the land to which our ancestors fled for religious liberty. You have lately been accused with being disorderly and rebellious by men in power who profess a great regard for order and the public good. And why don't you believe them and rest easy under their administrations? You tell us you cannot because you are taxed where you are not represented. And is it not really so with us? You do not deny the right of the British Parliament to impose taxes within her own realm; only complain that she extends her taxing power beyond her proper limits. And have we not as good right to say you do the same thing? And so that wherein you judge others you condemn yourselves? Can three thousand miles possibly fix such limits to taxing power as the difference between civil and sacred matters has already done? One is only a difference of space, the other is so great a difference in the nature of things as there is between sacrifices to God and the ordinances of man. This we trust has been fully proved....

And we have one difficulty in submitting to this power which our countrymen have not in the other case, that is, our case affects the conscience as theirs does not. And equal liberty of conscience is one essential article in our Charter which constitutes this government and describes the extent of our rulers' authority and what are the rights and liberties of the people. And in the confession of faith which our rulers and their ministers have published to the world they say, "God alone is Lord of the conscience and hath left it free from the doctrines and commandments of men which are in anything contrary to his word or not contained in it. So that to believe such doctrines or to obey such commands out of conscience is to betray true liberty of conscience, and the requiring of an implicit faith and an absolute blind obedience is to destroy liberty of conscience and reason also...."

In a celebrated oration for liberty, published last spring in Boston, a maxim was recited which carries its own evidence with it which is this, "No man can give that which is another's." Yet have not our legislature from time to time made acts to empower the major part of the inhabitants in towns and precincts to give away their neighbors' estates to what ministers they please! And can we submit to such doctrines and commandments of men and not betray true liberty of conscience! Every person is or ought to be benefited by civil government, and therefore they owe rulers honor and a tribute on that account. But the like cannot be truly said of an imposed minister, for as the gospel ministry is an ordinance of God and not of man so the obligation that any person or people are under to obey and support any man as a minister of Christ arises from the consideration of his appearing to them to resemble his Master in doctrine and conversation and from the benefit which people receive under their ministrations. From whence the law of equity makes the free communications of our carnal things to Christ's ministers to be a matter that as really concerns the exercise of a good conscience toward God as prayer and praise do, for they are both called sacrifices to him in the same chapter (Heb. 13:15–16).

Thus we have laid before the public a brief view of our sentiments concerning liberty of conscience and a little sketch of our sufferings on that account. If any can show us that we have made any mistakes either about principles or facts, we would lie open to conviction. But we hope none will violate the forecited article of faith so much as to require us to yield a blind obedience to them or to expect that spoiling of goods or imprisonment can move us to betray the cause of true liberty.... The foregoing appeal, having been examined and approved by many of his brethren, is presented to the public by their humble servant....

[William G. McLoughlin, ed., *Isaac Backus on Church, State, and Calvinism: Pamphlets, 1754–1789* (Cambridge, Mass.: Belknap Press, 1968), 309–42.]

– 19 –

Hannah Lee Corbin

While the eighteenth century witnessed the struggle for and victory of religious freedom in America, and the adoption of political documents that proclaimed equality, there were still many, in particular women and African slaves, who continued to suffer to put into practice the written laws of equality and freedom. Among those struggling for such goods was Hannah Lee Corbin (1728–83). Born into a prominent Virginia family of the planter aristocracy, Hannah was one of the sisters of Richard Henry Lee (1732–94), a political leader in the American Revolution, and cousin to Henry (Light-Horse Harry) Lee (1756–1818), famous American Revolutionary soldier and father of Confederate General Robert E. Lee. Hannah Lee grew up in the Anglican tradition and married Gawen Corbin in the Established Church. Mr. Corbin died, leaving Hannah a widow at the young age of thirty-two. A statement in his will declared that should she remarry or leave the county, Hannah would forfeit her estate. Nevertheless, she married the family physician, Richard Lingan Hall. And since prior to 1780 Virginia did not recognize Baptist marriages, Hannah Lee did not lose Peckatone Plantation and was able to pass it on to her daughter. Sometime between 1760 and 1762, a Baptist preacher by the name of David Thomas came to Virginia from Pennsylvania. He spoke to large audiences throughout the counties of the Northern Neck. Hannah went to hear Thomas and was converted to the Baptist view, although at the time there was no Baptist church in the five counties of the Northern Neck. She joined the Chappawamsi Baptist Church and was later a charter member of the Potomac Baptist Church. William Lumpkin observes that Baptist churches in colonial Virginia "offered to women the appeal of primitive Christianity to enter the faith on the same basis as men, and they argued that women are accepted equally with men as children of God" (Baptist History and Heritage, July 1973, 160). *Apparently Hannah made no secret about leaving the Anglican Church. In 1764 she was brought before the grand jury of Westmoreland County "for not appearing at her parish Church, for six months past." Leon McBeth notes that "women assumed a larger church role among Separate Baptists, assisting in baptisms, serving at the communion table, even preaching at church meetings"* (The Baptist

Heritage, 231). Along with other important Virginia Baptist women like Margaret Meuse Clay and Martha Stearns Marshall, Hannah Lee Corbin was such a leader in the church. As Anne Hutchinson in the preceding century had been, Hannah Lee was in the advance guard of women's suffrage and feminism. The following letters indicate her convictions about the equal status of women in both political and religious spheres and her life in view of the gospel story of Jesus, whom she called "the Despised Gallilean."

A Follower of the Despised Gallilean

From Letters to Her Sister Alice

I am not surprised that you seem to have a mean opinion of the Baptist religion. I believe most people that are not of that profession are persuaded we are either Enthusiasts or Hypocrites. But my dear Sister the followers of the Lamb have been ever esteemed so, this is our Comfort and that we know in whom we have believed.

I have wrote to my Brother [Richard Henry] & I beg you will use your interest with him to do something for the poor desolate widows.

A Response from Her Brother Richard Henry Lee

Chantilly, March 17, 1778

My Dear Sister,

Distressed as my mind is and has been by a variety of attentions, I am ill able by letter to give you the satisfaction I could wish on the several subjects of your letter. Reasonable as you are and friendly to the freedom and happiness of your country, I should have no doubt giving you perfect content in a few hours' conversation. You complain that widows are not represented, and that being temporary possessors of their estate ought not to be liable to the tax. The doctrine of representation is a large subject, and it is certain that it ought to be extended as far as wisdom and policy can allow; nor do I see that either of these forbid widows having property from voting, notwithstanding it has never been the practice either here or in England. Perhaps 'twas thought rather out of character for women to press into those tumultuous assemblages of men where the business of choosing representatives is conducted. And it might also have been considered as not so necessary, seeing that the representatives themselves, as their immediate constituents, must suffer the tax imposed in exact proportion as does all other property taxed, and that, therefore, it could not be supposed that taxes would be laid where the public good did not demand it. This, then, is the widow's security as well as that of the never married women, who have lands in their own right, for both of whom I have the highest respect, and would at any time give my consent to establish their right of voting....

The English Parliament nor their representatives would pay a farthing of the tax they imposed on us but quite otherwise. Their property would have been exonerated in exact proportion to the burthens they laid on ours. Oppressions, therefore, without end and taxes without reason or public necessity would have been our fate had we submitted to British usurpation. For my part I had much rather lease my children free than in possession of great nominal wealth, which would infallibly have been the case with all American possessions had our property been subject to the arbitrary taxation of a British Parliament....I believe there is no instance in our new government of any unnecessary placemen, and I know the rule is to make their salaries moderate as possible, and even these moderate salaries are to pay tax. But should Great Britain gain her point, where we have one placeman we should have a thousand and pay pounds where we pay pence; nor should we dare to murmur under pain of military execution. This, with the other horrid concomitants of slavery, may well persuade the American to lose blood and pay taxes also rather than submit to them....

A Letter to Her Sister Alice, Fall of 1780

My Dear Sister,

Five of your dear letters I have received without ever having an opportunity...to answer one of them. The bonnet & other things came safe as did the money but the most valuable part the books I never have got. You express a fear in your third letter that I may have gone back after putting my hand to the plough, but my dear Sister I hope so dreadful an evil will never happen to me. I hope I shall never live to see the day that I don't love God, for there can be nothing I know befall me so horrible as to be left to myself....And surely never poor mortal had so much reason to sing Free Grace as your Sister, that my exalted Redeemer should mercifully snatch me from the fire when so many thousands infinitely better by nature have been permitted to sin on till they have sunk to endless misery. Glory be to my God for his pardoning Grace, his redeeming Love....I think the scheme of raising money for the soldiers would be good if we had it in our power to do it. But we are so heavily taxed that we are unable without selling our principal estate to find ourselves common support. I am thankful that my lot is not among the high & the great, for I know that the rich & great are not the favorites of Heaven because their riches is all employed to gratify their own ambition & though they profess themselves Christians they neither obey the commands or precepts of the Gospel but amass & heap up riches without knowing who shall gather them. Blessed are the poor in spirit etc. Such think little of worldly Grandeur....

If my Brother Arthur is come I hope to see him notwithstanding I follow the despised Gallilean — Blessed be God that put it in my heart to do it, to follow Him thro' good report & evil report. My Dear Sister I hope we shall meet at the Right Hand of Glory.

[Ethel Armes, ed., *Stratford Hall: The Great House of the Lees* (Richmond, Va.: Garrett and Massie, Inc., 1936).]

– 20 –

John Leland

Though a native of Massachusetts, John Leland (1754–1841) is best remembered for his struggles for religious liberty in Virginia. Raised a Congregationalist, Leland was an avid reader of Scripture and of John Bunyan's Pilgrim's Progress. *When he was eighteen he experienced Christian conversion and was baptized by a Baptist minister. In 1776 Leland and his wife, Sallie Devine, moved to Virginia where he pastored various small Baptist congregations and worked as an itinerant preacher. Anglicanism was the established religion in Virginia, and Leland with all the baptists struggled under persecution from both ecclesial and civil authorities. After a "second" ordination in 1786 (some Virginia Baptists had questioned the authenticity of his ordination in Massachusetts), Leland became one of the main leaders of the Separate Baptists in the South. Known for his humorous, witty, and bold sermons, Leland spoke tirelessly on behalf of religious liberty, the disestablishment of the church, and against slavery. A self-educated man, he read widely and was well informed on the major issues of the day. His letters to and personal friendship with Thomas Jefferson and James Madison were highly influential in the passing of a bill that established religious freedom in Virginia (1786) and in the Bill of Rights that amended the Federal Constitution (1789). In 1791 Leland returned to Massachusetts where he continued preaching and writing, serving also in the state House of Representatives from 1811 to 1813. Leland's most famous work,* The Rights of Conscience Inalienable *(1791), lays out the author's many arguments defending full religious liberty. In his many sermons and speeches, Leland called for a moderate Calvinism and emphasized the necessity of evangelical fervor among Baptists. He argued that it was not the state's responsibility or right to enforce or spread the gospel, thus suggesting that Constantinianism was more harmful than helpful for the propagation of the gospel. It was the duty of each individual Christian to share the Good News with sinners. During his time in Virginia, Leland baptized over one thousand people.*

A Blow at the Root

Social pollution influences men to work ill to their neighbors, to prevent which civil government was appointed. "The law was not made for a righteous man, but for the lawless and disobedient." "The powers that be, are ordained of God." Rulers are God's ministers. That civil government in the hands of men, is an evil of itself, admits of no doubt. The vast expense to the community — the pride and cruelty of those in power — the intrigue and chicanery made use of by aspiring, avaricious men to gain seats of importance, and the arts and dissimulation used to keep their real designs out of view, prove the hypothesis that government is an evil, but with all these horrid features, it is a choice among evils — in fact, a necessary evil, to prevent greater evils. In this case, one of those instances appears, where, of two evils, the least is a chosen good.

How extensive this government is, is a point in which legislators, philosophers, and men in general, are greatly divided. Some suppose, that when government is formed and organized, those in office have power to make all civil, municipal, sumptuary and religious laws, and that any disregard of those laws, is a moral evil: they seem to pin their life, liberty, property, body and soul on the sleeve of their rulers, and abundance of those in power, love to have it so. If rulers were infallible in wisdom and goodness, there would be no danger in this scheme, but as all Adam's children are a bad breed, the scheme is very exceptionable.

Perhaps the legitimate designs of government cannot be better defined, than by saying, "it is to preserve the lives, liberties and property of the many units that form the whole body politic." For these valuable purposes, individuals have, in certain cases, to expose their lives in war to defend the state — to give up a little of their liberty, and be controlled by the general will, and part with a little of their property to compensate those who should be employed to secure the rest.

Government is, when rightly understood, the most economical means that men make use of, to secure themselves and be happy.

When a constitution of government is formed, it should be simple and explicit, the powers that are to be vested in, and the work to be performed by each department, should be defined with the utmost perspicuity, and this constitution should be attended to as scrupulously by men in office, as the Bible should be by all religionists. For either of the departments of government to deviate from the constitution, with a view to do good, is criminal, for if the honorable servants of the people forsake their political Bible, for a supposed good, they will soon forsake it for a real evil. Let the people first be convinced of the deficiency of the constitution, and remove the defects thereof, and then, those in office can change the administration upon constitutional ground.

If men were now as virtuous as their great progenitor was at first, it is probable they would need some distributive laws; but the idea of a code of penal laws among such innocent beings, would be inadmissible.

But the idea of such innocent beings is not now to be realized in fact among men. "All have sinned." It would, however, be a great blessing to mankind, if they were so virtuous as to have a few laws sufficient to restrain and direct them; for where there is a vast number of laws in a political body, there will be but few of the people who have leisure to read, and capacity to understand them; in such a labyrinth, the legislature will almost inevitably injure one act by another; besides, where only a few are learned in the law, it gives those few an undue advantage over others; further, such a maze of laws, like a cobweb, will entangle the innocent flies, but support the venomous spiders. And yet, where many vices reign, if there are not many laws, there will be many cases left to the will of the judge, and this gives the judge such an amazing importance both to legislate and judge of the law, and fact, that all who are interested, will seek to bribe the judge. And, if his temptations of bribes and importance do not overcome him, and induce him to pervert law and judgment, it will be because he is one of a thousand.

The conclusion is, that while men are so vicious, they must adopt the medium, between having too many, and too few laws; and above all, let them seek to become more virtuous, which is the direct way to escape the evils just pointed out; for when men observe the golden rule, of "doing unto all men as they would be done by," no just laws will do them any hurt.

But the means of procuring wealth, ease and comfort; the right of private judgment and free debate, and the liberty of conscience, are inalienable. These are not surrendered up to the general will, by individuals, when they enter into society; but each retains them in his own sovereign breast. The last of these, which is liberty of conscience, I shall now attend unto.

Whenever any right which men possess in a state of nature, is surrendered up to government, it is to be paid at least, with an equivalent: indeed, with something superior; but government cannot reward individuals with anything equally valuable with the liberty of their conscience.

He who is obliged by law to sin against his own conscience, cannot have his loss made good.

To be definite in expression, by the liberty of conscience, I mean, the inalienable right that each individual has, of worshipping his God according to the dictates of his conscience, without being prohibited, directed, or controlled therein by human law, either in time, place, or manner.

If the worship of God is to be controlled by law, who shall make that law? Shall the Pope? Have not the long succession of Popes, given incontestable evidence that they have been fallible? And shall fallible men make laws to direct us how to worship an infallible God? In all Protestant countries the idea is justly exploded; but kings, parliaments, and legislative bodies, have undertaken the solemn work, with but little solemnity. How have they succeeded? One year make a law, and the next alter, repeal, or add unto it. Does God annually, or periodically change? If not, these law makers change; and are changeable men competent to direct men how to worship an unchangeable God? ...

The first settlers of Massachusetts had left the rod of oppression in England, and fled to America for freedom; but not fully understanding that religious opinions were not under the control of civil government, in 1635, they passed a sentence of banishment against Roger Williams, because he opposed the interference of law in matters of religion; and three months afterwards, they made an attempt to seize him, and send him back to England; but he fled to Providence, and obtained a grant of land from the Narraganset Indians.

Governor Haines pronounced the sentence of banishment against Williams, but Haines soon got distressed in Massachusetts, and went to Connecticut; and when Mr. Williams saw him at his house, in Hartford, Haines said to him: "I must confess to you that the Most Wise God hath provided and cut out this part of the world, for a refuge and receptacle for all sorts of consciences." But had the fathers of Massachusetts believed the confession of Haines, they would not have proceeded, in 1652, and years afterwards, to imprison, whip, and pass sentence of banishment against the Baptists; and nail up their meeting house because they built it without a license from the ruling powers. Nor would they have hung the Quakers, as they did in 1659, '60 and '61....

About sixty years past, a very general revival of religion took place in New England; soon afterwards, a very considerable separation from the established religion followed, which occasioned abundance of distraints and imprisonments. For about forty of the last years, the Baptists have chiefly borne the lash; for no other society has arisen to any considerable importance. The point in debate is this: the law of the state says that, where the majority of a town, parish or precinct, choose a preacher, and contract with him for his hire, it shall be levied upon all within the limits of said town, parish or precinct, according to poll and property; and that it shall be collected in legal form, and distrained for, if not paid without. It also makes the same provision for building and repairing meeting-houses. It has hitherto been the case, that in most of the towns the Baptists have been the minority; consequently, they have been distrained upon, and imprisoned, because they would not pay their money voluntarily to preachers in whom they did not place confidence, nor approve of their sentiments; and to build meeting-houses where they did not choose to worship. He must be a poor logician,

who does not trace this oppression back to its origin, to that rotten
nest-egg, which is always hatching vipers: I mean the principle of intruding the laws of men into the kingdom of Christ, which kingdom is
not of this world. . . . Pardon me, my hearers, if I am over-warm. I lived
in Virginia fourteen years. The beneficent influence of my hero was too
generally felt to leave me a stoic. What may we not expect, under the
auspices of hearer, while Jefferson presides, with Madison in state by
his side. Now the greatest orbit in America is occupied by the bright-
est orb: but, sirs, expect to see religious bigots, like cashiered officers,
and displaced statesmen, growl and gnaw their galling bands, and, like
a yelping mastiff bark at the moon, whose rising they cannot prevent.

Let us then adore that God who has been so favorable to our land,
and nation — praise him for all that is past — trust him for all that is to
come, and not ascribe that to man which is due to God alone.

[L. F. Green, ed., *The Writings of the Late Elder John Leland* (New York: G. W. Wood,
1845), 235–55.]

Come, Thou Fount of Every Blessing

Come, thou fount of every blessing, tune my heart to sing thy grace;
Streams of mercy never ceasing, call for songs of loudest praise:
Teach me some melodious sonnet, sung by flaming tongues above;
Praise the mount! I'm fixed upon it, mount of thy redeeming love.

Here I raise my Ebenezer; hither by thy help I'm come;
And I hope, by thy good pleasure, safely to arrive at home:
Jesus sought me when a stranger, wand'ring from the fold of God;
He, to rescue me from danger, interposed his precious blood.

O to grace how great a debtor daily I'm constrained to be!
Let thy grace, Lord, like a fetter, bind my wand'ring heart to thee:
Prone to wander, Lord, I feel it, prone to leave the God I love;
Here's my heart, Lord, take and seal it, seal it for thy courts above.

Robert Robinson (1758)

Part Four

TO BE AN APOSTOLIC CHURCH

The Nineteenth Century

Introduction

The Nineteenth Century

Kenneth Scott Latourette called the nineteenth century the "Great Century" *(A History of Christianity)*. Not since the apostolic era had the wider church produced such missionary activity, experienced such evangelical vitality, or faced such theological uncertainty. It would be wrong to suggest that the nineteenth century was the beginning of Protestant missions or that Baptists alone began the movement. Seeds were planted in the preceding century. The Society for the Propagation of the Gospel in foreign parts was founded in 1701 to extend the ministry of the Anglican Church overseas and to evangelize non-Christians. By 1732 the Moravians sent missionaries to the West Indies and then to Greenland. Yet Protestantism in general, unlike Catholicism, was not greatly concerned about missionary work in foreign lands. The forming of the Baptist Missionary Society in 1792 was part of a new movement, with William Carey as its initial appointment and India its first field. By 1800 the BMS had nine missionaries working in evangelism, Bible translation, Christian education, and publishing. Soon there were mission societies scattered throughout Europe, Great Britain, and the United States.

Americans Adoniram and Ann Judson set out for India in 1812 as Congregationalist missionaries. By the time they arrived in Calcutta the Judsons were convinced Baptists. The General Missionary Convention (also known as the Triennial Convention) was formed in 1814 to support the work of the Judsons and future American Baptist missionaries. By mid-century Baptist congregations began cropping up in Germany, Scandinavia, France, and southern Europe due largely to the efforts of Johann G. Oncken, who lived by the motto "Every Baptist is a missionary." Not all Baptists, however, embraced this commitment to missions. Some resisted and others opposed it out of ministerial jealousy, fear of centralization, suspicion about fund-raising, and their own hyper-Calvinism. In *Thoughts on Missions* (1820), John Taylor of Kentucky called GMC organizer Luther Rice "a modern Tetzel" and said that missionaries "love money like a horse leech loves blood." But in the end missionary theology prevailed in Baptist life. As the folks back home sang "We've a story to tell to the nations," this unprecedented expansion of foreign missions continued, spreading the light from India to the continents of South America, Africa, and China.

The Great Century was also marked by evangelical vitality. This vitality was especially evident in North America. Timothy Dwight, president of Yale and grandson of Jonathan Edwards, kindled fires of revival that spread throughout New England in 1802 and continued to burn for decades. The western flank of the "Second Great Awakening" began in 1801 in Cane Ridge, Kentucky. As revival preachers with little or no formal education learned to present the simple message of salvation to camp meeting congregations, the lengthy and communally guided conversion experience of Puritan theology was shortened into an instantaneous and self-interpreting conversion event (Leonard, "Getting Saved in America," 111–27). Methodist circuit riders and Baptist farmer-preachers successfully extended the revivals onto the frontier, resulting in rapid growth of Methodist and Baptist populations. Interestingly, the participatory role of women among the Separate Baptists, which increased after the "First Great Awakening," diminished during the receding revivals of the nineteenth century as men began to assume control of the governing structures in the new churches.

In the third decade of the century, revival broke out again in New York through the preaching of Charles G. Finney, who introduced "new measures" such as "the prayer of faith," in which the unconverted were prayed for publicly by name, and the "anxious seat," where those under conviction would listen to the sermon. Finney's *Lectures on Revivals of Religion* (1835) gave a systematic account of this new evangelical theology. It emphasized the competency of individuals to make decisions about God, thus "Arminianizing" popular religion in America and moving it further away from the Calvinism of the eighteenth century. Dwight L. Moody, who preached in large meetings throughout the United States and Great Britain, and Sam P. Jones, "the Moody of the South," gave shape to the revivalist tradition in the second half of the century. By the end of the century, the evangelical revivals had established a powerfully "born again" Protestantism on both sides of the Atlantic rooted in the practices of biblicism, conversionism, evangelism, and activism (Noll, et al., *Evangelicalism*, 6, 128–31, 365–67; and Bebbington, *Evangelicalism in Modern Britain*, 2–17).

While the theological contours of popular religion in the nineteenth century were defined by revivals at home and missions abroad, the academy faced the challenge of growing theological uncertainty. Protestant theology was occupied all century long with a rescue effort — saving the theological enterprise and Christianity itself from the threat of the Enlightenment. In his magisterial two-volume study, Claude Welch outlines the theology of the century around three questions *(Protestant Thought in the Nineteenth Century)*. The first third of the century was dominated by the question of "the possibility of theology." The towering figures of the period were G. W. F. Hegel and Friedrich Schleiermacher — both professors at the University of Berlin. Hegel proposed that the development of ideas could be understood as a dialectical process in which a "thesis" was followed by an "antithesis." In the ensuing conflict the two were *aufgehoben,* which carried a double meaning of being done away with and preserved at a higher level as a "synthesis." Because Hegel thought that philosophy alone was capable of expressing all the dimensions of life in purely conceptual terms, he argued that Christianity could be preserved and vindicated as the Absolute Religion only by being transformed (*aufgehoben*) into philosophy. This transformation, however, meant the death of the personal transcendent God of traditional theism and the advent of Absolute (or Universal) Spirit.

Schleiermacher offered a way to retain the traditional piety and language of the Christian faith, although recast to accommodate "modern" belief. He contended that religion could not be reduced to a set of doctrines or ideas. It belonged to the realm of "feeling." Consequently, the truth of the Christian religion was available, not in rationality or morality, but in affections. In England Samuel Taylor Coleridge joined Schleiermacher in the Romantic protest against Rationalism, and in France Auguste Sabatier propagated Schleiermacher's interpretation of doctrine as the symbolic expression of religious feelings.

In the second third of the century, Protestant theology was largely concerned with "the possibility of Christology." How could the historical figure of Jesus be an object of faith in a modern world? In 1835 David Friedrich Strauss published his monumental *Leben Jesu,* translated into English in 1846 as *The Life of Jesus Critically Examined.* Strauss applied modern historiographical canons to the New Testament and concluded (in good Hegelian fashion) that the portrait of Jesus in the Gospels was neither factually accurate (as the orthodox asserted) nor historically false (as the rationalists contended) but was mythically true. The historical reconstruction of Strauss could not be ignored, but few others followed the same path. Humanists like Ludwig Feuerbach and Ralph Waldo Emerson turned away from the humanity of Christ to celebrate the human spirit. The Princeton theology of Charles Hodge and Benjamin B. Warfield and the Mercersberg theology of Philip Schaff and John W. Nevin looked back to the Reformed tradition for help in resisting the new historicism: the first through a revised Protestant scholasticism and the second in a revived Protestant catholicism. In different ways F. D. Maurice and Horace Bushnell developed a "critical orthodoxy" by providing historicized versions of Anglican and Protestant doctrine. At the margins of Protestant theology, and almost entirely overlooked by his contemporaries, Søren Kierkegaard reflected on "the absolute qualitative distinction" between God and humanity and the paradox of the incarnation.

The final third of the century turned on the question of Christianity and culture. Christian theologians such as Ernst Troeltsch offered "objective" accounts of the Christian religion among other religions; they borrowed from the social sciences: sociology (Durkheim and Weber), anthropology (Tylor and Frazer), and psychology (James and Freud). It was also during the last decades of the century that Protestant theology began to wrestle with the implications of the hard sciences, especially Darwin's theory of evolution. The publication of Albrecht Ritschl's *The Christian Doctrine of Justification and Reconciliation* (1870–74) offered a definitive account of the moral influence view of the atonement and established him as the dominant Protestant theologian of the late nineteenth century.

Liberalism reached its apogee in Adolf Harnack's immensely popular book *What Is Christianity?* (1900). By employing the methods of historical science, Harnack proposed that it was possible to grasp the "essence" of Christianity, that is, to strip off the husks of tradition and lay bare the kernel of the primitive gospel. The results of this "purely historical survey" disclose that the simple message of Jesus was not about miracles that did not happen, demons that do not exist, or the apocalypse that is not near. Rather, the teaching of Jesus could be summarized under three themes: the kingdom of God, the fatherhood of God, and the commandment of love. In the final analysis, Christianity is a matter between God and the individual: "God and the soul, the soul and its God" (*What Is Christianity?* 56). Thus Protestant liberalism attempted to rescue the faith by adapting it to modernity.

While Protestants meant to *rescue* Christianity, Catholics wanted to *preserve* it. At one extreme, the Catholic theological faculty at Tübingen dominated by J. A. Möhler was following Kant and Schleiermacher. At the other extreme was the attempt to shore up the faith against modernity with the *Syllabus of Errors* issued by Pius IX in 1864. It created much heat but offered little light. Between these extremes was John Henry Newman, who participated in the Anglo-Catholic revival (or Tractarian Movement) within the Anglican Church. The goal of the movement was to reclaim a true *via media* between Roman Catholicism and Evangelical Protestantism. The first tract was written by Newman and addressed the apostolic succession of the bishops as "the real ground on which our authority is built." Eventually Newman concluded that the appeal to antiquity could not be maintained within the Anglican Church, and he became a Roman Catholic. In his *Essay on the Development of Christian Doctrine* (1878), Newman offered a historicist defense of apostolicity suggesting that the church is able to manifest, publish, and interpret the unchanging faith to an ever-changing world and in so doing demonstrates its capability of inexhaustible expansion.

Missionary activity, evangelical vitality, and theological uncertainty shaped three competing understandings among Baptists about what it means to be faithful to apostolic Christianity: whether to be a church that is *missionary*, or *primitive*, or *successionist*. From the missionary activity of Carey, Judson, and Oncken they learned that like the first generation of believers, modern Christians were also "sent out" (the literal meaning of the Greek word *apostolos*). Thus, Baptists in the Great Century came to embrace the theology of the apostolic church as *a missionary church*. The unprecedented expansion appears at first blush to be merely an extension of Christendom (i.e., the link of church and nation) in the wake of colonialism, but as missiologist Wilbert Shenk observes, the modern missionary movement was "both a powerful last thrust of Christendom and an important instrument in bringing about [its] dissolution" ("The 'Great Century' Reconsidered," 158). How did the spread of Christianity lead to the end of Christendom?

By some early nineteenth-century accounts, taking the gospel to foreign lands was still as much about "civilizing the heathen" as it was about "christianizing" them. When this was embodied as a missionary strategy, it was a form of cultural imperialism. Admittedly, colonial powers sometimes opened the doors for missionaries, but they also closed the doors to missions, as the East India Company did to the BMS. Providentially, the gospel was often spread by evangelists with little or no direct connection to any denominational mission. For example, Christianity became established in Africa through indigenous apostles like Walter Wadé Harris (in Ivory Coast), Sampson Oppong (in Ghana), Garrick Braide (in the Niger delta), and Simon Kimbangu (in Belgian Congo). Rather than exporting a westernized version of Christendom, missionaries often found themselves responding to initiatives from within local communities of African Christianity.

With few exceptions the culture of the "Christian nations" did not fit the contexts of Asia or Africa. Consequently, the theology and strategy of missions gradually shifted away from extending Christian civilization to evangelizing and converting unbelievers. Some missionaries like Hudson Taylor, founder of the China Inland Mission, went so far as to forsake Western customs and conform to the habits of life among the indigenous people. As Christians on the mission fields began to exercise the "free church" practices taught by missionaries, Western colonial powers were caught in a contradiction: the expansionist ideology of Christendom could be maintained only by unchristian coercion. By helping indigenous Christians respond to the gospel from where *they* were, not from where the missionaries were, the gospel became "contextualized" in a new setting. Not surprisingly, missionary reflections on the contextualization of the gospel ran parallel to the academic discussions about Christianity and culture. In the long run, the kind of churches planted by Carey and the Judsons made colonialism untenable. Thus, the so-called Great Century should be seen as preeminently a "free church" (i.e., baptist) effort and not merely an extension of Christendom.

Yet Baptists labored to practice the "free church" theology that they preached. Nowhere was this struggle more important than in the United States, and no issue was more controversial for missions than slavery. The Triennial Convention, formed in 1814 to support foreign missions, began losing momentum when a letter was received in 1833 from the Baptist Union of England. The letter urged American Baptists to "effect the speedy overthrow" of the slave system, abolished that same year in Great Britain. A divisive controversy ensued. Abolitionists invoked the lines of argument made earlier by fellow Baptist David Barrow in *Slavery Examined* (1808). Proslavery voices joined Richard Furman in appealing to "the right of holding slaves [as] clearly established in the Holy Scriptures" (in *An Exposition of the Views of Baptists Relative to the Coloured Population*, 1823). The schism became final with the establishment in 1845 of the Southern Baptist Convention, which did not exclude slaveholders from missionary service. (Methodists and Presbyterians, ideologically divided like Baptists, also split along the Mason-Dixon line.) Even more important, the SBC was committed to the perpetuation of Southern values and principles as the embodiment of Christian culture. The Christendom consciousness of Southern Baptists is evident in its 1861 endorsement of "the noble course" of the Confederacy in opposing "our enemies." Even after the Civil War, Southern Baptists clung to the belief that what the Confederacy failed to establish with its armies would ultimately triumph through the superior principles of christianized Southern culture.

John Leadley Dagg, himself a strong proponent of slavery, echoed the missionary theology that "it is our duty to labor faithfully and perseveringly to bring all men to the knowledge of the truth." Indeed, Baptists in the South perceived themselves as "God's last and only hope" for world evangelization (Leonard, *God's Last and Only Hope*, 11–15). But just as the "free church" theology conflicted with and eventually overcame the coercive ideology of Christendom on the foreign mission fields, so the ugly story of slavery and the Civil War is a reminder that Southern Christendom was maintained in contradiction with its avowed "free church" theology of missions. Given this milieu, it is understandable that many African Americans were attracted to the militant abolitionism of David Walker's *Appeal* (1829) and a few to the violent example of Nat Turner's revolt (1831). As the selection from Alice Armstrong testifies, when it came to missions, the cultural captivity of

Southern churches extended to the silencing of women. But Southern Baptists were not the only churches in cultural captivity. Although independent black Baptist congregations and associations grew in great numbers through the nineteenth century, northern Baptists persistently ignored and marginalized the voices of former slaves and of free blacks like Rufus Perry and William Bishop Johnson, despite their remarkably prophetic and creative writings, which are excerpted in this part. To be sure, Baptists in the Great Century were deeply committed to being an apostolic, or missionary body, but their coercive extension and maintenance of Christendom reflects the enduring bias of race, class, and gender.

A second sense of apostolicity engendered by the evangelical revivals and akin to the aim of historicist research in religious studies was the desire to restore or recapture the experience of earliest (i.e., biblical) Christianity. These Baptists advocated the recovery of apostolicity by seeking to be *a primitive church*. Baptists, Methodists, and Presbyterians (the big three denominations in the Great Century) were all beneficiaries of the vitality produced by the evangelical revivals. Two selections in this chapter (the conversion narrative of Noah Davis and the sermon of Charles Spurgeon) witness to the growing evangelical consensus that the essential trait of biblical Christianity was genuine conversion. But the revivals also gave rise to the fragmentation of established denominations and the proliferation of new movements. It was a confusing time for Baptists as they struggled to understand their connection to the apostolic faith as recorded in the pages of the New Testament. From the transitional years of the postrevolutionary period to the Jacksonian era (1824–41), the lofty republican ideals of Jefferson gradually gave way to the common democratic beliefs of the people. This spirit of democracy was expressed in the popular demand for "private judgment" and the conviction that God's truth is immediately accessible to all people by going straight to Scripture. The selection by Francis Wayland is representative of this growing democratization in Baptist theology (see Hatch, *The Democratization of American Religion*, 1989).

Populist religion and the concern about apostolicity led to divisive controversies among Baptists. For William Miller of Vermont, the primitive church was the eschatological people of God. He became convinced by his study of biblical prophecy that Jesus would return in 1843. Preaching to audiences in the thousands, Miller denounced mainstream denominations as part of the great "falling away" and swept many Baptists into the Adventist movement. In the first third of the century, from New England to New York and Pennsylvania to Ohio, Abner Jones and Elias Smith called out thousands from the Baptists to reconstitute New Testament Christianity and form a "Christian" denomination. With the motto "No creed but the Bible" and a populist hermeneutic based on the "inalienable right" of every person to interpret the New Testament for himself or herself, Alexander Campbell began the Reforming Baptist movement. Campbell's restorationist message spread throughout Kentucky and the southern United States, leading huge numbers of Baptists to join the "Christians," or Disciples of Christ. By 1860 the movement claimed over two hundred thousand adherents. For these restorationists, the apostolic church was evidenced by unity.

Other Baptists united around a theology that identified apostolicity as adherence to the indelible marks of true religion, matching the growing uncertainty and search for foundations in the wider theological context. Their apostolic church was *a successionist church*. The most controversial and divisive successionist movement of the century was Landmarkism. Firebrand preacher J. R. Graves and his associates, A. C. Dayton and J. M. Pendleton, asserted that congregations that manifested the characteristics of right faith (believers not infants), correct mode of baptism (immersion not effusion), and proper authority (New Testament churches not religious societies) could trace an unbroken continuity directly to Jesus and the apostles. For Landmarkers, Baptists alone could lay claim to apostolicity. The SBC meeting in 1859 rejected several Graves-sponsored initiatives and reelected anti-Landmarker R. B. C. Howell as convention president, but the theology of Landmarkism continued to exert influence on Baptist life well into the twentieth century, as evidenced by J. M. Carroll's *Trail of Blood*. By reducing the apostolic faith to a set of propositions, Landmarkism anticipated fundamentalism, which would not reach full flower until the first quarter of the twentieth century. Yet by the 1890s many Baptists in North America began to join other Evangelical Protestants in rejecting the theology of liberalism and uniting around the "fundamentals" of the faith: an inerrant Bible, a virgin-born Savior, a substitutionary atonement, a bodily resurrection, and authentic miracles (Marsden, *Fundamentalism and American Culture*, 104–8).

In broad terms the response of rising Baptist fundamentalism mirrored the antimodernist strategy of traditional Catholicism (e.g., the *Syllabus of Errors*), and the path of incipient Baptist liberalism followed the accommodationist trajectory of modern Protestant thought. Yet unlike mainline Protestants, Baptists were cautious about incorporating modern theology into their churches. Perhaps because there was little perceived threat from within, they were also slow in addressing the theological uncertainty of modernity, although as the century began Robert Hall Jr. sounded a prophetic alarm about the dangers of "modern infidelity." In March of 1887 a piece entitled "The Down Grade" appeared in the *Sword and Trowel* published by C. H. Spurgeon. A series of articles followed, charging that socinianism, universalism, and higher criticism were widely held among Baptist clergy. Spurgeon met with such strong opposition that he withdrew from and was censured by the Baptist Union, never again to return. The controversy may have been resolved in favor of Spurgeon's opponents, but he had correctly perceived both the accommodation to modernity and the theological issues with which Baptist theology would continue to wrestle. His warning against "looking within to find the misty warrants of your experience" (the foundation of liberalism) shows that he observed the "turn to the subject" in nineteenth-century Protestant thought, although by arguing that the only sufficient justification for faith is a common sense understanding of God's command in Scripture (the foundation of fundamentalism) he also failed to resist the Siren songs of modernity. As the Great Century drew to a close, Baptists struggled to hold to the apostolic faith in a world coming of age.

– 21 –

Robert Hall Jr.

When Robert Hall Sr. (1728–91) preached before the 1779 meeting of the Northampton (England) Association of Particular Baptists, he appealed to the messengers to "take up the stumblingblock out of the way of my people" (Isaiah 57:14). The sermon was enthusiastically received and subsequently published under the title Help to Zion's Travelers. *Hall's* Help *had a softening effect on the hard shell of hyper-Calvinism, preparing the way for the evangelical theology of Andrew Fuller and William Carey. At age nine his son, Robert Hall Jr. (1764–1831), was already reading the works of Jonathan Edwards, who along with Fuller remained a formative influence on his theology. The younger Hall studied at Bristol Baptist Academy and King's College, Aberdeen, earning a master's degree. He twice served the Broadmead Church in Bristol (1785–90 and 1826–31), first as an associate and later as pastor, where he followed the celebrated Baptist leader John Ryland Jr. (1753–1825). His other pastorates included the Stone Yard Church of Cambridge (1791–1806), where he succeeded the learned but erratic Robert Robinson (1735–90), and the Harvey Lane Church of Leicester (1807–25). Hall defended the freedom of the church and the press from state control, and he advocated the causes of labor and the poor. He was a proponent of open communion and the general atonement. The publication of his sermon "Modern Infidelity Considered" in 1801 occasioned his great popularity and earned him a place as one of the most highly acclaimed Baptist voices of his day. Although the argument is directed against deism, skepticism, and atheism (i.e., modern infidelity), Hall was cautious about the modern project as a whole (the infidelity of modernity). Contending earnestly "for the faith which was once delivered unto the saints" (Jude 3), it was Hall's conviction that "the intrinsic excellence of [the Christian] religion needs not the aid of external appendages; but that, with or without a dowry, her charms are of sufficient power to fix and engage the heart" (Author's Preface in* The Works of Robert Hall, *2:7). Hall's piece is a reminder that whether in modernity, premodernity, or postmodernity, for Baptist theology the truth lies in gospel foolishness.*

Modern Infidelity Considered

As the Christian ministry is established for the instruction of men, throughout every age, in truth and holiness, it must adapt itself to the ever-shifting scenes of the moral world, and stand ready to repel the attacks of impiety and error, under whatever form they may appear. The church and the world constitute two societies so distinct, and are governed by such opposite principles and maxims, that, as well from this contrariety, as from the express warnings of scripture, true Christians must look for a state of warfare, with this consoling assurance, that the church, like the burning bush beheld by Moses in the land of Midian, may be encompassed with flames, but will never be consumed.

When she was delivered from the persecuting power of Rome, she only experienced a change of trials. The oppression of external violence was followed by the more dangerous and insidious attacks of internal enemies. The freedom of inquiry claimed and asserted at the reformation, degenerated, in the hands of men who professed the principles without possessing the spirit of the reformers, into a fondness for speculative refinements; and consequently into a source of dispute, faction, and heresy. While Protestants attended more to the points on which they differed than to those on which they agreed; while more zeal was employed in settling ceremonies and defending subtleties, than in enforcing plain revealed truths; the lovely fruits of peace and charity perished under the stones of controversy.

In this disjointed and disordered state of the Christian church, they who never looked into the interior of Christianity were apt to suspect, that to a subject so fruitful in particular disputes must attach a general uncertainty; and that a religion founded on revelation could never have occasioned such discordancy of principle and practice among its disciples. Thus infidelity is the joint offspring of an irreligious temper, and unholy speculation, employed, not in examining the evidences of Christianity, but in detecting the vices and imperfections of professing Christians. It has passed through various stages, each distinguished by higher gradations of impiety; for when men arrogantly abandon their guide, and willfully shut their eyes on the light of heaven, it is wisely ordained that their errors shall multiply at every step, until their extravagance confutes itself, and the mischief of their principles works its own antidote. That such has been the progress of infidelity will be obvious from a slight surrey of its history.

Lord Herbert, the first and purest of our English free-thinkers, who flourished in the beginning of the reign of Charles the First, did not so much impugn the doctrine or the morality of the Scriptures, as attempt to supersede their necessity, by endeavoring to show that the great principles of the unity of God — a moral government, and a future world — are taught with sufficient clearness by the light of nature. Bolingbroke, and some of his successors, advanced much farther, and attempted to invalidate the proofs of the moral character of the Deity, and consequently all expectations of rewards and punishments; leaving the Supreme Being no other perfections than those which belong to a first cause, or almighty contriver. After him, at a considerable distance, followed Hume, the most subtle, if not the most philosophical of the deists; who, by perplexing the relations of cause and effect, boldly aimed to introduce an universal skepticism, and to pour a more than Egyptian darkness into the whole region of morals. Since his time skeptical writers have sprung up in abundance, and infidelity has allured multitudes to its standard: the young and the superficial by its dexterous sophistry, the vain by the literary reputation of its champions, and the profligate by the licentiousness of its principles. Atheism, the most undisguised, has at length begun to make its appearance.

Animated by numbers, and emboldened by success the infidels of the present day have given a new direction to their efforts, and impressed a new character on the ever-growing mass of their impious speculations.

By uniting more closely with each other, by giving a sprinkling of irreligion to all their literary productions, they aim to engross the formation of the public mind; and, amidst the warmest professions of attachment to virtue, to effect an entire disruption of morality from religion. Pretending to be the teachers of virtue, and the guides of life, they propose to revolutionize the morals of mankind; to regenerate the world by a process entirely new; and to rear the temple of virtue, not merely without the aid of religion, but on the renunciation of its principles, and the derision of its sanctions. Their party has derived a great accession of numbers and strength from events the most momentous and astonishing in the political world, which have divided the sentiments of Europe betwixt hope and terror; and which, however they may issue, have, for the present, swelled the ranks of infidelity. So rapidly, indeed, has it advanced since this crisis, that a great majority on the continent, and in England a considerable proportion of those who pursue literature as a profession, may justly be considered as the open or disguised abettors of atheism....

Permit me to close this discourse with a few serious reflections. There is much, it must be confessed, in the apostasy of multitudes, and the rapid progress of infidelity, to awaken our fears for the virtue of the rising generation; but nothing to shake our faith; nothing which scripture itself does not give us room to expect. The features which compose the character of apostates, their profaneness, presumption, lewdness, impatience of subordination, restless appetite for change, vain pretensions to freedom and to emancipate the world, while themselves are the slaves of lust, the weapons with which they attack Christianity, and the snares they spread for the unwary, are depicted in the clearest colours by the pencil of prophecy: "Knowing this first" (says Peter), "that there shall come in the last days scoffers, walking after their own lusts" (2 Pet. 3:3). In the same epistle he more fully describes the persons he alludes to; "as chiefly them which walk after the flesh, in the lust of uncleanness, and despise government; presumptuous are they, self-willed, they are not afraid to speak evil of dignities; [...] sporting themselves in their own deceivings, having eyes full of adultery, and that cannot cease from sin; beguiling unstable souls: [...] for when they speak great swelling words of vanity, they allure through the lusts of the flesh, through much wantonness, those that were clean escaped from them who live in error; while they promise them liberty, they themselves are the servants of corruption" (2 Pet. 2:10, 13–14, 18–19). Of the same characters Jude admonishes us "to remember that they were foretold as mockers, who should be in, the last time, who should walk after their own ungodly lusts. These be they (he adds) who separate themselves (by apostasy), sensual, not having the Spirit" (Jude 18). Infidelity is an evil of short duration. "It has" (as a judicious writer observes) "no individual subsistence given it in the system of prophecy. It is not a beast; but a mere putrid excrescence of the papal beast: an excrescence which though it may diffuse death through every vein of the body on which it grew, yet shall die along with it" (Andrew Fuller, *The Gospel Its Own Witness*). Its enormities will hasten its overthrow....

Religion being primarily intended to make men *wise unto salvation*, the support it ministers to social order, the stability it confers on government and laws, is a *subordinate species* of advantage which we should have continued to enjoy, without reflecting on its cause, but for the development of deistical principles, and the experiment which has been made of their effects in a neighbouring country. It had been the constant boast of infidels, that their system, more liberal and generous than Christianity, needed but to be tried to produce an immense accession of human happiness; and Christian nations, careless and supine, retaining little of religion but the profession, and disgusted with its restraints, lent a favourable ear to these pretensions. God permitted the trial to be made. In one country, and that the centre of Christendom, revelation underwent a total eclipse, while atheism, performing on a darkened theatre its strange and fearful tragedy, confounded the first elements of society, blended every age, rank, and sex, in indiscriminate proscription and massacre, and convulsed all Europe to its centre; that the imperishable memorial of these events might teach the last generations of mankind to consider religion as the pillar of society, the safeguard of nations, the parent of social order, which alone has power to curb the fury of the passions, and secure to every one his rights; to the laborious the reward of their industry, to the rich the enjoyment of their wealth, to nobles the preservation of their honours, and to princes the stability of their thrones....

Having been led by the nature of the subject to consider chiefly the manner in which skeptical impiety affects the welfare of states, it is the more requisite to warn you against that most fatal mistake of regarding religion as an engine of policy; and to recall to your recollection that the concern we have in it is much more as *individuals* than as *collective bodies,* and far less temporal than eternal. The happiness which it confers in the present life comprehends the blessings which it scatters by the way in its march to immortality. That future condition of being which it ascertains, and for which its promises and truths are meant to prepare us, is the ultimate end of human societies, the final scope and object of present existence, in comparison of which all the revolutions of nations, and all the vicissitudes of time, are light and transitory. *Godliness has, it is true, the promise of the life that now is;* but chiefly *of that which is to come.* Other acquisitions may be requisite to make men great; but, be assured, the religion of Jesus is alone sufficient to make them good and happy. Powerful sources of consolation in sorrow, unshaken fortitude amidst the changes and perturbations of the world, humility remote from meanness, and dignity unstained by pride, contentment in every station, passions pure and calm, with habitual serenity, the full enjoyment of life, undisturbed by the dread of dissolution or the fear of an hereafter, are its invaluable gifts. To these enjoyments, however, you will necessarily continue strangers, unless you resign yourselves wholly to its power; for the consolations of religion are reserved to reward, to sweeten, and to stimulate obedience. Many, without renouncing the profession of Christianity, without formally rejecting its distinguishing doctrines, live in such an habitual violation of its laws, and contradiction to its spirit, that, conscious they have more to fear than to hope from its truth, they are never able to contemplate it without terror. It haunts their imagination, instead of tranquilizing their hearts, and hangs with depressing weight on all their enjoyments and pursuits. Their religion, instead of comforting them under their troubles, is itself their greatest trouble, from which they seek refuge in the dissipation and vanity of the world, until the throbs and tumults of conscience force them back upon religion. Thus suspended betwixt opposite powers, the sport of contradictory influences, they are disqualified for the happiness of both worlds; and neither enjoy the pleasures of sin, nor the peace of piety. Is it surprising to find a mind thus bewildered in uncertainty, and dissatisfied with itself, courting deception, and embracing with eagerness every pretext to mutilate the claims and enervate the authority of Christianity: forgetting that it is of the very essence of the religious principle to preside and control, and that it is impossible to *serve God and mammon?* It is this class of professors who are chiefly in danger of being entangled in the snares of infidelity. . . .

Within the limits of this discourse it would be impracticable to exhibit the evidences of Christianity; nor is it my design; but there is one consideration, resulting immediately from my text, which is entitled to great weight with all who believe in the one living and true God as the sole object of worship. The Ephesians, in common with other Gentiles, are described in the text as being, previous to their conversion, *without God in the world* (Eph. 2:12); that is, without any just and solid acquaintance with his character, destitute of the knowledge of his will, the institutes of his worship, and the hopes of his favour; to the truth of which representation whoever possesses the slightest acquaintance with pagan antiquity must assent. Nor is it a fact less incontestable, that, while human philosophy was never able to abolish idolatry in a single village, the promulgation of the gospel overthrew it in a great part (and that the most enlightened) of the world. If our belief in the unity and perfections of God, together with his moral government, and exclusive right to the worship of mankind, be founded in truth, they cannot reasonably be denied to be truths of the first importance, and infinitely to outweigh the greatest discoveries in science; because they turn the hopes, fears, and interests of man into a totally different channel from that in which they must otherwise flow. Wherever these principles are first admitted, there a new dominion is erected, and new system of laws established.

But since all events are under divine direction, is it reasonable to suppose that the great Parent, after suffering his creatures to continue for ages ignorant of his true character, should at length in the course of his providence, fix upon falsehood, and that alone, as the effectual method of making himself known; and that what the virtuous exercise of reason in the best and wisest men was never permitted to accomplish, he should confer on fraud and delusion the honor of effecting? It ill comports with the majesty of truth, or the character of God, to believe that he has built the noblest superstructure on the weakest foundation; or reduced mankind to the miserable alternative either of remaining destitute of the knowledge of himself, or of deriving it from the polluted source of impious imposture. We therefore feel ourselves justified on this occasion, in adopting the triumphant boast of the great apostle: "Where is the wise, where is the scribe, where is the disputer of this world? Hath not God made foolish the wisdom of this world? For that, in the wisdom of God, the world by wisdom knew not God, it pleased God by the foolishness of preaching to save them that believe" (1 Cor. 1:20–21).

[Robert Hall Jr., "Modern Infidelity Considered," in *The Works of Robert Hall* (London: Henry G. Bohn, 1851), 2:13–60.]

– 22 –

John Leadley Dagg

Native Virginian John Leadley Dagg (1794–1884) is widely regarded as one of the wisest and most scholarly theologians Baptists in nineteenth-century America produced. Dagg, converted at the age of fifteen, described this moment as "a joyful sense of acceptance with God." After serious study the young Dagg became convinced by the theology of believers baptism and was forthwith baptized into the fellowship of the Ebeneezer Church in Loudoun County, Virginia. Upon his ordination in 1817, Dagg held pastorates of several churches in Virginia and Pennsylvania, where he was instrumental in organizing Baptist missionary and educational work. He joined the faculty of Mercer University in 1843 and was named president two years later, a position he held until 1856. His most important work is the Manual of Theology, *published in 1857. Dagg's Theology appears to be dependent upon a simple biblicism, as he proposes to derive doctrine by going "straight to Scripture." Yet, as Brooks Holifield observes, "religious conservatism in the Old South was always as much a matter of philosophical as of biblical considerations" (Holifield,* The Gentlemen Theologians, *125). To a lesser degree than his contemporary James Petigru Boyce (1827–88), Dagg reflected the common sense assumptions of Scottish philosophy and the Calvinistic influence of the Princeton theology. His theology follows an order traditional in Protestant orthodoxy (i.e., God, sin, Christ, the Holy Spirit, etc.), but each doctrine is introduced by identifying a corresponding "duty" (i.e., to love God, to repent, to believe in Christ, to live and walk in the Spirit, etc.). In effect, Dagg was suggesting that the truth of Christian doctrine was self-evident by its commensurability with Christian piety. In the following selection, Dagg summarizes six "particular duties" under which Baptists must labor.*

The Duty of Baptists

Although the truth of God does not need human authority, or the patronage of great names, it is nevertheless the Divine pleasure to make it known to the world by human instrumentality; and this instrumentality needs to be adapted to the purpose for which it is employed. If God has commissioned a sect everywhere spoken against, to make known truth which the wise and learned have overlooked, that sect ought to understand the service to which they have been appointed, and ought to fulfil the prescribed duty firmly, faithfully, and in the fear of the Lord. As men designed for a peculiar service, let us, by earnest and constant endeavor, seek to ascertain the will of him to whose supreme authority we yield all our powers, and let us diligently and perseveringly obey that will, whether men revile or praise.

1. It is our duty to maintain the ordinances of Christ, and the church order which he has instituted, in strict and scrupulous conformity to the Holy Scriptures.

If the investigations of the sacred volume, which have been attempted in this work, have not been unsuccessful, the great body of Christ's professed followers have wandered from the right way. They have established ecclesiastical organizations which are not in accordance with his will; and have corrupted the ceremonies of worship which he instituted. These errors have the sanction of age, and of men venerable for their wisdom. To maintain our peculiarities in opposition to such influences has the appearance of bigotry and narrow-mindedness; and, if they are peculiarities which God's word does not require, we ought to relinquish them. But if we have attained to a knowledge of the Divine will, on points where the great mass of our fellow Christians have mistaken it, a duty of solemn responsibility is imposed on us, to hold fast what we have received, and defend the truth specially committed to our charge.

The plea is often urged that there are good men in all the denominations, and that the various forms of Religion, being alike consistent with piety, are matters of minor importance, and ought to be left to the preferences of individuals. If we do not readily admit this plea in its full extent, we are perhaps understood to deny that piety can be found out of our own party, or to claim undue deference to our judgment in religious matters. But whether men understand us or not, we are bound to obey God in everything. No command which he has given can be so unimportant that we are at liberty to disobey it at our pleasure. When the finger of God points out the way, no place is left to us for human preferences. And when we know the will of God, we are not only bound to obey for ourselves, but also to teach others to obey, so far as they are brought under the influence of our instruction. We may, without arrogant assumption, declare what we are firmly persuaded to be the will of God; and we must then leave every one to the judgment of him to whom all must give account. The man who can disobey God, because the thing commanded is of minor importance, has not the spirit of obedience in his heart; and the man who, knowing the will of God, forbears to declare it, because the weight of human authority is against him, fears men more than God.

2. It is our duty, while rendering punctilious obedience to all the commands of God, to regard the forms and ceremonies of Religion as of far less importance than its moral truths and precepts.

One of the earliest corruptions of Christianity consisted in magnifying the importance of its ceremonies, and ascribing to them a saving efficacy. With this superstitious reverence of outward forms, a tendency was introduced to corrupt these forms, and substitute ceremonies of human invention for the ordinances of God. To restore these ordinances to their original purity, and, at the same time, to understand and teach that outward rites have no saving efficacy, appears to be a service to which God has specially called the Baptists. We are often charged with attaching too much importance to immersion; but the notion that baptism possesses a sacramental efficacy finds no advocates in our ranks. It introduced infant baptism, and prevailed with it; and it still lingers among those by whom infant baptism is practiced. Our principles, by restricting baptism to those who are already regenerate, subvert the doctrine of baptismal regeneration, and exhibit the ceremony in its proper relation to experimental Religion. To give due prominence to spirituality above all outward ceremony, is an important service to which God has called our denomination.

3. It is our duty to hold and exhibit the entire system of Christian doctrine in all its just proportions.

An important advance is made in the proper exhibition of Christian truth, when ceremony is rendered duly subordinate to spirituality. This gives an opportunity to adjust the parts of the system in their proper harmony. An additional security for the preservation of sound doctrine is found in the converted church-membership which our principles require. The church universal is the pillar and ground of the truth, because it consists of those who love the truth; and in proportion as local churches are formed of the same materials, they are prepared to stand as bulwarks against heresy. This service Baptist churches have been known to render to the cause of truth. The general agreement of Baptist churches, in doctrine as well as church order, is a fact which gives occasion for devout gratitude to God. Let it be our continued care never to distort the beautiful system of divine truth by magnifying any part of it beyond its just proportion, or suppressing any part of the harmonious whole.

Because we differ from other professors of Religion in our faith and practice respecting the externals of Religion, we are under a constant temptation to make too much account of these external peculiarities. Against this temptation we should ever struggle. If we magnify ceremony unduly, ye abandon our principles, and cease to fulfil the mission to which the Head of the church has assigned us.

4. It is our duty to maintain lives of holy obedience in all things.

Many persons have the form of godliness who are strangers to its power. They render obedience to ceremonial precepts, while they neglect weightier matters of moral obligation. But a punctilious observance of ceremonies has no necessary connexion with remissness in more important duties. In an affectionate family, the children who strive to please their parents, and gratify their wishes in the most trivial concerns, are expected to be most dutiful in things of greatest moment. Such children of our heavenly Father ought Baptists to be. We claim to obey his will more fully in the outward forms of Religion than any other people. Consistency requires that we should be more obedient also in matters of highest importance. It is highly offensive to God, if, while we neglect his most important commands, we attempt to please him with mere outward service. His omniscient eye detects the attempted fraud, and his holiness detests it. Even short-sighted men discover the cheat, and contemn our hypocrisy. The reputation of Religion suffers by our unfaithfulness, and men, who observe our conduct, become confirmed in unbelief, to their everlasting ruin. Persons who do not profess to obey God in all things, may, with less pernicious effect, neglect his holy precepts; but Baptists ought to be holy in all things. Our profession requires us to be the best people in the world; and it should be our constant effort to walk according to this profession.

5. It is our duty to labor faithfully and perseveringly to bring all men to the knowledge of the truth.

We claim that we execute the commission which Christ gave to his apostles more fully than other Christian denominations. This commission requires us to preach the gospel to every creature; and we ought to be foremost in obeying it. This obligation has been felt by some of our faith and order, and all of us ought to feel it. The English Baptists have the honor of being foremost in the work of modern missions; and the names of Carey, and his fellow-laborers, who were the pioneers in this difficult service, deserve to be had in lasting remembrance. The names of Judson and Rice appear among the foremost in the history of American missions; and the conversion of these men to the Baptist faith may be regarded as a special call of God on American Baptists to labor for the spread of the gospel throughout the earth. On the Continent of Europe, Oncken and his noble band of associates, are, by their laborious and successful efforts in the Redeemer's cause, but fulfilling the obligations which every Baptist should feel. Voluntary devotion to Christ, and immediate responsibility to him, are conspicuous in our distinguishing peculiarities; and we ought to be conspicuous among the followers of Christ, by our labors or sufferings in his cause.

6. It is our duty to promote the spiritual unity of the universal church, by the exercise of brotherly love to all who bear the image of Christ.

Various schemes have been proposed by the wisdom of men for amalgamating the different Christian denominations. All these originate in the erroneous conception that the unity of the universal church must be found in external organization. To effect the union sought for, compromises are required of the several parties, and the individual conscience must yield to the judgment of the many. All these schemes of amalgamation are inconsistent with the Baptist faith. We seek spiritual unity. We would have every individual to stand on Bible ground, and to take his position there, in the unbiased exercise of his own judgment and conscience. There we strive to take our position; and there, and there only, we invite our brethren of all denominations to meet us. We yield everything which is not required by the word of God; but in what this word requires, we have no compromise to make. We rejoice to see, in many who do not take our views of divine truth, bright evidence of love to Christ and his cause. We love them for Christ's sake; and we expect to unite with them in his praise through eternal ages. We are one with them in spirit, though we cannot conform to their usages in any particular in which they deviate from the Bible. The more abundantly we love them, the more carefully we strive to walk before them in strict obedience to the commands of our common Lord. And if they sometimes misunderstand our motives, and misjudge our actions, it is our consolation that our divine Master approves; and that they also will approve, when we shall hereafter meet them in his presence.

[J. L. Dagg, *A Treatise on Church Order* (Charleston, S.C.: Southern Baptist Publication Society, 1858), 299–304.]

– 23 –

Alice Armstrong

With the exception of Southern Baptists, by 1872 women in the major Protestant denominations of North America had already established national organizations for missions education and promotion. Throughout the 1870s and 1880s there was a growing sense of urgency among Southern Baptists that women could uniquely contribute to the cause of world evangelization. Yet there was lingering opposition. In 1885 the SBC had even changed its constitution to exclude women as messengers. One of those indomitable souls who challenged the conservative resistance and awakened the women's missionary conscience was Alice Armstrong (1846–1928). Part of a prominent Baptist family in Baltimore, Maryland, Alice Armstrong was the older sister of the more well-known Annie Armstrong (1850–1938), who was to become the long-time corresponding secretary (and sometime irascible leader) of the Woman's Missionary Union. Alice herself served as a writer and editor of missions publications. The paper "Special Obligations of Woman to Spread the Gospel" was delivered at the 1888 organizational meeting of the WMU, held in the basement of the Broad Street Methodist Church in Richmond, Virginia. Armstrong's paper, when printed and distributed in the Southern states, was instrumental in garnering broad support for the women's movement among Baptists, much as the writings of Helen Barrett Montgomery would advance the role of women a generation later among Northern Baptists. Leon McBeth comments that "no cause has so awakened Baptist women as missions" (Women in Baptist Life, 99). It might also be added that no one has so awakened the missionary conscience of Baptists in the United States to missions as women.

Special Obligations of Woman
to Spread the Gospel

There is, possibly, no thinkable subject too minute to serve as a fulcrum for the see-saw of varying human opinion. If this be true of minor matters, how emphatically true it becomes of larger and more vital questions, where self-interest, habit, circumstances, education, make a conflict of opinion inevitable; and the judgment stands between all these multiplied forces, trying to steady itself. If, however, the human judgment, so liable to err, and to be unduly influenced, can have the aid of a divine revelation, can have a "thus saith the Lord" to confirm its balance, there ought to be no further indecision. In the world-wide question before us to-day, "Woman's obligation to spread the Gospel," we are in precisely that blessed position, where tiresome halting or painful wavering is alike needless. God's word comes to us in plain command and instructive example; and all we are left to do in the case is to learn the one and follow the other. Hence the question is not, "Are we obliged to spread the Gospel?" That has been definitely settled by divine wisdom, and removes much rubbish out of the way of our thinking, leaving the track clear for the very practical question, "What is our obligation to spread the Gospel?"

Before we pursue this inquiry, let us refresh our memories with a review of the divine commission "to go and tell." The angel said unto the women, "Fear not ye, for I know that ye seek Jesus. He is risen. Go quickly and tell his disciples that he is risen from the dead." "And Jesus met them, saying, All hail! be not afraid; go tell my brethren, that they go into Galilee and there shall they see me." And the women "told all these things to the eleven and to all the rest." "Then the two disciples returned from Emmaus, and found the eleven and them that were with them." And "Jesus himself stood in the midst of them" and "opened their understanding," and said, "Ye are witnesses of these things." And He said again, "As my Father hath sent me, so send I you"; and He breathed on them, and said, "Receive ye the Holy Ghost." And, "Behold, I send the promise of my Father upon you, but tarry in Jerusalem till ye be endued with power from on high." "These all continued with one accord in prayer, with the women," and "there appeared unto them cloven tongues, like as of fire, and sat upon each of them, and they were all filled, and began to speak" as spoken by the prophet Joel: "On my servants and hand-maidens I will pour out my Spirit, and the daughters shall prophesy." "Whereof we are all witnesses."

The Old Testament and the New both bear record that earnest, godly women with willing hearts, ready hands and fire-crowned tongues, gave of their substance, their labor and their consecrated words for the cause of God and the good of their fellows. The mention of their loving, tender services, accompanied in some cases with the richest commendations of the Saviour, was not thought unworthy, nor yet unwomanly, and it has been ringing down the centuries, and will continue its sweet music till the latest echo of time.

Fortified with the divine command and approved example of Scripture, we can now confine our diligent attention to what is woman's obligation to spread the Gospel, its extent, and her fitness to fill it.

What is an obligation? An indebtedness for a favor, something owed for value received, which ought to be paid. Is it considered a matter of choice or of duty, to pay an accredited bill? What do we owe the Gospel? In common with all who receive it, there are the infinite values of forgiven sins, peace with God, joy in the Holy Ghost, an eternity of blessedness and sinless serving. But as women, as American women of this nineteenth century, what do we owe the Gospel? We have only to look across the seas and compare our mountain-heights of privilege with the degrading and hopeless lives of sisters in lands where the Gospel has not spread, to begin to understand a tithe of our obligations to that Gospel.

Look at the women of Siam, who are taught that their very being is but a curse for misdeeds in a former existence; whose highest hope for this world is to be sold to husbands with many another to share the doubtful honor; while the majority, not so favored, are gambled away by their own mothers as slaves. A return to life under more favorable circumstances is their only hope in death. Has the Gospel done anything for us, either in living or dying, for which we are indebted?

Look at the women of Syria, at whose birth forty days of mourning are observed; who may never enter a mosque because Allah does not care for women; who are ignored by their husbands abroad and beaten by them at home; whose loftiest ambition is a heaven to themselves; the male paradise is forbidden — scarcely a cause for regret under the cir-cumstances, we should think — and this heaven may only be secured through abject obedience to these same ferocious, despotic husbands. Wives, mothers, daughters, our blood boils, and we grow rebellious even at thoughts of such barbarous indignities cast upon women! What has made us to differ? The Gospel, the glad evangel of the love of Christ, which distinctly states that "in Christ there is neither male nor female," but has restored woman to her place by Adam's side, as his true help-meet.

Look again at the women of China. What an endless throng! Crip-pled from earliest youth; denied education, except in lessons of obedi-ence to, or through, male relatives; ranked with parrots and monkeys in the scale of intelligence; superstitious and vicious, the normal outgrowth of enforced ignorance. Does the comparison with ourselves show any cause for gratitude?

Africa's degraded millions stand before us. Cringing slaves, the most fortunate of them, living absolutely on the caprice of their brutal hus-bands, or sold as chattels with the estate of a male relative. Dusky ciphers, who can do nothing, but who must suffer much! O, Christ of God, we thank thee for the privilege of being and doing something!

The list is not exhausted. Here comes India's troop of children, wives at ten, and even at seven, deprived of mother love at these tender years.

But fortunate, thrice fortunate, these! It is the widows, widows some-times at seven years of age, upon whom paganism has poured out its vials of wrath and injustice. They may never change their sad condition. At once degraded by their misfortune from every form of favor, they for-ever become the slaves of all their fellows; separated by an impassable gulf of disgrace, they receive but curses and blows. Death alone may be their release from the torture of living.

Mothers of America, your little ones, in pain and trouble, find a sure refuge in your love. India's religion makes it a sin to show these little sorrowing ones the slightest sympathy or kindness. Twenty-one million widows are dragging out to-day their crushed and hopeless existence, eighty thousand under nine years of age! We have the truth with Christ's gladdest invitation: "Suffer the little ones to come unto me, for of such is the kingdom of heaven." The Gospel has given us a home, in which all the tenderest affections and gentlest amenities of life are encouraged and strengthened, and where childhood may be built up upon the model of Him "who went about doing good."

But there is a shame and disgrace which comes closer home to us Americans than India's widows or Africa's degraded ciphers: Mor-monism is spreading its leprous fingers even over our own Southern land, and drawing into its deadly grasp the ignorant and unsuspecting. Alaska, too, over which floats our own day, is dominated by supersti-tions and practices in open day, which can rival for grossness any other land under the sun. Infidelity, which ever debases woman, is pouring into our country through the flood-gate of emigration. And last, but by no means least, Romanism, in its teachings and tendencies, as un-scriptural, as un-American, and as unrelenting as Mormonism, with its stealthy, tiger-like stride, is making advance, which is surely, but not slowly, pre-empting the great West beyond the Mississippi, much the larger half of our country, and intrenching itself here, in our very midst. Its late efforts to pervert the negroes of the south and to secure control of Southern emigration, are portentous of coming evil. Rome in America to-day is said to be stronger than Rome on the Tiber.

Christian women of America, with these facts to stir our keenest womanly sympathies, our truest patriotism and deepest gratitude; what is the extent of our obligations to spread the Gospel at home and abroad? The answer is not far to seek: the difference between our ele-vated position to-day and that of the most degraded of Alaska's witches or Africa's fetish worshippers, is the exact measure of our earthly obli-gation to spread the Gospel. And the length of the plummet line which reaches from Heaven's battlements to the lowest hell, alone can limit our spiritual obligations to give the glad tidings of salvation to those who know it not.

Woman's Fitness

Should a naturalist see for the first time the wing of a bird, he could judge from its construction, its adjustment of parts, that it was intended for easy and successful progress through the air. The fin of a fish is the best oar that ever worked in an oar-lock. The foot of man is a wondrous mechanical contrivance for movement. Did God so graciously care for the material growth and well-being of his creatures, and had he no regard for the spiritual and eternal progress of immortal souls? Were his invention and wisdom at fault, just at the point where failure would be most fatal? We know it could not be so. We know it is not so. The Gospel of Jesus Christ, the universal remedy, when applied, for universal sin, was put into the hands of man and woman alike, to be distributed to the sin-sick and the dying, to neighbors at home and abroad. And the instruments, designed and finished in part, by the great Masterworkman, were no clumsy, haphazard tools, but wondrously prepared and adapted, by their likenesses, and yet by their subtle differences, for the one work, with its infinite variety of departments.

How is woman specially fitted for the work of spreading the Gospel?

With a tenderer heart and keener sensibilities than man, she can take in a fuller measure of the love of Christ. Is she to take it in as the Dead Sea absorbs the sweet waters of the Jordan, and not to give it out again in all the fullness in which she receives it? Can this possibly be God's purpose in her richer endowment of reception? The same tenderness which draws her to Christ, widens her sympathies towards all whom she may help. Tact, that intangible something which woman possesses, that adapts her to her circumstances, has its widest and most fruitful field for exercise in the Lord's vineyard. Patience to do and yet wait for results is peculiarly a woman's lot, and is, at the same time, a large factor in favor of her success in Christian endeavor, whose law is, "first the blade, then the ear, and afterward the full corn in the ear." In the division of life's duties, made guardian of little things, woman has learned the inestimable importance of littles, in their individual worth and aggregate value; hence, she does not despise the day of small things. With a nimbleness of perception in adapting means to ends, acquired through the numberless and unexpected calls of daily life, her invention in this line, call it intuition, if you please, or quick-wittedness, is of large value in Christian work.

Besides these wondrous, God-given endowments, which, by universal consent, woman possesses, there are other latent abilities which only await opportunity for development, to further enrich her and make her an instrument better fitted still for the Master's use. Shall this Damascus blade, upon which the Divine Artificer has expended much of his cunningest workmanship, shall it be idly sheathed in its scabbard, afraid of soil or damage, while the battle of error, sin and death is wildly raging everywhere?

In addition to peculiar fittedness for work, suppose we clearly see there is work waiting for her, which only women can do — work among pagan women, to whom only women have access; work among women and children in our own land, from which man, by nature, habit and circumstances, is debarred. Is not this nice fitting of woman's capabilities into a place which she alone can fill, like the ball in the socket, is not this a direct message from above, "The Master is come and calleth for thee?"

An aroused will, guided by the promised aid of the Holy Spirit, and inspired by Scripture precept and example, can make us Southern Baptist women a power for good undreamt of in our past history; a power for good which will cost us not one whit of womanliness, but which will develop that womanliness into a genuine helpfulness, thinking, planning, acting, along its own special lines, and in thorough harmony with all other lines, for bringing in the kingdom of the Lord. Can one woman do this alone? No. But one woman's zeal can kindle another's, and she another's, and so on, *ad infinitum.* However, this is not gospel arithmetic. David says of the power of good against evil: "One shall chase a thousand, and two shall put ten thousand to flight." If true of the power of good over evil, how grandly more true of Christian zeal in its efforts to fire other Christian zeal, which has cooled through inaction.

Just at this point comes in the aid of a general organization, a representative body which has delegated powers to stimulate and to sustain every such beginning of zealous work and to crystallize it into permanent form. This organization does not seek to work apart from the individual Church, nor in spite of the Church, but through and by the Church, supplying asked-for help through counsel and information.

Because neither our grandmothers nor we ever had an organization, and because there have been hung up in elevated places over the harvest field, scarecrows of possible evils, do not let us blindly close our eyes to the known and positive good which has been the result of organization wherever tried, north, south, east, or west, the world around. We Southern Baptist women are strikingly like all other people, and may be benefited after a similar fashion. This is common sense. Perhaps it may be commonplace, too, for a concluding remark. But, if religious work is ever to amount to anything in this very work-a-day, practical world, against evil, which Satan has contrived to make very practical and commonplace, religious work must be largely constructed on principles of common sense.

[Alice Armstrong, "Special Obligation of Woman to Spread the Gospel" (Baltimore: Maryland Baptist Mission Room, 1888).]

– 24 –

Charles Haddon Spurgeon

Charles Haddon Spurgeon (1834–92) was the most renowned Free Church preacher of his day in Great Britain, and assuredly the best-known Baptist. This "prince of preachers" was born in humble circumstances, converted in a Methodist chapel at age fifteen, baptized in the Lark River, and accepted into a Baptist church. After brief schooling he became a Baptist pastor near Cambridge. From there he was called to the New Park Street Baptist Church of London and enlarged it to become the Metropolitan Tabernacle, whose building seated six thousand people. There he preached for over thirty years. Many thousands were converted and baptized in the course of his ministry, and many more were instructed by the Calvinist faith that he shared with most other British nonconformists of whatever denomination. In that faith Spurgeon found no obstacle to evangelism. The evangelical Calvinism he preached is the heritage of Andrew Fuller and Robert Hall Jr. (see previous selections). For Spurgeon the warrant of faith was not clear evidence of one's election but rather the simple summons of the gospel: "Believe on the Lord Jesus Christ, and thou shalt be saved" (Acts 16:31). Self-educated but well-educated, he devoted his life to preaching an evangelistic message to all comers. He remains one of the most popular and widely published preachers among Baptists and other evangelical Christians. The following sermon, based on the text "He that believeth on him is not condemned" (John 3:18), was originally delivered on February 17, 1861, at Exeter Hall in London, a common meeting place for evangelical Christians. Of this sermon Spurgeon himself said that it "has been translated for the aborigines of New Zealand, and some thousands have been distributed. The reading of it . . . has led to . . . conversions among Europeans and natives." Here shortened, it illustrates his style and displays some of his chief convictions.

None but Jesus

I intend this morning, by God's help, to put together sundry thoughts upon faith, each of which I may have uttered in your hearing at different times, but which have not been collected into one sermon before, and which, I have no doubt, have been misunderstood from the want of their having been put together in their proper consecutive order....

I. First, THE OBJECT OF FAITH, or to what faith looks.

I am told in the Word of God to believe — What am I to believe? I am bidden to look — to what am I to look? What is to be the object of my hope, belief, and confidence? The reply is simple. The object of faith, to a sinner, is Christ Jesus. How many make a mistake about this, and think they are to believe on *God the Father!* Now, belief in God is a result of faith in Jesus. We come to believe in the eternal love of the Father as the result of trusting the precious blood of the Son. Many men say, "I would believe in Christ if I knew that I were elect." This is coming to the Father, and no man can come to the Father except by Christ. It is the Father's work to elect; you cannot come directly to him, therefore you cannot know your election until first you have believed on Christ the Redeemer, and then through redemption you can approach the Father and know your election. Some, too, make the mistake of looking to the work of God *the Holy Spirit.* They look within to see if they have certain feelings, and if they find them their faith is strong, but if their feelings have departed from them, then their faith is weak, so that they look to the work of the Spirit which is not the object of a sinner's faith. Both the Father and the Spirit must be trusted in order to complete redemption, but for the particular mercy of justification and pardon, the blood of the Mediator is the only plea. *Christians* have to trust the Spirit after conversion, but the sinner's business, if he would be saved, is not with trusting the Spirit, nor with looking to the Spirit, but looking to Christ Jesus, and to him alone. I know your salvation depends on the whole Trinity, but yet the first and immediate object of a sinner's justifying faith is neither God the Father nor God the Holy Ghost, but God the Son, incarnate in human flesh, and offering atonement for sinners....

On nothing else must thou trust; he is to be the only prop and pillar of thy confidence; and all thou addest thereunto will be a wicked anti-christ, a rebellion against the sovereignty of the Lord Jesus. But take care if your faith save you, that while you look to Christ in all these matters, you view him as being *a substitute.* This doctrine of substitution is so essential to the whole plan of salvation, that I must explain it here for the thousandth time. God is just, he must punish sin; God is merciful, he wills to pardon those who believe in Jesus. How is this to be done? How can he be just and exact the penalty — merciful, and accept the sinner? He doeth it thus: he taketh the sins of his people and actually lifteth them up from off his people to Christ, so that they stand as innocent as though they had never sinned, and Christ is looked upon by God as though he had been all the sinners in the world rolled into one. The sin of his people was taken from their persons, and really and actually, not typically and metaphorically, but really and actually laid on Christ. Then God came forth with his fiery sword to meet the sinner and to punish him. He met Christ. Christ was not a sinner himself; but the sins of his people were all imputed to him. Justice, therefore, met Christ as though he had been the sinner — punished Christ for his people's sins — punished him as far as its rights could go — exacted from him the last atom of the penalty, and left not a dreg in the cup. And now, he who can see Christ as being his substitute, and puts his trust in him, is thereby delivered from the curse of the law. Soul, when thou seest Christ obeying the law, thy faith is to say, "He obeys that for his people." When thou seest him dying, thou art to count the purple drops and say, "Thus he took my sins away." When thou seest him rising from the dead, thou art to say, "He rises as the head and representative of all his elect." And when thou seest him sitting at the right hand of God, thou art to view him there as the pledge that all for whom he died shall most surely sit at the Father's right hand. Learn to look on Christ as being in God's sight as though he were the sinner. "In him was no sin." He was *"the just,"* but he suffered for the unjust. He was the righteous, but he stood in the place of the unrighteous; and all that the righteous ought to have endured, Christ has endured once for all, and put away their sins forever by the sacrifice of himself. Now, this is the great object of faith. I pray you, do not make any mistake about this, for a mistake here will be dangerous, if not fatal. View Christ, by your faith, as being in his life, and death, and sufferings, and resurrection, the substitute for all whom his Father gave him — the vicarious sacrifice for the sins of all those who will trust him with their souls. Christ, then, thus set forth, is the object of justifying faith. . . . The object of faith, then, is Christ as the substitute for sinners. God in Christ, but not God apart from Christ, nor any work of the Spirit, but the work of Jesus only must be viewed by you as the foundation of your hope.

II. Secondly, THE REASON OF FAITH, or why doth any man believe, and whence doth his faith come?

"Faith cometh by *hearing.*" Granted; but do not all men hear, and do not many still remain unbelieving? How, then, doth any man come by his faith? To his own experience his faith comes as the result of a *sense of need.* He feels himself needing a Saviour; he finds Christ to be just such a Saviour as he wants, and therefore because he cannot help himself, he believes Jesus. Having nothing of his own, he feels he must take Christ or else perish, and therefore he doeth it because he cannot help doing it. He is fairly driven up in a corner, and there is but this one way of escape, namely, by the righteousness of another; for he feels he cannot escape by any good deeds, or sufferings of his own, and he cometh to Christ and humbleth himself, because he cannot do without Christ, and must perish unless he lay hold of him. But to carry the question further back, where does that man get his sense of need? How is it that he, rather than others, feels his need of Christ? It is certain he has no more necessity for Christ than other men. How doth he come to know, then, that he is lost and ruined? How is it that he is driven by the sense of ruin to take hold on Christ the restorer? The reply is, this is *the gift of God;* this is the work of the Spirit. No man comes to Christ except the Spirit draw him, and the Spirit draws men to Christ by shutting them up under the law to a conviction that if they do not come to Christ, they must perish. Then by sheer stress of weather, they tack about and run into this heavenly port. Salvation by Christ is so disagreeable to our carnal mind, so inconsistent with our love of human merit, that we never would take Christ to be our all in all, if the Spirit did not convince us that we were wanting at all, and did not so compel us to lay hold on Christ.

But, then, the question goes further back still; how is it that the Spirit of God teaches some men their need, and not other men? Why is it that some of you were driven by your sense of need to Christ, while others go on in their self-righteousness and perish? There is no answer to be given but this, "Even so, Father, for so it seemed good in thy sight." It comes to divine sovereignty at the last. The Lord hath "hidden those things from the wise and prudent, and hath revealed them unto babes." According to the why in which Christ put it — "My sheep, hear my voice"; "ye believe not because ye are not of my sheep, as I said unto you." Some divines would like to read that — "Ye are not my sheep, because ye do not believe." As if believing made us the sheep of Christ; but the text puts it — "Ye believe not, because ye are not of my sheep." "All that the Father giveth me shall come to me." If they come not, it is a clear proof that they were never given; for those who were given of old eternity to Christ, chosen of God the Father, and then redeemed by God the Son — these are led by the Spirit, through a sense of need to come and lay hold on Christ. No man yet ever did, or ever will believe in Christ, unless he feels his need of him. No man ever did or will feel his need of Christ, unless the Spirit makes him feel, and the Spirit will make no man feel his need of Jesus savingly, unless it be so written in the eternal book, in which God hath surely, engraved the names of his chosen. So, then, I think I am not to be misunderstood on this point, that the reason of faith, or why men Believe, is God's electing love working through the Spirit by a sense of need, and so bringing them to Christ Jesus.

III. Thirdly, THE GROUND OF THE SINNER'S FAITH, or on what ground he dares to believe on the Lord Jesus Christ.

My dear friends, I have already said that no man will believe in Jesus, unless he feels his need of him. But you have often heard me say, and I repeat it again, that I do not come to Christ pleading that I feel my need of him; my reason for believing in Christ, is not that I *feel* my need of him, but that I *have* a need of him. The ground on which a man comes to Jesus, is not as *a sensible* sinner, but as a *sinner,* and nothing but a sinner. He will not come unless he is awakened; but when he comes, he does not say, "Lord, I come to thee because I am an awakened sinner, save me." But he says, "Lord, I am a *sinner;* save me." Not his awakening, but his sinfulness is the method and plan upon which he dares to come. You will, perhaps, perceive what I mean, for I cannot exactly explain myself just now. If I refer to the preaching of a great many Calvinistic divines, they say to a sinner, "Now, *if you feel* your need of Christ, if you have repented so much, *if* you have been harrowed by the law to such-and-such a degree, then you may come to Christ on the ground that you are an awakened sinner." I say that is false. No man may come to Christ on the ground of his being an awakened sinner; he must come to him *as a sinner.* When I come to Jesus, I know I am not come unless I am awakened, but still, I do not come as awakened. I do not stand at the foot of his cross to be washed because I have repented; I bring nothing when I come but sin. A sense of need is a good feeling; but when I stand at the foot of the cross, I do not believe in Christ because I have got good feelings, but I believe in him whether I have good feelings or not.

> Just as I am without one plea,
> But that thy blood was shed for me,
> And that thou bidst me come to thee,
> O Lamb of God, I come.

Faith is getting right out of yourself and getting into Christ. I know that many hundreds of poor souls have been troubled because the minister has said, "If you feel your need, you may come to Christ." "But," say they, "I do not feel my need enough; I am sure I do not." Many a score letters have I received from poor troubled consciences, who have said, "I would venture to believe in Christ to save me if I had a tender conscience; if I had a soft heart — but oh, my heart is like a rock of ice which will not melt. I cannot feel as I would like to feel, and therefore I must not believe in Jesus." Oh! down with it, down with it! It is a wicked anti-Christ; it is flat Popery! It is not your soft heart that entitles you to believe. You are to believe in Christ to renew your heard heart, and come to him with nothing about you but sin. The ground on which a sinner comes to Christ is that he is dead, and not that he knows he is dead; that he is lost, and not that he knows he is lost. I know he will not come unless he does know it, but that is not the ground on which he comes. It is the secret reason why, but it not the public positive ground which he understands. . . . The only thing you can bring to Christ is your sin and your wickedness. All he asks is that you will come empty. If you have anything of your own, you must leave all before you come. If there be anything good in you, you cannot trust Christ, you must come with nothing in your hand. Take him as all in all, and that is the only ground upon which a poor soul can be saved — as a sinner, and nothing but a sinner.

IV. Fourthly, THE WARRANT OF FAITH, or why a man dares to trust in Christ.

Is it not imprudent for any man to trust Christ to save him, and especially when he has no good thing whatever! Is it not an arrogant presumption for any man to trust Christ? No, sirs, it is not. It is a grand and noble work of God the Holy Spirit for a man to give the lie to all his sins, and still to believe and set to his seal that God is true, and believe in the virtue of the blood of Jesus. But why does any man dare to believe in Christ, I will ask you now. "Well," saith one man, "I summoned faith to believe in Christ because I did feel there was a work of the Spirit in me." You do not believe in Christ at all. "Well," says another, "I thought that I had a right to believe in Christ, because I felt somewhat." You had not any right to believe in Christ at all on such a warrant as that. What is a man's warrant then, for believing in Christ? Here it is. Christ tells him to do it, that is his warrant. Christ's word is the warrant of the sinner for believing — not what he feels nor what he is, nor what he is not, but that Christ has told him to do it. The Gospel runs thus: "Believe on the Lord Jesus Christ and thou shalt be saved. He that believeth not shall be damned." Faith in Christ, then, is a commanded duty as well as a blessed privilege, and what a mercy it is that it is a duty; because there never can be any question but that a man has a right to do his duty. Now, on the ground that God commands me to believe, I have a right to believe, be I who I may. The gospel is sent to every creature. Well, I belong to that tribe; I am one of the "every" creatures, and that gospel commands me to believe. I cannot be wrong in obeying a command of God. Now, it is a command of God given to every creature, that he should believe on Jesus Christ whom God hath sent. This is your warrant, sinner, and a blessed warrant it is, for it is one which hell cannot gainsay, and which heaven cannot withdraw. You need not be looking within to find the misty warrants of your experience. You need not be looking to your works, and to your feelings, to get some dull and insufficient warrants for your confidence in Christ. You may believe Christ because he tells you to do so. That is a sure ground to stand on, and one which admits of no doubt....

"Yes," says one, "but I have been a drunkard, a swearer, or lascivious, or profane." Then you are a sinner, you have not gone further than the uttermost, and he is able to save you still. "Ay," saith another, "but you do not know how my guilt has been aggravated." That only proves you to be a sinner, and that you are commanded to trust Christ and be saved. "Ay," cries yet another, "but you do not know how often I have rejected Christ." Yes, but that only makes you the more a sinner. "You do not know how hard my heart is." Just so, but that only proves you to be a sinner, and still; proves you to be one whom Christ came to save. "Oh, but sir, I have not any good thing. If I had, you know, I should have something to encourage me." The fact of your not having any good thing, just proves to me that you are the man I am sent to preach to. Christ came to save that which was lost and you have said only proves that you are lost, and therefore he came to save you. Do trust him — do trust him. "But if I am saved," saith one, "I shall be the biggest sinner that ever was saved." Then the greater music in heaven when you get there; the more glory to Christ, for the bigger the sinner the more honor to Christ when at last he shall be brought home. "Ay, but my sin has abounded." His grace shall much more abound. "But my sin has reached even to heaven." Yes, but his mercy reaches above the heavens. "Oh! but my guilt is as broad as the world." Yes, but his righteousness is broader than a thousand worlds. "Ay, but my sin is scarlet." Yes, but his blood is more scarlet than your sins, and can wash the scarlet out by a richer scarlet. "Ay, but I deserve to be lost, and death and hell are for my damnation." Yes, and so they may, but the blood of Jesus Christ can cry louder than either death or hell; and it cries to-day, "Father, let the sinner live." Oh! I wish I could get this thought out of my own mouth, and get it into your heads, that when God saves you, it is not because of anything in you, it is because of something in himself. God's love has no reason except in his own bowels; God's reason for pardoning a sinner is found in his own heart, and not in the sinner. And there is as much reason in you why you should be saved, as why another should be saved, namely, no reason at all. There is no reason in you why he should have mercy on you, but there is no reason wanted, for the reason lies in God, and in God alone.

V. And now I come to the conclusion, THE RESULT OF FAITH, or how it speeds when it comes to Christ.

The text says, "He that believeth is not condemned." There is a man there who has just this moment believed; he is not condemned. But he has been fifty years in sin, and has plunged into all manner of vice; his sins, which are many, are all forgiven him. He stands in the sight of God now as innocent as though he had never sinned. Such is the power of Jesus' blood, that "he that believeth is not condemned." Does this relate to what is to happen at the day of Judgment? I pray you look at the text, and you will find it does not say, "He that believeth *shall* not be condemned," but he *is* not; he is not now. And if he is not now, then it follows that he never shall be; for having believed in Christ, that promise still stands, "He that believeth is not condemned." I believe to-day I am not condemned; in fifty years time that promise will be just the same — "He that believeth is not condemned." So that the moment a man puts his trust in Christ, he is freed from all condemnation — past, present and to come; and from that day he stands in God's sight as though he were without spot or wrinkle, or any such thing. "But he sins," you say. He does indeed, but his sins are not laid to his charge. They are laid to the charge of Christ of old, and God can never charge the offence on two — first on Christ, and then on the sinner. "Ay, but he often falls into sin." That may be possible; though if the Spirit of God be in him he sinneth not as he was wont to do. He sins by reason of infirmity, not by reason of his love to sin, for now he hateth it.

But mark, you shall put it in your own way if you will, and I will answer, "Yes, but though he sin, yet is he no more guilty in the sight of God, for all his guilt has been taken from him, put on Christ — positively, literally, and actually lifted off from him, and put upon Jesus Christ. Do you see the Jewish host? There is a scapegoat brought out; the high priest confesses the sin of the people over the scapegoat's head. The sin is all gone from the people, and laid upon the scapegoat. Away goes the scapegoat into the wilderness. Is there any sin left on the people? If there be, then the scapegoat has not carried it away. Because it cannot be *here* and *there too*. It cannot be carried away and left behind too. "No," say you, "Scripture says the scapegoat carried away the sin; there was none left on the people when the scapegoat had taken away the sin. And so, when by faith we put our hand upon the head of Christ, does Christ take away our sin, or does he not? If he does not, then it is of no use our believing in him: but if he doth really take away our sin, then our sin cannot be on him and on us too; if it be on Christ, we are free, clear, accepted, justified, and this is the true doctrine of justification by faith. As soon as a man believeth in Christ Jesus, his sins are gone from him, and gone away forever. They are blotted out now. What if a man owe a hundred pounds, yet if he has got a receipt for it, he is free; it is blotted out; there is an erasure made in the book, and the debt is gone. Though the man commit sin, yet the debt having been paid before even the debt was acquired, he is no more a debtor to the law of God. Doth not Scripture say, that God has cast his people's sins into the depths of the sea? Now, if they are in the depths of the sea, they cannot be on his people too. Blessed be his name, in the day when he casts our sins into the depth of the sea, he views us as pure in his sight.

Oh! for faith to lay hold on this. Oh! for an overpowering faith that shall get the victory over doubts and fears, and make us enjoy the liberty wherewith Christ makes men free. Go home, ye that believe in Christ, and go to your beds this night, and say, "If I die in my bed, I cannot be condemned." Should you wake the next morning, go into the world and say, "I am not condemned." When the devil howls at you, tell him, "You may accuse, but I am not condemned." And if sometimes your sins rise,

say, "I know you, but you are all gone forever — I am not condemned."
And when your turn shall come to die, shut your eyes in peace.

> Bold shall you stand in that great day,
> For who aught to your charge can lay?

Fully absolved, by grace you shall be found at last, and all sin's
tremendous curse and blame shall be taken away, not because of anything you have done. I pray you do all you can for Christ out of
gratitude, but even when you have done all, do not rest there. Rest
still in the substitution and the sacrifice. Be you what Christ was in his
Father's sight, and when conscience awakens, you can tell it that Christ
was for you all that you ought to have been, that he has suffered all
your penalty; and now neither mercy nor justice can smite you, since
justice has clasped hands with mercy in a firm decree to save that man
whose faith is in the cross of Christ. The Lord bless these words for his
sake. Amen.

[Charles Haddon Spurgeon, *Spurgeon's Sermons* (New York: Sheldon and Co. and Boston:
Gould and Lincoln, 1857–60), 7:259–76.]

– 25 –

Noah Davis

Southern evangelical Christians, black and white, shared a social and spiritual ethos united by the common experience of conversion (see Donald G. Mathews, Religion in the Old South, *xv). By some estimates, in the 1830s there were as many as 140,000 black Southerners who were members of evangelical churches. One quarter of the Baptists were black. Typical of Southern evangelical religion was Noah Davis (1804– 66). Born a slave on a farm in Madison County, Virginia, Davis worked as a carpenter and an apprentice boot and shoe maker. Although Davis would become a prominent Baptist leader, his Christian conversion began in a Methodist meeting. At the age of twenty-seven, he was baptized and licensed to preach. With the help of sympathetic white Christians, Davis bought his freedom and became the pastor of the Saratoga Street African Baptist Chapel of Baltimore, Maryland, where he continued to work for the liberation of his own family. Proceeds from the sale of Davis's* Narrative, *published in 1859, went toward the manumission of his last two children still held in slavery. The autobiographical narrative provided by Davis is fairly representative of evangelical conversion. Yet it is important to note that his experience, as reported here, is neither unmediated nor self-interpreted. Family, church, even unregenerate shopmates help Davis know that he is truly converted. This communal strand was tightly bound to the conversion narratives of previous generations but would be only loosely connected to the growing privatization of religious experience in late nineteenth- and early twentieth-century America. Davis's account is a reminder that Baptist theology is a conversionist theology and that salvation is discerned and worked out within community.*

If I Was Only Converted

Just about the close of my apprenticeship, and as I began to feel myself a man, I commenced to visit the girls, which induced me to go still more frequently to church.

At that time, there were four churches in Fredericksburg. The colored people had apartments for worship with the white people, at each of these churches. They were Methodist, Presbyterian, Episcopalian and Baptist.

I had no particular preference for any one of these denominations, more than another, but went wherever my favorites went. One night a young lady invited me to go to the Methodist church, where a prayer-meeting was to be held. During the meeting, a venerable old gentleman rose to his feet, and related an account of the sudden death of a young lady, which he had read in a newspaper. When he related that solemn circumstance, it so affected me, that I felt as if I was about to die, in a sudden manner also.

Having always, from parental training, purposed in my mind to become religious before I died, I thought that now was the time to begin to pray. But I could not try to pray in the church, for I was afraid that the girls would laugh at me. Yet I became so troubled, that I left the house, girls and all, intending, to seek some place where I might pray. But to my horror and surprise, when I got out of the church, this reflection occurred to me, "God is in heaven, and you are on earth: — how can He hear you?" O, what distress of mind I now felt! I began to wonder how God could hear my prayer; for, sure enough, He was in heaven, and I on the earth. In my perplexity, I started for home.

Just before I reached the shop, where I slept, this thought struck me, if possible with more force than the former reflection: "God does see you!" It really appeared to me as if I could see that God was indeed looking at me; and not only so, but I felt that He had been looking at me all my life. I now said to myself, "It is of no use for me to pray. — If God has seen all my wickedness, as I feel that He has, then there is no mercy for me."

So I ran to my lodging-place, and tried to hide myself in a dark room. But this was useless; for it appeared that God could see me in the dark, as well as in the light.

I now felt constrained to beg for mercy, and spent the time in trying to obtain pardon for my sins. But the morning came, and the hour drew near for the hands to go to work, and I was still unhappy.

I felt so very different to what I had always felt, that I tried to examine my impressions of the previous night, to learn if it was true that God did see me or not; for I thought my imagination might have deceived me.

Up to this time, I was not fully convinced that God knew all about me. So I began to study about the matter. As I sat on the shoe-bench, I picked up a bunch of bristles, and selecting one of the smallest, I began to wonder, if God could see an object so small as that. No sooner had this inquiry arose in my heart, than it appeared to me, that the Lord could not only see the bristle, but that He beheld me, as plainly as I saw the little object in my hand; and not only so, but that God was then looking through me, just as I would hold up a tumbler of clear water to the sun and look through it. This was enough. I felt that I must pray, or perish; and now I began to pray.

But it really seemed, that the more I prayed the less hope there was for me. Still I could not stop praying; for I felt that God was angry with me. I had sinned against his holy laws; and now, if He should cut me off, and send me to hell, it was but right. These thoughts followed me day and night, for five weeks, before I felt relief. At length, one day, while sitting on my shoe bench, I felt that my time had come when I must die. What troubled me most, was that I should have to appear before God, in all my sins; — O, what horror filled my soul at the thought!

I began to wonder what I must do. I knew I was not prepared for death and the Judgment. It is true that two of my shopmates, at that time, were members of the church; but they did not seem to care for my soul. All the rest of the hands were as wicked as myself. "What shall I do?" was in my mind, all the time I sat at work.

The reflection occurred to me, "Your mother is a Christian; it may be she can save you." But this suggestion appeared to be offensive to God. Then came another thought, — "As my master was a rich man, could he not do something to help me?" But I found no relief in either,... and while I sat thus, hoping and praying, light broke into my mind — all my trouble left me in an instant.

I felt such a love and peace flowing in my soul, that I could not sit longer; I sprang to my feet, and cried out, "Glory to God!" It seemed to me, that God, whom I had beheld, a few seconds previously, angry with me, was now well-pleased. I could not tell why this great change had taken place in me; and my shopmates were surprised at my conduct, saying, that I must be getting crazy. But, just at this moment, the thought came into my mind, that I was converted; still, as I felt so very different from what I had expected to feel, I could not see how that could be. I concluded to run and see my mother, and ask her how people felt, when they got converted. So I went, right away, to my mother's house, some five or six squares from the shop.

When I reached the door of her house, it appeared to me that everything was new and bright. I went in, and sat down. Mother asked me how I was. I told her, I felt *right smart*. This was a new sound from me; for my answers to this question had long been — "*poorly.*" But now came the trial; to ask mother how people felt, when they were converted. I felt ashamed to ask the question; so I went into another room; and seeing a hymn book lying on the table, I took it up. The first hymn that struck my sight began with these words:

> When converts first begin to sing,
> Their happy souls are on the wing —
> Their theme is all redeeming love;
> Fain would they be with Christ above.
> With admiration they behold
> The love of Christ, which can't be told.

These lines expressed my feelings precisely, and being encouraged from them, I went to my mother, and asked her the question — "How do people feel, when they get converted?" She replied, "Do you think you are converted?" Now, this was a severe trial; for, although I felt that I was really changed, yet I wanted to hear from her, before I could decide whether I was actually converted, or not. I replied, "No." Then she said, "My son, the devil makes people think themselves converted sometimes." I arose, and left immediately, believing, that the devil had made a fool of me. I returned to my shop, more determined to pray than ever before.

I arrived, and took my seat, and tried to get under that same weight that I had felt pressing me down, but a short while before. But it seemed to me that I could not; and, instead of feeling sad, I felt joyful in my heart; and while trying to pray, I thought the Saviour appeared to me. I thought I saw God smiling upon me, through Christ, His Son. My soul was filled with love to God and Jesus Christ. It appeared to me, I saw a fullness in Jesus Christ, to save every sinner who would come to Him. And I felt, that if I was only converted, I would tell all sinners how precious the Saviour was. But I could not think myself converted yet, because I could not see what I had done, for God to pardon my sins. Still I felt a love to Him for what He had done for my soul.

Then I began to think upon my shopmates — and, O what pity ran through my soul for them. I wished to pray for them; but I felt so unworthy, that I could not do it. At last I promised the Lord that if He would convert my soul, I would talk to them.

It was several months after that, before I was made to realize this to be the work of God; and when it was made plain, O what joy it did bring to my poor soul!

I shortly became a member of the Baptist church, and was baptized, in company with some twenty others, by Rev. Geo. F. Adams, who was then pastor of the Baptist church in Fredericksburg, September 19, 1831. This church then contained about three hundred colored members.

[Noah Davis, *A Narrative of the Life of Rev. Noah Davis, A Colored Man* (Baltimore: John F. Weishampel, Jr. 1859), 18–25.]

– 26 –

Francis Wayland

The conventional wisdom among Baptists in North America is that on biblical grounds their forebears championed "the absolute right of private judgment in all matters of religion" (Wayland, Notes on the Principles and Practices of Baptist Churches, 132). Winthrop Hudson observes that contrary to this popular belief, the individualistic account of Baptist identity "was derived from the general cultural and religious climate of the nineteenth century rather than from any serious study of the Bible" (Baptist Concepts of the Church, 215). No one was more responsible for so defining and popularizing this version of the Baptist heritage than Francis Wayland (1796–1865). A graduate of Union College and Andover Theological Seminary, Wayland served for five years as pastor of the historic First Baptist Church of Boston, Massachusetts (1821–26). During the subsequent twenty-eight years, while president of Brown University, Wayland became one of the most influential Baptist voices in North America. From his position as editor of the American Baptist Magazine, *he gained the confidence of the faithful by describing himself as just "an old fashioned Baptist" and appealing to "the sturdy common sense of the masses of our Brethren." He successfully advocated the "society" method of missions in the Triennial Convention. A series of Wayland's essays from the* Examiner *(a denominational periodical) were collected and published as* Notes on the Principles and Practices of Baptist Churches. *Immensely popular, the book tells more about Wayland and the democratization of American religion than about the earlier generations of Baptists he meant to describe.*

Baptist Principles and Practices

In my last paper I took occasion to observe that while the Baptists, with other evangelical denominations, held the doctrine of the exclusive spirituality of the church of Christ, to them belonged the honor of holding this fundamental truth in its purity and simplicity, and of rejecting every principle and practice at variance with it. I also alluded to the fact that infant baptism cannot be maintained without involving some belief opposed to this fundamental article of vital Christianity. We may at various times have become lax in our discipline, and have failed to carry out in practice the principles which we believe. In such cases, all we need is to seek out the old paths and walk therein, to act, in a word, according to our established belief; and "we are ourselves again." On the contrary, those who hold to practices founded on beliefs at variance with this doctrine, cannot be thus rectified. Their principles are contradictory, and to carry them all out to their legitimate results, must lead either to inextricable confusion, or else to the subversion of some fundamental doctrine of the gospel.

But this is not the only tenet by which our denomination has been always distinguished.

1. As a natural and inspired consequence of the doctrine of the spirituality of the church, we have ever held to that of the universal priesthood of believers. We have always proclaimed that every child of God has the right, in his own person, of drawing near to God through the intercession of the one only Mediator and High Priest. Hence we reject all notions of the necessity of human mediators, and with it, all belief in the holiness of a priesthood, and in general of an ecclesiastical caste. While we believe that men are to be set apart for the duties of the ministry in whom we see the evidence of ministerial gifts, yet, that it is the church itself — by which I mean not the clergy, but the whole body of Christians which sets them apart; and that when thus appointed to this work, they are, by this act, rendered no better or holier than their brethren. They are not thus made lords over God's heritage, but servants of the church, appointed to minister in spiritual things. They have no authority, either individually or collectively, to legislate for their brethren, but are, in all respects, just as any other believers, subject to the law of Christ. This, in a country like our own, where the press is free and the church cannot wield the arm of the state, may seem a matter of secondary moment. But let anyone cast his eyes over the past history of Christianity, and observe the universal tendency of teachers of Religion to constitute themselves into a priesthood, to assert dominion over the conscience, and to use the power which they have usurped for their own advantage, and to the extinction of piety, and he will, I think, come to a very different conclusion. No more fatal error has, in all ages, dogged the footsteps of the church of Christ, than the belief in the official holiness of the teacher of Religion, and the necessity of a human mediator, in some sort, to appear on our behalf before God. From this belief have been developed those various forms of ecclesiastical hierarchy, which now, with their appalling weight, press down the masses of Europe, and hold them bound in the fetters of spiritual ignorance and sin.

2. Another truth which has always been inscribed on our banner is, the absolute right of private judgment in all matters of Religion. We have always believed that the New Testament was not given by God to a priesthood, to be by them diluted, compounded, and adulterated, and then retailed by the pennyworth to the people; but, on the contrary, that the whole revelation in its totality, in all its abundance of blessing, with all its solemn warnings, and its exceeding great and precious promises, is a communication from God to every individual of the human race. It is given to the minister in no higher, or better, or different sense, than it is given to every one who reads it. Every one to whom it comes is bound to study it for himself, and govern his life by it. The wisdom of Omniscience has tasked itself to render this communication plain, so that he that runs may read, and that a wayfaring man, though a fool, need not err therein. The Holy Spirit has, moreover, been sent to assist every one who will, with an humble and devout heart, seek to understand it. With such a revelation, and such spiritual aid, every man is required to determine for himself what is the will of God. Seeking to know his duty in this manner, he will not fail to discern it. He has, therefore, no excuse for disobedience. He cannot plead before God that he could not know his will. He cannot excuse himself before his Judge on the ground that his ministers deceived him. The revelation was made to the man himself, and the means were provided for his understanding of it. "Every one of us must give account for *himself* unto God." Such are the views which we have always entertained.

3. Allied to this is another like unto it. As I have before remarked, we have always held to the perfect sufficiency of the Scriptures to teach us in all matters pertaining to Religion. We, moreover, believe that the New Testament, the word spoken by the Son of God from heaven, and by the apostles whom he himself inspired, was given not to one nation, but to the whole human race for all coming time, and that by this word we are to decide upon the obligatoriness of every part of the older revelation. It is, therefore, in this sense, our only *rule* of faith and practice. To every precept of it bow implicitly as God's last, best, and final revelation of his will to mankind. We judge the Fathers, as they are called, by the New Testament. We judge tradition and the rites and usages of men by the same law. We appeal "to the Word and the testimony, and if they speak not according to this word, it is because there is no light in them." Hence we are delivered from the yoke of antiquity, tradition, and ecclesiastical usurpation, and rejoice in the liberty wherewith Christ has made us free.

We hear much at present, which indicates the dissatisfaction of honest and able men with the Christian church as it now exists in Europe, and to some extent in this country. It is surely not without foundation. We hear of various projects for a reformation of Christianity. None of these projects can, however, reach the evil. It will never be reached, and the world will never be reformed, until Christians prune off all the beliefs and usages which have been ingrafted on the church, as it was left by the apostles, and in simplicity and truth adopt for their only and sufficient rule, the New Testament, as it was committed to them by our Lord and Saviour.

4. Another article of our belief, and the last that I will mention, is that the church of Christ is distinct from every other association of men, and is wholly and absolutely independent of the civil power. The authority we plead for this belief is found in the reply of Peter and John to the Jewish Sanhedrin: "Whether it be right in the sight of God to hearken unto you more than unto God, judge ye, for we cannot but speak the things which we have seen and heard." We accordingly have ever believed that the state has no authority to legislate in matters pertaining to the conscience. When man violates the rights of man, the state may interfere, and prevent or punish the wrong. But, in matters which concern our relations to God, the state has no jurisdiction. It has no right to take cognizance of our duties to God. Hence it is guilty of wrong, if it prohibit or annoy any form of Religion, if it favor one more than another, if it restrict the exercise of any form of devotion, either public or private, or in any manner whatever interfere in the matter of religious belief or practice. Such was the view taken of this subject by Roger Williams, and hence, when he established a commonwealth, its fundamental principle was perfect freedom in religious concernments; or, as he so well designated it, "soul liberty." No man of his age had so clear conceptions of the rights of conscience as the founder of Rhode Island, and no one had ever carried them so honestly to their legitimate conclusions. I go further: no one has yet been able either to take from or add to the principles of religious liberty which he so simply and powerfully set forth. They stand as imperishable monuments to his fame, like the obelisks of LUXOR, on which the chiseling of every figure is now just as sharply defined as when, three thousand years since, they were left by the hand of their designer....

Here, then, is the peculiar glory of the Baptists. While they have suffered persecution at the hands of almost all the dominant sects that emerged from the Reformation, their garments have never been defiled by any violation of the rights of conscience. What Roger Williams claimed for himself, he as freely granted to others. He tells us: "I desire not that liberty to myself which I would not freely and impartially weigh out to all the consciences of the world beside." "All these consciences, yea, the very consciences of the Papists, Jews, etc., ought freely and impartially to be permitted their several worships, their ministers of worships, and what way of maintaining them they freely choose." And this, be it remembered, was said, and a government was established in conformity to it, at a time when, out of the little colony of Rhode Island and Providence Plantations, there was not a foot of the habitable earth where a Baptist could, without molestation, worship God according to the dictates of his own conscience. And at a later day, when there was not a colony in America in which the charter of a Baptist college could have been obtained, Brown University was incorporated. True to their principles, our fathers inserted a provision in the charter of this institution, by which the various sects in Rhode Island: Baptists, Episcopalians, Congregationalists and Quakers, in proportion to their then population, should forever constitute the government of the college. Such has ever been the constitution of this seat of learning.

Of the unspeakable importance of the principles to which I have thus alluded, there can now be no controversy. The doctrines of the spirituality of the church, the right of private judgment, the perfect sufficiency of the Scriptures as a rule of faith and practice, and the absolute separation of Church and State, are admitted to be the articles by which, the church of Christ must either stand or fall. The truths which Roger Williams first exemplified in his own little colony, are now the glory of his great republic; and they are at this moment agitating the millions of every nation of Europe. They must ere long make the circuit of the earth. And these other doctrines are now disturbing, the repose of ritual and formal Christianity everywhere, and the churches can never "shake themselves from the dust, and put on their beautiful garments," until they are universally adopted.

The Baptists may then lay claim, to say the least, to as high moral distinction as can be awarded to any sect in Christendom. They have borne testimony to the most important doctrines of revelation, in their unadulterated purity and simplicity. From each sect in turn, they have, for bearing this testimony, suffered scorn, contumely, reproach, and persecution. When they have obtained the power to persecute in turn, they used that power only to return good for evil, by granting to their persecutors every right which they claimed for themselves. When any sect can lay claim to higher or more honorable distinction, we will bow before them, and cheerfully yield them Christian precedence.

Such being the facts known to all the world, have we any reason to be ashamed of our fathers? When the very principles for which they suffered are now acknowledged to lie at the foundation, not only of pure Christianity, but of all civil and religious liberty, shall we hide our light under a bushel, and blush to bear testimony to eternal truth? After having so long stood in the vanguard of that noble host who have contended for apostolic Christianity and the inalienable rights of conscience, now that the victory is half achieved, and our principles are arousing the nations, shall we lay down our arms, furl our banners, and retire ingloriously from the combat? I know not what may be your answer, but I know what would have been the answer of Roger Williams.

[Francis Wayland, *Notes on the Principles and Practices of Baptist Churches* (New York: Sheldon, Blakeman, and Co., 1857), 130–39.]

27

Alexander Campbell

After the American Revolution, a growing number of preachers from New England to Kentucky began raising concerns about the fragmentation of Protestant Christianity. In his 1809 Declaration and Address, *Thomas Campbell (1763–1854) expressed the "desire to adopt and recommend such measures, as would give rest to our brethren throughout all the churches; — as would restore unity, peace, and purity, to the whole church of God." By the 1830s these forces consolidated around two convictions: "the union of all Christians and the restoration of primitive Christianity" (Garrison,* An American Religious Movement, *14). The most celebrated and influential of these restorationists was Thomas Campbell's son, Alexander (1788–1866). The younger Campbell followed his father from Scotland to North America in 1807. With the motto "Where the Scriptures speak, we speak, and where they are silent, we are silent," Alexander Campbell rejected the creedalism of Presbyterian theology in favor of simple biblicism and embraced believers baptism in place of infant baptism. Yet Campbell's theology remained deeply under the influence of the philosophy of John Locke and Scottish common sense realism. In 1823 Campbell founded a periodical called* The Christian Baptist, *but tensions eventually led him to break with other Baptists. His followers joined forces with those of Barton Stone (1772–1844). They renounced denominationalism and called themselves "disciples of Christ" and "Christians." The following selection is from the preface of Campbell's seminal work,* The Christian System, *published in 1866.*

The Union of Christians and
the Restoration of Primitive Christianity

Since the full development of the great apostasy foretold by Prophets and Apostles, numerous attempts at reformation have been made. Three full centuries, carrying with them the destinies of countless millions, have passed into eternity since the Lutheran effort to dethrone the *Man of Sin.* During this period many great and wonderful changes have taken place in the political, literary, moral, and religious conditions of society. That the nations composing the western half of the Roman empire have already been greatly benefited by that effort, scientifically, politically, and morally, no person acquainted with either political or ecclesiastical history can reasonably doubt. Time, that great arbiter of human actions, that great revealer of secrets, has long decided that all the reformers of the Papacy have been public benefactors. And thus the Protestant Reformation is proved to have been one of the most splendid eras in the history of the world, and must long be regarded by the philosopher and the philanthropist as one of the most gracious interpositions in behalf of the whole human race.

We Americans owe our national privileges and our civil liberties to the Protestant Reformers. They achieved not only an imperishable fame for themselves, but a rich legacy for their posterity. When we contrast the present state of these United States with Spanish America, and the condition of the English nation with that of Spain, Portugal, and Italy, we begin to appreciate how much we are indebted to the intelligence, faith, and courage of Martin Luther and his heroic associates in that glorious reformation.

He restored the Bible to the world in A.D. 1534, and boldly defended its claims against the impious and arrogant pretensions of the haughty and tyrannical See of Rome. But, unfortunately, at his death there was no Joshua to lead the people, who rallied under the banners of the Bible, out of the wilderness in which Luther died. His tenets were soon converted into a new state Religion, and the spirit of reformation which he excited and inspired was soon quenched by the broils and feuds of the Protestant princes, and the collisions of rival political interests, both on the continent and in the islands of Europe....

While philosophy, mysticism, and politics drove the parties to every question into antipodal extremes; while justification by metaphysical faith alone; while the forms and ceremonies of all sects begat the "Spirit alone" in the mind of George Fox; while the Calvinian five points generated the Arminian five points; and while the Westminster Creed, though unsubscribed by its makers, begot a hundred others, — not until within the present generation did any sect or party in Christendom unite and build upon the Bible alone.

Since that time, the first effort known to us to abandon the whole controversy about creeds and reformations, and to restore primitive Christianity, or to build alone upon the Apostles and Prophets, Jesus Christ himself the chief corner, has been made.

Tired of new creeds and new parties in Religion, and of the numerous abortive efforts to reform the reformation; convinced from the Holy Scriptures, from observation and experience, that the union of the disciples of Christ is essential to the conversion of the world, and that the correction and improvement of no creed, or partisan establishment in Christendom, could ever become the basis of such a union, communion, and co-operation, as would restore peace to a church militant against itself, or triumph to the common salvation; a few individuals, about the commencement of the present century, began to reflect upon the ways and means to restore primitive Christianity.

This led to a careful, most conscientious, and prayerful examination of the grounds and reasons of the present state of things in all the Protestant sects. On examination of the history of all the platforms and constitutions of all these sects, it appeared evident as mathematical demonstration itself, that neither the Augsburg articles of faith and opinion, nor the Westminster, nor the Wesleyan, nor those of any state creed or dissenting establishment, could ever improve the condition of things, restore union to the church, peace to the world, or success to the gospel of Christ.

As the Bible was said and constantly affirmed to be the Religion of Protestants, it was for some time a mysterious problem why the Bible alone, confessed and acknowledged, should work no happier results than the strifes, divisions, and retaliatory excommunications of rival Protestant sects. It appeared, however, in this case, after a more intimate acquaintance with the details of the inner temple of sectarian Christianity, as in many similar cases, that it is not the acknowledgment of a good rule, but the walking by it, that secures the happiness of society. The Bible in the lips, and the creed in the head and in the heart, will not save the church from strife, emulation and schism. There is no moral, ecclesiastical, or political good, by simply acknowledging it in word. It must be obeyed.

In our ecclesiastical pilgrimage we have occasionally met with some vehement declaimers against human written creeds, and pleaders for the Bible alone, who were all the while preaching up the opinions of *saint* Arius or *saint* Athanasius. Their sentiments, language, style, and general views of the gospel were as human as auricular confession, extreme unction, or purgatorial purification.

The Bible alone is the Bible only, in word and deed, in profession and practice; and this alone can reform the world and save the church. Judging others as we once judged ourselves, there are not a few who are advocating the Bible alone, and preaching their own opinions. Before we applied the Bible alone to our views, or brought our views and religious practices to the Bible, we plead the old theme, — "The Bible alone is the Religion of Protestants." But we found it an arduous task, and one of twenty years' labour, to correct our diction and purify our speech according to the Bible alone; and even yet we have not wholly practically repudiated the language of Ashdod. We only profess to work and walk by the rules which will inevitably issue in a pure speech, and in right conceptions of that pure, and holy, and celestial thing called Christianity, — in faith, in sentiment, and in practice.

A deep and abiding impression that the power, the consolations, and joys — the holiness and happiness — of Christ's Religion were lost in the forms and ceremonies, in the speculations and conjectures, in the feuds and bickerings of sects and scheme, originated a project many years ago for uniting the sects, or rather *the Christians* in all the sects, upon a clear and scriptural bond of union, — upon having a *"thus saith the Lord,"* either in express terms, or in approved precedent, "for every article of faith, and item of religious practice." This was offered in the year 1809, in the "Declaration and Address" of the Washington Association, Pennsylvania. It was first tendered to the parties that confessed the Westminster creed: but equally submitted to the Protestants of every name, making faith in Christ and obedience to him the only *test* of Christian character, and the only *bond* of church union, communion, and co-operation. It was indeed approved by all; but adopted and practiced by none, except the few, or part of the few, who made the future. . . .

We flatter ourselves that the principles are now clearly and fully developed by the united efforts of a few devoted and ardent minds, who set out determined to sacrifice every thing to truth, and follow her wherever she might lead the way: I say, the principles on which the church of Jesus Christ — all believers in Jesus as the Messiah — can be united with honor to themselves, and with blessings to the world; on which the gospel and its ordinances can be restored in all their primitive simplicity, excellency, and power, and the church shine as a lamp that burneth to the conviction and salvation of the world: — I *say, the principles* by which these things can be done are now developed, as well as the *principles themselves,* which together constitute *the original gospel* and *order of things* established by the Apostles.

The object of this volume is to place before the community in plain, definite, and perspicuous style, the *capital principles* which have been elicited, argued out, developed, and sustained in a controversy of *twenty-five years,* by the tongues and pens of those who rallied under the banners of the Bible alone. The principle which was inscribed upon our banners when we withdrew from the ranks of the sects was, *"Faith in Jesus as the true Messiah, and obedience to him as our Lawgiver and King, the* ONLY TEST *of Christian character, and the* ONLY BOND *of Christian union, communion, and co-operation, irrespective of all creeds, opinions, commandments, and traditions of men."*

This cause, like every other, was first plead by the tongue; afterwards by the pen and the press. The history of its progress corresponds with the history of every other religious revolution in this respect — that different points, at different times, almost exclusively engrossed the attention of its pleaders. We began with the *outposts* and *vanguard* of the opposition. Soon as we found ourselves in possession of one post our artillery was turned against another; and as fast as the smoke of the enemy receded we advanced upon his lines.

The first piece that was written on the subject of the great position appeared from the pen of THOMAS CAMPBELL, Senior, in the year 1809. An association was formed that year for the dissemination of the principles of reformation; and the piece alluded to, was styled "The Declaration and Address of the *Christian Association* of Washington, Pennsylvania."

The constitutional principle of this "Christian Association" and its object are clearly expressed in the following resolution: — "That this society, formed for the sole purpose of promoting simple evangelical Christianity, shall, to the utmost of its power, countenance and support such ministers, and such only, as exhibit a manifest conformity to the *Original Standard,* in conversation and doctrine, in zeal and diligence; only such as reduce to practice the *simple original* form of Christianity, expressly exhibited upon the sacred page, without attempting to inculcate any thing of human authority, of private opinion, or inventions of men, as having any place in the constitution, faith, or worship of the Christian church; or any thing as matter of *Christian Faith* or duty for which there cannot be produced a *'thus saith the Lord,'* either in express terms or by approved precedent."

The ground occupied in this resolution afforded ample documents of debate. Every inch of it was debated, argued, canvassed for several years, in Pennsylvania, Virginia, and Ohio. On this bottom we put to sea, with scarcely hands enough to man the ship. We had head-winds and rough seas for the first seven years, a history of which would be both curious and interesting.

But, to contradistinguish this plea and effort from some others almost contemporaneous with it, we would emphatically remark, that, while the remonstrants warred against human creeds, evidently because those creeds warred against their own private opinions and favorite dogmas, which they wished to substitute for those creeds, — this enterprise, so far as it was hostile to those creeds, warred against them, not because of their hostility to and private or favorite opinions which were desired to be substituted for them, but because those human institutions supplanted the Bible, made the word of God of non-effect, were fatal to the intelligence, union, purity, holiness, and happiness of the disciples of Christ, and hostile to the salvation of the world.

Unitarians, for example, have warred against human creeds, because those creeds taught Trinitarianism. Arminians, too, have been hostile to creeds, because those creeds supported Calvinism. It has, indeed, been alleged that all schismatics, good and bad, since the days of John Wycliffe, and long before, have opposed creeds of human invention because those creeds opposed them. But so far as this controversy resembles them in its opposition to creeds, it is to be distinguished from them in this all-essential attribute, — viz.: that *our opposition to creeds arose from a conviction that, whether the opinion in them were true or false, they were hostile to the union, peace, harmony, purity, and joy of Christians, and adverse to the conversion of the world to Jesus Christ.*

Next to our personal salvation, two objects constituted the *summum bonum,* the supreme good, worthy of the sacrifice of all temporalities. The first was the union, peace, purity, and harmonious co-operation of Christians, guided by an understanding enlightened by the Holy Scriptures; the other the conversion of sinners to God. Our predilections and antipathies on all religious questions arose from, and were controlled by, those all-absorbing interests. From these commenced our campaign against creeds. We had not at first, and we have not now, a favorite opinion or speculation which we would offer as a substitute for any human creed or constitution in Christendom.

We were not, indeed, at first apprized of the havoc which our *principles* would make upon our *opinion.* We soon, however, found our principles and opinions at war on some points; and the question immediately arose, *whether shall we sacrifice our principles to our opinions, or our opinions to our principles?* We need not say that we were compelled to the latter, judging that our principles were better than our opinions. Hence, since we put to sea on board this bottom, we have been compelled to throw overboard some opinions once as dear to us as they now are to those who never thought of the difference between principle and opinion.

Some of those opinions (as the most delicate and tender buds are soonest blighted by the frost) immediately withered, and died under the first application of our principles. Infant baptism and infant sprinkling, with all infantile imbecility, immediately expired in our minds, soon as the *Bible alone* was made the only measure and standard of faith and duty. This foundation of the Pedobaptist temple being instantly destroyed, the whole edifice leaning upon it became a heap of ruins. We explored the ruins with great assiduity, and collected from them all the materials that could be worked into the Christian temple; but the piles of rubbish that remained were immense. . . .

The CHRISTIAN BAPTIST, in *seven* annual volumes, being the first of these publications, and affording such a *gradual* development of all these principles as the state of the public mind and the opposition would permit, is, in the judgment of many of our brethren who have expressed themselves on the subject, better adapted to the whole community as it now exists, than our other writings. In this judgment I must concur; and to it especially, as well as to all other publications since commenced, I would refer the reader who may be solicitous to examine these principles more fully, and to consider the ordeal through which they have passed.

Having paid a very candid and considerate regard to all that has been offered against these principles, as well as having been admonished from the extremes into which some of our friends and brethren have carried some points, I undertake this work with a deep sense of its necessity, and with much anticipation of its utility, in exhibiting a concentrated view of the whole ground we occupy, of rectifying some extremes, of furnishing new means of defense to those engaged in contending with this generation for primitive Christianity.

Having also attentively considered the most vulnerable side of every great question, and re-examined the terms and phrases which have occasioned most opposition and controversy, whether from our own pen or that of any of our brethren, our aim is now to offer to the public a more matured view of such cardinal principles as are necessary to the right interpretation of the Holy Scriptures, both in requiring and communicating a correct knowledge of the Christian Institution, of such principles as are requisite to the discovery of truth and the exposure of error, as well as in a revised and corrected republication of the principal Extras of the Millennial Harbinger, to lay before the reader the elements of the gospel itself, and of the worship most acceptable to God, through Jesus Christ our Lord.

[Alexander Campbell, *The Christian System* (Cincinnati: H. S. Bosworth, 1866), 3–11.]

28

James Milton Carroll

James Milton Carroll (1852–1931) was a prominent Texas Baptist pastor and college president. His contribution remains overshadowed by his more famous brother Benjamin Harvey Carroll (1843–1914), denominational leader and founding president of Southwestern Baptist Theological Seminary. Yet J. M. Carroll's pamphlet The Trail of Blood *left an enduring legacy among Baptists in the South and Southwest. Published posthumously in 1931,* The Trail of Blood *reproduced the successionist theory of Baptist origins that had been advanced a century earlier in G. H. Orchard's book* A Concise History of Baptists, *which was republished and distributed by Landmark firebrand J. R. Graves in 1855. The spirit of Landmarkism has been captured in the following verse:*

> *Not at the River Jordan,*
> *But in the flowing stream,*
> *Stood John the Baptist preacher*
> *When he baptized Him.*
>
> *John was a Baptist preacher*
> *When he baptized the Lamb;*
> *Then Jesus was a Baptist,*
> *And thus the Baptists came.*

According to Landmarkers, there is a direct baptismal succession of Baptist churches through the history of Christianity, which as Carroll suggests, is traced by a crimson trail of martyrs' blood. In this conviction he joins the Anabaptist writers of the Martyrs Mirror. *The Landmark successionist theory of apostolic origins, however, ran counter to the Campbellite claim that their churches alone restored primitive Christianity. Both were convictionally true. Neither was historically accurate.*

The Trail of Blood

I want now to call your attention to some of the landmarks, or ear-marks of this Religion — the Christian Religion. If you and I are to trace it down through 20 long centuries, and especially down through 1,200 years of midnight darkness, darkened by rivers and seas of martyr blood, then we will need to know well these marks. They will be many times terribly disfigured. But there will always be some indelible mark. But let us carefully and prayerfully beware. We will encounter many shams and make-believes. If possible, the very elect will be betrayed and deceived. We want, if possible, to trace it down through credible history, but more especially through the unerring, infallible, words and marks of Divine truth.

Some Unerring, Infallible Marks

If in going down through the centuries we run upon a group or groups of people bearing not these distinguishing marks and teaching other things for fundamental doctrines, let us beware.

1. Christ, the author of this Religion, organized His followers or disciples into a Church. And the disciples were to organize other churches as this Religion spread and other disciples were "made."

2. This organization or church, according to the Scriptures and according to the practice of the Apostles and early churches, was given two kinds of officers and only two — pastors and deacons. The pastor was called "Bishop." Both pastor and deacons to be selected by the church and to be servants of the church.

3. The churches in their government and discipline to be entirely separate and independent of each other. Jerusalem to have no authority over Antioch; nor Antioch over Ephesus; nor Ephesus over Corinth, and so forth. And their government to be congregational, democratic. A government of the people, by the people, and for the people.

4. To the church were given two ordinances and only two, Baptism and the Lord's Supper. These to be perpetual and memorial.

5. Only the "saved" were to be received as members of the church (Acts 2:47). These saved ones to be saved by grace alone without any works of the law (Eph. 2:5, 8, 9). These saved ones and they only, to be immersed in the name of the Father, Son and Holy Spirit (Matt. 28:19). And only those thus received and baptized, to partake of the Lord's Supper, and the supper to be celebrated only by the church, in church capacity.

6. The inspired scriptures, and they only, in fact, the New Testament and that only, to be the rule and guide of faith and life, not only for

the church as an organization, but for each individual member of that organization.

7. Christ Jesus, the founder of this organization and the savior of its members, to be their only priest and kin, their only Lord and Lawgiver, and the only head of the churches. The churches to be executive only in carrying out their Lord's will and completed laws, never legislative, to amend or abrogate old laws or to make new ones.

8. This Religion of Christ to be individual, personal, and purely voluntary or through persuasion. No physical or governmental compulsion. A matter of distinct individual and personal choice. "Choose you" is the scriptural injunction. It could be neither accepted nor rejected nor lived by proxy nor under compulsion.

9. Mark well! That neither Christ nor His apostles, ever gave to His followers, what is know today as a denominational name, such as "Catholic," "Lutheran," "Presbyterian," "Episcopal," and so forth — unless the name given by Christ to John was intended for such, "The Baptist," "John the Baptist" (Matt. 11:11 and 10 or 12 other times). Christ called the individual follower "disciple." Two or more were called "disciples." The organization of disciples, whether at Jerusalem or Antioch or elsewhere, was called Church. If more than one of these separate organizations were referred to, they were called Churches. The word church in the singular was never used when referring to more than one of these organizations. Nor even when referring to them all.

10. I venture to give one more distinguishing mark. We will call it — Complete separation of Church and State. No combination, no mixture of this spiritual Religion with a temper of "Religious Liberty," for everybody....

First Period A.D. 30–500

The first of these changes from New Testament teachings embraced both policy and doctrine. In the first two centuries the individual churches rapidly multiplied and some of the earlier ones, such as Jerusalem, Antioch, Ephesus, Corinth, etc., grew to be very large; Jerusalem, for instance, had many thousand members (Acts 2:41; 4:4, 5:14), possibly 25,000 or even 50,000 or more. A close student of the book of Acts and Epistles will see that Paul had a mighty task even in his day in keeping some of the churches straight. See Peter's and Paul's prophecies concerning the future (II Pet. 2:12; Acts 20:29–31. See also Rev., second and third chapters).

These great churches necessarily had many preachers or elders (Acts 20:17). Some of the bishops or pastors began to assume authority not given them in the New Testament. They began to claim authority over other and smaller churches. They, with their many elders, began to lord it over God's heritage (III John 9). Here was the beginning of an error which has grown and multiplied into many other seriously hurtful errors. Here was the beginning of different orders in the ministry running up finally to what is practiced now by others as well as Catholics. Here began what resulted in an entire change from the original democratic policy and government of the early churches. This irregularity began in a small way, even before the close of the second century. This was possibly the first serious departure from the New Testament church order.

Another vital change which seems from history to have had its beginning before the close of the second century was on the great doctrine of Salvation itself. The Jews as well as the Pagans, had for many generations, been trained to lay great stress on Ceremonials. They had come to look upon types as anti-types, shadows as real substances, and ceremonials as real saving agencies. How easy to come thus to look upon baptism. They reasoned thus: The Bible has much to say concerning baptism. Much stress is laid upon the ordinance and one's duty concerning it. Surely it must have something to do with one's salvation. So that it was in this period that the idea of "Baptismal Regeneration" began to get a fixed hold in some of the churches.

The next serious error to begin creeping in, and which seems from some historians (not all) to have begun in this same century and which may be said to have been an inevitable consequence of the "baptismal regeneration" idea, was a change in the subjects of baptism. Since baptism has been declared to be an agency or means to salvation by some erring churches, then the sooner baptism takes place the better. Hence arose "infant baptism." Prior to this "believers" and "believers" only, were regarded as proper subjects for baptism. "Sprinkling" and "pouring" are not now referred to. These came in much later. For several centuries, infants, like others, were immersed. The Greek Catholics (a very large branch of the Catholic church) up to this day, have never changed the original form of baptism. They practice infant baptism but have never done otherwise than immerse the children. . . .

Thus it will be noted that during the first three centuries three important and vital changes from the teachings of Christ and His Apostles had their beginnings. And one significant event took place. Note this summary and recapitulation:

1. The change from the New Testament idea of bishop and church government. This change grew rapidly, more pronounced, and complete and hurtful.

2. The change from the New Testament teachings as to Regeneration to "baptismal regeneration."

3. The change from "believers baptism" to "infant baptism." (This last, however, did not become general nor even very frequent for more than another century.)

"Baptismal regeneration" and "infant baptism." These two errors have, according to the testimony of well-established history, caused the shedding of more Christian blood, as the centuries have gone by, than all other errors combined, or than possibly have all wars, not connected with persecution, if you will leave out the recent "World War." Over 50,000,000 Christians died martyr deaths, mainly because of their rejection of these two errors during the period of the "dark ages" alone — about twelve or thirteen centuries.

Three significant facts, for a large majority of the many churches, are clearly shown by history during these first three centuries.

1. The separateness and independence of the Churches.

2. The subordinate character of bishops or pastors.

3. The baptism of believers only....

Up to this period, notwithstanding much and serious persecutions, Christianity has had a marvelous growth. It has covered and even gone beyond the great Roman Empire. Almost, if not all the inhabited world has heard the gospel. And, according to some of the church historians, many of the original churches organized by the Apostles are yet intact, and yet loyal to Apostolic teachings. However, as already shown, a number of very marked and hurtful errors have crept in and gotten a permanent hold among many of the churches. Some have become very irregular.

Persecutions have become increasingly bitter. Near the beginning of the fourth century comes possibly the first definite government edict of persecution. The wonderful growth of Christianity has alarmed the pagan leaders of the Roman Empire. Hence Galerius, the emperor, sent out a direct edict of more savage persecution. This occurred Feb. 24, 303 A.D. Up to this time Paganism seems to have persecuted without any definite laws to that effect.

But this edict failed so utterly in its purpose of stopping the growth of Christianity, that this same emperor, Galerius, just eight years thereafter (A.D. 311) passed another edict recalling the first and actually granting toleration — permission to live the Religion of Jesus Christ. This was probably its first favorable law.

By the beginning of the year A.D. 313, Christianity has won a mighty victory over paganism. A new emperor has come to the throne of the Roman Empire. He evidently recognized something of the mysterious power of this Religion that continued to grow in spite of persecution.

History says that this new emperor who was none other than Constantine had a wonderful realistic vision. He saw in the skies a fiery red cross and on that cross written in fiery letters these words — "By this thou shalt conquer." He interpreted it to mean that he should become a Christian. And that by giving up paganism and that by attaching the spiritual power of the Christian Religion onto the temporal power of the Roman Empire the world could be easily conquered. Thus the Christian Religion would in fact become a whole world Religion, and the Roman Empire a whole world empire.

So under the leadership of Emperor Constantine there comes a truce, a courtship and a proposal of marriage. The Roman Empire through its emperor seeks a marriage with Christianity. Give us your spiritual power and we will give you of our temporal power.

To effectually bring about and consummate this unholy union, a council was called. In A.D. 313, a call was made for a coming together of the Christian churches or their representatives. Many but not all came. The alliance was consummated. A Hierarchy was formed. In the organization of the Hierarchy, Christ was dethroned as head of the churches and Emperor Constantine enthroned (only temporarily, however) as head of the church.

The Hierarchy was the definite beginning of a development which finally resulted into what is now known as the Catholic, or "universal" church. It might be said that its indefinite beginnings were near the close of the second and beginning of the third century, when the new ideas concerning bishops and preacher church government began to take shape.

Let it be definitely remembered that when Constantine made his call for the council, there were very many of the Christians (Baptists) and of the churches, which declined to respond. They wanted no marriage with the state, and no centralized religious government, and no higher ecclesiastical government of any kind, than the individual church. These Christians (Baptists) nor the churches ever at that time or later, entered the hierarchy of the Catholic denomination.

Up to the organization of the Hierarchy and the uniting of church and state, all the persecution of Christianity has been done either by Judaism or Paganism. Now comes a serious change. Christians (in name) begin to persecute Christians. Constantine, desiring to have all Christians join with him in his new idea of a state Religion, and many conscientiously opposing this serious departure from New Testament teachings, he begins using the power of government to compel. Thus begin the days and years and even centuries of a hard and bitter persecution against all those Christians who were loyal to the original Christ and Apostolic teachings.

Remember that we are now noting the events occurring between the years A.D. 300 and 500. The Hierarchy organized under the leadership of Constantine, rapidly developed into what is now known as the Catholic church. This newly developing church joined to a temporal government, no longer simply an executive to carry out the completed laws of the New Testament, began to be legislative, amending or annulling old laws or enacting new ones utterly unknown to the New Testament.

One of the first of its legislative enactments, and one of the most subversive in its results, was the establishing by law of "infant baptism." By this new law, "Infant Baptism" becomes compulsory. This was done A.D. 416. Infants had been infrequently baptized for probably a century preceding this. Insofar as this newly enacted law became effective, two vital New Testament laws were abrogated — "Believers Baptism" and "Voluntary personal obedience in Baptism."

As an inevitable consequence of this new doctrine and law, these erring churches were soon filled with unconverted members. In fact, it was not very many years until probably a majority of the membership was composed of unconverted material. So the great spiritual affairs of God's great spiritual kingdom were in the hands of an unregenerate temporal power. What may now be expected? . . .

The course followed by the loyal churches soon, of course, incurred the hot displeasure of the state Religionists, many, if not most of whom, were not genuine Christians. The name "Christian," however, was from now on denied those loyal churches who refused to accept these new errors. They were robbed of that, and called by many other names, sometimes by one and sometimes by another, "Montanist," "Tertullianists," "Novationists," "Paterines," etc., and some at least because of their practice of rebaptizing those who were baptized in infancy, were referred to as "Ana Baptists." . . .

Now to sum up the most significant events of this first five-century period:

1. The gradual change from a democracy to a preacher-church government.

2. The change from salvation by grace to Baptismal Salvation.

3. The change from "believers' baptism" to "infant baptism."

4. The Hierarchy organized. Marriage of church and state.

5. Seat of empire changed to Constantinople.

6. Infant baptism established by law and made compulsory.

7. Christians begin to persecute Christians.

8. The "Dark Ages" begin 426.

9. The sword and torch rather than the gospel become the power of God (?) unto salvation.

10. All semblance of "Religious Liberty" dies and is buried and remains buried for many centuries.

11. Loyal New Testament churches, by whatever name called, are hunted and hounded to the utmost limit of the new Catholic temporal power. Remnants scattered over the world are finding uncertain hiding places in forests and mountains, valleys, dens and caves of the earth....

[J. M. Carroll, *The Trail of Blood* (Lexington, Ky.: Ashland Baptist Church, 1931), 8–19]

– 29 –

Nat Turner

Crazed killer or legendary hero? What is often lost in the denigration and celebration of Nat Turner (1800–31) is the supremely religious character of the man who inspired the slave rebellion of 1831 in Southampton County, Virginia. Stephen Oates observes that Turner "grew to manhood with the words of the prophets roaring in his ears" (The Fires of Jubilee, 26). He spent many hours in prayer and fasting and was known as "the Prophet." As he searched the Scriptures, Nat discovered that proslavery preachers had overlooked warrants against enslavement (e.g., Exodus 21:16; Deuteronomy 24:7). Although he was never officially received into or ordained by any organized church, Nat Turner identified himself as a Baptist preacher. In 1827 he baptized himself and a notorious white sinner in the waters of Pearson's Mill Pond. Turner denounced the injustice of slavery and warned of impending judgment that would precede the coming Jubilee. A series of apocalyptic visions confirmed his reading of Scripture. A solar eclipse in February 1831 and sun spots in August of the same year were taken as signs that Judgment Day was at hand. Turner and his followers marched toward Jerusalem, the county seat of Southampton, to "slay utterly old and young, both maids, and little children, and women" (Ezekiel 9:6). This was the same biblical text cited by the militant Anabaptists at Münster three centuries earlier. The end was no less tragic. In all about sixty whites and an estimated two hundred blacks were killed. The insurrectionists including Turner were captured and hanged. Along with Anne Hutchinson, Turner contributes to the mystical and prophetic streams of Baptist theology, though he joined many others in rejecting nonviolence. The following selection is part of his confessions, given to attorney Thomas Gray. Although certainly not Turner's exact words, it truthfully represents his theological standpoint.

I Had a Vision

Having soon discovered to be great, I must appear so, and therefore studiously avoided mixing in society, and wrapped myself in mystery,

241

devoting my time to fasting and prayer — By this time, having arrived
to man's estate, and hearing the scriptures commented on at meetings, I
was struck with that particular passage which says: "Seek ye the kingdom of Heaven and all things shall be added unto you." I reflected much
on this passage, and prayed daily for light on this subject — As I was
praying one day at my plough, the spirit spoke to me, saying, "Seek ye
the kingdom of Heaven and all things shall be added unto you. Question — what do you mean by the Spirit? Ans. The Spirit that spoke to
the prophets in former days — and I was greatly astonished, and for two
years prayed continually, whenever my duty would permit — and then
again I had the same revelation, which fully confirmed me in the impression that I was ordained for some great purpose in the hands of the
Almighty. Several years rolled round, in which many events occurred to
strengthen me in this my belief. At this time I reverted in my mind to
the remarks made of me in my childhood, and the things that had been
shown me — and as it had been said of me in my childhood by those by
whom I had been taught to pray, both white and black, and in whom
I had the greatest confidence, that I had too much sense to be raised,
and if I was, I would never be of any use to any one as a slave. Now
finding I had arrived to man's estate, and was a slave, and these revelations being made known to me, I began to direct my attention to this
great object, to fulfil the purpose for which, by this time, I felt assured
I was intended. Knowing the influence I had obtained over the minds
of my fellow servants, (not by the means of conjuring and such like
tricks — for to them I always spoke of such things with contempt) but
by the communion of the Spirit whose revelations I often communicated
to them, and they believed and said my wisdom came from God. I now
began to prepare them for my purpose, by telling them something was
about to happen that would terminate in fulfilling the great promise that
had been made to me — About this time I was placed under an overseer,
from whom I ran away — and after remaining in the woods thirty days,
I returned, to the astonishment of the negroes on the plantation, who
thought I had made my escape to some other part of the country, as my
father had done before. But the reason of my return was, that the Spirit
appeared to me and said I had my wishes directed to the things of this
world, and not to the kingdom of Heaven, and that I should return to
the service of my earthly master — "For he who knoweth his Master's
will, and doeth it not, shall be beaten with many stripes, and thus have
I chastened you." And the negroes found fault, and murmured against
me, saying that if they had my sense they would not, serve any master in the world. And about this time I had a vision — and I saw white
spirits and black spirits engaged in battle, and the sun was darkened —
the thunder rolled in the Heavens, and blood flowed in streams — and I
heard a voice saying, "Such is your luck, such you are called to see, and

let it come rough or smooth, you must surely bare it." I now withdrew myself as much as my situation would permit, from the intercourse of my fellow servants, for the avowed purpose of serving the Spirit more fully — and it appeared to me, and reminded me of the things it had already shown me, and that it would then reveal to me the knowledge of the elements, the revolution of the planets, the operation of tides, and changes of the seasons. After this revelation in the year 1825, and the knowledge of the elements being made known to me, I sought more than ever to obtain true holiness before the great day of judgment should appear, and then I began to receive the true knowledge of faith. And from the first steps of righteousness until the last, was I made perfect; and the Holy Ghost was with me, and said, "Behold me as I stand in the Heavens" — and I looked and saw the forms of men in different attitudes — and there were lights in the sky to which the children of darkness gave other names than what they really were — for they were the lights of the Saviour's hands, stretched forth from east to west, even as they were extended on the cross on Calvary for the redemption of sinners. And I wondered greatly at these miracles, and prayed to be informed of a certainty of the meaning thereof — and shortly afterwards, while laboring in the field, I discovered drops of blood on the corn as though it were dew from heaven — and I communicated it to many, both white and black, in the neighborhood — and I then found on the leaves in the woods hieroglyphic characters, and numbers, with the forms of men in different attitudes, portrayed in blood, and representing the figures I had seen before in the heavens. And now the Holy Ghost had revealed itself to me, and made plain the miracles it had shown me — For as the blood of Christ had been shed on this earth, and had ascended to heaven for the salvation of sinners, and was now returning to earth again in the form of dew — and as the leaves on the trees bore the impression of the figures I had seen in the heavens, it was plain to me that the Saviour was about to lay down the yoke he had borne for the sins of men, and the great day of judgment was at hand. About this time I told these things to a white man, (Etheldred T. Brantley) on whom it had a wonderful effect — and he ceased from his wickedness, and was attacked immediately with a coetaneous eruption; and blood oozed from the pores of his skin, and after praying and fasting nine days, he was healed, and the Spirit appeared to me again, and said, as the Saviour had been baptised so should we be also — and when the white people would not let us be baptised by the church, we went down into the water together, in the sight of many who reviled us, and were baptised by the Spirit — After this I rejoiced greatly, and gave thanks to God. And on the 12th of May, 1828, I heard a loud noise in the heavens, and the Spirit instantly appeared to me and said the Serpent was loosened, and Christ had laid down the yoke he had borne for the sins of men, and that I should take it on and fight against the Serpent, for the time was fast approaching when the first should be last and the last should be first. Ques. Do you not find yourself mistaken now? Ans. Was not Christ crucified? And by signs in the heavens that it would make known to me when I should commence the great work — and until the first sign appeared, I should conceal it from the knowledge of men — And on the appearance of the sign, (the eclipse of the sun last February) I should arise and prepare myself, and slay my enemies with their own weapons.

[Thomas R. Gray, *The Confessions of Nat Turner* (Baltimore: Lucas and Deaver, 1831).]

30

Rufus Perry

In the antebellum Southern United States, white preachers and slave-owners justified slavery as a divinely ordained institution. One of the popular biblical texts used to support their view was the curse of Canaan (Genesis 9:25–27). Since Canaan was supposed to be the ancestor of the (Hamitic) Negro people, servitude was their station in life. Into such a world Rufus Perry (1834–95) was born a slave in Smith County, Tennessee. Yet he refused to allow this stigmatizing theology to determine his life. When Perry was eighteen, he escaped to Canada. He was converted in 1854 and began preparation for the Christian ministry at Kalamazoo (Michigan) Theological Seminary with the class of 1861. Later that same year he was ordained as the pastor of the Second Baptist Church of Ann Arbor and went on to minister in three other churches in Canada and the United States. He served as editor, publisher, and denominational leader in the Consolidated American Baptist Missionary Convention, a short-lived merger between the American Baptist Missionary Convention and the Western and Southern Missionary Baptist Convention that began 1866 and lapsed in 1877. In his magisterial work, The Cushite *(1893), Perry argued that prejudice, rooted in poor theology, is dependent on bad history. If, as he believed, it could be demonstrated "that the ancient Egyptians, Ethiopians and Libyans . . . were the ancestors of the present race of Ham, then the Negro of the nineteenth century may point to them with pride; and . . . cherish the hope of a return to racial celebrity, when in the light of a Christian civilization, Ethiopia shall stretch out her hands unto God"* (The Cushite, *x). Only now has the wisdom of his insight come of age.*

Prejudice against the Negro Modern

That prejudice which arrays itself against the Negro, subjecting good citizens of this race to insult, mean injustice, and the most cruel forms of outrage, is of modern date and American nativity. It is not innate, else it would have always existed, and similarly operated among all other peoples. It is not a cause, but rather an effect whose cause is the Negro's condition and modern history. His color serves only as an immediate and constant expose of his ethnical identity. Otherwise the blame, if any, were with the Creator, and that prejudice were absolute and not blameworthy.

Between racial affinity and racial prejudice, there is a wide distinction. The one is born of God; the other is born of the devil. The works of the one are benevolent; the works of the other, malevolent. This affinity may prefer what is more homogeneous to what is more foreign without injustice to the unpreferred; and this it always does except in cases of anomalous exception. On the other hand, racial prejudice, when unbridled or unresisted, irrationally rejects, arrogantly dominates, and mercilessly abuses those against whom it is directed. It is wholly a creature of circumstance. It may be generated and fostered by Religion, as in the case of the Jews; by condition, as in the case of the Negro and the Indian; or by national custom, as in the case of the Chinese. But it is an anthropological malady that may be cured, else the Christian doctrine of redemption is a farce. There are two panaceas or remedies. One is the possession of a pure Christianity; the other is a removal of the cause by a favorable change of condition.

The Ethiopian has regarded white as a symbol of impurity and unrighteousness. The white man, on the other hand has so regarded black. The Ethiopian says: "as white as the devil." The white man says: "as black as the devil." The Ethiopian, three hundred years ago, painted Christ and the Virgin Mary black; but wicked men and devils, he painted white. Christ in his Passion he painted black; but Judas, Annas, Caiaphas, Pilate, Herod, and the Jews, he painted white. He painted Michael black; but the devil, white. (See Dr. Russell's *History of Nubia and Abyssinia,* p. 275). This shows that color, as a symbol of purity and justice, is arbitrary and unphilosophical, and merely accommodative in its racial application.

When the Cushite, as a race, shall again excel or equal the white man in learning and material acquisition, then, as in the days of his ancient celebrity, he will find no trouble on account of his color. Or, when the white man shall have become Christianized according to the letter and spirit of the New Testament, then he will see the meaning and feel the force of fatherhood in God and brotherhood in man, whether the man be European, Asiatic or African; whether he be white, yellow, or black.

The student of history can explore the whole field of ancient literature without finding anything more disparaging to the Negro than to others. In an inaugural address delivered January 5th, 1881, by Edward Wilmot Blyden., LL.D., president of Liberia College, he says:

I have noticed a few lines from Virgil, describing a Negress of the lower class, which are made to do duty on all occasions when the modern traducers of the Negro would draw countenance for their theories from the classical writers; but similar descriptions of the lower European races abound in their own literature. The lines are the following, used by Nott and Gliddon, and recently quoted by Dr. Winchell:

> Interdum clamat Cybalen; erat unica custos;
> Afra genus, tote patriam testante figura;
> Torta comam, labroque tumens, et fusca colorem,
> Pectore lata, jacens mammis, compressior alvo,
> Cruribus exilis, spatiosa prodiga planta;
> Continuis rimis calcanea scissa rigebant.

[Meanwhile he calls Cybale. She was his only (house) keeper. African by race, her whole figure attesting her fatherland; with crisped hair, swelling lip, and dark complexion; broad in chest, with pendant dugs and very contracted abdomen; with spindle shanks and broad enormous feet; her lacerated heels were rigid with continuous cracks.]

But hear how Homer, Virgil's superior and model, sings the praises of the Negro Euryabates, who signalized himself at the siege of Troy:

> A reverend herald in his train I knew,
> Of visage solemn, sad, but cable hue.
> Short *woolly curls* o'er-fleeced his bending head,
> O'er which a promontory shoulder spread.
> Euryabates, in whose large soul alone,
> Ulysses viewed an image of his own.

Dr. Blyden was urging the study of the Greek and Latin languages and literature as preferable instruments of culture; saying that "in those languages there is not, as far as I know, a sentence, a word, or a syllable disparaging to the Negro. He may get nourishment from them without taking in any race poison. They will perform no sinister work upon consciousness, and give no unholy bias to his inclinations." The ancient Assyrians and Persians, the Greeks and Romans all had a proper respect for the ethnological peculiarities of the Cushite.

When Darius of Persia feasted the magnates of his hundred and twenty-seven provinces, — the rulers of the Medes, the princes of Persia, and the generals of the Armies, he did not slight the distinguished men of India and Ethiopia. They too sat at his table and ate and drank to their satiety, (*Joseph. Antiq.* xi. 3, 2). On the day of Pentecost, there were at Jerusalem, among the many strangers, Egyptians and Libyans from the neighborhood of Cyrene. They were not Jews of the line of

Shem, whose tongue was Hebrew, else they would not have been numbered with those foreigners who heard the Apostles speak in their own tongues, wherein they were born, "the wonderful works of God." It is more probable that they were African Cushites, against whose physical nature no man of that age was stupid and impious enough to take exception.

Retrospection

From what has been shown, there is sufficient warrant for the conclusion:

1. That the ancient Cushite, the progenitor of the modern Negro, led the world for centuries in all that related to civilization and human progress. To this fact the holy scriptures bear testimony in saying (Acts vii. 22) that "Moses was learned in all the wisdom of the Egyptians, and was mighty in words and in deeds." This Egyptian learning came into Egypt from Ethiopia and went from Egypt into other parts of the world.

2. That the art of war, that prowess in man hunting inaugurated by Nimrod in the land of Shinar, soon reappeared in Ethiopia and, descending the Nile into Lower Egypt, there, as in Ethiopia, formed itself into a kind of military academy for the world, and subsequently sent out a Sesostris terrible in war, and a Shishak as skilled and brave as any general of the ancient Asiatic or European nations; or as any of the nineteenth century, not excepting Napoleon in Europe or Washington in America.

3. That the art of writing, originating first in pictorial symbols and then developing into phonetic characters, was imported by the Cushite priests of Ethiopia into Egypt; and from there they found their way to Phoenicia, Mesopotamia, Greece and other countries, finally returning to Egypt an alphabet of finer finish.

4. That religious thought, civil law, mechanical art and the science of medicine were all of like origin. The art of embalming the dead was a special department of medical science in which the Cushite physicians of Egypt excelled. Their embalming was so skillfully done that even now, after a lapse of more than three thousand years, it remains a witness to their scientific knowledge.

5. That, looking back over the centuries from the Christian era to Noah, and noting the rise and fall of great men and great nations we see none more conspicuous than the children of Ham. Greece had her Athens, and could boast of Homer, Herodotus, Plato, Solon, Socrates, and Demosthenes, and a host of other poets, historians, philosophers and orators, and of her great Alexander. Persia had her Cyrus the Great, her Cambyses, her Darius and her religious Zoroaster; China had her great cities walled in so that nothing could come in or go out but the

theosophic philosophy of her deified Confucius; Rome had her noted patricians, and, like Greece, her poets, orators, historians and generals, and begat for herself a great name; but before all these is the land of Ham, of Cush and the Cushite; the land chosen of God in which to train his peculiar people, and as a city of refuge for His own Son when Herod sought to slay him.

Africa had her Cushite Meroë, her Thebes, her Memphis, her sciences and her wonderful works of art; she had a great commercial traffic with the nations of the East, borne from country to country by numerous caravans. She had her high priests, whose sacred hieroglyphics bespoke their reverence for their gods. She had a thousand thousand soldiers, infantry and cavalry, with generals of unequalled prowess; she had her astronomers, physicians, and wise men, men of deeds rather than of words, of actions rather than of theory. She had her Sesostris, her Memnon, her Shishak, her Zerah, her Nitocris, her Queen of Sheba, her Candaces, and her long line of great Pharaohs mentioned in the sacred Scriptures. She had her Hannibal and her Terence, the one distinguished for being the greatest general with whom the Romans ever measured swords, and the other for giving polish to the Roman tongue, and for giving expression to a philanthropic sentiment, than which even the Christian age produces nothing grander: *"Homo Sum, humani nil a me alienum puto"* (I am a man, and I consider nothing foreign to me that relates to man). This brief expression, just eight words, contains all the law and the prophets, and it is as precious as the "golden rule" of sacred writ.

Now what the Cushite was, certainly has some bearing on an intelligent judgment of what he is, and is to be. It should inspire him with an ambition to emulate his forefathers; for if to the memory of the distinguished Negroes of modern times we add the historic facts reaching from Menes to the Christian era attesting the greatness of the ancient Cushites, of whom we are lineal descendants, it were pusillanimous in us, and dishonoring to our ancestors, to be ashamed of either our color or our name.

[Rufus L. Perry, *The Cushite: The Descendants of Ham from Noah to the Christian Era* (Springfield, Mass.: Willey and Co., 1893), 154–61.]

31

William Bishop Johnson

*In the late nineteenth century, African American Baptists were, as James Melvin Washington observes, a "frustrated fellowship" (*Frustrated Fellowship, *Macon, Ga.: Mercer University Press, 1986). They were frustrated by the racism that excluded them from equal participation in the two major white Baptist denominations. The racism of Southern Baptists was overt as they demanded that the "inferior" Negro people accept the supremacy of their white brethren. The racism of Northern Baptists was more covert, but their inaction equally failed to welcome black churches into their ranks. In the meantime, African American Baptists remained divided into several competing conventions. In 1894, from the pages of* The National Baptist Magazine, *which he served as editor, and from the pulpit of the Second Baptist Church of Washington, D.C., where he held forth as pastor, William Bishop Johnson (1858–?) began to call for a union of this frustrated fellowship. The result was the formation of the National Baptist Convention in 1895. A graduate of Wayland Seminary in Richmond, Virginia, Johnson returned as a professor in 1882, and he remained a champion of theological education for African Americans. The sermon "The Scourging of a Race" captures Johnson's vision of racial and spiritual unity in the gospel. He develops his message with a typological reading of the biblical text. The Negro people are Israel. The years of wilderness wandering are the forty years since emancipation. Adversity is God's scourge. It is a wonderful example of the baptist vision: "a trope of mystical identity binding the story now to the story then, and the story then and now to God's future yet to come"(McClendon,* Doctrine, *45).*

The Scourging of a Race

The hour of trial is upon us. Nearly forty years have rolled into the deathless past and the American Negro has contributed his part to the world's civilization, and to the peace and progress of the American people, under the most discouraging and humiliating conditions that have confronted any people in all history. It will be conceded that the peculiar economic and social surroundings of the Negro American are not of his making. He was made an element in the life of this republic without his consent and has for nearly three hundreds years' residence in this country been a source of solicitude, a problematical quantity in our national equation, which we seem as far from satisfactorily solving to-day as when we first commenced its solution....

The mighty achievements of the Negro stand like the granite walls of a Gibraltar; the silent and permanent progress he is still making, in spite of all obstacles thrown in his way, will be written up by some future historian. It is with the present I wish to deal. Nearly forty years of freedom find us more heavily burdened than ever. Before our eyes, we have seen swept away, everything that stands for citizenship, and that helps to make a people happy and prosperous. Now, why should the Negro be scourged so unmercifully after these years of sacrifice and service, in a land he has helped to enrich, and which he still helps to beautify and maintain?...

"When a man's ways please the Lord He maketh even his enemies to be at peace with him." Do the ways of the race please the Lord? God is in all history, and all history has a unit because God is in it. Providence is the light of history and the soul of the world. It is only when we see God in history that we get at its clear significance and truth. God's providence is the golden thread that passes through the entire web of human destiny and gives it its strength and beauty and consistency.

National calamities mean more than individual ones, because they affect a wider circle, since nations represent more than the individual. Nations live longer than individuals, hence they make a record, more stable and lasting; their positions as creators of ideals and sentiment is vastly more far-reaching than the individual. What is true of nations is also true to a lesser extent of races. Now, when God deals with a nation or race, and permits that race to prosper or retrograde, he has some mighty object in view — either that of punishment or reward. Whatever punishment God extends to individuals or nations, on earth, is intended for their reformation, not always their utter destruction. If they hear and repent, God will be merciful to them and help them. If they persist in their evil course, God will utterly destroy them or cut them short of their glory. God punishes nations on earth; individuals in eternity.

This was true with God's dealing with the Egyptians, Babylonians, Grecians, Romans, and especially so of the Israelites, whose history during the forty years migration in the wilderness I have selected as a parallel of the Negro's forty years of meanderings in the land of freedom. I find many parallel lines and I shall show how God scourged Israel forty years....

Their disobedience was so marked, the forgetfulness of God so frequent, that only Caleb and Joshua were permitted to see the promised land, after forty years of toil, privation, sorrow, danger, disappointment, death, and expectancy in the wilderness. Truly,

> God moves in a mysterious way,
> His wonders to perform,
> He plants his footsteps on the sea,
> And rides upon the storm.

There is a close analogy between God's dealing with Israel and his way with the Negro, especially since emancipation. We all know in the dark, dark days of slavery, our mothers and fathers called upon the God of heaven to be liberated. They wanted to breathe liberty's atmosphere, and they promised God to serve him, even better, when slavery's chain had been bursted and they could worship him under their own vine and fig tree. We also know how *Providence* brought the creation of sentiment in the republic against slavery.

God is still with us. His sleepless eye is ever upon us. His arms, everlasting, are still around us. He is still our Sun and Shield. He still gives grace and glory. No good thing does he withhold from those who walk uprightly. But while God loves us still, we must not forget his word, which says, "Whom the Lord loveth, he chastened."

Let us look at the evils that have overtaken us as a people in the last few years and see if God is not permitting our enemies to scourge us as he did Israel. God has no new way to deal with nations or races. He says, "If any man will serve me, him will my father honor." And this honor is to be conferred in life as well as in death.

> The hill of Zion yields
> A thousand sacred sweets,
> Before we reach the heavenly fields,
> Or walk the golden streets.

He has been applying this rule of service and reward, since our first parents stood amidst Eden's bowers; clad in innocency and dwelling in perpetual union with their God.

What is the scourge he is using to bring the Negro Race to duty? No one will deny that we are forgetting God; we have spent too much time with the development of the intellect at the expense of our moral and spiritual natures. God has made man a symmetrical being — put within him a trinity of forces — the intellect, will, sensibilities. He intended that no man should be properly trained until all these forces had been governed and disciplined. He intends that the mighty powers of the soul should be directed to God and his law that the heart should be made responsive to duty to God and man. . . .

The attempt of our enemies to humiliate, crush, and destroy the Negro, is one way God is applying the scourge to the race. In every section of this country race hatred and prejudice is on the increase. In many places where its poisonous breath has never been felt before; in sections, noted, heretofore, for fairness and justice, it has forced men to forget the common laws of humanity, and join the howling mob that cries, "Down with the Negro!" "Kill him!" "Lynch him!"

The fact that in all the South, vitiated and devilish public sentiment born of ignorance and sectional prejudice has placed upon the statute books laws that force the railway companies to provide a separate coach for Negroes; and that puts no premium upon *respectability* nor *financial worth,* but says to the immoral, criminal, and diseased, "Go mingle with the moral purity, best brain and character of your race; huddle in the dirt and filth of a separate coach, and pay the same fare as those who ride in a luxurious adjoining car," and this in a country of boasted liberty; the friend of suffering humanity abroad, while festering crowds are suffering within our own gates.

This legislation intended to humiliate the best Negro; to crush his manhood and destroy his race pride, is the scourge in the hands of the Almighty, driving the Negroes together and preparing them to surprise the world in racial unity and self-protection.

The disenfranchisement of the Negro, by which he is reduced to a political nonentity, is another scourge with which God is whipping the Negro to acquire property and education. It is simply making him a stronger man in the community, and while it robs him of the badge of citizenship, it brings him to the point where he finds it to his advantage to build character and make himself so thoroughly an essential element of progress and prosperity that an exalted public sentiment will be created against this relic of human selfishness, American prejudice and race legislation, which will bring the South to its senses and sweep it forever from among a people whose declaration of independence declares all men "free and equal."

Such *legislation as Jim Crow car laws* cannot live long among a free people and at this stage of civilization that is everywhere putting a premium upon *worth,* not color; upon *character,* rather than accident of birth. The fact that *the Negro is not secure in his life and property,* but is ruthlessly lynched under any pretext or exiled from home because he has an opinion and expressed it, is another scourge. That such an appalling sentiment could exist; such a dangerous and deadly unwritten law could be sustained, in a country like this, shows an unjust and wicked public sentiment that sustains it. Here are the courts that guarantee a fair and impartial trial to the humblest citizen, ignored and a state of anarchy and mob violence placed in their stead. Men administer law to suit themselves, in the face of duly appointed administrators, appointed by the State and elected by the suffrages of the people.

There are but few places in America where the lives and property of Negroes are secure. The civilized world knows this. Our fame as a nation of lynchers, who does not believe in the courts we, ourselves, have established, but resorts to lawlessness and murder is international universal. This lawless spirit among us takes the American people out of the list of humanitarians and classifies them with the Russian Massacre, Chinese Boxers, and African Cannibals. Lynching is now an American pastime. And no one can tell when the most representative Negro will be subjected to the noose or provide a roast for a howling mob.

All this makes the Negro unhappy and creates in him a temptation to be unpatriotic when the nation's life is in danger and puts him out of harmony with everything American. The Negroes do not intend to leave America, and the American people might as well arrange to take him along. Assimilate them as a part of the people; and let them go up or down upon their own merits. If they cannot stand the severe pressure of competition with other people; if they have not in them the natural qualities that can fight resistance, legitimate resistance; if they cannot stand the crucial fires, along with others, then they ought to die and be forgotten.

God is permitting all this lawlessness, this flagrant injustice, this ingratitude of the American people for the Negroes, who gave their lives to save this country against the white men who plotted to ruin it; God permits these things to come upon us, that we may be made perfect through suffering and ready for the battle that will come some day in this country between right and wrong; between the weak and strong. Because a race is once backward is no sign it will always be so. Japan is an illustration of how "a little one may become a thousand," and how that same little one will some day surprise the world.

The American people are as unreasonable as they are unjust. They damn us if we do; and they damn us if we don't do. The Negro has reduced his illiteracy at a greater rate than any other people. He has shown that an education does for him what it does for every man — makes him conscious of his relation to others; improves his condition; makes him a better citizen and a nobler man. And yet we are told the educated Negro is a failure, and that education unfits him for service. Whatever may be the criminal record of the race in this country, it is not made up of the educated Negroes.

They have not contributed to the prison houses and the great army of those who care not for law and order. The door of opportunity has been closed and barred in their faces, and they have been denied the smallest chance to succeed among the people, yet we find them in possession of sterling character, church, school, and private property; their homes are models of refinement and their children clothed in neat and becoming apparel. Can the Anglo-Saxon say as much? Does he forget the large percentage of educated criminals, who hold positions of public trust? Are there annals yet to be told of those who languish in prison cells because of the malfeasance in office of those who hold positions of public trust? Is there another people, judging from grand jury indictments, and judicial decisions, who hold a more just title to outlawry, thievery, bribery, embezzlement, robbery, murder, and every other crime found in the catalogue of criminology than the white people, and do not the educated classes among them find a large representation in jails and prisons?

Now, if education ruins, whom does it ruin, the *Negro,* or the *white man?* No one need worry about the Negro and his education; he has such a fine start up the steeps of knowledge, that only God can hinder them from reaching the Pierian heights. All these evils are the scourge of the Almighty, provoking the Negro to a larger faith in God, and a more devout Christian life and service. The lives of our fathers were marked by prayer to God for direction and protection. The lives of their children must be characterized by the same. It means heaven's sympathy; heaven's assistance; heaven's protection.

The hour has come when the race must fall upon its knees and in the name of that God that hears the cries of the oppressed; that Christ whose sacred heart is filled with sympathy and whose holy and omnific arm is always outstretched in behalf of those who love him, and who declares no weapon formed against us shall prosper, and every tongue that rises in judgment shall be condemned — call, with unwavering faith, for help against the mighty; against those who fill the earth with widows and cause the orphan's heart to bleed.

When a man's ways please the Lord he maketh even his enemies to be at peace with him. See to it that our *ways* please the Lord. That the heart beat of the race is in union with God and in harmony with his law. See to it that no other gods shall take the place of him who weigheth the mountains in scales and the hills in a balance and who meteth out the heavens with a span and holdeth the waters in the hollow of his hand. Let us turn our faces toward the God of heaven, acknowledging our sins and finding forgiveness in the blood of a crucified Redeemer.

Then shall our enemies turn from us; then shall the Lord return to Zion and everlasting songs of deliverance shall be upon our tongue; and the desert and solitary place shall clap their hands and men shall beat their swords into ploughshares and their spears into pruning hooks. Nation shall not lift up sword against Nation, neither shall they learn war any more. And the loftiness of man shall be bowed down and the haughtiness of men shall be made low and the Lord alone shalt be exalted in that day.

[William Bishop Johnson, *The Scourging of a Race*, 7th ed. (Washington, D.C.: Beresford, Printer, 1904), 1–17.]

– 32 –

Curtis Lee Laws

Born in Loudoun County, Virginia, and educated at Crozer Theological Seminary, Curtis Lee Laws (1868–1946) was a pastor, editor, and denominational leader. He served two prominent pastorates: the First Baptist Church of Baltimore, Maryland (1893–1908), where he became famous for his widely distributed sermon "The Fiery Furnace and Soul Liberty" and the Greene Avenue Baptist Church of Brooklyn, New York (1908–13). In that sermon preached in 1904, Laws commended the civil disobedience of English baptists (conservatives and liberals) who suffered together for their resistance against the use of tax revenues to promote sectarian teaching. When Laws became the editor of the Watchman Examiner *in 1913 (a position he held until 1938), it enjoyed the largest circulation of any Baptist periodical in the North and established him as a trusted voice of historic Baptist principles. Concerned about the advance of liberalism in seminaries and churches, Laws and others issued a call for a conference on the fundamentals of New Testament faith just prior to the 1920 meeting of the Northern Baptist Convention in Buffalo, New York. In his reporting of the "side lights" of that convention, Laws coined the term* fundamentalist *for those "who still cling to the great fundamentals and who mean to do battle royal" for the faith. Yet he was far from the spirit of fundamentalism that E. J. Carnell later described as orthodoxy grown cultic. Laws' definition of fundamentalism was deliberately broad, not divisively narrow. It required neither inerrancy nor dispensationalism — the growing shibboleths of antimodernists. Fundamentalism, for Laws, was essentially an attempt to reaffirm theological orthodoxy and promote biblical Christianity. These aims were not unlike those of Pope Pius X in his condemnation of modernism. But in contrast to the more factious voices in the fundamentalist movement of W. B. Riley, T. T. Shields, and J. Frank Norris, Laws was ever a denominational loyalist who believed that "Baptists ought to be big enough and wise enough and Christ-like enough to discuss all their differences in the fear of God and in the spirit of Christ."*

The Fiery Furnace and Soul Liberty

To celebrate the destruction of Jerusalem and his victory over the nation of Judah, Nebuchadnezzar, King of Babylon, set up a golden image
in the plain outside the city. Its immensity and grandeur were designed
to display the power and dominion of Babylon and its god. When
all the Babylonian officials had assembled for the dedication of this
colossus, a herald proclaimed that, by edict of the king, all the people
should bow down and worship this image at the sound of the music.
But the three friends and associates of Daniel could not be cajoled or
coerced into obedience to this command of the king. As in the days
of the apostles, these Jewish heroes hesitated not an instant between
obedience to the law of God and to the command of the king. They
courteously but courageously said to the tyrannical king: "O king, we
have no need to answer thee in this matter. If you fulfill your threat,
our God whom we serve is able to deliver us from the burning fiery
furnace, and He will deliver us out of thy hands, O king. But if not,
be it known unto thee, O king, that we will not serve thy god, nor
worship the golden image which thou hast set up" (Dan. 3:16–18).
This is a bold and heroic declaration of soul liberty. They were dealing with an unenlightened heathen king. In his wrath he threw them
into the fiery furnace. They were willing to suffer for their convictions,
but they were not willing to live contrary to their convictions. Their
God delivered them from their peril, and so our God, who is "the
same yesterday, today and forever" (Heb. 13:8), will, in His own good
time and by methods of His own choosing, deliver His people who
are willing to suffer rather than to abandon the truth.... [Laws then
traces the heritage of religious liberty from the days of the Anabaptists
forward.]

Religious Liberty Imperiled

A fortnight ago, in a sermon preached from this pulpit, I incidentally referred to the combined efforts of the English Parliament and the Church
of England to crush out the free churches of England and Wales, and I
called upon the Archbishop of Canterbury, now visiting in this country,
to enlighten our people upon this return to mediaeval barbarism upon
the part of the great religious body of which he is the head. My exact
words were these:

> The Archbishop of Canterbury, as the primate of all England and
> the head of the establishment, is largely responsible for the sec-
> tarian education law, and being in this country he has a good

opportunity to teach us his authority for the adoption of a system which is contrary to all laws of justice and contrary to the will of God — a system which seeks to control the individual conscience. Thank God for the non-conformists, and that there are thousands in England today who would die at the stake rather than be forced to submit to the dictation of the established Church, of the king and of the Parliament when their deliverances are contrary to the plain teaching of God's word. It is generally thought that religious liberty has been attained in all countries of high civilization, and the Archbishop of Canterbury will find little sympathy among the American ministers and laymen of the Protestant Episcopal Church for a law which is a disgrace to the great Christian body of which he is the head.

I meant no personal discourtesy to the Archbishop, who once was a low churchman, and who, before his elevation to his present high office, extended many courtesies to non-conformists. But he represents an institution, he is the head of the established Church. The established Church is responsible for the law. The Archbishop must be willing to bear this responsibility, and I am sure that he is.

To my great surprise, distinguished Protestant Episcopal ministers here in Baltimore have taken exception to my words. I had not supposed that there was a well-informed and patriotic man in America who would endorse the cunning effort of the English establishment to enforce the teachings of Episcopacy upon the children of other denominations in the schools supported by the state. I am confident that the ministers who are apologizing for their distinguished visitor would not have the public schools of Baltimore run in the interests of Episcopacy. The friendly discussion which has followed the publication of this brief and incidental reference to the present religious and educational controversy in Great Britain proves, first, that many people among us desire more information upon this important question, and second, that there may be some people among us (very few, let us hope) who are not enthusiastic supporters of the doctrine of soul liberty, not withstanding the deliverances of the Constitution of the United States, under the protection of which they live and prosper. . . . [Laws continues explaining the sectarian school act passed by Parliament in 1902–3 and gives a brief history of education law in England.]

Passive Resistance and How It Has Worked

The free churches determined not to receive state aid for the support of their own schools, and they were equally determined not to pay the school rate for the support of other sectarian schools. They were quite prepared to suffer any inconvenience or indignity or outrage for the sake of their conscientious convictions. They might have refused to resist the law and fled before their persecutors, as did the Pilgrim Fathers of the long ago. But these men love their country, which they have helped to make, and they do not propose to be driven out of it. They might have stultified their consciences and paid the rate, becoming peace-at-any-price men. They might have followed in the footsteps of their fathers, who in 1688 united in a revolution against ecclesiastical tyranny. We may rejoice that, instead, our brethren have simply refused to pay the rate, courteously but courageously declaring that in good conscience they cannot pay to have false and pernicious doctrines taught in the schools. Since the days of John Bunyan passive resistance has been the weapon by which non-conformists have won most of their victories. The immortal tinker expressed himself in these quaint words: "I told him the law has provided two ways of obeying — the one to do that which I let my conscience believe I am bound to actively, and when I cannot obey actively, then I am willing to lie down and suffer what they shall do to me...."

When the non-conformists declared that they were willing to suffer for their consciences, they knew what was facing them. They were ridiculed by the Church papers for saying that the education act might end in the imprisonment of free church ministers and laymen throughout the country. The prophecy has come true. In the *Daily News* of London Dr. John Clifford, the leader of the movement, has recently given the history of the first year of "passive resistance." The bright side of the picture is that many noble-hearted Church of England people have joined the movement and are standing with the non-conformists, and that Roman Catholics have also expressed their purpose to share the fortunes of the persecuted. Dr. Clifford declares that it is more than a religious revolt of the free churches; that it is "essentially a citizens revolt against the intrusion of Parliament, led by the Bishops, into the realm of conscience, and the distinctive fact is that these citizens are undeniably amongst the best assets of the nation." The weak-kneed are becoming more courageous, the people are enlisting, the Church is awakening to the fact that the movement is growing with alarming rapidity. But there is a dark side to the picture. During the year there have been 21,871 summons issued to coerce men and women into paying the school tax. Nine hundred and seventy-one sales of property, representing many thousands of individual owners, have taken place. Twenty-two of the freemen of one of the most highly civilized nations of the world have been thrust into prison, to sleep on prison beds and to eat prison fare, that the Church of England may use the schools supported by the state for proselytizing to her own communion the children of non-conformist parents. At this time nearly 2000 arrests are being made each week. Several Baptists have been imprisoned, and I glory in their heroism.

Another Baptist preacher was imprisoned long ago by the same authority, but we had all felt that the established Church had become civilized since the days of John Bunyan. Thank God for the passive resisters who refuse to be coerced by a priest-ridden government, who refuse to sit calmly down and have their liberties stolen from them. These are the men whom the Archbishop of Canterbury has had the effrontery to call "anarchists." They include in their ranks such men as John Clifford, Alexander Maclaren, Principal Fairbairn, Reginald J. Campbell, Thomas Spurgeon, G. Campbell Morgan, Frederick B. Meyer, W. J. Dawson, J. Monroe Gibson, Bendel Harris, Silvester Horne, Henry S. Lunn, W. Robertson Nicoll, J. H. Shakespeare, Mark Guy Pearce and many more of equal note, and thousands more of equal nobility of character — clergymen, ministers, journalists, teachers, manufacturers, merchants, jurists and statesmen.

The Duty and Privilege of Americans

Without popular government in the truest sense, our co-religionists in England and Wales are at the mercy of a Parliament dominated by the Bishops of the Church of England. The establishment is boldly striking at the life of non-conformity. The policy of both government and Church savors of the Inquisition of the Middle Ages. The nonconformists are too strong and too determined to flee the persecution as did the Pilgrims and Puritans. They will stand their ground and die if necessary for religious freedom. This is a battle in which the whole civilized world should be interested. The like of it has never been known before. For England to swing out of line in the onward march of civilization and return to the ideals of the sixteenth century is pitiable, but that her noblest sons and daughters should be humiliated and persecuted for conscience's sake in this age is diabolical. As American citizens it is our duty to protest when one of the most cherished principles of our own civilization is being tramped under the feet of a nation which rejoices in our friendship. If the American press would agitate this matter, speaking its mind upon this reversal of the twentieth-century ideals, from purely political motives the English government would give instant attention.

As members of the same churches and denominational bodies, many of us have a special privilege. Our brethren over the sea profoundly appreciate the interest which we are taking in their struggle, and they rejoice in every expression of sympathy and affection which reaches them from our country. They are not posing as martyrs, nor pleading for sympathy, but they would be either more or less than human if they were not strengthened by the knowledge that the English-speaking world is wishing them God-speed.

The Protestant Episcopal Church of America is facing a splendid opportunity and at the same time an awful responsibility. In their hearts the broad-minded and Christlike ministers and laymen of American Episcopacy can have no sympathy with the motives and methods of the Church of England as expressed in this educational act. It is mere subterfuge to lay the guilt of this matter at the door of Parliament. Now, if our Episcopal brethren will be true to their own convictions and speak as they feel, their protest in this matter will shake the English establishment from center to circumference....

At such a time as this we shall all feel inclined to smile and to forgive our Episcopal brethren the presumption of calling themselves the American National Church, and we shall rejoice if conditions here are improved by the Archbishop's visit. But we do devoutly pray that *The Churchman* may be right as to the Archbishop's own enlightenment. He needs it, or, at least, his Church needs it, and the need is pressing and imperative. Again I say, I rejoice in the opportunity which God has placed before our Episcopal brethren. The two Churches have no organic connection, and yet their relations are such that the mother Church will be glad to listen to her more enlightened daughter, and let us hope that the daughter will do her full duty.

Before the Archbishop of Canterbury leaves this country he ought to know how Americans feel about religious liberty. He would hardly dare call us "anarchists" as he calls the passive resisters among our co-religionists in England. The Archbishop, a good and great man, deserves to be treated with every courtesy, but if our religious leaders do their duty, he will hear many a ringing protest against the tyranny of the Church of which he is the head. His policy ought to receive no sympathy. In this land of the free no guest can be treated with discourtesy. In this land of the brave no man among us will be a coward when the liberties of our brethren are threatened. May our God sustain and strengthen His children in their time of trial. May they be patient and gentle and forgiving like the Master. May they be saved from using the weapons of this world in their battle for soul liberty. The victory will surely come, and with it other and grander victories for the truth.

> New occasions teach new duties;
> Time makes ancient good uncouth.
> We must upward still and onward
> Who would keep abreast of Truth.
> Lo, before us gleam her camp-fires;
> We ourselves must pilgrims be,
> Launch our Mayflower and steer boldly

Through the desperate winter sea,
Nor attempt the future's portal
With the past's blood-rusted key.

[Curtis Lee Laws, *The Fiery Furnace and Soul Liberty* (Baltimore: First Baptist Church of Baltimore, 1904).]

Shall We Gather at the River

Shall we gather at the river,
Where bright angel feet have trod;
With its crystal tide forever
Flowing by the throne of God?

Yes, we'll gather at the river,
The beautiful, the beautiful river;
Gather with the saints at the river
That flows by the throne of God.

On the margin of the river,
Washing up its silver spray,
We will walk and worship ever,
All the happy golden day.

Ere we reach the shining river,
Lay we every burden down;
Grace our spirits will deliver,
And provide a robe and crown.

Soon we'll reach the shining river,
Soon our pilgrimage will cease;
Soon our happy hearts will quiver
With the melody of peace.

Robert Lowry (1864)

Part Five

TO BE A
RIGHTEOUS CHURCH

The Twentieth Century

Introduction

The Twentieth Century

Readers who consult the table of contents can see a difference in the twentieth-century chapter of this book even before they read it: a far greater number of theologians show up in this century. It has been difficult to limit the choices even to these. We have followed our rule of including, among baptist theologians, only those whose life work is complete (with very few exceptions, ones no longer living) and only those who have been — and will be — widely read. Yet this points to a difficulty that lengthens our list: it is hard to distinguish recent theologians of fleeting fame from those whose work is going to endure. Such discernment becomes increasingly difficult as we approach the present; doubtless some we include will hardly be remembered at the end of the twenty-first century, yet we cannot say which. There is another reason for the greater numbers: the baptist movement has grown and is more widely spread than ever; to be truthful we needed to include theologians from every continent and from every people. Meanwhile, the movement has grown in importance in the regions covered in earlier chapters: In Britain and especially in America baptist communities of many sorts have come of age and produced theological work that demands attention.

And what a century! Perhaps none since the sixteenth has been so religiously tumultuous, and none since the seventeenth or before so churned by political upheaval. The rise of nation-states in Europe at the beginning of the modern period was followed in the twentieth century by their rise around the entire globe, all clamoring for a place on the world stage as the colonial age receded. The devastating Thirty Years War of the 1600s has been dwarfed by far greater destruction in two World Wars in the 1900s, followed not by a just peace but by a gigantic deadlock between (U.S. and Soviet) nuclear superpowers surrounded by unending strife among less powerful nations. People cry peace, peace, when there is no peace (cf. Jeremiah 6:14, 8:11). Meanwhile the development of science and technology, already exceeding comprehension in the 1800s, was dwarfed by the scientific and technological "explosions" of the century now ending — not omitting the literal explosion of atom bombs in warfare (U.S. against Japan, 1945) and the ominous rumble of continuing "test" nuclear bomb explosions underground. One recalls that Baptist historian Kenneth Scott Latourette, writing his multivolume history of Christian missions at mid-century, titled his twentieth-century volume "Advance through Storm." The storms are evident; is there indeed advance?

At least in some ways there has been Christian advance. For the baptist movement, we believe the principal advance has been a discovery, or rather a rediscovery, of the biblical demand that God's baptizing, obedient, evangelistic, missionary people shall be also a *righteous* people, that God's church shall be a righteous church. The terrors and tribulations of this century have extended a cry as loud as any Macedonian call: show us true virtue; save us from our own injustice! Baptists have heard that cry, and baptist theology has set out to answer in a variety of ways.

Baptist theological development in this century as in the past has occurred in the light of, and sometimes in conversation with, the Protestant and Catholic theologies of the century. Though baptist thought remained, at century's end, almost uncharted territory for Christian theologians of other persuasions, just as Anabaptist thought had been in earlier centuries, there were some faint signs that the baptist contribution was noticed. More impressive (and for present concerns more relevant) was the attention paid by baptists to these others. There are (at this writing) no great baptist graduate universities or other centers of theological reflection, so able students from baptist churches have often gone to others' universities, religious or secular, and have learned others' ways of thought, sometimes to the near exclusion of their own. Consequently, the selections that follow have been written by baptist theologians not only deeply aware of their own Christian heritage but well educated in that of others and aware of the environing culture both share.

As the century began, two features of American Protestant theology were harbingers of change. One was modernism; the other was the social gospel. Interestingly, though both were wider-than-baptist Christian movements, each was furnished with Baptist leadership. The Divinity School at the University of Chicago, of Baptist origin, was a center of modernism; Rochester Seminary, especially because of Walter Rauschenbusch, was a focus of social gospel reflection. The social gospel, however, in this regard unlike modernism, went well beyond the schools, constituting a mass movement of spiritual awakening in American churches, accompanied by hymns, driven by prayer, and fulfilled in many works of love and mercy. Since Baptists Douglas Clyde Macintosh (a Chicago graduate) and Harry Emerson Fosdick (a New York pastor), both modernists, are represented below, as is Walter Rauschenbusch, who is known as father of the social gospel, there is no need to say more about these important early-century movements here.

Protestant theology began to change dramatically after the First World War (1914–18). So sharp was the shift that historian Claude Welch regards 1914–18, and not 1900, as the actual turning point between the centuries. Certainly the years from 1900 to 1918 saw a continuation of older modes of Protestant thought — liberal Protestantism and its modernist version as well as scholastic Protestantism and its fundamentalist version. In the new arrangement of life among European survivors of the Great War, a new spirit appeared: liberalism had nothing more to offer; Protestant theology must return to its sixteenth-century sources (and through these to biblical sources). The new movement was thus labeled neo-orthodoxy, though as wags put it, it was professedly not new and certainly not orthodox. Nevertheless, neo-orthodoxy constituted a vigorous renaissance of Christian thought. Here the great names were Karl Barth and Emil Brunner in Switzerland, the Baillie brothers (John and Donald) in Scotland, and the Niebuhr brothers (Reinhold and H. Richard) in America. Germans Rudolf Bultmann and Paul Tillich steered their own courses, marginal with respect to these others. In any case, neo-orthodoxy waned as the twentieth century closed, and varied new currents of Protestant theology followed. Protestants in the United States borrowed selectively from liberation theology, not always recognizing the difference created by their North American setting and history; they borrowed from many other sources as well. In the short run, at least, the spectrum of Protestant thought shattered into fragments by century's end, with little evidence of unity or continuity among the shards. One line of division separated theologians who emphasized the immanence (i.e., this-worldly presence) of God from those who emphasized God's transcendence (see Stanley J. Grenz and Roger E. Olson, *Twentieth-Century Theology: God and the World in a Transitional Age*). A still broader study of the century is provided by David F. Ford, editor, *The Modern Theologians: An Introduction to Christian Theology in the Twentieth Century*.

Catholic theology in the century underwent its own profound changes. For the most part Catholic theologians had not previously come to terms with the nineteenth century's new history — biblical history, church history, social history — that by this time challenged Catholic even more than Protestant self-understanding. As the century opened, the most prominent sign of meeting that challenge was Catholic modernism, whose great names were Alfred Loisy in France and George Tyrrell and Friedrich von Hügel in Britain. Its stated goal was to recast the time-honored Catholic faith in modern thought forms. Modernism was formally condemned by Pope Pius X in 1907, but since the problems it addressed persisted, Catholic modernism went underground and continued to affect quiet Catholic scholars who eventually emerged in milder-than-modernist dress at Vatican Council II (1962–65). All the Catholic theologians who dominated the latter part of the century were formed by that Council. They included in Europe Karl Rahner and the sometimes rebellious Hans Küng, and in the two-thirds world, liberation theologians such as Peruvian priest Gustavo Gutiérrez and Brazilian Leonardo Boff. Liberation theology, encouraged by Roman Catholic bishops at a notable conference at Medellín, Colombia, in 1968, found that the revisionary doctrines of Vatican II applied to the class-riven societies of Latin America in ways somewhat parallel to revolutionary Marxism. Rather than pass along tired dogmas, theologians could now consult the insights of poor, faithful Catholics who were meeting in Latin American "basic communities" to read Scripture, talk about their common lives, and discover liberation in the gospel. Such theology attended to *praxis* (practice) in order to call into question oppressive societies and replace them with more just ones.

Having already noted the strong Baptist participation in early-century Protestant liberalism both in its more theoretical form (modernism) and in its applied form (the social gospel), we can now add other ways twentieth-century baptist theologies paralleled Protestant and Catholic directions. The older liberalism had its parallel in the cautious experientialism of Edgar Young Mullins. As with modernism, many major fundamentalists were Baptists. While our selection passes over prominent ones such as Canadian T. T. Shields and Texan J. Frank Norris, it includes a reading from Carl F. H. Henry, leading intellectual theorist of the new evangelicalism that was a self-correction of earlier fundamentalism. Those nearest neo-orthodoxy in this chapter are Walter Thomas Conner and Dale Moody. Conner, the more original thinker, quietly reacted against his teachers Rauschenbusch and Mullins while continuing with them to resist fundamentalism; Moody, best at transmitting European thought to America, was deeply influenced by Barth and was a student and friend of Emil Brunner.

More surprising, in view of historic baptist challenges to Catholicism, are the strong parallels between baptist thinkers and Latin American liberation theology. In fact, it was the baptists who came first. The selections in this and the preceding chapter from social gospel and African American theologians and from English theologian and activist Muriel Lester illustrate this point clearly enough: already in the nineteenth century some of these thinkers had displayed a style of reflection that sprang from the common life of their people, uttered a cry for redemptive justice as old as the slave spirituals, and skillfully read the Bible as a liberating social document. All these features were later echoed (though usually in ignorance of their baptist predecessors) by the South American liberationists. Moreover, social gospelers and black theologians were free from the European scholasticism that weighed upon such Latin American theologians as Gutiérrez and Segundo. While rarely given the name "liberation theologians," North Americans such as Walter Rauschenbusch, Benjamin Mays, Howard Thurman, Martin King, and J. Deotis Roberts (here not represented by a selection since happily he is still living) right along with Central American Baptist liberationist Orlando Costas and African Osadolor Imasogie, show a dimension of baptist thought left unrecognized in some collections of "Baptist theologians," while at the same time these workers are ignored by Protestant and Catholic literature — an omission that perpetuates old sixteenth-century biases.

In these ways baptist theologies have addressed the spiritual yearning and the hunger and thirst for righteousness that mark this century's course. Not all the problems were solved; not all sharers of the task rest easily together. Note, too, that the twentieth century is not fully represented here, since many of its active workers are still alive and well, and thus fall outside the parameters we have adopted for this book of roots. Yet in the midst of the tensions and tragedies of the world noted at chapter's outset, these penetrating reflections have appeared. In them, in assorted ways and varying degrees, (1) fidelity to Scripture and to Jesus Christ its center, (2) relevance to world need, and (3) consistency with the baptist heritage of earlier centuries once more emerged. Readers are urged to watch for the reappearance of these notes and to measure the authenticity of each selection by their appearance or absence.

– *33* –

Augustus Hopkins Strong

August Hopkins Strong (1836–1921) was born to privilege. The son of a wealthy newspaperman, he was brother to the founder of East-man Kodak and a close personal friend of John D. Rockefeller, a place in life considerably more affluent than that of most theologians in this volume. Nevertheless, Strong devoted his life selflessly to students and churches of lesser means. Educated at Yale and Rochester (Baptist) Sem-inary, he served as pastor of Baptist churches in Massachusetts and Ohio before returning to Rochester as seminary president and professor of theology — posts he held for forty years. From 1876 on he produced successive editions of a massive Systematic Theology *comparable to the similar work by Princeton Presbyterian Charles Hodge. As a theolo-gian, Strong is best understood as a mediating figure; he was richly informed by the conservative Calvinist heritage that had shaped most British and American Baptists of his day, but he realized that mod-ern science and Scripture scholarship offered scholastic Calvinism hard challenges. Consequently, he tried to maintain the best of the old while accommodating the new beliefs. He supported this rationally by postu-lating a belief in God, the self, and the external world, which he labeled "ethical monism," a philosophy that owed much to German idealism. In touch with the times, he did not rule out human evolution as had Hodge; for Strong, evolution was simply God's creative method. The present selection, dealing with miracles, is from the 1907 edition of* Sys-tematic Theology: *It shows Strong's style of outlining his argument in larger print and supporting it with evidence of various sorts in finer print; here for brevity a portion of the finer print material is omitted.*

Miracles as Attesting a Divine Revelation

I. Definition of Miracle

A. Preliminary Definition. — A miracle is an event palpable to the senses, produced for a religious purpose by the immediate agency of

272

God; an event therefore which, though not contravening any law of nature, the laws of nature, if fully known, would not without this agency of God be competent to explain.

This definition corrects several erroneous conceptions of the miracle: — (*a*) A miracle is not a suspension or violation of natural law; since natural law is in operation at the time of the miracle just as much as before. (*b*) A miracle is not a sudden product of natural agencies — a product merely foreseen by him who appears to work it; it is the effect of a will outside of nature. (*c*) A miracle is not an event without a cause; since it has for its cause a direct volition of God. (*d*) A miracle is not an irrational or capricious act of God; but an act of wisdom, performed in accordance with the immutable laws of his being, so that in the same circumstances the same course would be again pursued. (*e*) A miracle is not contrary to experience; since it is not contrary to experience for a new cause to be followed by a new effect. (*f*) A miracle is not a matter of internal experience, like regeneration or illumination; but is an event palpable to the sense, which may serve as objective proof to all that the worker of it is divinely commissioned as a religious teacher....

... The definition given above is intended simply as a definition of the miracles of the Bible, or, in other words, of the events which profess to attest a divine revelation in the Scriptures. The New Testament designates these events in a two-fold way, viewing them either subjectively, as producing effects upon men, or objectively, as revealing the power and wisdom of God. In the former aspect they are called *terata,* "wonders," and *semeia,* "signs" (John 4:48; Acts 2:22). In the latter aspect they are called *dunameis,* "powers," and *erga,* "works" (Mat. 7:22; John 14:11). See H. B. Smith, Lect. on Apologetics, 90– 116, esp. 94 — "*semeion,* sign, marking the purpose or object, the moral end, placing the event in connection with revelation." The Bible Union Version uniformly and properly renders *teras* by "wonder," *dunamis* by "miracle," *ergon* by "work," and *semeion* by "sign." Goethe, Faust: "Alles Vergängliche ist nur ein Gleichniss: Das Unzulängliche wird hier Ereigness" — "Everything transitory is but a parable; The unattainable appears as solid fact." So the miracles of the New Testament are acted parables, — Christ opens the eyes of the blind to show that he is the Light of the world, multiplies the loaves to show that he is the Bread of Life, and raises the dead to show that he lifts men up from the death of trespasses and sins....

B. Alternative and Preferable Definition. — A miracle is an event in nature, so extraordinary in itself and so coinciding with the prophecy or command of a religious teacher or leader, as fully to warrant the conviction, on the part of those who witness it, that God has wrought it with the design of certifying that this teacher or leader has been commissioned by him.

This definition has certain marked advantages as compared with the preliminary definition given above: — (*a*) It recognizes the immanence of God and his immediate agency in nature, instead of assuming an antithesis between the laws of nature and the will of God. (b) It regards the miracle as simply an extraordinary act of that same God who is already present in all natural operations and who in them is revealing his general plan. (c) It holds that natural law, as the method of God's regular activity, in no way precludes unique exertions of his power when these will best secure his purpose in creation. (d) It leaves it possible that all miracles may have their natural explanations and may hereafter be traced to natural causes, while both miracles and their natural causes may be only names for the one and self-same will of God. (e) It reconciles the claims of both science and religion: of science, by permitting any possible or probable physical antecedents of the miracle; of religion, by maintaining that these very antecedents together with the miracle itself are to be interpreted as signs of God's special commission to him under whose teaching or leadership the miracle is wrought.

Augustine, who declares that "Dei voluntas rerum natura est," defines the miracle in De Civitate Dei, 21:8 — "Portentum ergo fit non contra naturam, sed contra quam est nota natura." He says also that a birth is more miraculous than a resurrection, because it is more wonderful that something that never was should begin to be, than that something that was and ceased to be should begin again. E. G. Robinson, Christ. Theology, 104 — "The natural is God's work. He originated it. There is no separation between the natural and the supernatural. The natural is supernatural. God works in everything. Every end, even though attained by mechanical means, is God's end as truly as if he wrought by miracle." Shaler, Interpretation of Nature, 141, regards miracle as something exceptional, yet under the control of natural law; the latent in nature suddenly manifesting itself; the revolution resulting from the slow accumulation of natural forces. In the Windsor Hotel fire, the heated and charred woodwork suddenly burst into flame. Flame is very different from mere heat, but it may be the result of a regularly rising temperature. Nature may be God's regular action, miracle its unique result. God's regular action may be entirely free, and yet its extraordinary result may be entirely natural. With these qualifications and explanations, we may adopt the statement of Biedermann, Dogmatik, 581–91 — "Everything is miracle, — therefore faith sees God everywhere; Nothing is miracle, — therefore science sees God nowhere...."

Miracle is an immediate operation of God; but, since all natural processes are also immediate operations of God, we do not need to deny the use of these natural processes, so far as they will go, in miracle. Such wonders of the Old Testament as the overthrow of Sodom and Gomorrah, the partings of the Red Sea and of the Jordan, the calling down of fire from heaven by Elijah and the destruction of the army of Sennacherib, are none the less works of God when regarded as wrought by the use of natural means. In the New Testament Christ took water to make wine, and took the five loaves to make bread, just as in ten thousand vineyards to-day he is turning the moisture of the earth into the juice of the grape, and in ten thousand fields is turning carbon into corn. The virgin-birth of Christ may be an extreme instance of parthenogenesis which Professor Loeb of Chicago has just demonstrated to take place in other than the lowest forms of life and which he believes to be possible in all. Christ's resurrection may be an illustration of the power of the normal and perfect human spirit to take to itself a proper body, and so may be the type and prophecy of that great change when we too shall lay down our life and take it again. The scientist may yet find that his disbelief is not only disbelief in Christ, but also disbelief in science. All miracle may have its natural side, though we now are not able to discern it; and, if this were true the Christian argument would not one whit be weakened, for still miracle would evidence the extraordinary working of the immanent God, and the impartation of his knowledge to the prophet or apostle who was his instrument....

2. Possibility of Miracle

An event in nature may be caused by an agent in nature yet above nature. This is evident from the following considerations:

(*a*) Lower forces and laws in nature are frequently counteracted and transcended by the higher (as mechanical forces and laws by chemical, and chemical by vital), while yet the lower forces and laws are not suspended or annihilated, but are merged in the higher, and made to assist in accomplishing purposes to which they are altogether unequal when left to themselves.

By nature we mean nature in the proper sense — not "everything that is not God," but "everything that is not God or made in the image of God"; see Hopkins, Outline Study of Man, 2–8, 259. Man's will does not belong to nature, but is above nature....

(*b*) The human will acts upon its physical organism, and so upon nature, and produces results which nature left to herself never could accomplish, while yet no law of nature is suspended or violated. Gravitation still operates upon the axe, even while man holds it at the surface of the water — for the axe still has weight (cf. 2 Ki. 6:5–7).

Versus Hume, Philos. Works, 4:130 — "A miracle is a violation of the laws of nature." Christian apologists have too often needlessly embarrassed their argument by accepting Hume's definition. The stigma is entirely undeserved. If man can support the axe at the surface of the water while gravitation still acts upon it, God can certainly, at the prophet's word, make the iron to swim, while gravitation still acts upon it. But this last is miracle....

(*c*) In all free causation, there is an acting without means. Man acts upon external nature through his physical organism, but, in moving his physical organism, he acts directly upon matter. In other words, the human will can use means, only because it has the power of acting initially without means....

(*d*) What the human will, considered as a supernatural force, and what the chemical and vital forces of nature itself, are demonstrably able to accomplish, cannot be regarded as beyond the power of God, so long as God dwells in and controls the universe. If man's will can act directly

upon matter in his own physical organism, God's will can work immediately upon the system which he has created and which he sustains. In
other words, if there be a God, and if he be a personal being, miracles
are possible. The impossibility of miracles can be maintained only upon
principles of atheism or pantheism....

(e) This possibility of miracles becomes doubly sure to those who see
in Christ none other than the immanent God manifested to creatures.
The Logos or divine Reason who is the principle of all growth and
evolution can make God known only by means of successive new im-
partations of his energy. Since all progress implies increment, and Christ
is the only source of life, the whole history of Creation is a witness to
the possibility of miracle....

"A man builds a house. In laying the foundation he uses stone and mortar,
but he makes the walls of wood and the roof of tin. In the superstructure he
brings into play different laws from those which apply to the foundation. There
is continuity, not of material, but of plan. Progress from cellar to garret requires
breaks here and there, and the bringing in of new forces: in fact, without the
bringing in of these new forces the evolution of the house would be impossible. Now substitute for the foundation and superstructure living things like
the chrysalis and the butterfly; imagine the power to work from within and not
from without; and you see that true continuity does not exclude but involves
new beginnings...."

3. Probability of Miracles

A. We acknowledge that, so long as we confine our attention to nature,
there is a presumption against miracles. Experience testifies to the uniformity of natural law. A general uniformity is needful, in order to make
possible a rational calculation of the future, and a proper ordering of
life....

...G. D. B. Pepper: "Where there is no law, no settled order, there can be
no miracle. The miracle presupposes the law, and the importance assigned to
miracles is the recognition of the reign of law. But the making and launching of
a ship may be governed by law, no less than the sailing of the ship after it is
launched. So the introduction of a higher spiritual order into a merely natural
order constitutes a new and unique event." Some Christian apologists have erred
in affirming that the miracle was antecedently as probable as any other event,
whereas only its antecedent improbability gives it value as a proof of revelation.
Horace: "Nec deus intersit, nisi dignus vindice nodus inciderit."

B. But we deny that this uniformity of nature is absolute and universal. (a) It is not a truth of reason that can have no exceptions, like
the axiom that a whole is greater than its parts. (b) Experience could
not warrant a belief in absolute and universal uniformity, unless experience were identical with absolute and universal knowledge. (c) We
know, on the contrary, from geology, that there have been breaks in this

uniformity, such as the introduction of vegetable, animal and human life, which cannot be accounted for, except by the manifestation in nature of a supernatural power....

C. Since the inworking of the moral law into the constitution and course of nature shows that nature exists, not for itself, but for the contemplation and use of moral beings, it is probable that the God of nature will produce effects aside from those of natural law, whenever there are sufficiently important moral ends to be served thereby....

...This is proved by the Incarnation. The Christian sees in this little earth the scene of God's greatest revelation. The superiority of the Spiritual to the physical helps us to see our true dignity in the creation, to rule our bodies, to overcome our sins. Christ's suffering shows us that God is no indifferent spectator of human pain. He subjects himself to our conditions, or rather in this subjection reveals to us God's own eternal suffering for sin. The atonement enables us to solve the problem of sin.

D. The existence of moral disorder consequent upon the free acts of man's will, therefore, changes the presumption against miracles into a presumption in their favor. The non-appearance of miracles, in this case, would be the greatest of wonders....

E. As belief in the possibility of miracles rests upon our belief in the existence of a personal God, so belief in the probability of miracles rests upon our belief that God is a moral and benevolent being. He who has no God but a God of physical order will regard miracles as an impertinent intrusion upon that order. But he who yields to the testimony of conscience and regards God as a God of holiness, will see that man's unholiness renders God's miraculous interposition most necessary to man and most becoming to God. Our view of miracles will therefore be determined by our belief in a moral, or in a non-moral, God....

4. The amount of testimony necessary to prove a miracle is no greater than that which is requisite to prove the occurrence of any other unusual but confessedly possible event.

Hume, indeed, argued that a miracle is so contradictory of all human experience that it is more reasonable to believe any amount of testimony false than to believe a miracle to be true....

The argument is fallacious, because

(a) It is chargeable with a *petitio principii*, in making our own personal experience the measure of all human experience. The same principle would make the proof of any absolutely new fact impossible. Even though God should work a miracle, he could never prove it. (b) It involves a self-contradiction, since it seeks to overthrow our faith in human testimony by adducing to the contrary the general experience of men, of which we know only from testimony. This general experience, moreover, is merely negative, and cannot neutralize that which is positive, except upon principles which would invalidate all testimony whatever. (c) It requires belief in a greater wonder than those which it would escape. That multitudes of intelligent and honest men should against all their interests unite in deliberate and persistent falsehood, under the circumstances narrated in the New Testament record, involves a change in the sequences of nature far more incredible than the miracles of Christ and his apostles....

5. Evidential Force of Miracles

(a) Miracles are the natural accompaniments and attestations of new communications from God. The great epochs of miracles — represented by Moses, the prophets, the first and second comings of Christ — are coincident with the great epochs of revelation. Miracles serve to draw attention to new truth, and cease when this truth has gained currency and foothold.

Miracles are not scattered evenly over the whole course of history. Few miracles are recorded during the 2500 years from Adam to Moses. When the N.T. Canon is completed and the internal evidence of Scripture has attained its greatest strength, the external attestations by miracle are either wholly withdrawn or begin to disappear. The spiritual wonders of regeneration remain, and for these the way has been prepared by the long progress from the miracles of power wrought by Moses to the miracles of grace wrought by Christ. Miracles disappeared because newer and higher proofs rendered them unnecessary. Better things than these are now in evidence....

(e) The resurrection of our Lord Jesus Christ — by which we mean his coming forth from the sepulcher in body as well as in spirit — is demonstrated by evidence as varied and as conclusive as that which proves to us any single fact of ancient history. Without it Christianity itself is inexplicable, as is shown by the failure of all modern rationalistic theories to account for its rise and progress.

In discussing the evidence of Jesus' resurrection, we are confronted with three main rationalistic theories:

I. The *Swoon-theory* of Strauss. This holds that Jesus did not really die. The cold and the spices of the sepulcher revived him. We reply that the blood and water, and the testimony of the centurion (Mark 15:45), proved actual death. The rolling away of the stone, and Jesus' power immediately after, are inconsistent with immediately preceding swoon and suspended animation. How was his life preserved? where did he go? when did he die? His not dying implies deceit on his own part or on that of his disciples.

II. The *Spirit-theory* of Keim. Jesus really died, but only his spirit appeared. The spirit of Jesus gave the disciples a sign of his continued life, a telegram from heaven. But we reply that the telegram was untrue, for it asserted that his body had risen from the tomb. The tomb was empty and the linen cloths showed an orderly departure. Jesus himself denied that he was a bodiless spirit: "a spirit hath not flesh and bones, as ye see me having" (Luke 24:39). Did "his flesh see corruption" (Acts 2:31)? Was the penitent thief raised from the dead as much as he? Godet, Lectures in Defence of the Christian Faith. lect. i: A dilemma for those who deny the fact of Christ's resurrection: Either his body remained in the hands of his disciples, or it was given up to the Jews. If the disciples retained it, they were impostors: but this is not maintained by modern rationalists. If the Jews retained it, why did they not produce it as conclusive evidence against the disciples?

III. The *Vision-theory* of Renan. Jesus died, and there was no objective appearance even of his spirit. Mary Magdalene was the victim of subjective hallucination, and her hallucination became contagious. This was natural because the Jews expected that the Messiah would work miracles and would rise from the dead. We reply that the disciples did not expect Jesus' resurrection....

6. Counterfeit Miracles

Since only an act directly wrought by God can properly be called a miracle, it follows that surprising events brought about by evil spirits or by men, through the use of natural agencies beyond our knowledge, are not entitled to this appellation. The Scriptures recognize the existence of such, but denominate them "lying wonders" (2 Thess. 2:9).

These counterfeit miracles in various ages argue that the belief in miracles is natural to the race, and that somewhere there must exist the true. They serve to show that not all supernatural occurrences are divine, and to impress upon us the necessity of careful examination before we accept them as divine.

False miracles may commonly be distinguished from the true by (*a*) their accompaniments of immoral conduct or of doctrine contradictory to truth already revealed — as in modern spiritualism; (*b*) their internal characteristics of inanity and extravagance — as in the liquefaction of the blood of St. Januarius, or the miracles of the Apocryphal New Testament; (*c*) the insufficiency of the object which they are designed to further — as in the case of Apollonius of Tyana, or of the miracles said to accompany the publication of the doctrines of the immaculate conception and of the papal infallibility; (*d*) their lack of substantiating evidence — as in mediaeval miracles, so seldom attested by contemporary and disinterested witnesses; (*e*) their denial or undervaluing of God's previous revelation of himself in nature — as shown by the neglect of ordinary means, in the cases of Faith-cure and of so-called Christian Science.

Only what is valuable is counterfeited. False miracles presuppose the true. Fisher, Nature and Method of Revelation, 283 — "The miracles of Jesus originated faith in him, while mediaeval miracles follow established faith. The testimony of the apostles was given in the face of incredulous Sadducces. They were ridiculed and maltreated on account of it. It was no time for devout dreams and the invention of romances." The blood of St. Januarius at Naples is said to be contained in a vial, one side of which is of thick glass, while the other side is of thin. A similar miracle was wrought at Hales in Gloucestershire. St. Alban, the first martyr of Britain, after his head is cut off, carries it about in his hand. In Ireland the place is shown where St. Patrick in the fifth century drove all the toads and snakes over a precipice into the nether regions. The legend however did not become current until some hundreds of years after the saint's bones had crumbled to dust at Saul, near Downpatrick (see Hemphill, Literature of the Second Century, 180–82). Compare the story of the book of Tobit (6–8), which relates the expulsion of a demon by smoke from the burning heart and liver of a fish caught in the Tigris, and the story of the Apocryphal New Testament (I, Infancy), which tells of the expulsion of Satan in the form of a mad dog from Judas by the child Jesus. On counterfeit miracles in general, see Mozley, Miracles, 15, 161; F. W. Farrar, Witness of History to Christ, 72; A. S. Farrar, Science and Theology, 298; Tholuck, Vermischte Schriften, 1:27; Hodge, Syst. Theol., 1:630; Presb. Rev., 1881: 687–719.

Some modern writers have maintained that the gift of miracles still remains in the church. Bengel: "The reason why many miracles are not now wrought is not so much because faith is established, as because unbelief reigns." Christlieb: "It is the want of faith in our age which is the greatest hindrance to the stronger and more marked appearance of that miraculous power which is working here and there in quiet concealment. Unbelief is the final and most important reason for the retrogression of miracles." Edward Irving, Works, 5:464 — "Sickness is sin apparent in the body, the presentiment of death, the forerunner of corruption. Now, as Christ came to destroy death, and will yet redeem the body from the bondage of corruption, if the church is to have a first fruits or earnest of this power, it must be by receiving power over diseases that are the first fruits and earnest of death." Dr. A. J. Gordon, in his Ministry of Healing, held to this view. See also Boys, Proofs of the Miraculous in the Experience of the Church; Bushnell, Nature and the Supernatural, 446–92; Review of Gordon, by Vincent, in Presb. Rev., 1883:475–593; Review of Vincent, in Presb. Rev., 1884:49–79.

In reply to the advocates of faith-cure in general, we would grant that nature is plastic in God's hand; that he can work miracles when and where it pleases him; and that he has given promises which, with certain Scriptural and rational limitations, encourage believing prayer for healing in cases of sickness. But we incline to the belief that in these later ages God answers such prayer, not by miracle, but by special providence, and by gifts of courage, faith and will, thus acting by his Spirit directly upon the soul and only indirectly upon the body. The laws of nature are generic volitions of God, and to ignore them and disuse means is presumption and disrespect to God himself. The Scripture promise to faith is always expressly or impliedly conditioned upon our use of means: we are to work out our own salvation, for the very reason that it is God who works in us; it is vain for the drowning man to pray, so long as he refuses to lay hold of the rope that is thrown to him. Medicines and physicians are the rope thrown to us by God; we cannot expect miraculous help, while we neglect the help God has already given us; to refuse this help is practically to deny Christ's revelation in nature. Why not live without eating, as well as recover from sickness without medicine? Faith-feeding is quite as rational as faith-healing. To except cases of disease from this general rule as to the use of means has no warrant either in reason or in Scripture. The atonement has purchased complete salvation, and some day salvation shall be ours. But death and depravity still remain, not as penalty, but as chastisement. So disease remains also. Hospitals for Incurables, and the deaths even of advocates of faith-cure, show that they too are compelled to recognize some limit to the application of the New Testament promise....

[Augustus Hopkins Strong, *Systematic Theology*, 12th ed. (Philadelphia: Judson, 1907), 117–33.]

34

Edgar Young Mullins

Edgar Young Mullins (1860–1928) was born just a year later than Walter Rauschenbusch (see Rauschenbusch below) and was like his better-known Baptist contemporary strongly influenced by the liberal Protestant thought of his century. Mullins was born in Mississippi and grew up in East Texas during the poor times that followed the Civil War; he was savingly converted in young adulthood and after study at Southern Baptist Seminary, Louisville, was a pastor in Baltimore and in Massachusetts. In Baltimore he sought to lead his people in practicing the social gospel, but when he became president of Southern Seminary at a time when its struggles between liberals and traditionalists were intense, he left aside his earlier social concerns and concentrated upon the issues that agitated his constituency. Three polarizing issues preoccupied him: the struggle with "Landmark" Baptists (the heirs of J. R. Graves) over Baptist roots; the Calvinist-Arminian battle over divine sovereignty and human freedom; and the modernist-fundamentalist battle over the proper response to modernity. Not clearly a partisan of either side in any of these Baptist battles, Mullins made it the task of his leadership to steer the seminary and the denomination at home and abroad into tranquility beyond each of them. His best-known work (besides his theological textbook The Christian Religion in Its Doctrinal Expression *of 1917, often reprinted), is* The Axioms of Religion *(1908). In it Mullins sought to obviate all three controversies: against the Landmarkers, the one true Baptist root was each individual's religious liberty or (as he phrased it) soul competency; reaching past the Calvinist struggle, human freedom was not opposed to divine sovereignty but was God's own gift to humanity; and third, the doctrinal claims of Fundamentalism must yield to the deeper claim of Baptists to restore original, experiential Christianity. The present selection, drawn from* Axioms, *sets Mullins' attempt at reconciliation in a wider framework of criticism of non-Baptists. Today's reader should realize that the pope of Mullins' day, Pius X, was trying hard to suppress his own rebellious "Americanists," such as bishops John England and John Ireland, who might well have been closer to Mullins, though he does not acknowledge them. Yet Mullins' polemic is not so much unfair as partly out of touch (and by*

now, out of date as well) in its grasp of Roman Catholicism. Mullins' in-
dividualism was closely in harmony with the rugged individualism of the
era of Theodore Roosevelt, and he brought it to bear upon the earlier
communitarianism of Baptist life in the South.

The Soul's Competency in Religion

. . . If the principle of the competency of the soul in religion under God
is a distinctive Baptist contribution to the world's thought, a vital element in the Baptist message to the race, then it ought to appear to be
such when compared with the points of view of various other Christian bodies. Under this process of comparison I think the candid reader
will recognize without difficulty that this is a distinguishing mark of the
Baptists. He will also perceive its simplicity, and indeed universality as
an underlying assumption in New Testament Christianity, while at the
same time he will discover in it a comprehensive criterion of judgment
for classifying the various existing ecclesiastical bodies of Christendom.

Romanists and the Soul's Competency in Religion

First, then, compare the principle of the competency of the soul in religion with Roman Catholicism. It can be shown historically without the
slightest difficulty that the formative principle of the Roman Catholic
system is the direct antithesis to the doctrine of the soul's competency.
Romanism, in other words, asserts at every point the soul's incompetency in religion. From beginning to end Romanism conceives of the
human spirit as dependent in religion upon other human spirits. It regards the soul as incompetent to deal alone with God. This is not only
the outward expression and practical result of the Roman hierarchical
system; it is also the avowed theory of the church, proclaimed without hesitation. The laity are dependent upon the priesthood. Each lower
order in the hierarchy is dependent upon the next above it, and all together are under the necessity of drawing instruction for the intellect and
the rule for the moral and religious life from the infallible head of the
church in Rome.

In every particular of the ecclesiastical and religious life of the Roman
Catholic, the soul's incompetency is assumed. All the seven sacraments
illustrate the statement in a striking way. The soul's capacity to deal
with Christ and receive revelation at his hands is denied in baptism.
For through baptism alone as administered by the authorized priesthood
(save in certain emergencies) can the regenerating efficacy of Christianity
reach the soul. Outside the church is no salvation. Christ and the soul
alone are not equal to the redemptive task. The only competent hands

are human and priestly. The same principle inheres in the administration of the Lord's Supper. Its power is nothing until the elements are changed by the priestly touch into the body and blood of Christ. Communion with Christ is thus taken out of the realm of spirit and transferred to the realm of matter, and the material elements necessary to the communion are held in the form of an ecclesiastical monopoly by a human priesthood. Auricular confession also assumes that in prayer man is incompetent to deal directly with God. A human priest must pronounce absolution. The penance also which the priest imposes raises a barrier between the broken heart and the forgiving Father in heaven, and asserts that his pardoning love instead of rolling in like a tide upon the penitent soul expands and contracts in accordance with the severity or leniency of an erring human mediator. Again, Christ cannot call a man into his ministry, and no man can respond to that call, outside the line of apostolic succession. The sacrament of orders limits Christ's ministry to an ecclesiastical chain which at no point must be broken, and at once pronounces the decree of condemnation upon all others, and asserts that the alleged direct call into the ministry from Christ himself is a delusion.

The sacrament of extreme unction, which is applied to the dying, is another form of the Romanist assertion of the soul's incompetency. God's grace in the heart cannot fit a man for the exodus through death out of this life into the next. Not until the priest, with oil consecrated by the bishop, has anointed the dying in the figure of the cross, on eyes, ears, nostrils, mouth, the palms of the hands and soles of the feet, is the soul prepared to make its exit. The soul is thus made competent for death only through priestly mediation. The fetters of this bondage to a mortal and human priesthood are not broken even when death has severed spirit from body; for even then the gates of purgatory fly open only through priestly intercession upon earth.

And finally the doctrine of papal infallibility combined with that of an authoritative tradition forbids all private or divergent interpretations of Scripture. To discover and proclaim an interpretation of the word of God which contravenes in any essential particular that which bears the stamp of traditional or papal approval, is for the Catholic to invoke upon his head the anathema of the church.

Thus from beginning to end and throughout its very fiber Romanism rears its ecclesiastical structure on the denial of the soul's competency in religion. There is not a leaf on this vast tree which is not ribbed and modeled in rigid obedience to its one constructive ideal, the soul's incapacity to attend to religion for itself. While not desiring in the slightest measure to abate the value or importance of the good Roman Catholicism has done in its benevolent and philanthropic work, one is compelled to say that in its ecclesiastical theory it is not only against the spirit of human development and progress, but is inconsistent with the

Christianity of Christ. If there is any one thing which stands out above others in crystal clearness in the New Testament it is Christ's doctrine of the soul's capacity, right, and privilege to approach God directly and transact with him in religion.

Protestantism Also Inconsistent

We look next at the Baptist principle of the competency of the soul in religion in its relation to Protestantism in general. We find here, of course, important modifications of the case as it stands with Roman Catholicism. But all the churches which adhere to infant baptism or episcopacy in any form come short of the New Testament principle in certain important respects. These bodies in fact represent a dualistic Christianity. They attempt to combine the Romish principle of incompetency with the antithetic principle of competency. In insisting upon the doctrine of justification by faith they recognize the principle of competency; but in retaining infant baptism or episcopacy they introduce the opposite view. Infant baptism takes away from the child its privilege of individual initiative in salvation and lodges in the hands of parents or sponsors the impossible task of performing an act of religious obedience for another. Such a view is as an axe laid to the root of obedience, and destroys its essential nature as such.

It thus appears that current Protestantism attempts to harmonize two principles which are essentially contradictory to each other. There are in other words two ways of being saved, and two ways of entering a Presbyterian or Episcopal church. One way is by personal obedience. The applicant for church-membership who has not been baptized relates a Christian experience which of course involves justification by faith in Christ. He is received and baptized upon this profession of faith and thus obeys for himself. Another, who was baptized in infancy, also applies for church-membership and is received on the strength of that baptism. In the one case the candidate obeyed for himself, in the other his sponsors obeyed for him. The two principles are fundamentally opposed. It is not surprising, therefore, that Pedobaptist churches have great difficulty in explaining the status of baptized infants in the church. Are they church-members or not? New England Congregationalists struggled over the question for a long time in colonial days, and they have never attained a satisfactory solution of the problem as we shall see in a later chapter.

The same difficulties exist to-day in all Pedobaptist denominations. No intelligible view of the status of baptized infants in the church can possibly be set forth which does not contradict the doctrine of justification by faith and personal obedience which is also held by these same churches. The reason is that in the one case the competency of the soul in religion is affirmed — that is, in justification by faith and personal obedience; and in the other that competency is denied — that is, in infant baptism and sponsorial or parental obedience.

The New Testament principle of the soul's competency is violated also in all forms of church polity which retain episcopacy and any other form of ecclesiastical oligarchy. But as the principle of democracy in church government is to receive attention in later chapters, further discussion of this point is omitted here.

In concluding our remarks on the relation of the Baptist doctrine of the soul's competency in religion to Pedobaptist ideas, it is only necessary to remark that the latter adopt at one point and contradict at another a principle which reaches its fullness in the Baptist polity and general view of Christianity. The Baptists have consistently applied the principle at every point. Their aim is to restore original Christianity in its completeness to the human race.

The Soul's Competency and Modern Progress

We must consider next the relation of the doctrine of competency to modern life and progress. This also will be discussed in later portions of the book. Meantime a few words by way of general outline. Properly understood the doctrine of the soul's competency in religion is the summary of our progressive life and civilization. The religious principle is always the dominant force which gives its leading characteristics to any civilization. The competency of man in religion is the competency of man everywhere. Every significant movement of our day is one form or another of that high purpose of man to make his way back to God. Art is simply the assertion of man's inherent capacity for beauty, the claim that he is competent to trace out in time all the subtle lines of grace, all the varied hues and forms of a manifold and wonder-crowded universe. Art is simply the march of the beauty lover along the highways of a variegated creation, forward and upward until he stands face to face with Him who is the infinitely Beautiful.

Science is the corresponding quest for truth, the assertion that the soul was made for truth, its competency to find and its capacity for truth, its deathless struggle for truth until it stands in the presence of Him who is the Truth.

Agnosticism a Belated Philosophy

Philosophy also simply asserts the competency of man in the realm of speculative thought. Christian theism is the only possible philosophy for the man who accepts our fundamental principle of the soul's competency. For it asserts God's ability to communicate a revelation to man and man's capacity to receive it and to communicate with God. Agnosticism, which denies the competency of the human intellect, is the Roman Catholicism of philosophy, and is a belated view of human ability in the intellectual sphere. Many who lean toward agnosticism in their theological attitude need to reexamine their foundations and discover its real intellectual and spiritual affinities.

Again, politics and government and the social institutions assume man's moral competency, his capacity for moral progress under God in a well-ordered society. Society is the bold assertion that under God's leadership eternal right will be attained in the human sphere. If you let the gold and the pearl stand for the highest moral values; if you let the walls of jasper and their twelve foundations stand for the reign of moral law; if you let the sunless yet resplendent heavens above stand for the light and glory of truth in its triumph in the human soul; and if you let the hallelujahs of the tearless and shadowless and triumphant multitude in white stand for a purified social order, then you have in the unmatched glory and beauty of the New Jerusalem which the prophet saw descending from heaven to earth, the fitting symbol of what is going on in the world all about us — man under God achieving for himself an ideal social order. The absence of the temple from the perfected city means that all life will become a temple, all its manifestations an act of worship. The absence of the sun means that all light and all truth are now ours through the indwelling God. The absence of labor from the city means that now achievement is spontaneous. Culture, religion, morality, are all blended into a perfect harmony of achieving and progressing humanity.

The Fountain of Discontent

It is man's deathless conviction of his competency to achieve this goal that opens in his bosom the fountain of eternal discontent. A symbol of his progress toward his goal is a sculptor carving out of the marble his vision, rejoicing in it for a time, and then destroying it or setting it aside and beginning his work on another block and making a better statue; forever achieving and yet forever repudiating his achievement until he achieves the image of God in himself through God's grace. All this and more is implicit in our view of the competency of the soul in religion. America is the arena which God has supplied for the free and full play of the principle, and from here it is destined to spread until it covers the earth.

It will be observed that man's competency as thus outlined is a competency under God. In religion the counterpart of this truth is God's revelation in Christ, the divine competency, so to speak, to approach man on the basis of his divinely constituted human nature, and in keeping with his mental and moral faculties. And the history of religion shows that without the divine initiative, without revelation, without grace, man failed to find God. His competency, therefore, is not apart from God's approach. The Scriptures are the record of God's approach to man in Christ. These become to us the medium through which truth finds us, and without them Christ would inevitably pass into eclipse, and men would wander helpless, like a rudderless ship driven by tide and tempest. He would thus repeat the sad failures of the past, seen in all the superstitious, and ceremonial, and speculative attempts to find God.

[E. Y. Mullins, *The Axioms of Religion* (Philadelphia: Judson, 1908), 59–69.]

35

Helen Barrett Montgomery

*A daughter of upper-middle-class parents, Helen Barrett (1861–1934),
after graduating from stylish Wellesley College, returned to her home to
become a church and civic leader. Her father, Adoniram Judson Barrett
(named after the pioneer Baptist missionary to Burma), was a pastor in
Rochester, New York; her mother, Emily Barrows, was a schoolteacher.
Helen Barrett organized a big adult Sunday school class in her parents'
Lake Avenue Baptist Church, became a strong leader in civic reform and
social welfare at a time when women civic leaders were rare (her plumb
line was Rochester professor Walter Rauschenbusch's social gospel), and
eventually married a businessman, William A. Montgomery, who later
became an executive in the newly founded General Motors Corporation
and who strongly supported her in her Christian work. Helen Barrett
Montgomery helped organize the Baptist women of New York State and
later of all the North in a Woman's American Baptist Foreign Mission
Society, serving as its president for eleven years. The Northern Baptist
Convention elected her as its first female president in 1921. She made
missionary tours of the Pacific and the Orient, wrote books describing what she saw, and became a literary sensation, selling more than
160,000 copies of one mission book,* The King's Highway. *In 1924 she
translated the first English New Testament version by a woman, the*
Centenary New Testament. *The present selection is drawn from one
of her mission reports. It is not surprising that one of Helen Barrett
Montgomery's friends was Susan B. Anthony, the leading feminist of
the day.*

Ladies Last

We live in a country where the discussion of "Woman's Rights" is ever
to the front. We are to study lands where they are just beginning to
recognize woman's wrongs — lands where the slogan "Ladies First" is
consistently and persistently "Ladies Last." The appeal to the women
of England and America was winged by the recital of the intolerable injustices and oppressions under which the women of the non-Christian

lands spent their lives; an appeal whose force fifty years has not dulled. For while there are terrible wrongs against women in our own land, there is this difference: the wrongs of Hindu, Chinese, and Moslem women are buttressed behind the sanctions of religion, and are endorsed by the founders of their faith; while in our own land these wrongs flaunt themselves against the spirit and the plain provisions of our religion. If women fully recognized the emancipatory nature of the pure religion of Jesus, the force of the religious missionary arguments would be tremendously strengthened.

In this brief summary of woman's life under the ethnic religions, we find that she is nowhere accepted as man's equal, nowhere free, nowhere educated, nowhere is her right to her person recognized. The brave words of James Russell Lowell, spoken at a great banquet in London after someone had alluded sneeringly to Christianity, may well close this survey of the subject.

"When the keen scrutiny of skeptics has found a place on this planet where a decent man may live in decency, comfort, and security, supporting and educating his children unspoiled and unpolluted, a place where age is reverenced, infancy protected, womanhood honored, and human life held in due regard — when skeptics can find such a place ten miles square on this globe, where the Gospel of Christ has not gone before and cleared the way and laid the foundations that made decency and security possible, it will then be in order for these skeptical literati to move thither and there ventilate their views. But so long as these men are dependent on the very religion which they discard for every privilege they enjoy, they may well hesitate to rob the Christian of his hope and humanity of its faith in that Saviour who alone has given to men that hope of Eternal Life which makes life tolerable and society possible, and robs death of its terrors and the grave of its gloom."

Such was the condition of womanhood in the vast non-Christian world confronting the women of Christendom, when these Women's Missionary Societies were organized. It was at once a challenge and an appeal, the most moving and powerful. Neither challenge nor appeal has weakened in the years that have elapsed. Perhaps today we see more clearly than was seen then the necessity of raising woman if we are to raise the race; know more fully than they the horrors of the servile life in which the majority of women the world over are forced to live. Yet there are certain specious arguments that need to be squarely met. It may be objected that American women, too, labored under great disadvantages; that they were shut from the schools, denied the control of their property, treated as subordinates and inferiors; and that in Christendom we have the white-slave trade, the red-light district, and other hateful and debasing traffics in womanhood. It may be inquired why we send Christianity to others when it has been powerless to control these great social injustices among ourselves?

In reply to these it may be wise first to point out that in the non-Christian world these disabilities and injustices are sanctioned by the recognized standards of the people.

Confucius and Muhammad, [the] Code of Manu, and Buddhist scriptures alike agree in assigning woman to a position of inferiority and subordination, and in treating her as a "scandal and a slave, a drudge and a disgrace, a temptation and a terror, a blemish and a burden." On the other hand, the Bible, as the authoritative source of Christianity, and the teachings of the greatest exponents of Christianity constantly honor women and inculcate purity of life. The evils that in Christian lands are recognized as sin, known to be contrary to all religious standards, and practiced only by those who do not accept these standards, are in non-Christian lands unashamed because embedded in the religious sanctions of the nation. Strictly speaking, there is no Christian nation, but only nations in process of becoming Christian. But even so, the steady pressure of Bible ideals, exerted slowly and against tremendous difficulties, has already brought a revolution in the position of women.

We have quoted somewhat freely from the scriptures of non-Christian religions in regard to the position of women; it is not amiss to refresh our memories on the Biblical teachings. There is no respect in which the Bible is in sharper contrast with all its contemporary literature. No study ought to waken greater loyalty in the hearts of Christian women than to see how all the reforms of Christendom which affect women are based squarely upon the principles of the Bible. As a stimulus to further study, consider the following points:

1. *The prominence assigned to women in the Bible.* — What a noble company it is — Eve, Rebecca, Rachel, Miriam, Deborah, Hannah, Huldah, Naomi, Ruth, the widow of Zarephath, the Shunamite, Vashti, Esther, the three Marys, Elisabeth, Anna, Dorcas, Lydia, Priscilla, Phoebe, Lois, Eunice, the Elect Lady. The perfect little pen sketches of godly women that adorn the pages of the Bible from its beginning to its end cannot be surpassed for tenderness and beauty. Meek wives and loving mothers are there; but there are also prophets, seers, judges, queens, deliverers, poets. High courage and noble daring are there, as well as love and renunciation. These women think as well as believe. It is hard to mention any quality of the woman of fully developed and harmonious personality which is not mirrored in one or more of these heroines of the Bible.

2. *The tone of moral purity that pervades the Bible.* — The deepest affront to womanhood is the levity and impurity with which the facts of sex have been approached in life and literature. If the Bible be contrasted with any of the ethnic faiths, with the myths of Greece and Egypt, with thought as recorded in carving and temple and hieroglyph, the white

glory of the Book shines out. Frankness there is in the Bible; the frank plainness of speech in regard to facts and vices which belongs to a primitive time and people, but of evil suggestion, of obscenity, of immoral beautifying of ugly sin under fine names, not a trace. All other bibles tried by this test fail; by this test the Bible stands without even the smell of fire about its garments. Where in all literature will one find such terrible, searching denunciation against impurity of life and thought, such faithful holding up of the consequences of evil?

The commandment against adultery, the stern legislation against the impurity which characterized ancient social life, the punishment of Sodom, the solemn warnings of the prophets, the broken-hearted confessions of sin and longings for purity that breathe through the Psalms are only the preparation for the all-consuming purity which Jesus taught and lived: the right hand to be cut off, the right eye to be plucked out, the secret thought of evil to be repented of. Paul moves in the very atmosphere of Jesus when he says, "Know ye not that your body is the temple of the Holy Ghost which is in you, which ye have of God, and ye are not your own? For ye are bought with a price, therefore glorify God in your body and in your spirit, which are God's."

3. *In the Bible are enunciated the principles which will finally lead to the complete emancipation of women.* — The legislation of the Old Testament, while partial and preparatory, and in that sense imperfect, is marked by a consideration for the rights of the weak and dependent, of women, children, the poor, the slave, that sets it apart from all other ancient literature.

The very account of the creation, "In the image of God created he him, male and female created he them," is strange to primitive thought. As someone has said of the beautiful garden story, "Eve was taken neither from man's head, to be his divinity, nor from his feet, to be his slave, but from his side, to be his companion and helper."

The gradual development of the doctrine of the individual in the teachings of the prophets laid the foundation for a democracy that should at last abolish the caste of sex. The democracy of the New Testament got its seal and inspiration in the teachings and practice of Jesus. He took up the old teaching of the prophets, obscured by the prejudice of centuries, brushed aside the dishonoring conventions which the rabbis had built up, and associated with women in the plane of a beautiful, free, human relationship. He sat wearied by the well conversing with a woman to the scandalizing of his disciples, who thought this quite beneath him as a holy man and rabbi. To women he reared the lovely memorial of his praise, and at the faith of women he marveled. Women followed him and ministered to him. He alone among religious teachers had a word of hope for the harlot, and to a woman he gave the first resurrection commission.

It is not strange if his disciples could not rise at once to the height of his example and his teaching. Paul labors hard to assure us that he is speaking quite on his own responsibility and is not at all inspired, though he thinks he understands the mind of Christ, when he writes those directions to the Corinthian church which have been a stumbling-block to so many. All these specific directions of his are to be read first in the light of conditions then existing in Greek society, summed up in his own words — "Let all things be done decently and in order"; second in the light of his own consistent practices, and third in the light of his own fully enunciated principles. When so regarded it is found that the remarkable freedom already developing among the Christian community was laying its women open to foul imputations in the rich Greek city, where the only women free to speak and associate with the men were women of loose character. Hence Paul's urgency that the cause be not imperiled by insisting on a liberty which was turning the unaccustomed heads of the women. According to his practice we find that women were his helpers in preaching and organization, that his letters and the Book of the Acts are dotted with little unconscious revelations of the position of influence which women already held in the young church life. But when it comes to principles, Paul, unencumbered by the need of practical adjustment that so bothers the best philosophers, lays down the Magna Charta of womanhood in a Christianity in which there is neither male nor female, bond nor free, but in which all are one in Christ Jesus. He sees clearly that the duty of subordination and service is laid on all alike in Christ's great democracy and only those who love most are most honored.

It does not yet appear what we shall be, but is already manifest that the spirit of Jesus as revealed to us in the word of his truth is already making a new world; not a man's world, hard, cruel, bitter toward the weak, nor a woman's world, weak, sentimental, tasteless, but a world of humanity in which for the first time the full orb of all the qualities that serve to mark the human shall have free course and be glorified.

It may be asked why, then, if the Christian Scriptures contain these teachings concerning women, there is so long delayed and imperfectly realized an expression of the same in social and political institutions. The answers are many: (1) The Bible is only in possession of a fraction of the people, and that only within the last two or three centuries. For ages the Book was either prohibited to the people by the hierarchy, or rendered inaccessible by its cost, or made of none effect by the illiteracy and sodden ignorance of the masses. (2) The Bible doctrines in regard to women are the last word in democracy, and the first word is just getting itself uttered. Step by step democracy must fight its way against the self-interest, the pride, the passion, and the prejudices of mankind. (3) A steady progress upward can be seen in Christian countries; laws are ameliorated, violence is curbed, child labor is limited, women do come to their rights in exact proportion as Christian ideals become dominant in a nation. (4) The influence of these principles can already be seen to begin to penetrate non-Christian lands in proportion as they come in contact with the religion, the institutions, the literature of Christian lands.

If, as we have seen, the ethnic faiths have no clear gospel for the emancipation of woman and child; if outside of Christian countries they still labor under the most cruel disabilities of both law and custom; if in our own land it is the spirit of the Gospel of Christ which most powerfully wars against intemperance, lust, and greed — woman's hereditary foes — the duty of Christian women to put within the reach of their sisters in other lands this good tidings of great joy is plain. The great Emancipator of the mother and child must be made known in every dark corner of the earth. In the title of our chapter is cleverly summed up by a recent writer on India, the difference between that land and our own — "Ladies First," "Ladies Last," there stand two warring theories of life. In the one insolent strength triumphs over weakness, greed takes what it can get, the wise oppress the ignorant. Helpless because she bears the child in her bosom, woman is pushed to the wall. In the other the very spirit of the Christ is incarnate. Shoulders are strong not to shove, but to bear burdens, wise men are to learn of the child-like, the masters are to be chief servants of all.

[Helen Barrett Montgomery, *Western Women in Eastern Lands* (New York: Macmillan, 1910), 66–75.]

36

Walter Rauschenbusch

Walter Rauschenbusch (1861–1918), an urban pastor and later a professor at Rochester Theological Seminary, is rightly honored as the father of the social gospel. The son of German-born parents, Rauschenbusch labored in a slum area of New York City as rising tides of immigration and industrialization produced wretched living conditions in American cities. Though his earlier training had emphasized forgiveness for personal sin and the joy of individual fellowship with Christ, Rauschenbusch found his congregants were being destroyed not so much by inward need (à la Bunyan) as by social forces beyond any individual's control. He studied the prophets of the Old Testament, contemporary social analyses, and, supremely, the character and example of Jesus to discover a gospel that would liberate society. Conversion, he found, was meant for societies as well as individuals. America was a land where converted individuals lived in an unconverted economic and political culture, but the good news was that this could change; the social order could be Christianized. This theme became the banner for generations of Baptist and other Christian leaders, especially in the industrial North. The social gospel as a movement succumbed to discouragement and cynicism after the World Wars, but it had an enduring aftermath. In the 1930s came the Democratic Party's New Deal, which brought social gospel themes to practical politics as "social security" and "welfare," concepts previously unknown to this national government, and applied them to poor Southern blacks and whites as well as to urban Northern poor. The "Christian realism" of Rauschenbusch's theological successor Reinhold Niebuhr was a much darker version of the social gospel. Finally, the (mainly black and therefore largely Baptist) civil rights movement of the 1960s, focused by Martin Luther King Jr., renewed and expanded Rauschenbusch's vision by calling for the "beloved community" — a human fellowship beyond privilege and violence. It is interesting to speculate upon the difference it might have made to American Christian history had Rauschenbusch's and Mullins' (see Mullins' selection above) places been reversed — what if the white Baptist South had felt early on the impact of Rauschenbusch's devotion to remedying social ills while the increasingly secular North had experienced the healing touch of Mullins' sophisticated version of soul religion?

The Kingdom of God

If theology is to offer an adequate doctrinal basis for the social gospel, it must not only make room for the doctrine of the kingdom of God, but give it a central place and revise all other doctrines so that they will articulate organically with it.

This doctrine is itself the social gospel. Without it, the idea of redeeming the social order will be but an annex to the orthodox conception of the scheme of salvation. It will live like a Negro servant family in a detached cabin back of the white man's house in the South. If this doctrine gets the place which has always been its legitimate right, the practical proclamation and application of social morality will have a firm footing.

To those whose minds live in the social gospel, the kingdom of God is a dear truth, the marrow of the gospel, just as the incarnation was to Athanasius, justification by faith alone to Luther, and the sovereignty of God to Jonathan Edwards. It was just as dear to Jesus. He too lived in it, and from it looked out on the world and the work he had to do.

Jesus always spoke of the kingdom of God. Only two of his reported sayings contain the word "church," and both passages are of questionable authenticity. It is safe to say that he never thought of founding the kind of institution which afterward claimed to be acting for him.

Yet immediately after his death, groups of disciples joined and consolidated by inward necessity. Each local group knew that it was part of a divinely founded fellowship mysteriously spreading through humanity, and awaiting the return of the Lord and the establishing of his kingdom. This universal church was loved with the same religious faith and reverence with which Jesus had loved the kingdom of God. It was the partial and earthly realization of the divine society, and at the parousia the church and the kingdom would merge.

But the kingdom was merely a hope, the church a present reality. The chief interest and affection flowed toward the church. Soon, through a combination of causes, the name and idea of "the kingdom" began to be displaced by the name and idea of "the church" in the preaching, literature, and theological thought of the church. Augustine completed this process in his *De Civitate Dei*. The kingdom of God which has, throughout human history, opposed the kingdom of sin, is today embodied in the church. The millennium began when the church was founded. This practically substituted the actual, not the ideal church for the kingdom of God. The beloved ideal of Jesus became a vague phrase which kept intruding from the New Testament. Like Cinderella in the kitchen, it saw the other great dogmas furbished up for the ball, but no prince of theology restored it to its rightful place. The Reformation, too, brought no renascence of the doctrine of the kingdom; it had only eschatological value, or was defined in blurred phrases borrowed from the church. The present revival of the kingdom idea is due to the combined influence of the historical study of the Bible and of the social gospel.

When the doctrine of the kingdom of God shriveled to an undeveloped and pathetic remnant in Christian thought, this loss was bound to have far-reaching consequences. We are told that the loss of a single tooth from the arch of the mouth in childhood may spoil the symmetrical development of the skull and produce malformations affecting the mind and character. The atrophy of that idea which had occupied the chief place in the mind of Jesus, necessarily affected the conception of Christianity, the life of the church, the progress of humanity, and the structure of theology. I shall briefly enumerate some of the consequences affecting theology. This list, however, is by no means complete.

1. Theology lost its contact with the synoptic thought of Jesus. Its problems were not at all the same which had occupied his mind. It lost his point of view and became to some extent incapable of understanding him. His ideas had to be rediscovered in our time. Traditional theology and the mind of Jesus Christ became incommensurable quantities. It claimed to regard his revelation and the substance of his thought as divine, and yet did not learn to think like him. The loss of the kingdom idea is one key to this situation.

2. The distinctive ethical principles of Jesus were the direct outgrowth of his conception of the kingdom of God. When the latter disappeared from theology, the former disappeared from ethics. Only persons having the substance of the kingdom ideal in their minds, seem to be able to get relish out of the ethics of Jesus. Only those church bodies which have been in opposition to organized society and have looked for a better city with its foundations in heaven, have taken the Sermon on the Mount seriously.

3. The church is primarily a fellowship for worship; the kingdom is a fellowship of righteousness. When the latter was neglected in theology, the ethical force of Christianity was weakened; when the former was emphasized in theology, the importance of worship was exaggerated. The prophets and Jesus had cried down sacrifices and ceremonial performances, and cried up righteousness, mercy, solidarity. Theology now reversed this, and by its theoretical discussions did its best to stimulate sacramental actions and priestly importance. Thus the religious energy and enthusiasm which might have saved mankind from its great sins, were used up in hearing and endowing masses, or in maintaining competitive church organizations, while mankind is still stuck in the mud. There are nations in which the ethical condition of the masses is the reverse of the frequency of the masses in the churches.

4. When the kingdom ceased to be the dominating religious reality, the church moved up into the position of the supreme good. To promote

the power of the church and its control over all rival political forces was equivalent to promoting the supreme ends of Christianity. This increased the arrogance of churchmen and took the moral check off their policies. For the kingdom of God can never be promoted by lies, craft, crime, or war, but the wealth and power of the church have often been promoted by these means. The medieval ideal of the supremacy of the church over the state was the logical consequence of making the church the highest good with no superior ethical standard by which to test it. The medieval doctrines concerning the church and the papacy were the direct theological outcome of the struggles for church supremacy, and were meant to be weapons in that struggle.

5. The kingdom ideal is the test and corrective of the influence of the church. When the kingdom ideal disappeared, the conscience of the church was muffled. It became possible for the missionary expansion of Christianity to halt for centuries without creating any sense of shortcoming. It became possible for the most unjust social conditions to fasten themselves on Christian nations without awakening any consciousness that the purpose of Christ was being defied and beaten back. The practical undertakings of the church remained within narrow lines, and the theological thought of the church was necessarily confined in a similar way. The claims of the church were allowed to stand in theology with no conditions and obligations to test and balance them. If the kingdom had stood as the purpose for which the church exists, the church could not have fallen into such corruption and sloth. Theology bears part of the guilt for the pride, the greed, and the ambition of the church.

6. The kingdom ideal contains the revolutionary force of Christianity. When this ideal faded out of the systematic thought of the church, it became a conservative social influence and increased the weight of the other stationary forces in society. If the kingdom of God had remained part of the theological and Christian consciousness, the church could not, down to our times, have been salaried by autocratic class governments to keep the democratic and economic impulses of the people under check.

7. Reversely, the movements for democracy and social justice were left without a religious backing for lack of the kingdom idea. The kingdom of God as the fellowship of righteousness, would be advanced by the abolition of industrial slavery and the disappearance of the slums of civilization; the church would only indirectly gain through such social changes. Even today many Christians cannot see any religious importance in social justice and fraternity because it does not increase the number of conversions nor fill the churches. Thus the practical conception of salvation, which is the effective theology of the common man and minister, has been cut back and crippled for lack of the kingdom ideal.

8. Secular life is belittled as compared with church life. Services rendered to the church get a higher religious rating than services rendered to the community.

Thus the religious value is taken out of the activities of the common man and the prophetic services to society. Wherever the kingdom of God is a living reality in Christian thought, any advance of social righteousness is seen as a part of redemption and arouses inward joy and the triumphant sense of salvation. When the church absorbs interest, a subtle asceticism creeps back into our theology and the world looks different.

9. When the doctrine of the kingdom of God is lacking in theology, the salvation of the individual is seen in its relation to the church and to the future life, but not in its relation to the task of saving the social order. Theology has left this important point in a condition so hazy and muddled that it has taken us almost a generation to see that the salvation of the individual and the redemption of the social order are closely related, and how.

10. Finally, theology has been deprived of the inspiration of great ideas contained in the idea of the kingdom and in labor for it. The kingdom of God breeds prophets; the church breeds priests and theologians. The church runs to tradition and dogma: the kingdom of God rejoices in forecasts and boundless horizons. The men who have contributed the most fruitful impulses to Christian thought have been men of prophetic vision, and their theology has proved most effective for future times where it has been most concerned with past history, with present social problems, and with the future of human society. The kingdom of God is to theology what outdoor color and light are to art. It is impossible to estimate what inspirational impulses have been lost to theology and to the church, because it did not develop the doctrine of the kingdom of God and see the world and its redemption from that point of view.

These are some of the historical effects which the loss of the doctrine of the kingdom of God has inflicted on systematic theology. The chief contribution which the social gospel has made and will make to theology is to give new vitality and importance to that doctrine. In doing so it will be a reformatory force of the highest importance in the field of doctrinal theology, for any systematic conception of Christianity must be not only defective but incorrect if the idea of the kingdom of God does not govern it.

The restoration of the doctrine of the kingdom has already made progress. Some of the ablest and most voluminous works of the old theology in their thousands of pages gave the kingdom of God but a scanty mention, usually in connection with eschatology, and saw no connection between it and the Calvinistic doctrines of personal redemption.

The newer manuals not only make constant reference to it in connection with various doctrines, but they arrange their entire subject matter so that the kingdom of God becomes the governing idea.

In the following brief propositions I should like to offer a few suggestions, on behalf of the social gospel, for the theological formulation of the doctrine of the kingdom. Something like this is needed to give us "a theology for the social gospel."

1. The kingdom of God is divine in its origin, progress and consummation. It was initiated by Jesus Christ, in whom the prophetic spirit came to its consummation, it is sustained by the Holy Spirit, and it will be brought to its fulfillment by the power of God in his own time. The passive and active resistance of the kingdom of evil at every stage of its advance is so great, and the human resources of the kingdom of God so slender, that no explanation can satisfy a religious mind which does not see the power of God in its movements. The kingdom of God, therefore, is miraculous all the way, and is the continuous revelation of the power, the righteousness, and the love of God. The establishment of a community of righteousness in mankind is just as much a saving act of God as the salvation of an individual from his natural selfishness and moral inability. The kingdom of God, therefore, is not merely ethical, but has a rightful place in theology. This doctrine is absolutely necessary to establish that organic union between religion and morality, between theology and ethics, which is one of the characteristics of the Christian religion. When our moral actions are consciously related to the kingdom of God they gain religious quality. Without this doctrine we shall have expositions of schemes of redemption and we shall have systems of ethics, but we shall not have a true exposition of Christianity. The first step to the reform of the churches is the restoration of the doctrine of the kingdom of God.

2. The kingdom of God contains the teleology of the Christian religion. It translates theology from the static to the dynamic. It sees, not doctrines or rites to be conserved and perpetuated, but resistance to be overcome and great ends to be achieved. Since the kingdom of God is the supreme purpose of God, we shall understand the kingdom so far as we understand God, and we shall understand God so far as we understand his kingdom. As long as organized sin is in the world, the kingdom of God is characterized by conflict with evil. But if there were no evil, or after evil has been overcome, the kingdom of God will still be the end to which God is lifting the race. It is realized not only by redemption, but also by the education of mankind and the revelation of his life within it.

3. Since God is in it, the kingdom of God is always both present and future. Like God it is in all tenses, eternal in the midst of time. It is the energy of God realizing itself in human life. Its future lies among the

mysteries of God. It invites and justifies prophecy, but all prophecy is fallible; it is valuable in so far as it grows out of action for the kingdom and impels action. No theories about the future of the kingdom of God are likely to be valuable or true which paralyze or postpone redemptive action on our part. To those who postpone, it is a theory and not a reality. It is for us to see the kingdom of God as always coming, always pressing in on the present, always big with possibility, and always inviting immediate action. We walk by faith. Every human life is so placed that it can share with God in the creation of the kingdom, or can resist and retard its progress. The kingdom is for each of us the supreme task and the supreme gift of God. By accepting it as a task, we experience it as a gift. By laboring for it we enter into the joy and peace of the kingdom as our divine fatherland and habitation.

4. Even before Christ, men of God saw the kingdom of God as the great end to which all divine leadings were pointing. Every idealistic interpretation of the world, religious or philosophical, needs some such conception. Within the Christian religion the idea of the kingdom gets its distinctive interpretation from Christ. (a) Jesus emancipated the idea of the kingdom from previous nationalistic limitations and from the debasement of lower religious tendencies, and made it world-wide and spiritual. (b) He made the purpose of salvation essential in it. (c) He imposed his own mind, his personality, his love and holy will on the idea of the kingdom. (d) He not only foretold it but initiated it by his life and work. As humanity more and more develops a racial consciousness in modern life, idealistic interpretations of the destiny of humanity will become more influential and important. Unless theology has a solidaristic vision higher and fuller than any other, it cannot maintain the spiritual leadership of mankind, but will be outdistanced. Its business is to infuse the distinctive qualities of Jesus Christ into its teachings about the kingdom, and this will be a fresh competitive test of his continued headship of humanity.

5. The kingdom of God is humanity organized according to the will of God. Interpreting it through the consciousness of Jesus we may affirm these convictions about the ethical relations within the kingdom: (a) Since Christ revealed the divine worth of life and personality, and since his salvation seeks the restoration and fulfillment of even the least, it follows that the kingdom of God, at every stage of human development, tends toward a social order which will best guarantee to all personalities their freest and highest development. This involves the redemption of social life from the cramping influence of religious bigotry, from the repression of self-assertion in the relation of upper and lower classes, and from all forms of slavery in which human beings are treated as mere means to serve the ends of others. (b) Since love is the supreme law of Christ, the kingdom of God implies a progressive reign of love

in human affairs. We can see its advance wherever the free will of love supersedes the use of force and legal coercion as a regulative of the social order. This involves the redemption of society from political autocracies and economic oligarchies; the substitution of redemptive for vindictive penology; the abolition of constraint through hunger as part of the industrial system; and the abolition of war as the supreme expression of hate and the completest cessation of freedom. (c) The highest expression of love is the free surrender of what is truly our own, life, property, and rights. A much lower but perhaps more decisive expression of love is the surrender of any opportunity to exploit men. No social group or organization can claim to be clearly within the kingdom of God which drains others for its own ease, and resists the effort to abate this fundamental evil. This involves the redemption of society from private property in the natural resources of the earth, and from any condition in industry which makes monopoly profits possible. (d) The reign of love tends toward the progressive unity of mankind, but with the maintenance of individual liberty and the opportunity of nations to work out their own national peculiarities and ideals.

6. Since the kingdom is the supreme end of God, it must be the purpose for which the church exists. The measure in which it fulfills this purpose is also the measure of its spiritual authority and honor. The institutions of the church, its activities, its worship, and its theology must in the long run [each] be tested by its effectiveness in creating the kingdom of God. For the church to see itself apart from the kingdom, and to find its aims in itself, is the same sin of selfish detachment as when an individual selfishly separates himself from the common good. The church has the power to save in so far as the kingdom of God is present in it. If the church is not living for the kingdom, its institutions are part of the "world." In that case it is not the power of redemption but its object. It may even become an anti-Christian power. If any form of church organization which formerly aided the kingdom now impedes it, the reason for its existence is gone.

7. Since the kingdom is the supreme end, all problems of personal salvation must be reconsidered from the point of view of the kingdom. It is not sufficient to set the two aims of Christianity side by side. There must be a synthesis, and theology must explain how the two react on each other.

The entire redemptive work of Christ must also be reconsidered under this orientation. Early Greek theology saw salvation chiefly as the redemption from ignorance by the revelation of God and from earthliness by the impartation of immortality. It interpreted the work of Christ accordingly, and laid stress on his incarnation and resurrection. Western theology saw salvation mainly as forgiveness of guilt and freedom from punishment. It interpreted the work of Christ accordingly, and laid stress on the death and atonement. If the kingdom of God was the guiding idea and chief end of Jesus — as we now know it was — we may be sure that every step in his life, including his death, was related to that aim and its realization, and when the idea of the kingdom of God takes its due place in theology, the work of Christ will have to be interpreted afresh.

8. The kingdom of God is not confined within the limits of the church and its activities. It embraces the whole of human life. It is the Christian transfiguration of the social order. The church is one social institution alongside of the family, the industrial organization of society, and the state. The kingdom of God is in all these, and realizes itself through them all. During the Middle Ages all society was ruled and guided by the church. Few of us would want modern life to return to such a condition. Functions which the church used to perform, have now far outgrown its capacities. The church is indispensable to the religious education of humanity and to the conservation of religion but the greatest future awaits religion in the public life of humanity.

[Walter Rauschenbusch, *A Theology for the Social Gospel* (New York: Macmillan, 1917), 131–45.]

37

Douglas Clyde Macintosh

Douglas Clyde Macintosh (1877–1948) was born, converted, baptized, and educated (finishing at McMaster College) in Ontario, Canada, before going on to the University of Chicago for his Ph.D. This first decade of the twentieth century was the heyday of Chicago modernism; theologians there optimistically treated religious experience as a sure foundation for a new Christian theology, fit for modern men and women. Invited to teach at Yale, Macintosh brought this training there with him, but he also brought the indelible memory of his early evangelistic Christian convictions as a youth in Ontario. In time he developed his own theological method that brought the two together: the universe operated according to law, and the laws of the spiritual realm were as invariant and dependable as those of the physical realm. Thus, anyone who made a "right religious adjustment" (abbreviated RRA) received the promised blessing as surely as those who drank water had their thirst quenched. This spiritual reliability made it possible to treat theology as a science of the spirit, and Macintosh's teaching and writing explored theology's (empirical) scientific character. An interesting fact about Canadian Macintosh's long residence in Connecticut is that when he applied for United States citizenship, the U.S. government required him to swear his willingness to bear arms in its defense. A convinced Baptist pacifist, Macintosh was unable to do this; the consequent denial of citizenship, appealed, rose to the U.S. Supreme Court, where his application was rejected. Yale, however, retained him as a professor, and he completed his teaching career there.

Theology as an Empirical Science

In undertaking to formulate the laws of empirical theology we naturally presuppose both the general fact of revelation and particular facts of revelation, such as have been discussed in the preceding sections. In accepting such facts as empirical data for our science, we are taking the position, as indicated above, that in experimental religion at its best there is objectively valid religious perception. A more detailed exposition and defense of our position than we have offered above would lead us into the philosophy of religion, and so beyond the intended scope of the present volume.

In experimental religion, as in all experiential life, there are factors which are constant and others which are variable. Now the possibility of formulating empirical laws depends upon the discovery of constant relations in the midst of experienced variations. Among the constants involved in the present instance are nature with its laws, and certain aspects of the social environment and of human nature in general. The most important constant for theology, however, is the being and character of God. This is the Constant of empirical theological laws. The God whose existence, in the light of permanently successful religious experience, we are justified in assuming, has been defined above as the necessary objective Factor in religious experience, or the Object of active religious dependence, or the Source of salvation, i.e., of religious deliverance from evil. Other preliminary definitions, sufficient to mark off the religious Object from other objects are the following: the objective Source of that inner or spiritual preparedness for whatever the future may bring which is achieved through the right sort of religious adjustment; or again, the Power, not identical with our empirical selves, nor with the merely physical or merely human environment, which makes for righteousness in and through us according as we relate ourselves to it in a certain discoverable way. This is the Reality which we have called the Holy Spirit. Beyond what is here involved we do not attempt to anticipate the results of theological theory; the character of God is what we have to investigate by our empirical procedure. We simply assume (in the scientifically tentative or empirical way) that God has character and will therefore be found to be dependable, when we have found out what we ought to depend upon the religious Object for. It is involved in what we have already said, that God is a constant Source of unfailing spiritual power. Of course to assert dependable character is not necessarily to deny free agency. Moreover, even with all the constants involved, we do not claim that theology is or ever can become an exact science. We may not be able to make an exact quantitative prediction of the results of experimental religion in any individual case, because of the many more or less unknown factors and at least one factor which is not completely predetermined. But the quality and direction characteristic of the Constant's action may be learned through empirical investigation.

Among the variables which tend to enter as factors into religious experience are certain phases of the social environment and of the individual training and outfit of ideas. Often these are constants relatively to some collections of religious data, and variables relatively to others. But the two most important variables, at least within the individual religious subject, are the quality and degree of responsiveness of nature or constitution, and the particular religious adjustment adopted. According to the variation from individual to individual, and from one time to another within the same individual, the results of the religious adjustment come quickly or slowly, and steadily or unsteadily. For example, the conditions of right religious adjustment being fulfilled and persisted in, there are some persons into whose lives there will be a gradually increasing incoming of the divine, and others in whose cases the incoming may be delayed for some time, and then, when the constitutional resistance has been overcome, it may manifest itself suddenly. However, the influence of the social religious environment may counteract the tendency to slowness and unsteadiness. But in general there would seem to be at least four possible types, due to constitutional and environmental differences, viz. (1) that of quick but unsteady returns, (2) that of slow but steady returns, (3) that of quick and steady returns, and (4) that of slow and unsteady returns.

But the most important variable, especially for our present purpose, is the particular religious adjustment adopted by the individual. What we are interested in formulating is the right religious adjustment, i.e., the one which is at the same time critically justifiable and most effective for good. It is that adjustment to the religious Object which is necessary in order to realize those values for the sake of which individuals are and ought to be experimentally religious.

It may be worth while to point out the mistaken nature of the notion often entertained that the adjustment is primarily or even exclusively intellectual, i.e., that there is a law of religious experience the sole and sufficient human condition of which is correct religious opinion, or belief. Experience has long ago and time after time refuted this idea. To be sure, among the Jews in the days of primitive Christianity belief in Jesus as the Messiah seemed the condition of the Christian experience of salvation; but this was because, under the special circumstances of that people at that time, such a belief was the cue to a whole series of practical attitudes, which were the real condition of the religious experience. But for most people in "Christian" communities to-day, the doctrine that Jesus was the Messiah, or Christ, is a commonplace of traditional teaching and belief; it has practically no spiritual dynamic at all. The "right religious adjustment" must be sought primarily in the volitional rather than in the intellectual realm.

According to scientific empirical procedure, in seeking to determine the most effective intellectually justifiable religious adjustment, we should first go as far as we can in deducing theological hypotheses from the general presuppositions of theology and the special theological assumption of the existence of the religious Object (as defined in preliminary fashion), together with the general principle of the dependableness of that Object. We should then supplement the rather bare and abstract content of these hypotheses by having recourse to the scientific imagination, with its suggestions drawn from prescientific religious experience. Finally the hypotheses thus constructed and speculatively elaborated should be used as working hypotheses and submitted to the test of practical experience, and in the light of the result classified as refuted or partially verified or completely verified. One would do well, however, definitely to compare his tentative results with those of others, paying special attention to testimonies of those most expert in securing successful religious adjustments.

But the process of the discovery of empirical laws may be greatly facilitated if we remember that in the religious life and experience of Jesus we find the supreme instance of success in experimental religion. We have already referred to the three main factors in Jesus' spiritual ministry as the presenting in his teaching and perhaps even more in the spirit discernible in his action, of (1) the true moral ideal for man, (2) the true religious ideal for man, and (3) the true revelation of God. Here we are concerned with all three of these, but especially with the second. The religious example of Jesus has its significance and value largely because of the chief end for the sake of which he was religious, viz., the promotion of moral efficiency in the interests of true human welfare. For Jesus has his transcendent greatness chiefly through the fact that he was at once a social and a religious genius; he discovered the true worth of man and the true way to God. It is true that in Jesus Christ as revelation of God, we have the objective Factor to which religious adjustment has to be made, not only better represented but better presented than elsewhere, and thus at the same time giving us a greater certainty of the divine Reality than we should otherwise have been able to have in systematically beginning our own religious experience. But it is the religious example of Jesus which we find especially illuminating at this point. It is not without ample justification that an experienced and well-known religious worker has expressed the first definite step toward the essentially Christian religious experience in the following declaration: "It is my purpose, with the help of God, to pay what it costs to be a sincere follower of Jesus Christ."

Assisted by these considerations we may analyze into the following chief elements what has been found to be at once the most effective and, we would claim, a critically justifiable religious adjustment. First, then, there must be concentration of attention, with the aid of appropriate guiding ideas, upon the Object of religious dependence, identified with the Source of religious deliverance, with special reference to a thoroughly moral end which represents "the soul's sincere desire." There must also be a whole-hearted or absolute self-surrender to the divine

Being, a consecration and abandon of one's self to be worked upon and through by the divine Power; and at the same time an absolute dependence upon God with reference to the thoroughly moral and sincerely desired end which is to be realized with the assistance of the divine Power. It is also important that there be a willed responsiveness, or readiness for active expression, as the divine Being may seem to guide and impel. This is the really essential thing in faith. It involves trusting God; it is venturing to go ahead with one's own part in the process, counting upon God for adequate grace and power for the fulfillment of the duty before us. It is well, to be sure, to cultivate the habit of waiting before God for the necessary "enduement with power"; but one should not be too dilatory any more than he should be too precipitate. And finally, there should be a steady persistence in the religious attitude just described. What is to be maintained here, then, is that the laws of empirical theology may be thrown into generalized form in a statement to the effect that, on condition of the above-described religious adjustment on man's part, God produces in human life and character certain moral experiences and qualities, with tendencies toward certain further consequences.

Before proceeding to a detailed statement of the principal theological laws, however, some further general observations may be recorded. It would seem that there may be, and are, within the limits of a "right religious adjustment," various differentiations of the faith attitude. The most important factor in this variation, perhaps, is the nature of the moral objective entertained. For example, the faith-attitude which seeks patience under affliction will be somewhat different from that which aims at power for service; and so where the objectives are firmness and gentleness respectively.

Again, it may be remarked, the laws of empirical theology, if they are to keep close to the facts, will frequently have to embody a sliding scale of results varying in proportion to the earnestness and persistence of the individual will with reference to religious adjustment. This is especially true of the growth of spiritual character under religious influence, and of the emotional phases of religious experience. But it is not always possible to formulate a uniformly sliding scale. The most notable exception is bound up with the fact that, so far as special enduement with power for service and for the overcoming of temptation is concerned, there are no results, comparatively speaking, until the consecration or self-surrender is at least intended to be total and absolute. Again, this condition having been fulfilled, the results tend to vary with attention and prayer, and so to fall into a sliding scale, but only up to a certain point; for there seems to be, in the case of persons of ordinary constitutions, a "law of diminishing returns" after a certain point has been reached. For example, for most people it is probably not true that two hours spent continuously in prayer will produce twice as much in the way of spiritual uplift and power as would result from a single hour thus occupied. On the other hand, there are persons of mystical temperament who seem to get very slight returns until they have persisted in their devotions far beyond what is customarily regarded as a reasonable time. And probably nobody is ever justified in saying that he has at any time exhausted the possibilities of spiritual uplift bound up with the right sort of experimental religion. There seems always, in spite of any law of diminishing returns, an inexhaustible possibility of more of the divine....

[Douglas Clyde Macintosh, *Theology as an Empirical Science* (New York: Macmillan, 1919), 140–45.]

38

Harry Emerson Fosdick

Fundamentalism, the early twentieth-century theological movement that A. H. Strong and others like him sought to contain or redirect, nevertheless flourished. Its theological opponents gave themselves various names such as "the New Theology," but came in time to be known as Protestant Modernists, thinkers who made a valiant if unstable attempt to translate Christian faith into the thought-forms of the times. As such, the modernist movement could be considered conservative, *but it was fiercely criticized by the fundamentalists or self-styled orthodox, who held that modernism in its effort to adjust to new thought abandoned too much of old Christianity. Harry Emerson Fosdick (1878–1969), pastor, author, sometime theological lecturer, came like Strong from intensely Baptist territory in upstate New York (Fosdick was born in Buffalo). He was educated at interdenominational Union Theological Seminary, New York, where his chief theological mentor was William Newton Clarke, a Baptist, and where his inspiration was the writing of Walter Rauschenbusch. Fosdick served as a Baptist pastor, then as an army chaplain during World War I, and next, without renouncing his Baptist connections, as pastor of First Presbyterian Church, New York City (1918–25). At First Presbyterian, Fosdick preached and later published the famous sermon, "Shall the Fundamentalists Win?" which challenged three essentials of that rising movement — the virgin birth of Jesus, biblical inerrancy, and a literal Second Coming. None of them were essential or fundamental, Fosdick claimed, to authentic Christianity. In 1930 he became pastor of the new interdenominational Riverside Church in New York, founded with Rockefeller money. There he exercised an influential ministry until retirement in 1946. Though the following selection is taken from a book published during his years of Presbyterian service, it is consistent with Fosdick's liberal standpoint and representative of many Baptist thinkers in his generation who adopted liberal assumptions about the foundational role of religious experience in their attempts to support Christian belief.*

Progressive Christianity

Obviously, the point where this progressive conception of Christianity comes into conflict with many widely accepted ideas is the abandonment which it involves of an external and inerrant authority in matters of religion. The marvel is that that idea of authority, which is one of the historic curses of religion, should be regarded by so many as one of the vital necessities of the faith. The fact is that religion by its very nature is one of the realms to which external authority is least applicable. In science people commonly suppose that they do not take truth on any one's authority; they prove it. In business they do not accept methods on authority; they work them out. In statesmanship they no longer believe in the divine right of kings nor do they accept infallible dicta handed down from above. But they think that religion is delivered to them by authority and that they believe what they do believe because a divine Church or a divine Book or a divine Man told them.

In this common mode of thinking, popular ideas have the truth turned upside down. The fact is that science, not religion, is the realm where most of all we use external authority. They tell us that there are millions of solar systems scattered through the fields of space. Is that true? How do we know? We never counted them. We know only what the authorities say. They tell us that the next great problem in science is breaking up the atom to discover the incalculable resources of power there waiting to be harnessed by our skill. Is that true? Most of us do not understand what an atom is, and what it means to break one up passes the farthest reach of our imaginations; all we know is what the authorities say. They tell us that electricity is a mode of motion in ether. Is that true? Most of us have no first hand knowledge about electricity. The motorman calls it "juice" and that means as much to us as to call it a mode of motion in ether; we must rely on the authorities. They tell us that sometime we are going to talk through wireless telephones across thousands of miles, so that no man need ever be out of vocal communication with his family and friends. Is that true? It seems to us an incredible miracle, but we suppose that it is so, as the authorities say. In a word, the idea that we do not use authority in science is absurd. Science is precisely the place where nine hundred and ninety-nine men out of a thousand use authority the most. The chemistry, biology, geology, astronomy which the authorities teach is the only science which most of us possess.

There is another realm, however, where we never think of taking such an attitude. They tell us that friendship is beautiful. Is that true? Would we ever think of saying that we do not know, ourselves, but that we rely on the authorities? Far better to say that our experience with friendship has been unhappy and that we personally question its utility! That, at least, would have an accent of personal, original experience in it. For here we are facing a realm where we never can enter at all until we enter, each man for himself.

Two realms exist, therefore, in each of which first-hand experience is desirable, but in only one of which it is absolutely indispensable. We can live on what the authorities in physics say, but there are no proxies for the soul. Love, friendship, delight in music and in nature, parental affection — these things are like eating and breathing; no one can do them for us; we must enter the experience for ourselves. Religion, too, belongs in this last realm. The one vital thing in religion is first-hand, personal experience. Religion is the most intimate, inward, incommunicable fellowship of the human soul. In the words of Plotinus, religion is "the flight of the alone to the Alone." You never know God at all until you know him for yourself. The only God you ever will know is the God you do know for yourself.

This does not mean, of course, that there are no authorities in religion. There are authorities in everything, but the function of an authority in religion, as in every other vital realm, is not to take the place of our eyes, seeing in our stead and inerrantly declaring to us what it sees; the function of an authority is to bring to us the insight of the world's accumulated wisdom and the revelations of God's seers, and so to open our eyes that we may see, each man for himself. So an authority in literature does not say to his students: The Merchant of Venice is a great drama; you may accept my judgment on that — I know. Upon the contrary, he opens their eyes; he makes them see; he makes their hearts sensitive so that the genius which made Shylock and Portia live captivates and subdues them, until like the Samaritans they say, "Now we believe, not because of thy speaking: for we have heard for ourselves, and know." That is the only use of authority in a vital realm. It can lead us up to the threshold of a great experience where we must enter, each man for himself, and that service to the spiritual life is the Bible's inestimable gift.

At the beginning, Christianity was just such a first-hand experience as we have described. The Christian fellowship consisted of a group of men keeping company with Jesus and learning how to live. They had no creeds to recite when they met together; what they believed was still an unstereotyped passion in their hearts. They had no sacraments to distinguish their faith — baptism had been a Jewish rite and even the Lord's Supper was an informal use of bread and wine, the common elements of their daily meat. They had no organizations to join; they never dreamed that the Christian gospel would build a church outside the synagogue. Christianity in the beginning was an intensely personal experience.

Then the Master went away and the tremendous forces of human life and history laid hold on the movement which so vitally he had begun. His followers began building churches. Just as the Wesleyans had to leave the Church of England, not because they wanted to, but because the Anglicans would not keep them, so the Christians, not because they planned to, but because the synagogue was not large enough to hold them, had to leave the synagogue. They began building creeds; they had to. Every one of the first Christian creeds was written in sheer self-defense. If we had been Christians in those first centuries, when a powerful movement was under way called Gnosticism, which denied that God, the Father Almighty, had made both the heaven and the earth, which said that God had made heaven indeed but that a demigod had made the world, and which denied that Jesus had been born in the flesh and in the flesh had died, we would have done what the first Christians did: we would have defined in a creed what it was the Christians did believe as against that wild conglomeration of Oriental mythology that Gnosticism was, and we would have shouted the creed as a war cry against the Gnostics. That is what the so-called Apostles' Creed was — the first Christian battle chant, a militant proclamation of the historic faith against the heretics; and every one of its declarations met with a head-on collision some claim of Gnosticism. Then, too, the early Christians drew up rituals; they had to. We cannot keep any spiritual thing in human life, even the spirit of courtesy, as a disembodied wraith. We ritualize it: we bow, we take off our hats, we shake hands, we rise when a lady enters. We have innumerable ways of expressing politeness in a ritual. Neither could they have kept so deep and beautiful a thing as the Christian life without such expression.

So historic Christianity grew, organized, creedalized, ritualized. And ever as it grew, a peril grew with it, for there were multitudes of people who joined these organizations, recited these creeds, observed these rituals, took all the secondary and derived elements of Christianity, but often forgot that vital thing which all this was meant in the first place to express: a first-hand, personal experience of God in Christ. That alone is vital in Christianity; all the rest is once or twice or thrice removed from life. For Christianity is not a creed, nor an organization, nor a ritual. These are important but they are secondary. They are the leaves, not the roots; they are the wires, not the message. Christianity itself is a life.

If, however, Christianity is thus a life, we cannot stereotype its expressions in set and final forms. If it is a life in fellowship with the living God, it will think new thoughts, build new organizations, expand into new symbolic expressions. We cannot at any given time write "finis" after its development. We can no more "keep the faith" by stopping its growth than we can keep a son by insisting on his being forever a child. The progressiveness of Christianity is not simply its response to a progressive age; the progressiveness of Christianity springs from its own inherent vitality. So far is this from being regrettable, that a modern

Christian rejoices in it and gladly recognizes not only that he is thinking thoughts and undertaking enterprises which his fathers would not
have understood, but also that his children after him will differ quite
as much in teaching and practice from the modernity of to-day. It has
been the fashion to regard this changeableness with wistful regret. So
Wordsworth sings in his sonnet on Mutability:

> Truth fails not; but her outward forms that bear
> The longest date do melt like frosty rime,
> That in the morning whitened hill and plain
> And is no more; drop like the tower sublime
> Of yesterday, which royally did wear
> Its crown of weeds, but could not even sustain
> Some casual shout that broke the silent air,
> Or the unimaginable touch of Time."

Such wistfulness, however, while a natural sentiment, is not true to
the best Christian thought of our day. He who believes in the living
God, while he will be far from calling all change progress, and while
he will, according to his judgment, withstand perverse changes with
all his might, will also regard the cessation of change as the greatest
calamity that could befall religion. Stagnation in thought or enterprise
means death for Christianity as certainly as it does for any other vital
movement. Stagnation, not change, is Christianity's most deadly enemy,
for this is a progressive world, and in a progressive world no doom is
more certain than that which awaits whatever is belated, obscurantist
and reactionary.

[Harry Emerson Fosdick, *Christianity and Progress* (London: Nisbet and Co., 1922),
57–65.]

39

Muriel Lester

Born into a prosperous and prominent Baptist family, Muriel Lester (1883–1968) devoted her life to solidarity with the poor. In 1898 Lester was converted and baptized into the Fillebrook Baptist Church in Essex County, England. The writings of Leo Tolstoy became a catalyst for her second conversion, another spiritual change after she had already begun her Christian pilgrimage. This experience, she later wrote, "changed the very quality of life for me." As Lester began to associate with the poor in the East End of London, she became increasingly disappointed with the inability of the institutional church to effect real social transformation. In 1914 Muriel and her sister Verona established a community center known as Kingsley Hall for the East End of London. Paul Dekar notes that "Lester owed to her Baptist inheritance a passion to live fully in the light of Resurrection power" (For the Healing of the Nations, 225). During the First World War she joined and in 1933 began serving as traveling secretary for the Fellowship of Reconciliation (the leading international pacifist organization). Guests at Kingsley Hall included American Catholic Worker Dorothy Day and Indian activist Mahatma Gandhi. A tireless advocate for peace and justice, Lester sought always to give voice to the cares of "God's other children" — the poor, the marginalized, the disenfranchised. She authored some thirteen books. It Occurred to Me and her subsequent volumes carry the power of her simple yet deeply spiritual autobiographical style. Gandhi wrote of Lester, "She endeavors every moment of her life to practice what she professes and preaches in her writings" (cited in Richard Deats, Ambassador of Reconciliation, 3).

The Disciplined Life

In Germany and Russia they specialize in the disciplined life. Our lives have to be even more disciplined. We must out-train the totalitarians, out-match their "intrepidity, contempt for comfort, surrender of private interest, obedience to command" with a superior courage, frugality, loyalty and selflessness. Our job is bigger than theirs. It is to spread the

Kingdom of Heaven, the Rule of God. Our business is to stop war, to purify the world, to get it saved from poverty and riches, to make people like each other, to heal the sick, and comfort the sad, to wake up those who have not yet found God, to create joy and beauty wherever we go, to find God in everything and in everyone.

Without confidence the body politic tends to disintegrate. Without confidence business is impossible. Without confidence we can do nothing. There is power, unseen, indefinable, inherent in the stuff of the life which always responds to confidence. How can we link all of ourselves to this power? What must we do to acquire the strength of spirit, the carefree joy without which life is a lame and rather smirched affair? Are there any rules? During the past few years groups of people, young mostly — in America, in Berlin, in Vienna, in Fanø and in England — have met together at odd and awkward hours to work out a set of techniques for living the disciplined life. Here are some:

To disarm — not only our bodies by refusing to kill, or to make killing instruments in munitions factories — but to disarm our minds of anger, pride, envy, hate and malice. We should stop praying the Lord's Prayer until we can see that "Our Father" means we are "tied to the same living tether" not only with fellow countrymen but with everybody on this planet. In this perspective, righteous indignation is soon found to be a noxious growth, fostered by the pleasure we feel unconsciously in comparing our imagined rectitude with the obvious evil of other nations. Owning up to our own share of blame in any awkward situation that arises in international as well as home or church or social life, is a pre-condition of getting a new start made. Usually it is the most sensible and perhaps least blameworthy person who makes the first move. He may not be conscious of any particular guilt of his own, but he takes it for granted that, being in general a sinner, he had some hand in it, and he sets the healing process going [by] not excusing himself, and by shouldering his share of the general blame. No matter how morally superior we feel, this fact remains: no one can suddenly become our enemy because he happens to have been born the other side of a river, or strip of sea, and two governments have signed a bit of paper called an ultimatum. Violence creates violence. This applies to our mental moods. Our anger, pride, envy, hate, malice and "righteous indignation" are murderous. However deep they have twined into our personality, we must pluck them out though such drastic uprooting may entail agony. Self-pity also has to go. Self-pity is a perfect preparation for dictatorship.

What we call non-violence is not enough. It may still be camouflaged cowardice. Non-violence to be effective must be allied with the vow of truth. To pretend that the aggressor is not aggressing, as was done by certain great powers during the rape of Manchuria and the destruction of Spain, is to stultify personality; it is to destroy morale and imperil the future by destroying the ability to think straight. Gandhi's followers train themselves to speak the truth without fear and without exaggeration; to tell it to people who do not want to hear it, or in the quarters where the telling of it may lose them their jobs or land them in jail. Gandhi was obeying the vow of truth when he declared that the British government was "Satanic" but that they the British people must be loved and on occasion copied, for they have certain virtues which the Indian lacks, just as the Indian has virtues which the British lack.

But even non-violence plus truth is not enough. There is a third necessity — non-co-operation. This takes sublime courage; the courage not to raise one's hand and say "Heil Hitler"; the courage of Japanese soldiers who have refused to kill Chinese. War-resistance implies non-co-operation. If our country were suddenly Hitlerized, or Stalinized, we should have to refuse to keep the imposed laws at whatever cost. This implies that we must make ourselves spiritually and physically fit to endure torture.

We must keep at the top of our form, ready for anything. It is rather an insult to God to make it appear that He is such a bad engineer as to be continually turning out machines that don't work. Poise, endurance, strength, the serenity that comes from the open-air life — all these things characterized Jesus. To walk three or four miles a day is one step in this direction. (Mr. Ford will somehow survive.) The body is the temple of something far more holy than we may suspect. Holiness means health, wholeness and completeness. To let the Spirit of God thus rule our lives eventually brings real fulfillment. On that basis problems such as sex solve themselves. And voluntary simplicity becomes exhilarating just as going without pie sharpens the alertness and staying power of a long distance runner.

We must face the fact that the present economic order is not God's. Why do we wait for revolutions or elections? Why not begin now to readjust our personal economic life? "If you possess superfluities, while your brethren lack necessities, you are possessing the goods of others and are therefore stealing." A growing number of people realize that they have a right to the satisfaction of their needs, physical and cultural, but beyond that their property is not really theirs at all. According to the law of the land it belongs to them. According to the law of God it belongs to the people who need it — God's other children. It's rather a lark working out all these common sense ideas, even in the midst of a distraught and distressing world. We might meet with like-minded people, a group of three is enough to begin with, and state how much money each of us received during the previous month by earning, income or gift, and exactly how we spent it; confessing thus the measure of our greed and our need with equal frankness. The persistence of the worship of the golden calf is due in part to a secrecy and pride and false sanctity with which we treat money matters.

We discuss with our friends our thoughts, our religious ideas, our love affairs, but we rarely let them know our income. We might leave out one meal a week, not only to provide a little fund for the propagation of our ideas, but to recall our errant thought to the hunger of many friends, and raise other people's standard of living by lowering our own. Ours, even in peacetime, not to promulgate vegetarianism, to despise the delight of chocolates, to fear the effects of nicotine, but it seems a bit vulgar to consume in a few seconds the price of a week's food for a Chinese family. The more we like candy, smokes and cakes, the more potent reminders they become, when we refuse to take them, of our unemployed friends and of the undernourished millions in the Orient. To do without dessert so that a Chinese child may be kept alive for a whole day (it costs three cents to do that!) does not rob one of energy. It enhances one's sense of solidarity. It makes one more alive.

There is a plenitude in the world of all good things; enough raw materials for food, fuel and clothing to satisfy the needs of every inhabitant of the globe. But we cannot enjoy too much cake while others have no bread. If you and I love God with all our hearts and all our wills and all our wits, we will not leave the job of breaking down barriers of class, nation or race to isolated efforts here and there. We will work together with other people in organized social pressures to distribute goods according to a sound economic plan so that the "haves" and "have-nots" shall gain equitable access to the abundance of this earth. Ought not all the Lord's people to be ready to speak out the truth, to face officials, magistrates, editors, archbishops and dictators, and give them a message of common sense in the name of God and the common people? "I claim no privileges that others cannot have the counterpart of on the same terms," said Eugene V. Debs. Can't we who are relatively over-privileged go a little way toward his position?

The idea of being stripped of superfluities is so that others may enjoy what otherwise we should be stealing from them. It is also so that we ourselves may be more athletic, more alert to expect "that of God" in every man we meet. Let us remember that it is far easier to love enemies whom we have never seen, who live hundreds of miles away, than our next-door neighbor whose dog or radio irritates us. The vertical barriers that separate country from country are easier to break through than the horizontal barriers that separate man from man in the same city; barriers between those of different races, class and character. When one has learned to recognize a spark of God's Spirit in the least reputable of one's neighbors, one has more power to drop all labels and to work for that justice which must underlie the making of peace.

The only way to get strong enough to keep at it is to practice the presence of God. We have to force ourselves to return many times in a morning from worry and self-pity, from fear and defeatism, from conceit and callousness, to the Unseen Reality of the Eternal. When we are overtaken in a fault, in sin, in a new realization of our own pitiful weakness and hypocrisy, we do not grieve overmuch. We lift up our hearts to God immediately as Brother Lawrence advises, not delaying a second, and we say: "Lord, I shall always go on doing such and such, unless I keep closer to Thee." Those who are not rooted deeply enough in God, who are not disciplined by prayer to face facts and repent of sins and gain power to make a fresh start, tend to project their self-disgust on to others. They lose confidence in the future, in life itself.

We keep silent, solitary, if possible, for half an hour a day. During this period we enjoy completely relaxed muscles and nerves. We walk or sit or lie and we let our breathing become slow, and deep and regular. The surprising restfulness that ensues at the end of fifteen minutes or so makes one understand that the rhythm of the Universe [is] God's, and is keeping our own bodies and minds sane and sound. God's Spirit breathed into man's nostrils the breath of life and he became a living soul. His Creative Spirit is also the Recreative Spirit. Our nights and our awakening are no longer haunted by apprehensions of things undone, by self-disgust, by dread of some coming ordeal, for each of these fears and shames is faced in the presence of God. How is it possible to dread an interview with anyone, when we know God will be the third Person present at that conversation? The world is God's, though one has to rally all one's forces to keep aware of the fact. The world is God's, though our breakfast coffee is spoilt by its proximity to a newspaper full of horrors.

We can no longer make the affirmation lightheartedly. Yet to confess that the world is not God's, to say He has failed, abdicated, that another method, not God's must be adopted, is to court disintegration, to commit the ultimate blasphemy. It would blacken the skies with bombing aeroplanes and with despair. For if we forcibly detach ourselves from our particular fears and hates, recriminations and regrets, if we submit ourselves to the cleansing power of events, we see that our narrow vision, our callous self-indulgence, our lazy, purposeless living, our profit-seeking, our tenacious hold on national, racial and personal privileges, have materially helped to create the present agony.

In quietness and confidence is our strength. From now on, we're committed to the exciting, dangerous but never dull talk of using all our available powers. It is because we have used only a fraction of our available powers that our bodies have been poisoned with silly, bitter, angry thoughts, or the sense that we have no place in the world.

We accept the fact that most of God's work is done slowly, remembering how long it takes Him to make a tree. Lots of His work is done in the dark, in secret, underground. Isn't it an honor for us to be given work like that, quiet and low and regular rather than the showy kind? We may face the firing squad. Again, nothing externally dramatic like that may ever happen to us. What difference?

Ours is to keep sensitive enough to be in contact with God daily, to practice life as an art. Many times a day we are to sharpen our hunger for that perfection which is the goal of all art by putting ourselves through certain necessary scales and exercises just as a good pianist does.

[Muriel Lester, *Training* (Nashville: Abingdon-Cokesbury, 1940), 3–10.]

– 40 –

Walter Thomas Conner

A quite different theological heritage than that of the preceding authors appears in the work of Walter Thomas Conner (1877–1952), the deeply respected teacher of present author McClendon. The age of theological liberalism (represented by all the preceding twentieth-century selections except A. H. Strong's) was followed in Protestantism by a "neo-orthodoxy," in which Christian theologians attempted a return to earlier theological exemplars. Conner falls in this class; though he studied with Strong and Rauschenbusch and later with Mullins, he was influenced by Europeans Barth and Gustaf Aulén and even more by Scripture: Conner thought the Bible shed essential light on the work of these later theologians. In 1945 he included in The Gospel of Redemption, *a revision of his earlier systematics, a section on the church — thus correcting E. Y. Mullins and others who had passed over that doctrine in their own theologies. A son of the Western plains, Conner was born in Arkansas, converted in Texas, and served for most of his days as professor at Southwestern Baptist Theological Seminary, where most were like himself Southwesterners. He had a keen ear for plain English language and spoke and wrote with a clarity few could excel. After his death, attempts were made to claim him for Calvinist hyper-orthodoxy and other right-wing causes, but his spoken and written words refute these claims — see his biography written by his student and colleague Stewart A. Newman:* W. T. Conner: Theologian of the Southwest. *In fact, as the following selection shows, Conner anticipated many of the theological moves later made by John Howard Yoder. Some today may learn with surprise that long before them he was emphasizing the centrality of the resurrection of Jesus Christ from the dead, was recognizing the indispensable role of Septuagint studies in understanding the Greek New Testament, and was looking to Asia to provide the next chapter in Christian theological development. He affirmed (against the orthodoxy of not a few generations) that in atonement God himself had suffered; so he was a "patripassian." Some of these emphases are evident in the following selection, which is drawn from one of his two mature systematic volumes (the other is* Revelation and God *[1936]). In Conner, Baptist theology began turning a decisive corner, though (perhaps because*

*they consigned him to his region and his denomination) few in his day
recognized the turn.*

The Cross as Victory Over Sin

The Ransom Theory

One of the earliest views with reference to the saving work of Christ
was known as the ransom theory. It was never formulated in any very
definite manner and could hardly be spoken of as a definite theory. It
prevailed more or less generally for something like a thousand years. It
had associated with it such outstanding names in Christian history as
Origen and Augustine. Since many of the names of the early church fathers were associated with the view, it is sometimes spoken of as the
"patristic" view. It was the nearest thing to a definite theory of the
atonement in Christian history until Anselm's day.

The view had for a scriptural background or foundation such passages as the saying of Jesus that the Son of man came to give his life a
ransom for many (Mark 10:45) and numerous other passages in which
his work is spoken of as a ransoming or redeeming from sin and its
power. When the question arose as to whom the ransom was paid, many
of the early fathers said that it was paid to the devil. In general outline,
with variations, the view was that the devil in the Fall acquired a right
over mankind; God redeemed man from his enslaved condition by de-
livering Christ in death to the devil, according to terms of an agreement.
But in the resurrection Christ overcame the devil and he was left de-
spoiled of both Christ and mankind. Sometimes an element of deceit
and trickery was introduced into the theory, in that the devil was offered Christ in death in exchange for the race. The devil was unaware of
Christ's divinity. Christ, however, being divine overcame the devil and
thus robbed him of his victim.

Sin as Opposition to God

Crude as this view was, it truly represents sin and salvation as a conflict
between God and the devil. It is a conflict that is more than human and
more than individual. It is a conflict between a kingdom of light and one
of darkness, between God at the head of the forces of righteousness and
Satan at the head of the forces of evil.

Some recent writers have indicated that a true view of Christ's saving
work would need to follow this line rather than the lines of the "moral"
or "penal" views.

As I understand them, they mean to say that we should think of Christ's saving work as being the overcoming of spiritual opposition to God and the death of Christ as the means by which this was accomplished. It seems to me that this is a true insight. From the beginning of human history sin has been opposition to God. Moreover, it has been more than a human conflict. Man fell, under temptation from a superhuman source. We wrestle not with flesh and blood alone. Sin is diabolical in its nature.

Moreover, sin develops over against righteousness. The higher the manifestation of righteousness the more subtle and intense does the opposition become. Paul speaks of "the passions of sins which were through the law" (Rom. 7:5). The law becomes an occasion for the development of sin. Most of the rest of the chapter is an exposition of what the apostle means by that statement. He indicates that before we come into possession of moral light sin is a slumbering principle in us. When we come to have moral light (the law) and learn what is right, we do not perform the right. Instead of that, sin awakens to energetic action and man is enslaved by its power. Only Christ can deliver from its power.

Jesus indicates that the condemnation of the people to whom he ministered would be greater than that of the people of Sodom and Gomorrah or of Tyre and Sidon. This was true because the people of Chorazin, Capernaum, and Bethsaida had greater light and privilege, and hence greater guilt. In John's Gospel Jesus says: "If I had not come and spoken unto them, they had not had sin"; and, "If I had not done among them the works which none other did, they had not had sin" (John 15:22, 24). Now, he says, they have no cloak or excuse for their sin. The thing that made their sin so terrible was that they had seen both him and the Father (v. 24). His presence in their midst as the light of the world meant that they must accept that light and turn to God or else turn irrevocably to sin and death. It is doubtless along this line that we are to understand the warning in Matthew 12:31. He was in their midst doing the works of God under the power of God's Spirit. They were blasphemously saying that his works were the works of the devil. They could not deny his mighty works, but they were saying that they were devilish in character. Anybody who would thus deliberately call white black was in danger of putting out his own spiritual eyes and so perverting his own moral nature that it would be a moral impossibility for God to save him. He would forever fix his own character in sin.

So we see that the character of sin is such and the character of God's holiness or righteousness is such that there is an inevitable conflict between the two. This conflict has been going on since the beginning of human history and will go on to its end. The Fourth Gospel refers to this conflict when it says: "The light shineth in the darkness, and the darkness did not apprehend [or better perhaps, overcome] it" (John 1:5). This conflict is represented in John's Gospel as a ceaseless struggle between light and darkness.

This view, of course, would be inconsistent with an absolute monism. It is based on the assumption that man has moral freedom and responsibility and that sin is real opposition to God. It is monotheistic in its interpretation of the world but not monistic. Sin is more than weakness or immaturity: it is voluntary rebellion against the will of God.

The Conflict in the Life of Jesus

The life of Jesus was one of conflict with evil all the way through. During his infancy the forces of evil were seeking to destroy him, so that his parents had to flee with him to Egypt. From his entrance into his public ministry, he was beset with trial and temptation, but was always victorious. So far as we are given light on his temptations and struggles, they centered in his mission and how he should fulfill that mission. His messianic mission was not a part of his life; it was all his life. He lived for the one thing of fulfilling his mission. His meat was to do his Father's will and complete the work that God had given him to do. The big question in his life was not whether he should do the work assigned him, but how he should do it. What method and means should he use to do the work assigned him? How should he proceed to inaugurate God's kingdom on earth? Should he appeal to spectacular methods, perform miracles that would astound the multitude and win a popular following? Should he appeal to military or physical force and subdue his enemies with irresistible power? Such questions as these formed the center of his struggle in the wilderness and in the great crises of his life, even up to Gethsemane.

He had come to establish the righteous reign of God among men. The question was what the nature of the reign should be and how it should be established. Evil must be dethroned; but how could that be done? The methods used to establish the reign of God must conform to the nature of the kingdom to be established. A spiritual reign could not be established by spectacular and military methods. God can reign in the lives of men only by their free consent and by their active cooperation. Hence the means used must be such as would secure that result. This could not be done by military or political power. God can use military power to destroy military power, but he cannot use military or political power to establish a spiritual kingdom. The history of Christianity is a demonstration of the futility of the use of carnal means and methods for promoting spiritual ends.

Jesus saw that love was the only power that would be effective in establishing a kingdom of love. He made love, therefore, the central principle in religion. But Jesus saw another thing. He saw that love in the kind of world in which he lived would be crucified. He warned the disciples that following him would mean persecution. He knew how the Old Testament prophets had been treated, and he knew what living a life of love would do to him and what it would mean to those who followed him. There is a significant statement about Cain in 1 John 3:11–12. It says that Cain slew his brother for the reason that his own works were evil while his brother's were good. The nature of sin is such that it fights the good. It would not be evil if it did not.

So Jesus was put to death because of his goodness. The evil forces of his day were bound to kill him. They could not live with him. What else could they do? They must kill him or cease to be evil. On the other hand, if Jesus had ceased using the method of love and had adopted the method of worldly force, he would have ceased to be righteous and would have lost the power of righteousness, the power of love. When the devil tried to get Jesus to compromise by worshiping him, Jesus saw that this was not the way to win but to lose. By compromising with evil Jesus would have lost all. His mission would have failed and evil would have triumphed.

John tells us that God is love (1 John 4:8, 16). This makes love the essence of God's being. The penal view [of atonement] tends to make retributive justice the fundamental or controlling attribute of God. The New Testament makes nothing more fundamental than love in God. Since God is love, to say that love and evil are in conflict with each other is to say that God and evil are in conflict. This was the guarantee that, in the case of Jesus, love should triumph over evil. When Jesus was executed as a malefactor, crucified between two criminals, it seemed that evil was definitely and finally victorious over righteousness and truth. He was hounded by envy, jealousy, and malice, accused by false witnesses and put to death as a criminal. Yet it is to be noted that the Jewish Sanhedrin condemned him to death on the ground of his own confession that he was the Messiah, the Son of God. The paradox seems to be that in pretense, on the surface, he was put to death as a malefactor and a criminal, but in reality he was condemned as the Messiah of God, the Savior of the world. It was sin that put him to death, and he was put to death as God's Messiah.

The Cross as the Climax of This Conflict

This conflict thus came to its climax in the cross of Christ. Here light and darkness, holiness and sin, God and the devil came into deadly combat. One side or the other must forever be conquered. Holiness and truth here forever conquered sin and evil. God could oppose sin in one of two ways. One is by punishing the sinner; the other is by redeeming him.

The former method gives a partial but true revelation of God. It reveals the element of retributive justice in God. The second method gives a final revelation of God's character as grace that saves. We do not come to the Christian conception of God until we know God as grace. In the future we may know more about God's grace, but we will never know him in any character that is higher than grace. Such is a moral impossibility. This gives finality in the revelation of God's character as grace.

The method of redemption nullifies sin; punishment only suppresses it. An evildoer may be restrained by justice; grace changes him into a saint.

In this view the cross was inevitable if the incarnation is granted. If Christ is God come as a sinless man into a fallen race, the cross was inevitable. In that case, the sinless Christ is sure to live a life of service to men and they are sure to crucify him. Each acts his part. This view not only brings the incarnation in line with the cross. It also makes redemption the work of God all the way through. It has been customary among advocates of the penal view, from the days of Anselm on, to regard the atonement as man's work, not God's, in the sense that it was held that it was the human nature of Christ that suffered, not the divine. It is true that Anselm and his followers held that Christ was divine, but they held that he suffered only in his human nature. His divine nature, it was said, gave added dignity to his person and hence gave increased value (infinite or practically so) to his sufferings. These sufferings had to be of infinite value to counterbalance the infinite indignity suffered by the honor (or justice) of God. But while the divine nature of Christ gave infinite value to his person and hence to his sufferings, it was held that the divine nature did not suffer, since God was impassible. He could not suffer.

The idea that Christ acted according to his two natures, either one governing his action according to the situation independently of the other while the other gave value to what he did, amounts to denying the reality of the incarnation. We are not here trying to solve the mystery of the incarnation, but we are arguing on the assumption of its reality. But if the natures lay side by side in his person and he could act according to either nature independently of the other, then God did not become man, he only took human nature as a kind of coat which was only a garment he wore, not a part of him. In that case God came near to man; he did not become man. This would not be a real incarnation.

Besides, if there was no divine suffering, there was no divine sacrifice for sins, and the redeeming death of Christ was a human act, not a divine achievement. This is not the New Testament view. The New

Testament view is that in Christ God became man and that his work in saving us — all his work in saving us — is God's work. God himself got under the burden of our sins. He achieved our redemption.

The revelation of God as love contradicts the idea that God cannot suffer. A God who loves must suffer when his world is invaded by sin and men are destroyed by it. To say that God does not suffer is to say that he does not care.

Victory Manifest in the Resurrection

When Jesus died on the cross it appeared that sin and death had conquered. But not so in reality. He triumphed over sin and death. He conquered death because he conquered sin. Peter was right when he said that he could not be holden of death (Acts 2:24). He seemed to be conquered by sin, but he had conquered sin and therefore rose victorious over death.

Thus the conflict between Christ and sin that culminated in death issued in resurrection. Sin and death go together. They are parts of one whole. Death is not something that God arbitrarily inflicts on the sinner. Dr. [E. Y.] Mullins talks about the sin-death principle. This is in line with the New Testament. Paul closely links sin and death in all his discussions. This comes out clearly in such passages as Romans chapters 5–8. "The wages of sin is death" (6:23). Those who live according to the flesh are about to die (8:13). The justified man is not under condemnation, because the law of the Spirit of life (the control of the Spirit that produces life) has freed him from the law (control) of sin and death. Sin and death are Siamese twins. They are inseparable.

The reason Christ conquered sin and death was because he was the incarnation of God. This conflict was not between man and sin. Sin had won that contest throughout history. But now God, in the person of Christ, entered the contest on behalf of man, and won in the conflict. The resurrection was the complete defeat of sin, death, and the devil. Jesus did not die as a victim; he died as a victor. His victory was manifest in the resurrection. He said that no man took his life from him. He laid it down of himself, and of himself he took it again (John 10:18). The penal theory treats Jesus as a victim, but he died as a conqueror. In dying he conquered death and Hades. The resurrection of Jesus is the watershed of New Testament Christianity. It marks the continental divide. To change the figure a little, it marks the point where we go up onto a higher plane, but we do not come down again.

The resurrection of Jesus was the elevation of his whole personality to a higher plane of being. It gives us a universal, spiritual Christ instead of a local, limited Christ. Many people look back with longing to the Christ of the Lake or the Galilean hills. It was evidently wonderful for the disciples to have Christ present with them in the flesh. But we today have something more wonderful than that. We have a Christ who in his resurrection was raised above the limitations of time and space....

[Walter T. Conner, *The Gospel of Redemption* (Nashville: Broadman, 1945), 112–20. Used by permission.]

– 41 –

Robert C. Walton

Robert Clifford Walton (1905?–85) was a theologian and Baptist pastor of unusual insight and depth. After education at Bristol, England, and at Regent's Park College, Oxford, he served Baptist churches in Lancashire and at Victoria Road, Leicester, until invited to become General Secretary of the Student Christian Movement in Schools, and then (in 1949) senior producer of religion programs for the British Broadcasting Corporation. In the latter role he developed programs on religion for instruction in British schools; thus much of his ministry was occupied with the religious education of youth. During the 1940s Walton helped to found an interdenominational spiritual fellowship, the Community of St. Julian in Sussex. Later he worked with the Baptist Renewal Group, which was interested in recovering a stronger view of church, ministry, and sacraments than recent Baptist generations had embraced, and a stronger ecumenism than was acceptable to the "evangelical" party (McBeth, The Baptist Heritage, *511–12.) For Walton and his allies, the church universal (denoted in the selection that follows by "Church" with a capital C) logically precedes the local church (always lowercase). Walton was well aware of the dominant nineteenth-century individualism to which American theologian E. Y. Mullins' concept of soul competency had paid such honor. Walton did not reject outright the claim of individualism, but to it he added a moderating note, the strong claim of Christian community. His concept of church as gathered community struck a deep chord that had been missed for many generations.*

The Community of the Church

One of the basic principles determining the life of both the primitive Church and the early Baptist movement was the conception of Christian community. Churchmanship was vital for both, not in the sense of adherence to a rigid ecclesiastical system, but in the sense that all Christians took the Church seriously and naturally found their full life within it. The local church in first century Ephesus and in seventeenth century

Bristol was a closely knit fellowship wherein all the members were one in the common life of the Body. Moreover, the relations existing between different churches reflected this deep sense of Christian community. In a very real sense the joy of one was the joy of all and the hurt of one was the hurt of all. In the first century, loyalty to the Apostles, not imposed but gladly given, a unity of faith, a common suffering in persecution, and generosity to the poor saints drew the churches together and made the one universal Church a reality to all Christians. In the seventeenth century the bonds forged by the Associations, Messengers and the [English] General Baptist Assembly, a common faith that the gathered church was of divine appointment, the threat and the reality of persecution, united scattered, self-governing churches into one fellowship. How deeply the early Baptists felt the need of denominational solidarity is shown by their determination in surmounting the formidable difficulties of travel. Only a genuine conviction that the Church is one, could have brought delegates together once a year to London from as far afield as Northamptonshire and Lincolnshire, and supported the Messengers and evangelists in their constant travelling.

Since the middle of the eighteenth century, under the disintegrating pressure of a new industrial system, this sense of community has been largely lost, not only in the Church, but still more in secular society. It is worth while to trace briefly the way this has happened in order that we may understand the situation which now challenges us. . . .

As the years of the eighteenth century went by, as trade and the Empire expanded and the Industrial Revolution changed the face of England, the religious fervor and sense of God's sole glory which characterized the Calvinist "Holy Community" was distilled away. The fellowship of the church, less vital now than in the seventeenth century, no longer disciplined certain broad aspects of life. Instead of the gathered society there was the confident individualist, in fact, independent of the Church's fellowship and discipline even when a member of it. He was as steady and ruthless as his Puritan ancestor, but concerned not with sanctifying the world, but with exploiting it. Laissez-faire, economic atomism, the ruthless struggle for markets, the exploitation of unorganized labor were the results. This, in its turn, reacted upon the churches and especially the Free Churches from whose ranks so many of the new industrial leaders came. The disintegrating pressure of this new individualism, unchecked by any sense of the will and glory of God, invaded our denomination, as it did others, and in much of our theology, as in the problems of church order, we are under its influence still.

In this situation modern man has three alternatives. Roman Catholic writers, such as Eric Gill and G. K. Chesterton, would have us defy the whole historical development of the past three hundred years, and recreate a medieval peasant society in the twentieth century. This program is, of course, absurdly impracticable, but even if it could be achieved, we should be unhappier men than we are because the historical changes of the past three centuries have conditioned us and given us such different desires, that we should be profoundly discontented with a less complex way of life. There would speedily be a new Peasants' Revolt in favor of a scientific industrial civilization.

The second alternative is to cling to what remains of nineteenth century individualism with its injustices and cruelties, its prizes for the few and its misery for the many. If, within the Church, we continue to see our future against this social background, the stream of history will bypass us, for individualism is everywhere discredited and men are searching for new forms of community life. Their quest is more subconscious than conscious at the moment, but this felt need may well revolutionize the structure of society. The rise of the totalitarian state, for all its horrors and its negation of essential Christian principles, bears witness to the frustrated loneliness of the ordinary man or woman weary of the heroic, futile struggle to be master of his fate and captain of his soul....

Here is the true alternative of the Christian Church, especially for Baptists in whose tradition there is just that kind of intimate community which modern man needs. It is the task of the Church to hold the balance between the old selfish individualism, and the drift to a condition of society where the individual is anonymous and a part of a soulless mass. A true community is one which stands between the individual and the State, saving him, on the one hand from isolation, and, on the other, from being an impersonal cog in the machine. To fulfill this task we need an adequate conception of the Church — such a conception, in fact, as Baptists held in the seventeenth century.

Within Christianity this deep desire of modern people is reflected in the attempt, in every denomination, to rethink the doctrine of the Church and to rediscover the solid values of life within a closely knit community. This is, indeed, a return to historical Christianity which is concerned not with what a man does with his solitariness, but with a distinctive type of communal life, largely created by and lived within a distinctive society — the Church.

This attempt to rediscover the true significance of the Church will inevitably lead each denomination to emphasize afresh its own insights. Our own denomination is, today, aggressively Baptist, and we should render small service to the One Catholic Church were we to minimize the contribution which God has given us to make to Christianity as a whole. Indeed our best contribution is to rethink our doctrine of the Church, the Ministry and the Sacraments. Nevertheless, there has come into existence during the past few years a new consciousness of the World Church, the universal Christian community which is in every

place. Baptists may fairly claim to have been pioneers, through William
Carey and his successors, in the creation of World Christianity, and loyalty to the past as well as a sensitive understanding of the way the Holy
Spirit is guiding us today, should lead us to find our place with all other
Christians; not only in the less comprehensive, though more intimate,
fellowship of the local church and the one denomination, but in the
worldwide community, the whole Christian society which stands over
against a hostile or indifferent pagan world. It is enrichment, not im-
poverishment, to be conscious that the local Baptist church to which
we belong is, like the church in Corinth, the Body of Christ, the local
manifestation of the Universal Church. It is enrichment not impoverish-
ment, to share with all other Christians in the Ecumenical Movement,
the ministry of reconciliation in all its varied forms, which Christ has
committed to us....

To sum up: a new demand for life in a true community, a deeply
entrenched capitalist system which the churches are said to support, but
which is under fire from fierce criticism, modern science with an increasingly comprehensive claim to direct the whole of life, and an unread
Bible to which we can no longer appeal because the world no longer accepts its authority; these are features of that background against which
we must now proclaim our message and do the work God has entrusted
to us. On the other hand, the encouraging features of the modern situation are the new determination of each denomination to rediscover its
distinctive contributions and insights and the new consciousness of the
World Church wherein those insights may be honored and used for the
service of God....

We have seen how amongst the historical conditions which shaped
the life of the primitive Church and of the Baptist movement, one factor
proved to be dominant. For the early Church it was the experience of
Christ risen and the Holy Spirit ever present. For the first Baptists it was
the Bible in their mother tongue and freedom to read it, and the new
life derived from it. What will be the dominant factor of the future?
Will it be a new social gospel which might win again the allegiance of
the working classes, or a new sense of community closely bound with
the Ecumenical Movement, or a new understanding of worship, and a
new sacramental fellowship which the Church alone can offer to needy
men and women? Or will it be some new thing which God will do,
of which as yet we have no knowledge? "The wind bloweth where it
listeth ... so is every one that is born of the Spirit." We do not yet know
the dominant fact of our time. We must wait for God to reveal it. We
desire, however, in this chapter to examine the idea of the Christian
community, and its impact upon social life, and the meaning of worship
as these things are known to us in our Baptist churches.

What kind of community do we, as Baptists, desire to create? Our first and major emphasis must be upon the fact that we are not members of a human society, but of a divine creation, led by the Holy Spirit, working under the guidance of God and disciplined by His judgments. As John Smyth said, "It is by virtue of the covenant God maketh with us" that our churches stand. To enter the fellowship of a Baptist church involves an act of personal decision, personal faith and self-surrender, but a church is called into existence and its life is maintained, not by the decision of men, but by the will of God. An entirely wrong and mischievous twist is given to the idea of Christian community if we apply Rousseau's theory of a "social contract" to our church life. Our churches are not groups of individuals who agree to live and work together for their common benefit. They are not self-created, self-appointed, self-governing and self-perpetuating bodies like tennis clubs and political parties. Their life is indeed historically conditioned, but this does not alter the fact that they are God's new creation, since He is the Lord of History....

A Baptist community is, first, a *free* community, though only and always because in Christ's service there is perfect freedom. He is the Head of the Body and the Lord of the Church, and the only freedom we ought to claim or desire is freedom to work within the pattern of His will. All lesser freedoms, our human individuality and nonconformity count for nothing beside the obligation to conform to Christ's purpose, which conformity is His statute and our song: His command and our delight....

Thus the second realm wherein we maintain our freedom is the *self-government* of the local congregation. The Edinburgh Report drew a distinction between "authoritarian" and "personal" types of churches, the former emphasizing the divine given-ness of objective criteria, as Scriptures, Creeds, and Orders, the latter stressing rather the individual experience of divine grace as the supreme reality in the life of the Church. The distinction goes deeper. Throughout the Christian era there have been two main views of the Church. On the first view it is a vast, efficiently organized, all-embracing religious corporation, owning property, walking with kings, having authority over, and occupying a central place in society by reason of its size, power and prestige. There is grandeur in this conception of the Church "terrible as an army with banners." There is danger too. A religious corporation so easily becomes a vested interest, bargaining and compromising because its possessions are in jeopardy. On the second view, which Baptists maintain, the Church is a spiritual fellowship composed of an innumerable number of small, compact groups, held together by a peculiar intensity of spiritual communion which binds in one both Jesus and the believer, and also each member to all the others. The simplicity of this makes a strong appeal to many minds but the danger is that each group so easily becomes a law unto itself, and its fellowship with the other groups a fiction and a sham....

Again, the early Baptists had a conception of ordered liberty. This can be seen in their emphasis on discipline. It was disorderly for a gifted brother to preach without the commission of his church. Moreover, this liberty with order was applied to the actions of churches. There was a right and a wrong way of calling a minister, and it was disorderly to call a man in the wrong way....

The third characteristic of the Baptist community is that it is composed of *responsible* members. This naturally follows from our doctrine of Believer's Baptism, and is expressed in the idea of the gathered church and the church meeting. Here, especially, it is necessary to keep firmly in mind the nature of the Church as a divine society and not a human institution. The church meeting is not primarily "democracy in action," nor a business meeting. Business has to be transacted; the method of doing so is "democratic" in that the matter in hand is fully discussed and decided by a majority vote, but the real significance of the church meeting — and we have largely forgotten it — lies deeper. It is the occasion when God speaks to the church as a church. The members gather together and wait — wait upon God. This waiting, however, is not merely passive: it is an action. The members gather together with their diversity of gifts — experience, wisdom, vision, skill in prayer — and when its spiritual resources are mobilized, the church waits for God to speak. "As they ministered to the Lord and fasted, the Holy Ghost said...."

The word of the Lord to the church thus assembled may be a word of command, or a message of consolation, or a judgment upon the church for its faithlessness. How often have we gone away from the church meeting with a deep sense of humility and correction, as the members of the Fenstanton church went away "acknowledging that they were in an evil way and resolved to amend"? In a church which knows what it means to be a community, the "exercise of godly discipline" will never merely be the denunciation of the sins of individuals, but rather the humiliation of the fellowship which has not been radiant enough to keep one of its members unspotted from the world. Discipline *by* the church may, at times, be necessary, but far more important is discipline *of* the church by the judgments of God.

It is in the church meeting that the principle of the priesthood of all believers is most adequately expressed in our church life. Here the church member is expected to exercise not so much his business ability, though that is of value, as his spiritual gifts; to contribute to the treasury of the church from his store of spiritual wisdom and experience....

[Robert C. Walton, *The Gathered Community* (London: Carey, 1946), 107–29.]

Carl F. H. Henry

Carl F. H. Henry (1913–) was born on Long Island, New York, to German immigrant parents who were only nominally Christian. During his boyhood he displayed a gift for journalism, reporting for and then editing the local weekly newspaper. After being savingly converted, however, his career plans seemed to change. He graduated from Wheaton College, earned a Th.D. at Northern Baptist Theological Seminary, and later (1949) a Ph.D. in philosophy from Boston University. Before receiving this last degree he had already begun to teach at newly founded, non-denominational Fuller Theological Seminary in California. While there he wrote two influential books, Remaking the Modern Mind *(1946) and* The Uneasy Conscience of Modern Fundamentalism *(1947), books which earned Henry a national reputation among Fundamentalists looking for a better conception of their Christian faith. Later Henry left Fuller to become founding editor of* Christianity Today, *an evangelical journal that led many of its fundamentalist readers into a new evangelicalism. Still later he left the journal and went on to write a six-volume introduction to evangelical theology titled* God, Revelation, and Authority *(1976–83).* The Uneasy Conscience, *from which the present selection is drawn, challenged conservative Christians to regain concern for the life of society as a whole and not just the conversion of individuals. A significant feature of Henry's brand of evangelicalism was his deliberate use of* modern *modes of argument, and this despite his outspoken scorn for "the modern mind." Time after time Henry's arguments were human-centered, universalizable, reductionist, and foundational, the very marks of philosophical modernity at Boston University during his study there (on Henry's philosophical modernity, see Nancey Murphy and James Wm. McClendon Jr., "Distinguishing Modern and Postmodern Theologies"). This marked his reasoning despite his intention to return to older ways of Christian thinking by "remaking the modern mind." Concretely, Henry's critique of dog-eat-dog capitalism would hardly have been enough for radical Baptists such as Muriel Lester or Howard Thurman. Yet for fundamentalist Baptists it was a beginning.*

The Dawn of a New Reformation

The need for a vital evangelicalism is proportionate to the world need. The days are as hectic as Nero's Rome, and they demand attention as immediate as Luke's Macedonia.

The cries of suffering humanity today are many. No evangelicalism which ignores the totality of man's condition dares respond in the name of Christianity. Though the modern crisis is not basically political, economic or social, fundamentally it is religious, yet evangelicalism must be armed to declare the implications of its proposed religious solution for the politico-economic and sociological context for modern life.

However marred, the world vessel of clay is not without some of the influence of the Master Molder. God has not left himself entirely without witness in the global calamity; he discloses himself in the tragedies as well as the triumphs of history. He works in history as well as above history. There is a universal confrontation of men and women by the divine Spirit, invading all cultures and all individual lives. There is a constructive work of God in history, even where the redemptive Gospel does not do a recreating work. The evangelical missionary message cannot be measured for success by the number of converts only. The Christian message has a salting effect upon the earth. It aims at a recreated society; where it is resisted, it often encourages the displacement of a low ideology by one relatively higher. Democratic humanitarianism furnishes a better context for human existence than political naturalism, except as it degenerates to the latter.

Modern evangelicalism need not substitute as its primary aim the building of "relatively higher civilizations." To do that is to fall into the error of yesterday's liberalism. Its supreme aim is the proclamation of redeeming grace to sinful humanity; there is no need for Fundamentalism to embrace liberalism's defunct social gospel. The divine order involves a supernatural principle, a creative force that enters society from outside its natural sources of uplift, and regenerates humanity. In that divine reversal of the self-defeating sinfulness of man is the only real answer to our problems of whatever political, economic, or sociological nature. Is there political unrest? Seek first, not a Republican victory, or a labor victory, but the kingdom of God and his righteousness. Then there will be added not necessarily a Republican or labor victory, but political rest. Is there economic unrest? Seek first, not an increase of labor wages coupled with shorter hours, with its probable dog-eat-dog resultant of increased commodity cost, but the divine righteousness; this latter norm will involve fairness for both labor and management. But there will be added not only the solution of the problems of the economic man, but also those of the spiritual man. There is no satisfying rest for modern civilization if it is found in a context of spiritual unrest. This is but another way of declaring that the Gospel of redemption is the most pertinent message for our modern weariness, and that many of our other so-called solutions are quite impertinent, to say the least.

But that does not mean that we cannot cooperate in securing relatively higher goods, when this is the loftiest commitment we can evoke from humanity, providing we do so with appropriate warning of the inadequacy and instability of such solutions. The supernatural regenerative grace of God, proffered to the regenerate, does not prevent his natural grace to all men, regenerate and unregenerate alike. Because he brings rivers of living water to the redeemed, he does not on that account withhold the rain from the unjust and just alike. The realm of special grace does not preclude the realm of common grace. Just so, without minimizing the redemptive message, the church ministers by its message to those who stop short of commitment, as well as to regenerate believers.

The implications of this for evangelicalism seem clear. The battle against evil in all its forms must be pressed unsparingly; we must pursue the enemy, in politics, in economics, in science, in ethics — everywhere, in every field, we must pursue relentlessly. But when we have singled out the enemy — when we have disentangled him from those whose company he has kept and whom he has misled — we must meet the foe head-on, girt in the Gospel armor. Others may resist him with inadequate weapons; they do not understand aright the nature of the foe, nor the requirements for victory. We join with them in battle, seeking all the while more clearly to delineate the enemy, and more precisely to state the redemptive formula.

These sub-Christian environments which result from an intermingling of Christian and non-Christian elements, however much they fail to satisfy the absolute demand of God, are for the arena of life more satisfactory than an atmosphere almost entirely devoid of its redemptive aspects. It is far easier, in an idealistic context, to proclaim the essential Christian message than it is in a thoroughly naturalistic context. Life means more in a context of idealism, because true meaning evaporates in a context of naturalism: for that reason, the preaching of a more abundant life finds a more favorable climate in the former. Though neither is to be identified with the kingdom of God, Anglo-Saxon democracy is a relatively better atmosphere by far than German totalitarianism was, and what made it better is the trace of Hebrew-Christian ideology that lingers in it.

While it is not the Christian's task to correct social, moral and political conditions as his primary effort apart from a redemptive setting, simply because of his opposition to evils he ought to lend his endorsement to remedial efforts in any context not specifically anti-redemptive, while at the same time decrying the lack of a redemptive solution. In

our American environment, the influences of Christian theism are still
abroad with enough vigor that the usual solutions are non-redemptive,
rather than anti-redemptive, in character. Such cooperation, coupled
with the Gospel emphasis, might provide the needed pattern of action
for condemning aggressive warfare in concert with the United Nations
Organization while at the same time disputing the frame of reference
by which the attempt is made to outlaw such warfare; for condemning racial hatred and intolerance, while at the same time protesting
the superficial view of man which overlooks the need of individual regeneration; for condemning the liquor traffic, while insisting that it is
impossible by legislation actually to correct the heart of man; for seeking justice for both labor and management in business and industrial
problems, while protesting the fallacy that man's deepest need is economic. This is to link the positive Christian message with a redemptive
challenge to the world on its bitterest fronts. Christian ethics will always resist any reduction of the good of the community to something
divorced from theism and revelation; its conviction that non-evangelical
humanism cannot achieve any lasting moral improvements in the world
as a whole because of the lack of an adequate dynamic will engender the
vigorous affirmation of a Christian solution.

Not that evangelical action stops here; this is hardly the beginning of
it. One of the fallacies of modern thought, with which non-evangelical
groups have been so much taken up in recent years, is that the mere
"passing of a resolution" or the "writing of a book" in which the proposed method was set forth, automatically constitutes a long step on the
road to deliverance. But too often the action stopped with the resolution
or the book. Western culture was flooded with solutions for deliverance, from every sort of idealism and humanism, during the very years
that it walked most rapidly to its doom. The same danger attends any
evangelical revival.

The evangelical task primarily is the preaching of the Gospel, in the
interest of individual regeneration by the supernatural grace of God,
in such a way that divine redemption can be recognized as the best
solution of our problems, individual and social. This produces within
history, through the regenerative work of the Holy Spirit, a divine society that transcends national and international lines. The corporate
testimony of believers, in their purity of life, should provide for the
world an example of the divine dynamic to overcome evils in every
realm. The social problems of our day are much more complex than
in apostolic times, but they do not on that account differ in principle.
When the twentieth century church begins to "outlive" its environment
as the first century church outreached its pagan neighbors, the modern
mind, too, will stop casting about for other solutions. The great contemporary problems are moral and spiritual. They demand more than

a formula. The evangelicals have a conviction of absoluteness concerning their message, and not to proclaim it, in the assault on social evils,
is sheer inconsistency. But the modern mood is far more likely to react
first on the level of Christianity as a life view, than at the level of Christianity as a world view. Obviously, from the evangelical viewpoint, the
two cannot be divorced. But from the non-evangelical viewpoint, a baptism of pentecostal fire resulting in a world missionary program and a
divinely-empowered Christian community would turn the uneasy conscience of modern evangelicalism into a new reformation — this time
with ecumenical significance.

[Carl F. H. Henry, *The Uneasy Conscience of Modern Fundamentalism* (Grand Rapids:
Eerdmans, 1947), 84–89.]

– 43 –

Howard Thurman

*The son of a Florida railroad gandy dancer (i.e., section worker),
Howard Thurman (1900–1981) resolved when he was a child never to
have anything to do with the church because of the injustice he perceived in it. Yet he came to spend his entire working life in church
colleges and in the church itself, changing it from within. His autobiography,* With Head and Heart, *describes young Thurman's baptism
in the Halifax River outside Daytona, as the congregation sang "Let's
go down to Jordan." Ordained by the First Baptist Church of Roanoke,
Virginia, scholar and spiritual leader, Thurman was pastor of Mount
Zion Baptist Church in Oberlin, Ohio, after graduation from Rochester
Theological Seminary. Eventually he became dean of the chapel at
Howard and later at Boston University, and still later he founded the
Church for the Fellowship of All Peoples in San Francisco, a congregation interracial and interdenominational in constituency but decidedly
baptist in flavor. Thurman saw early on that the message of the prophets
and Jesus addressed the situation of the "disinherited" in every time
and place. As Joseph R. Washington Jr., writes, "Thurman perceived
that those Protestants whose voices were the loudest in protest against
the inadequacies of the capitalistic system were conversely indifferent to
the Negro"* (Black Religion: The Negro and Christianity in the United
States, *107). That is, Thurman saw that efforts to reform the economic
and class structure, though necessary, usually left racism untouched.
Legend has it that once, invited to speak at Nashville's color-conscious
Fisk University chapel, Thurman, who was both small of stature and
coal-black in color, and who was nearly swallowed by his black ministerial gown, mounted the pulpit, whereupon a titter ran through the
light-brown student assembly. Turning to a large painting of Jesus on
the chapel wall, Thurman said aloud, "They're laughing at me, Jesus."
And then, still aloud, "They laughed at you, too, didn't they?" Then he
proceeded to deliver to a suddenly quieted chapel a message that challenged black (or light brown) racism along with white racism. Leaders
in the civil rights movement learned about gospel righteousness from
him, as did some white theologians. The following selection is drawn
from* Jesus and the Disinherited (1949), *a book Martin Luther King Jr.,*

kept in his briefcase as he traveled. In it, Thurman's aim was to show that Jesus himself faced sinful social structures but offered a (nonviolent) strategy of resistance. It provides a penetrating exposition of the original Jesus movement. Readers may want to compare this piece with the (much later) Orlando Costas selection.

Jesus and the Disinherited

Many and varied are the interpretations dealing with the teachings and the life of Jesus of Nazareth. But few of these interpretations deal with what the teachings and the life of Jesus have to say to those who stand, at a moment in human history, with their backs against the wall.

To those who need profound succor and strength to enable them to live in the present with dignity and creativity, Christianity often has been sterile and of little avail. The conventional Christian word is muffled, confused, and vague. Too often the price exacted by society for security and respectability is that the Christian movement in its formal expression must be on the side of the strong against the weak. This is a matter of tremendous significance, for it reveals to what extent a religion that was born of a people acquainted with persecution and suffering has become the cornerstone of a civilization and of nations whose very position in modern life has too often been secured by a ruthless use of power applied to weak and defenseless peoples.

It is not a singular thing to hear a sermon that defines what should be the attitude of the Christian toward people who are less fortunate than himself. Again and again our missionary appeal is on the basis of the Christian responsibility to the needy, the ignorant, and the so-called backward peoples of the earth. There is a certain grandeur and nobility in administering to another's need out of one's fullness and plenty. One could be selfish, using his possessions — material or spiritual — for strictly private or personal ends. It is certainly to the glory of Christianity that it has been most insistent on the point of responsibility to others whose only claim upon one is the height and depth of their need. This impulse at the heart of Christianity is the human *will to share* with others what one has found meaningful to oneself elevated to the height of a moral imperative. But there is a lurking danger in this very emphasis. It is exceedingly difficult to hold oneself free from a certain contempt for those whose predicament makes moral appeal for defense and succor. It is the sin of pride and arrogance that has tended to vitiate the missionary impulse and to make of it an instrument of self-righteousness on the one hand and racial superiority on the other....

We begin with the simple historical fact that Jesus was a Jew. The miracle of the Jewish people is almost as breathtaking as the miracle of

Jesus. Is there something unique, some special increment of vitality in the womb of the people out of whose loins he came, that made of him a logical flowering of a long development of racial experience, ethical in quality and Godlike in tone? It is impossible for Jesus to be understood outside of the sense of community which Israel held with God. This does not take anything away from him; rather does it heighten the challenge which his life presents, for such reflection reveals him as the product of the constant working of the creative mind of God upon the life, thought, and character of a race of men. Here is one who was so conditioned and organized within himself that he became a perfect instrument for the embodiment of a set of ideals — ideals of such dramatic potency that they were capable of changing the calendar, rechanneling the thought of the world, and placing a new sense of the rhythm of life in a weary, nerve-snapped civilization....

The second important fact for our consideration is that Jesus was a poor Jew. There is recorded in Luke the account of the dedication of Jesus at the temple: "And when the days of her purification according to the law of Moses were accomplished, they brought him...to the Lord; (as it is written in the law of the Lord, Every male that openeth the womb shall be called holy to the Lord;) and to offer a sacrifice according to that which is said in the law of the Lord, A pair of turtle doves, or two young pigeons." When we examine the regulation in Leviticus, an interesting fact is revealed: "And when the days of her purifying are fulfilled, for a son,...she shall bring a lamb of the first year for a burnt offering, and a young pigeon, or a turtle dove, for a sin offering.... And if she be not able to bring a lamb, then she shall bring two turtles, or two young pigeons; the one for a burnt offering and the other for a sin offering." It is clear from the text that the mother of Jesus was one whose means were not sufficient for a lamb, and who was compelled, therefore, to use doves or young pigeons....

The third fact is that Jesus was a member of a minority group in the midst of a larger dominant and controlling group. In 63 B.C. Palestine fell into the hands of the Romans. After this date the gruesome details of loss of status were etched, line by line, in the sensitive soul of Israel, dramatized ever by an increasing desecration of the Holy Land. To be sure, there was Herod, an Israelite, who ruled from 37 to 4 B.C., but in some ways he was completely apostate. Taxes of all kinds increased, and out of these funds, extracted from the vitals of the people, temples in honor of Emperor Augustus were built within the boundaries of the holy soil. It was a sad and desolate time for the people. Herod became the symbol of shame and humiliation for all of Israel....

In the main, there were two alternatives faced by the Jewish minority of which Jesus was a part. Simply stated these were to resist or not to resist. But each of these alternatives has within it secondary alternatives.

Under the general plan of nonresistance one may take the position of imitation. The aim of such an attitude is to assimilate the culture and the social behavior-pattern of the dominant group. It is the profound capitulation to the powerful, because it means the yielding of oneself to that which, deep within, one recognizes as being unworthy. It makes for a strategic loss of self-respect. The aim is to reduce all outer or external signs of difference to zero, so that there shall be no ostensible cause for active violence or opposition. Under some circumstances it may involve a repudiation of one's heritage, one's customs, one's faith. Accurate imitation until the facade of complete assimilation is securely placed and the antagonism of difference dissolved — such is the function of this secondary alternative within the broader alternative of nonresistance. Herod was an excellent example of this solution.

To some extent this was also the attitude of the Sadducees. They represented the "upper" class. From their number came the high priests, and most of the economic security derived from contemporary worship in the temple was their monopoly. They did not represent the masses of the people. Any disturbance of the established order meant upsetting their position. They loved Israel, but they seem to have loved security more. They made their public peace with Rome and went on about the business of living. They were astute enough to see that their own position could be perpetuated if they stood firmly against all revolutionaries and radicals. Such persons would only stir the people to resist the inevitable, and in the end everything would be lost. Their tragedy was in the fact that they idealized the position of the Roman in the world and suffered the moral fate of the Romans by becoming like them. They saw only two roads open before them — become like the Romans or be destroyed by the Romans. They chose the former.

The other alternative in the nonresistance pattern is to reduce contact with the enemy to a minimum. It is the attitude of cultural isolation in the midst of a rejected culture. Cunning the mood may be — one of bitterness and hatred, but also one of deep, calculating fear. To take up active resistance would be foolhardy, for a thousand reasons. The only way out is to keep one's resentment under rigid control and censorship.

The issue raised by this attitude is always present. The opposition to those who work for social change does not come only from those who are the guarantors of the status quo. Again and again it has been demonstrated that the lines are held by those whose hold on security is sure only as long as the status quo remains intact. The reasons for this are not far to seek. If a man is convinced that he is safe only as long as he uses his power to give others a sense of insecurity, then the measure of their security is in his hands. If security or insecurity is at the mercy of a single individual or group, then control of behavior becomes routine. All imperialism functions in this way. Subject peoples are held under control by this device.

One of the most striking scenes in the movie *Ben Hur* was that in which a Roman legion marches by while hundreds of people stand silently on the roadside. As the last soldier passes, a very dignified, self-possessed Jewish gentleman, with folded arms and eyes smoldering with the utmost contempt, without the slightest shift of his facial muscles spits at the heel of the receding legionary — a consummate touch. Such — in part, at least — was the attitude of the Pharisee. No active resistance against Rome — only a terrible contempt. Obviously such an attitude is a powder keg. One nameless incident may cause to burst into flame the whole gamut of smoldering passion, leaving nothing in its wake but charred corpses, mute reminders of the tragedy of life. Jesus saw this and understood it clearly.

The other major alternative is resistance. It may be argued that even nonresistance is a form of resistance, for it may be regarded as an appositive dimension of resistance. Resistance may be overt action, or it may be merely mental and moral attitudes. For the purposes of our discussion resistance is defined as the physical, overt expression of an inner attitude. Resistance in this sense finds its most dramatic manifestation in force of arms.

Armed resistance is apt to be a tragic last resort in the life of the disinherited. Armed resistance has an appeal because it provides a form of expression, of activity, that releases tension and frees the oppressed from a disintegrating sense of complete impotency and helplessness. "Why can't we do something? Something must be done!" is the recurring cry. By "something" is meant action, direct action, as over against words, subtleties, threats, and innuendoes. It is better to die fighting for freedom than to rot away in one's chains, the argument runs.

> Before I'd be a slave
> I'd be buried in my grave,
> And go home to my God
> And be free!...

The cause is just, it cannot fail. Any failure is regarded as temporary and, to the devoted, as a testing of character.

This was the attitude of the Zealots of Jesus' day. There was added appeal in their position because it called forth from the enemy organized determination and power. It is never to be forgotten that one of the ways by which men measure their own significance is to be found in the amount of power and energy other men must use in order to crush them or hold them back. This is at least one explanation of the fact that even a weak and apparently inconsequential movement becomes formidable under the pressure of great persecution. The persecution becomes a vote of confidence, which becomes, in turn, a source of inspiration, power, and validation. The Zealots knew this. Jesus knew this. It is a matter of more than passing significance that he had a Zealot among his little band of followers, indeed among the twelve chosen ones.

In the face of these alternatives Jesus came forth with still another. ...The solution which Jesus found for himself and for Israel, as they faced the hostility of the Greco-Roman world, becomes the word and the work of redemption for all the cast-down people in every generation and in every age. I mean this quite literally. I do not ignore the theological and metaphysical interpretation of the Christian doctrine of salvation. But the underprivileged everywhere have long since abandoned any hope that this type of salvation deals with the crucial issues by which their days are turned into despair without consolation. The basic fact is that Christianity as it was born in the mind of this Jewish teacher and thinker appears as a technique of survival for the oppressed. That it became, through the intervening years, a religion of the powerful and the dominant, used sometimes as an instrument of oppression, must not tempt us into believing that it was thus in the mind and life of Jesus. "In him was life; and the life was the light of men." Wherever his spirit appears, the oppressed gather fresh courage, for he announced the good news that fear, hypocrisy, and hatred, the three hounds of hell that track the trail of the disinherited, need have no dominion over them.

I belong to a generation that finds very little that is meaningful or intelligent in the teachings of the church concerning Jesus Christ. It is a generation largely in revolt because of the general impression that Christianity is essentially an otherworldly religion, having as its motto: "Take all the world, but give me Jesus." The desperate opposition to Christianity rests in the fact that it seems, in the last analysis, to be a betrayal of the Negro into the hands of his enemies by focusing his attention upon heaven, forgiveness, love, and the like. It is true that this emphasis is germane to the religion of Jesus, but it has to be put into a context that will show its strength and vitality rather than its weakness and failure. For years it has been a part of my own quest so to understand the religion of Jesus that interest in his way of life could be developed and sustained by intelligent men and women who were at the same time deeply victimized by the Christian church's betrayal of his faith....

The striking similarity between the social position of Jesus in Palestine and that of the vast majority of American Negroes is obvious to anyone who tarries long over the facts. We are dealing here with conditions that produce essentially the same psychology. There is meant no further comparison. It is the similarity of a social climate at the point of a denial of full citizenship which creates the problem for creative survival. For the most part, Negroes assume that there are no basic citizenship rights, no fundamental protection, guaranteed to them by the state, because their status as citizens has never been clearly defined. There has been for them little protection from the dominant controllers of society and even less protection from the unrestrained elements within their own group.

The result has been a tendency to be their own protectors, to bulwark themselves against careless and deliberate aggression. The Negro has felt, with some justification, that the peace officer of the community provides no defense against the offending or offensive white man; and for an entirely different set of reasons the peace officer gives no protection against the offending Negro. Thus the Negro feels that he must be prepared, at a moment's notice, to protect his own life and take the consequence therefor. Such a predicament has made it natural for some of them to use weapons as a defense and to have recourse to premeditated or precipitate violence.

Living in a climate of deep insecurity, Jesus, faced with so narrow a margin of civil guarantees, had to find some other basis upon which to establish a sense of well-being. He knew that the goals of religion as he understood them could never be worked out within the then-established order. Deep from within that order he projected a dream, the logic of which would give to all the needful security. There would be room for all, and no man would be a threat to his brother. "The kingdom of God is within." "The Spirit of the Lord is upon me, because he hath anointed me to preach the gospel to the poor."

The basic principles of his way of life cut straight through to the despair of his fellows and found it groundless. By inference he says, "You must abandon your fear of each other and fear only God. You must not indulge in any deception and dishonesty, even to save your lives. Your words must be Yea-Nay; anything else is evil. Hatred is destructive to hated and hater alike. Love your enemy, that you may be children of your Father who is in heaven."

[Howard Thurman, *Jesus and the Disinherited* (Nashville: Abingdon, 1949), 11–35.]

Benjamin Elijah Mays

Many Baptists and others who know the name and fame of Martin Luther King Jr. (one of whose writings appears in chapter 45 of this book) have no idea of the degree to which King's vision and elo- quence sprang from the long African American baptist heritage. Much that we learn from him came from the ecclesial breast at which he was suckled, which was the life and faith of the African American church. Perhaps the primary bearer of this tradition in the generation immediately preceding King's was Benjamin Elijah Mays (1894–1984), minister, educator, and outstanding spokesperson for Christian witness in the post-Reconstruction and pre-civil rights South. Born in rural South Carolina to parents who had themselves been slaves, Mays was educated at Bates College, was ordained a Baptist minister in 1921, and earned a Ph.D. from the University of Chicago in 1935. He alternated pastoring and teaching roles until Howard University made him dean of its School of Religion; then in 1940 he became president of More- house College in Atlanta (King's alma mater). Mays' principal writings include important sociological studies of black religious life in America: The Negro's Church (with Joseph W. Nicholson) and The Negro's God. His leadership affected not only King but other insightful black thinkers such as Joseph R. Washington Jr., and J. Deotis Roberts, though Mays was largely ignored by contemporary white Baptist leaders, South and North. The present address was delivered in Cleveland, Ohio, to a session of the Baptist World Alliance, 8th Congress, meeting there in 1950.

Christian Light on Human Relationships

For nineteen long centuries Christian light has been shining on human relationships. As Goodspeed translates John 1:5, "The Light is still shin- ing in the darkness, for the darkness has never been put out." This statement is applicable to our situation in 1950. War, economic injus- tice, political corruption, racial bigotry, chaos, confusion, fear, tragedy.

"The Light is still shining in the darkness" in 1950, "for the darkness has never been put out...."

The Christian light leads to the inevitable conclusion that God is the Father of all and that all men are brothers. If God is a common Father and if all men are brothers, then it follows that the human family is one. It belongs together. Even those who hold that God is Father of believers only and that only believers are brothers must also hold that nationality and race are not prerequisites for brotherhood.

Christian light penetrates deeper. It is all too easy to preach that all men are brothers and then act as if only some men are brothers. Christian light says, either all men are brothers, or no men are brothers. Either God is the Father of all men, or he is the Father of no man. Either the lives of all children are sacred, or the life of no child is sacred. If the Americans and the English are brothers, then the Americans and the Germans are brothers. If God is the Father of the Italians, he is the Father of the Ethiopians. If the life of the richest child is precious, then the life of the poorest child is precious. Either all or none.

In other words, the destiny of each individual wherever he resides on the earth is tied up with the destiny of all men that inhabit the globe. Whether we like it or not, we cannot do anything about it. The English poet and cleric John Donne has set the idea in language that is immortal:

No man is an Iland, intire of it selfe;
Every man is a peece of the Continent,
A part of the maine;
If a Clod bee washed away by the Sea,
Europe is the lesse, as well as if a Promontorie were,
As well as if a Mannor of thy friends of thine owne were:
Any man's death diminishes me, because I am involved in
       mankinde;
and therefore never send to know for whom the bell tolls;
It tolls for thee.

Everything I have said up to now proves only one thing. It proves that we know pretty well what Christian light is. It has been shining brilliantly across nineteen centuries. It is clear in our minds what kind of human relations should exist among nations. It is also clear that Christian light condemns the inhumanity of man to man in our economic life. It is equally clear that the corruption in political life is condemned by Christian light. We know what Christianity has to say about war and racial discrimination.

Yes, we have light! Christian light and scientific light! We are the most educated people known to history. We have more colleges and universities, more schools of theology, more technical and professional schools than any age in history. We are the most degreed people in the annals of time: D.D.s, LL.D.s, M.D.s, Litt.D.s, Ph.D.s — all kinds of D.s. We know more science than ever before, more physics, chemistry, mathematics, biology than any previous age. We know more philosophy, literature, and religion, and yet we are nearer destruction today than at any previous time. We have plenty of light, but like Pilate, we have more light than faith. Pilate had light — so much light that he admitted that he found no fault in Jesus, but Pilate could not stand up to the light he saw. And herein lies the tragedy of our time!

We know the horrors and tragedies of war. We know that wars are seldom if ever won, that one war sows the seeds for another war, and another and another. We know that World War I laid the foundation of World War II and that World War II laid the foundation of what may be World War III.

We have Christian light on war. And yet we go on fighting and preparing for it. If there is anything we learn from history, it's nothing. Twenty-five or thirty centuries ago when the Egyptians and the Babylonians couldn't settle their difference through peaceful means, they fought it out on the battlefield. In 1914 and in 1917 when we could not get together, we fought out our differences on the battlefields of Europe. Twenty centuries ago when the Romans and the Greeks couldn't get together, they went to war. In 1939 and 1941 when we couldn't settle our differences through peaceful means we fought it out on the battlefields of the world.

In 1950 the United Nations, Russia and the United States cannot settle their differences around the conference table, so we are shooting it out on the battlefields of Korea. We have nineteen centuries of Christian light on the subject of war, but the light still shines in darkness, for the darkness has never been put out.

We need more than light. And when war comes, we all become immoral. There is only one issue confronting a nation at war, and that is to win it. If it takes deception to win the war, we deceive. If it takes lying to win it, we lie. If it takes the starving of innocent women and children to win it, we starve them. If it takes the raping of women and girls in order to keep up the morale of the soldiers, we wink at it. If it takes the dropping of atomic bombs to win it, we drop atomic bombs. We all become immoral including the ministers of God. We need more than Christian light.

We have Christian light on cultural and race relations. And yet one of the most enlightened nations in history was responsible for the murder of 6,000,000 Jews. Despite Christian light we have a Christian church in South Africa which justifies its brutal Fascist, Nazi policy by an appeal to Scripture and theology. In Christian United States one of the most segregated institutions in America is God's church — segregated in the North, segregated in the South. Many of our so-called Christian statesmen will fight to the death any move to equalize opportunities for all peoples. It is clear that Christian light is not enough.

When it comes to business in human relations, we have plenty of light; and yet if a man can get ahead of his fellows by exploiting them, we Christians call it "good business." If a man can turn a business deal that will net him a hundred thousand dollars without working for it, we call him a good businessman. A politician running for office is concerned primarily with getting votes. He may appeal to religious or racial prejudice. But if he gets elected, we Christians say, "He is a good politician!" In all these areas, we seldom begin with what is Christian or just, what is right or honorable. We begin by asking what is expedient and how much will the traffic bear.

Christian light is not enough. We need the power of God unto salvation. "Except a man be born again, he cannot see the kingdom of God." Without redemption a man can see the Christian light in human relations and keep on hating his brother. Without redemption, we can know the truth and deliberately lie. Without redemption, we can see the high road beckoning us on and we can deliberately choose the low road. Every honest man knows from experience what Paul meant when he said in essence, I find myself doing that which I know I ought not to do. I find myself failing to do that which I know I ought to do. What is Paul saying? Paul is saying that light is not enough.

What then can we do to be saved? It is the responsibility of the church of Christ to launch an evangelistic campaign to convert men to God. We should begin first with ourselves, the ministers of Christ. Ask God, and mean it, to create within us a clean heart and renew a right Spirit within us. Ask him to purge our souls of sin and corruption. Let us submit our wills to God. We are not ready for an evangelistic campaign until the ministers themselves repent and are purified....

The early Christians had what I have in mind. Their faith and belief in God were not theoretical. They lived them and many died for their beliefs. And in so doing they changed the character of the world. We Christians of 1950 can do the same for our day if we repent of our sins, change our ways, take the offensive for righteousness, and trust God for results.

You may well ask what will happen to us if we do this. I do not know. I cannot tell you what will happen to our positions, nor to our social prestige if we insist that Christian people be thoroughly changed. What will happen to our economic security? I cannot tell you. I cannot even predict what will happen to our lives. But I don't believe that Jesus and Paul, Peter and John, Amos and Hosea, Luther and Knox, Ridley and Latimer, ever debated the question as to what would happen to them if they did God's will. These questions are beside the point. But if we have faith in Jesus Christ and believe in the Lord God, we will act, seek to do his will, and leave the consequences to him. God will take care of us. We do not follow the light we see because we trust ourselves and things rather than God. Nations trust their armies and navies, their airplanes and submarines and their atomic and hydrogen bombs and not God. If we cannot trust God, if we cannot convert men and women to God, our civilization is doomed. We need faith — the faith of Browning who said: "One who never turned his back, but marched breast forward, never doubted clouds would break, never dreamed though right were worsted wrong would triumph — held, we fail to rise, are baffled to fight better, sleep to wake."

The light is still shining in the darkness, for the darkness has never been put out.

[*Official Report of the Baptist World Alliance, 8th Congress* (Cleveland, Ohio, 1950).]

– 45 –

Martin Luther King Jr.

That Martin Luther King Jr.'s birthday (January 15, 1929) is an American national holiday suggests his great political importance, despite the fact that this Atlanta, Georgia, native and Baptist minister never held a public office. His name is synonymous with the twentieth-century American quest for righteous race relations. The national holiday implies (perhaps too optimistically) that the quest has successfully ended. Though he received a good education—at Morehouse College (B.A.), Crozer Theological Seminary (B.D.), and Boston University (Ph.D.) — if we seek the deepest sources of his witness, we discover them not merely in this training but in his Baptist upbringing, his ministry in Baptist churches, and in the Christian faith, which formed his strong convictions and provided his vital images (on King's black Baptist heritage see McClendon, Biography as Theology*). The Southern Christian Leadership Conference he headed and the wider civil rights movement of which it was a main part made a significant advance upon the social gospel by progressing from ministerial talk and writing to public nonviolent direct action by Christians against overt oppression. The present selection, one of King's best-known deliverances, was written during a 1963 Birmingham, Alabama, direct action campaign in which he had been arrested and jailed. It replied to a statement issued by several Birmingham white clergy who objected to the movement's style of protest. (One of the clergymen was Southern Baptist pastor Earl Stallings.) Most of the themes of King's other writings and speeches appear here in language rich with biblical imagery that powered his work. A genuine Baptist martyr, he was assassinated while working in yet another series of demonstrations, a civil rights campaign in Memphis, Tennessee, in 1968.*

Letter from Birmingham Jail

April 16, 1963

My Dear Fellow Clergymen:

While confined here in the Birmingham city jail, I came across your recent statement calling my present activities "unwise and untimely."

Seldom do I pause to answer criticism of my work and ideas. If I sought to answer all the criticisms that cross my desk, my secretaries would have little time for anything other than such correspondence in the course of the day, and I would have no time for constructive work. But since I feel that you are men of genuine good will and that your criticisms are sincerely set forth, I want to try to answer your statement in what I hope will be patient and reasonable terms.

I think I should indicate why I am here in Birmingham, since you have been influenced by the view which argues against "outsiders coming in." I have the honor of serving as president of the Southern Christian Leadership Conference, an organization operating in every Southern state, with headquarters in Atlanta, Georgia. We have some eighty-five affiliated organizations across the South and one of them is the Alabama Christian Movement for Human Rights. Frequently we share staff, educational, and financial resources with our affiliates. Several months ago the affiliate here in Birmingham asked us to be on call to engage in a nonviolent direct-action program if such were deemed necessary. We readily consented, and when the hour came we lived up to our promise. So I, along with several members of my staff, am here because I was invited here. I am here because I have organizational ties here.

But more basically, I am in Birmingham because injustice is here. Just as the prophets of the eighth century B.C. left their villages and carried their "thus saith the Lord" far beyond the boundaries of their home towns, and just as the Apostle Paul left his village of Tarsus and carried the gospel of Jesus Christ to the far corners of the Greco-Roman world, so am I compelled to carry the gospel of freedom beyond my own home town. Like Paul, I must constantly respond to the Macedonian call for aid.

Moreover, I am cognizant of the interrelatedness of all communities and states. I cannot sit idly by in Atlanta and not be concerned about what happens in Birmingham. Injustice anywhere is a threat to justice everywhere. We are caught in an inescapable network of mutuality, tied in a single garment of destiny. Whatever affects one directly, affects all indirectly. Never again can we afford to live with the narrow, provincial "outside agitator" idea. Anyone who lives inside the United States can never be considered an outsider anywhere within its bounds.

You deplore the demonstrations taking place in Birmingham. But your statement, I am sorry to say, fails to express a similar concern for the conditions that brought about the demonstrations. I am sure that none of you would want to rest content with the superficial kind of social analysis that deals merely with effects and does not grapple with underlying causes. It is unfortunate that demonstrations are taking place in Birmingham, but it is even more unfortunate that the city's white power structure left the Negro community with no alternative.

In any nonviolent campaign there are four basic steps: collection of the facts to determine whether injustices exist; negotiation; self-purification; and direct action. We have gone through all these steps in Birmingham. There can be no gainsaying the fact that racial injustice engulfs this community. Birmingham is probably the most thoroughly segregated city in the United States. Its ugly record of brutality is widely known. Negroes have experienced grossly unjust treatment in the courts. There have been more unsolved bombings of Negro homes and churches in Birmingham than in any other city in the nation. These are the hard, brutal facts of the case. On the basis of these conditions, Negro leaders sought to negotiate with the city fathers. But the latter consistently refused to engage in good-faith negotiation....

You may well ask: "Why direct action? Why sit-ins, marches and so forth? Isn't negotiation a better path?" You are quite right in calling for negotiation. Indeed, this is the very purpose of direct action. Nonviolent direct action seeks to create such a crisis and foster such a tension that a community which has constantly refused to negotiate is forced to confront the issue. It seeks so to dramatize the issue that it can no longer be ignored. My citing the creation of tension as part of the work of the nonviolent resister may sound rather shocking. But I must confess that I am not afraid of the word "tension." I have earnestly opposed violent tension, but there is a type of constructive, nonviolent tension which is necessary for growth. Just as Socrates felt that it was necessary to create a tension in the mind so that individuals could rise from the bondage of myths and half-truths to the unfettered realm of creative analysis and objective appraisal, so must we see the need for nonviolent gadflies to create the kind of tension in society that will help men rise from the dark depths of prejudice and racism to the majestic heights of understanding and brotherhood....

We know through painful experience that freedom is never voluntarily given by the oppressor; it must be demanded by the oppressed. Frankly, I have yet to engage in a direct-action campaign that was "well timed" in the view of those who have not suffered unduly from the disease of segregation. For years now I have heard the word "Wait!" It rings in the ear of every Negro with piercing familiarity. This "Wait" has almost always meant "Never." We must come to see, with one of our distinguished jurists, that "justice too long delayed is justice denied."

We have waited for more than 340 years for our constitutional and God-given rights. The nations of Asia and Africa are moving with jet-like speed toward gaining political independence, but we still creep at horse-and-buggy pace toward gaining a cup of coffee at a lunch counter. Perhaps it is easy for those who have never felt the stinging darts of segregation to say, "Wait." But when you have seen vicious mobs lynch your mothers and fathers at will and drown your sisters and brothers at whim; when you have seen hate-filled policemen curse, kick, and even kill your black brothers and sisters; when you see the vast majority of your twenty million Negro brothers smothering in an airtight cage of poverty in the midst of an affluent society; when you suddenly find your tongue twisted and your speech stammering as you seek to explain to your six-year-old daughter why she can't go to the public amusement park that has just been advertised on television, and see tears welling up in her eyes when she is told that Funtown is closed to colored children, and see ominous clouds of inferiority beginning to form in her little mental sky, and see her beginning to distort her personality by developing an unconscious bitterness toward white people; when you have to concoct an answer for a five-year-old son who is asking: "Daddy, why do white people treat colored people so mean?"; when you take a cross-country drive and find it necessary to sleep night after night in the uncomfortable corners of your automobile because no motel will accept you; when you are humiliated day in and day out by nagging signs reading "white" and "colored"; when your first name becomes "nigger," your middle name becomes "boy" (however old you are) and your last name becomes "John," and your wife and mother are never given the respected title "Mrs."; when you are harried by day and haunted by night by the fact that you are a Negro, living constantly at tiptoe stance, never quite knowing what to expect next, and are plagued with inner fears and outer resentments; when you are forever fighting a degenerating sense of "nobodiness"; then you will understand why we find it difficult to wait. There comes a time when the cup of endurance runs over, and men are no longer willing to be plunged into the abyss of despair. I hope, sirs, you can understand our legitimate and unavoidable impatience.

You express a great deal of anxiety over our willingness to break laws. This is certainly a legitimate concern. Since we so diligently urge people to obey the Supreme Court's decision of 1954 outlawing segregation in the public schools, at first glance it may seem rather paradoxical for us consciously to break laws. One may well ask: "How can you advocate breaking some laws and obeying others?" The answer lies in the fact that there are two types of laws: just and unjust. I would be the first to advocate obeying just laws. One has not only a legal but a moral responsibility to obey just laws. Conversely, one has a moral responsibility to disobey unjust laws. I would agree with St. Augustine that "an unjust law is no law at all."

Now, what is the difference between the two? How does one determine whether a law is just or unjust? A just law is a man-made code that squares with the moral law or the law of God. An unjust law is a code that is out of harmony with the moral law. To put it in the terms of St. Thomas Aquinas: An unjust law is a human law that is not rooted in eternal law and natural law. Any law that uplifts human personality is just. Any law that degrades human personality is unjust. All segregation statutes are unjust because segregation distorts the soul and damages the personality. It gives the segregator a false sense of superiority and the segregated a false sense of inferiority. Segregation, to use the terminology of the Jewish philosopher Martin Buber, substitutes an "I-it" relationship for an "I-thou" relationship and ends up relegating persons to the status of things. Hence segregation is not only politically, economically, and sociologically unsound, it is morally wrong and sinful. Paul Tillich has said that sin is separation. Is not segregation an existential expression of man's tragic separation, his awful estrangement, his terrible sinfulness? Thus it is that I can urge men to obey the 1954 decision of the Supreme Court, for it is morally right; and I can urge them to disobey segregation ordinances, for they are morally wrong....

I must make two honest confessions to you, my Christian and Jewish brothers. First, I must confess that over the past few years I have been gravely disappointed with the white moderate. I have almost reached the regrettable conclusion that the Negro's great stumbling block in his stride toward freedom is not the White Citizen's Counciler or the Ku Klux Klanner, but the white moderate, who is more devoted to "order" than to justice; who prefers a negative peace which is the absence of tension to a positive peace which is the presence of justice; who constantly says: "I agree with you in the goal you seek, but I cannot agree with your methods of direct action"; who paternalistically believes he can set the timetable for another man's freedom; who lives by a mythical concept of time and who constantly advises the Negro to wait for a "more convenient season." Shallow understanding from people of good will is more frustrating than absolute misunderstanding from people of ill will. Lukewarm acceptance is much more bewildering than outright rejection....

I had also hoped that the white moderate would reject the myth concerning time in relation to the struggle for freedom. I have just received a letter from a white brother in Texas. He writes: "All Christians know that the colored people will receive equal rights eventually, but it is possible that you are in too great a religious hurry. It has taken Christianity almost two thousand years to accomplish what it has. The teachings of Christ take time to come to earth." Such an attitude stems from a tragic misconception of time, from the strangely irrational notion that there is something in the very flow of time that will inevitably cure all ills. Actually, time itself is neutral; it can be used either destructively or constructively.

More and more I feel that the people of ill will have used time much more effectively than have the people of good will. We will have to repent in this generation not merely for the hateful words and actions of the bad people but for the appalling silence of the good people. Human progress never rolls in on wheels of inevitability; it comes through the tireless efforts of men willing to be co-workers with God, and without this hard work, time itself becomes an ally of the forces of social stagnation. We must use time creatively, in the knowledge that the time is always ripe to do right. Now is the time to make real the promise of democracy and transform our pending national elegy into a creative psalm of brotherhood. Now is the time to lift our national policy from the quicksand of racial injustice to the solid rock of human dignity....

Oppressed people cannot remain oppressed forever. The yearning for freedom eventually manifests itself, and that is what has happened to the American Negro. Something within has reminded him of his birthright of freedom, and something without has reminded him that it can be gained. Consciously or unconsciously, he has been caught up by the *Zeitgeist,* and with his black brothers of Africa and his brown and yellow brothers of Asia, South America and the Caribbean, the United States Negro is moving with a sense of great urgency toward the promised land of racial justice. If one recognizes this vital urge that has engulfed the Negro community, one should readily understand why public demonstrations are taking place. The Negro has many pent-up resentments and latent frustrations, and he must release them. So let him march; let him make prayer pilgrimages to the city hall; let him go on freedom rides and try to understand why he must do so. If his repressed emotions are not released in nonviolent ways, they will seek expression through violence; this is not a threat but a fact of history. So I have not said to my people: "Get rid of your discontent." Rather, I have tried to say that this normal and healthy discontent can be channeled into the creative outlet of nonviolent direct action. And now this approach is being termed extremist.

But though I was initially disappointed at being categorized as an extremist, as I continued to think about the matter I gradually gained a measure of satisfaction from the label. Was not Jesus an extremist for love: "Love your enemies, bless them that curse you, do good to them that hate you, and pray for them which despitefully use you, and persecute you." Was not Amos an extremist for justice: "Let justice roll down like waters and righteousness like an ever-flowing stream." Was not Paul an extremist for the Christian gospel: "I bear in my body the marks of the Lord Jesus." Was not Martin Luther an extremist: "Here I stand; I cannot do otherwise, so help me God." And John Bunyan: "I will stay in jail to the end of my days before I make a butchery of my conscience." And Abraham Lincoln: "This nation cannot survive half slave and half free." And Thomas Jefferson: "We hold these truths to be self-evident, that all men are created equal...." So the question is not whether we will be extremists, but what kind of extremists we will be. Will we be extremists for hate or for love? Will we be extremists for the preservation of injustice or for the extension of justice? In that dramatic scene on Calvary's hill three men were crucified. We must never forget that all three were crucified for the same crime — the crime of extremism. Two were extremists for immorality, and thus fell below their environment. The other, Jesus Christ was an extremist for love, truth and goodness, and thereby rose above his environment. Perhaps the South, the nation and the world are in dire need of creative extremists....

Let me take note of my other major disappointment. I have been so greatly disappointed with the white church and its leadership. Of course, there are some notable exceptions. I am not unmindful of the fact that each of you has taken some significant stands on this issue. I commend you, Reverend Stallings, for your Christian stand on this past Sunday, in welcoming Negroes to your worship service on a nonsegregated basis. I commend the Catholic leaders of this state for integrating Spring Hill College several years ago.

But despite these notable exceptions, I must honestly reiterate that I have been disappointed with the church. I do not say this as one of those negative critics who can always find something wrong with the church. I say this as a minister of the gospel, who loves the church; who was nurtured in its bosom; who has been sustained by its spiritual blessings and who will remain true to it as long as the cord of life shall lengthen.

When I was suddenly catapulted into the leadership of the bus protest in Montgomery, Alabama, a few years ago, I felt we would be supported by the white church. I felt that the white ministers, priests, and rabbis of the South would be among our strongest allies. Instead, some have been outright opponents, refusing to understand the freedom movement and misrepresenting its leaders; all too many others have been more cautious than courageous and have remained silent behind the anesthetizing security of stained-glass windows....

Yes, these questions are still in my mind. In deep disappointment I have wept over the laxity of the church. But be assured that my tears have been tears of love. There can be no deep disappointment where there is not deep love. Yes, I love the church. How could I do otherwise? I am in the rather unique position of being the son, the grandson and the great-grandson of preachers. Yes, I see the church as the body of Christ. But, oh! How we have blemished and scarred that body through social neglect and through fear of being nonconformists.

There was a time when the church was very powerful — in the time when the early Christians rejoiced at being deemed worthy to suffer for what they believed. In those days the church was not merely a thermometer that recorded the ideas and principles of popular opinion; it was a thermostat that transformed the mores of society.

Whenever the early Christians entered a town, the people in power became disturbed and immediately sought to convict the Christians for being "disturbers of the peace" and "outside agitators." But the Christians pressed on in the conviction that they were "a colony of heaven," called to obey God rather than man. Small in number, they were big in commitment. They were too God-intoxicated to be "astronomically intimidated." By their effort and example they brought an end to such ancient evils as infanticide and gladiatorial contests.

Things are different now. So often the contemporary church is a weak, ineffectual voice with an uncertain sound. So often it is an arch-defender of the status quo. Far from being disturbed by the presence of the church, the power structure of the average community is consoled by the church's silent — and often even vocal — sanction of things as they are.

But the judgment of God is upon the church as never before. If today's church does not recapture the sacrificial spirit of the early church, it will lose its authenticity, forfeit the loyalty of millions, and be dismissed as an irrelevant social club with no meaning for the twentieth century. Every day I meet young people whose disappointment with the church has turned into outright disgust.

Perhaps I have once again been too optimistic. Is organized religion too inextricably bound to the status quo to save our nation and the world? Perhaps I must turn my faith to the inner spiritual church, the church within the church, as the true *ekklesia* and the hope of the world. But again I am thankful to God that some noble souls from the ranks of organized religion have broken loose from the paralyzing chains of conformity and joined us as active partners in the struggle for freedom. They have left their secure congregations and walked the streets of Albany, Georgia, with us. They have gone down the highways of the South on tortuous rides for freedom. Yes, they have gone to jail with us. Some have been dismissed from their churches, have lost the support of their bishops and fellow ministers. But they have acted in the faith that right defeated is stronger than evil triumphant. Their witness has been the spiritual salt that has preserved the true meaning of the gospel in these troubled times. They have carved a tunnel of hope through the dark mountain of disappointment.

I hope the church as a whole will meet the challenge of this decisive hour. But even if the church does not come to the aid of justice, I have no despair about the future....

Before closing I feel impelled to mention one other point in your statement that has troubled me profoundly. You warmly commended the Birmingham police force for keeping "order" and "preventing

violence." I doubt that you would have so warmly commended the police force if you had seen its dogs sinking their teeth into unarmed,
nonviolent Negroes. I doubt that you would so quickly commend the
policemen if you were to observe their ugly and inhumane treatment
of Negroes here in the city jail; if you were to watch them push and
curse old Negro women and young Negro girls; if you were to see them
slap and kick old Negro men and young boys; if you were to observe
them, as they did on two occasions, refuse to give us food because we
wanted to sing our grace together. I cannot join you in your praise of
the Birmingham police department....

I wish you had commended the Negro sit-inners and demonstrators
of Birmingham for their sublime courage, their willingness to suffer and
their amazing discipline in the midst of great provocation. One day the
South will recognize its real heroes. They will be the James Merediths,
with the noble sense of purpose that enables them to face jeering and
hostile mobs, and with the agonizing loneliness that characterizes the
life of the pioneer. They will be old, oppressed, battered Negro women,
symbolized in a seventy-two-year-old woman in Montgomery, Alabama,
who rose up with a sense of dignity and with her people decided not to
ride segregated buses, and who responded with ungrammatical profun-
dity to one who inquired about her weariness: "My feets is tired, but my
soul is at rest." They will be the young high school and college students,
the young ministers of the gospel and a host of their elders, courageously
and nonviolently sitting in at lunch counters and willingly going to jail
for conscience' sake. One day the South will know that when these
disinherited children of God sat down at lunch counters, they were in
reality standing up for what is best in the American dream and for the
most sacred values in our Judaeo-Christian heritage, thereby bringing
our nation back to those great wells of democracy which were dug deep
by the founding fathers in their formulation of the Constitution and the
Declaration of Independence.

Never before have I written so long a letter. I'm afraid it is much too
long to take your precious time. I can assure you that it would have
been much shorter if I had been writing from a comfortable desk, but
what else can one do when he is alone in a narrow jail cell, other than
write long letters, think long thoughts and pray long prayers?

If I have said anything in this letter that overstates the truth and indicates an unreasonable impatience, I beg you to forgive me. If I have said
anything that understates the truth and indicates my having a patience
that allows me to settle for anything less than brotherhood, I beg God
to forgive me.

I hope this letter finds you strong in the faith. I also hope that circumstances will soon make it possible for me to meet each of you, not
as an integrationist or a civil-rights leader but as a fellow clergyman and

a Christian brother. Let us all hope that the dark clouds of racial prejudice will soon pass away and the deep fog of misunderstanding will be lifted from our fear-drenched communities, and in some not too distant tomorrow the radiant stars of love and brotherhood will shine over our great nation with all their scintillating beauty.

Yours for the cause of Peace and Brotherhood,
Martin Luther King, Jr.

– 46 –

Takashi Yamada

Earlier chapters of this book make clear that the authors recognize contemporary Baptists as a key part, though only a part, of a heritage wider and older than the Protestant Reformation of the 1500s, and thus of course older than the earliest English Baptist, John Smyth, and his comrades in the 1600s. This book includes theological writing from these early baptists, who existed under many names, such as baptist and Brethren (but to their enemies, only Anabaptist). Some took the name of their strong Dutch leader, Menno Simons (see chapter 5 above). Mennonites survive to the present and have preserved many early baptist traits and convictions. Among these traits, Mennonite baptists diligently obey the Great Commission: they hold the Christian world mission central. One of their Japanese converts is Takashi Yamada (1926?–). During World War II, Yamada, a student in the Japanese Naval Academy, with his classmates was challenged to volunteer as a Kamikaze pilot — flying one desperate suicide flight to destroy an American naval vessel, by then on the attack. Yamada felt that his training had involved deception, so he refused the call — and survived the war. Later, while working for a trading company in Kobe, he was invited to attend a Mennonite mission Bible study. When the study progressed to Acts 2, Yamada and others in the class requested baptism and proposed starting a church; despite the missionaries' reluctance to move so fast, the church began. Yamada himself was baptized in 1952 and became a minister in 1956. He has taught at Associated Mennonite Biblical Seminaries, Elkhart, Indiana, has been a leader in world Mennonite activity, and serves at present writing as pastor of Kobayashi (Mennonite Church) Brotherhood. His writings include a book on church growth translated as Experiments in Church Growth. *The Bible study that follows, based on Matthew 5:21–24, was his address to the Mennonite World Conference in Curitiba, Brazil, in 1972. Its theme, Jesus' teaching on forgiveness in the church, has been central to the baptist movement throughout its history; because of its central importance, this indispensable teaching is often called the Rule of Christ.*

Reconciliation in the Church

...So far we have tried to grasp some of the important meanings of our text. Now I would like to spend some time discussing our given topic, keeping in our minds what we have learned in the previous section.

A. Our Difficulties: "Reconciliation in the Church" Is a Somewhat Difficult Matter to Deal With

1a. The difficulty may come partially from the fact that we are inclined to have an idealistic image of the Christian church and a superficial idea of the unity of the church. Therefore we often cherish in ourselves idealistic images trying to evade facing the actual condition of disunity and conflicts. Or we sometimes pretend to put our primary emphasis on efforts in bringing people outside of the church to be reconciled to God, and by doing so, try to justify our own problems in the church. Another difficulty along this line is that a legalistic and moral approach does not work, since reconciliation is essentially what God causes among us when we come to know the certain ways the Spirit works, and yield ourselves to him.

b. In the New Testament the organic oneness in the relationships between Christ and believers, and among believers is described in various ways such as "vine and its branches," "the Shepherd and his sheep," and "the family of God or the Body of Christ and the members." Jesus, in his great prayer before the passion, prayed for the unity of believers. When the Holy Spirit descended on the *group* of disciples on the day of Pentecost, they experienced the reality of this spiritual oneness in an entirely unique and powerful way. There the *New Community* of faith and life was formed. It was based on mutual trusting in brotherly love.

c. Already in the early stage of the life of the primitive church, however, the unity was seriously threatened by the sharp conflict between the Jewish and the gentile Christians. Since then, throughout the history of the Christian church, there has not been a time that the whole church as an actual historical existence enjoyed perfect unity. The church has always suffered from disunity and conflicts within herself, and struggled for true unity and oneness. The message of the gospel of reconciliation has been entrusted to the church, and proclaimed and borne fruit in marvelous ways in human history. But at the same time the church has always needed reconciliation within herself.

d. I believe that one of the problems of the church on this point lies in that we often fail to grasp our Christian faith in the context of communal life on its practical level. So we tend to minimize our faith to the extent that at last faith may become a matter of individual possession for the sake of our own gains and happiness and "the passport to heaven." We fail to realize that the church is the area or fellowship in which we practice the way of righteousness and experience the reconciling power of Christ among us.

e. Another problem is, I believe, that we usually do not have sufficient understanding of the ways in which those principles of life in God's Kingdom function through the working of the Spirit of Christ in our fellowship. Here we need to understand the dynamic inner spiritual structure and function of the fellowship.

B. The Spiritual Structure and Function

a. I believe that the gospel of Jesus Christ creates a true responsible self in each one of us if we voluntarily and sincerely respond to it. When God said to Moses "I AM WHO I AM" (Exd. 3:14), he revealed himself as *the self-responsible Person* who was going to call out his own people in history "according to his good pleasure which he hath purposed in himself" (Eph. 1:9). He always speaks to us here and now in the midst of our actual situations. As we continue to respond consciously to him and his calling as the members of the Body of Christ, the chosen people of God in history, he nurtures the unique selfhood in us. This is entirely different from a kind of individualistic selfhood separated from God and his community. Since God speaks to us anew every time out of ever changing situations, we, on our side, always must be ready to open ourselves before him, breaking down our preconceptions, presuppositions and the old frame of references so that we may keep our personal encounter and dialogue with God and obey him anew in our life situations.

b. Significant life begins when we try to open ourselves before our fellowmen, and participate in the lives of each other in a vital way. However, this kind of meaningful relationship can be established only among men who have experienced this unique selfhood. And as we have learned already, this openness, uniqueness, and selfhood come from God. Therefore, in the Christian community of forgiven and forgiving fellowship, we truly encounter each other and participate in one another's lives. In this way we become true men and "are grown up in every way into him who is the head, into Christ" (Eph. 4:15).

c. A vital community life does not necessarily guarantee us smooth, easy and peaceful living; it is rather a challenging, exciting and adventurous way of living. In its normal healthy state, the Christian community has certain creative tensions between our vertical relations with God and our horizontal relations with our fellowmen. Creative tensions can be crucial tensions. There may be some personal conflicts among brothers that could lead the church to disaster.

d. Right in such difficult situations we really experience what it means to forgive our fellow brothers and to be forgiven by them only if we keep ourselves open to God and to our fellow men. Through these experiences we learn a precious lesson that we do need our fellow brothers, especially those who are in opposition and conflict with us so that we may be transformed by the Spirit of the living Christ.

e. Therefore we come to know that the living Christ is working as the creative Spirit who causes creative tensions in the fellowship, and stimulates the church to grow together. However, the living Christ is also the reconciling and healing Spirit working in the fellowship. The Apostle Paul often speaks about the various kinds of gifts of the Spirit given to each one of the members of the Body of Christ in the New Testament. Here is *the uniqueness* of each individual Christian. But he does not forget to add that those diverse gifts are given not for our own benefit, but for the sake of our brothers, and the whole Body (I Cor. 12:12–13). Here is *the responsibleness* of each member.

f. Here and there in the New Testament we find amazing diversity, critical tensions caused by sharp contrasts and differences, and even some personal crushes in the Christian fellowship. But right there we see the living Christ of the church stimulating, reconciling and healing, sometimes quickly and sometimes slowly, in his church.

g. If we take a second look at the teaching and the life of Jesus on earth in the light of the presence and the work of the living Christ in the church, we may begin to see the reality of God's kingdom on earth. The Spirit of Christ is dynamic power to give life to the inner spiritual structure and function of the Christian community.

C. Obstacles Standing in the Way of Keeping True Unity

a. Differences of opinion, emphasis and Christian experience can create misunderstandings and wrong, prejudiced images of our fellow men. Then we react against our fellow Christians, basing our actions on these false images of them that we have built up in our minds. Not only self-defending, self-insisting and self-justifying attitudes toward others, but also a closed, indifferent and non-participating attitude hinders reconciliation and unity in the church. Our particular ecclesiastical heritages and traditions, certain emphases on some aspects of church life, rituals, forms and customs need to be re-examined, and at the same time re-evaluated always in order that these may not cause serious disunity and disruptions among us; but rather that they may give life, abundance, and unique diversity to our fellowship.

D. Some Areas in Which Reconciliation Is Needed

a. From what we have discussed in this paper, it is obvious that the way to reconciliation is not in trying to heal disruptions or conflicts by leveling off differences and adjusting contrasts on the human level. Rather it is a dynamic act of the living Christ who brings together men from different backgrounds, having very different temperaments and ideas, and who lifts them up to a higher spiritual solidarity in and through these human differences. Only the living Christ can make it possible for us to "have power to comprehend with all the saints what is the breadth and length and height and depth, and to know the love of Christ which surpasses knowledge" (Eph 3:18, 19).

b. Today we hear that the human gaps caused by racial, economic, social, cultural, and generational differences are so deep even in the Christian church that the need for reconciliation is most urgent. However, this has been the problem of the church through all ages from the time of the early church to this age of the technological revolution. So it is not surprising to find the same problem of human gaps caused by exactly the same differences as mentioned above. As the church has struggled with and agonized over the problem, Christians have looked up to Christ and found him as the Reconciler.

c. Reconciliation in Christian fellowship in the so-called mission fields is something to which not much attention has been paid until the recent years of growing nationalism in Asian and African countries. This is, however, one of the areas where the real problems of the churches, both older and younger, are exposed plainly. Sometimes the seeds of disunity and conflicts are brought and planted into the naive fellowship of young native churches by the wrong denominationalism and particularistic group consciousness of the foreign missions. Authoritarian and paternalistic approaches and policies can hinder the healthy development of selfhood among native Christians, and distort the Christian gospel itself. An extreme type of absolute exclusivism and one-sided proclamation is very harmful in mission fields, and it is contradictory to the spirit of reconciliation. An attitude of resistance on the side of a younger church over against an older church for its authoritarian approach may cause some unhappy results in their mutual relationship. The older and younger can grow together by seeking for reconciliation in a positive way, and the younger may find that it can also help and contribute to the older.

d. Reconciliation is also needed among the churches in those areas where the tragic experiences of wars are still remembered deep in the hearts of the people. Ever since I became a Christian I have always found it strange that between our missionaries and us, Japanese Christians, the tragic war experiences in which both our nations were involved and in which we shared our responsibility for the war have been seldom taken up as a serious subject of discussion. Unconsciously or consciously, somehow we may have evaded the issue, probably because we thought it unhelpful to dig out that past unhappy incident now and argue about it. As I ponder on the matter of reconciliation in the church, I have come to see that the reconciling Christ touches and heals these sore spots in our hearts. Instead of saying some beautiful words of formal greeting to our brethren at this special occasion, I confess the sins of the Japanese nation and of myself in the past wars, and sincerely ask for forgiveness from you, my brothers in Christ.

e. Several years ago I was invited by the Taiwanese Mennonite Church to spend some time with them. While I was there, one day my dear Taiwanese friend, Pastor Lin, introduced me to one of his church members, a Chinese Christian who had once fought against the Japanese Army as a soldier when he was in mainland China. When we faced each other, it was this Chinese brother who first stretched out his right hand for shaking hands, saying, "We were once enemies of each other, but now we are brothers in Christ." I was struck and moved so deeply by what he did that I just could not help being choked up with tears. In World War II, I was in the Japanese Navy and fought against America. Pastor Lin's motherland had been occupied by Japan for 50 years, and because of it, his fellowmen had to participate in the war. With this tragic historical background, each one of us met together there, and found that we were brothers in Christ. Furthermore at the back of the conversion and Christian life of each one of the three of us, there were the toiling works of our missionary brothers from overseas. There I see the higher spiritual solidarity in Christ beyond our racial and cultural solidarity. The church is a community of God's people surpassing their racial, national and cultural human ties.

E. Concluding Words

a. The emergence of the church, her existence in history, and the proclamation of the gospel are the definite events of the last days in the whole plan of the saving act of God in man's history. The church is moving forward on the road of adventure for Christ in an eschatological tension, voluntarily and consciously taking in advance part of the full blessings of the day when God completes his work of redemption and reconciliation of the whole of mankind as well as of the universe. Only when we are experiencing the dynamic power of the reconciling Christ in our midst, can the church be an effective and powerful vessel for reconciling people in the world to God and among themselves.

b. Are we satisfied with a kind of average Christian life with mere repetition of going to church on Sundays, attending church committee meetings once in a while, offering fairly good amounts of money to the church treasury or foreign mission fund, engaging occasionally in some kind of social relief work as good Christian citizens, doing nothing bad but nothing really significant?

c. Or are we going to follow the path of Jesus and launch out into the adventurous life of those who belong to the community of God on earth, witnessing boldly to the reconciling power and grace of Christ in the world?

Am I really sure that I belong to this community of God?

[*Proceedings of the Ninth Mennonite World Conference*, Curitiba, Brazil, 1972, 7–25. Used by permission.]

– 47 –

Dale Moody

Dale Moody (1915–92) was converted at the age of twelve while on a horseback ride across his home ranch near Grapevine, Texas. He was educated at Texas' Baylor University and at the Southern Baptist Theological Seminary in Louisville, Kentucky. There among his teachers he especially admired theologian H. W. Tribble and missiologist W. O. Carver. Moody earned a second doctorate at Oxford University in the 1960s. From 1945, however, he had been teaching doctrinal theology at Southern. A vigorous scholar and public lecturer who never forgot his cowboy beginnings, despite his tender regard for others, or perhaps because of it, Moody relished theological controversy. Well informed in Christian tradition, his own highest authority was the New Testament. This priority inevitably brought him into conflict with Baptists shaped by one version of Calvinism, who maintained that "once saved, always saved" was the true scriptural position, while Moody vigorously insisted Scripture did not teach that. After his formal retirement, he continued to teach at Southern Seminary, but due to his controversial stance on this topic, his contract was not renewed in 1983. (Later the seminary recanted, making him professor emeritus.) He died firm in the conviction that on this and most other matters he was right and his opponents were wrong. The present selection reflects his side of the controversy about apostasy; it is taken from his summary doctrinal volume, The Word of Truth, *which in turn was based on his often-repeated seminary lectures.*

The Question of Apostasy

What does the New Testament mean by apostasy and related terms? A scriptural approach begins with the central issues and only then sets forth secondary questions of Scripture and tradition. After the meaning of apostasy as a New Testament teaching is clarified, then the controversies in church history may be evaluated.

Apostasy is not a term imposed upon the New Testament; it is a New

Testament term used in both a special and a general sense. The special sense in which the apostasy of many in the latter days ends in the great apostasy, or falling away, before the return of Christ, is discussed in the section on the consummation (see II Thess. 2:3 and I Tim. 4:1 for this sense). It is the possibility of apostasy that is ever present between immaturity and maturity in the life of faith that is the subject of this section (see Heb. 3:12 for this sense). This alone is the concern at present.

Apostasy in Scripture

Backsliding in the Old Testament is a general background for understanding the New Testament teachings on falling away from a personal faith in the Lord Jesus, but the New Testament should be interpreted in terms of the New Covenant. In the Old Covenant the unfaithfulness of Israel to the covenant may be called national apostasy as those who had turned to the Lord turned away from him. This was a special concern of the prophet Jeremiah. The nearest thing in the Old Testament to the New Testament teaching on apostasy would be willing sins or high-handed sins for which there were no sacrifices.

There are several warnings in the Synoptic Gospels about the danger that disciples may fall away, but perhaps the plainest passage is Luke's interpretation of the Parable of the Sower (8:9–15). Some only hear the word of God without believing it, but those in a second group "believe for a while and in a time of temptation fall away" (8:13). A. T. Robertson comments: "Ostensibly they are sincere and have a real start in the life of faith."

Superficial believers are not the only type that falls away. The thorny ground in the Parable of the Sower represents those who hear the word of God, "but as they go on their way they are choked by the cares and riches and pleasures of life, and their fruit does not mature" (8:14). Those who hold fast the word of God "in an honest and good heart" are the only ones that "bring forth fruit with patience" (8:15). It is amazing how preconceived dogmas blind so many to the realism of this parable. It happens before their eyes in so many ways, but they refuse to see what is so obvious.

The Acts of the Apostles records the story of Ananias and Sapphira, who were smitten dead because they lied to the Holy Spirit of God (5:11). Simon Magus "himself believed," but Peter pronounced the curse of God upon him. Paul was aware that "fierce wolves" would pounce upon the believers of Ephesus and "draw away disciples after them" (Acts 20:30). On this last passage A. T. Robertson has the salty statement: "There is a false optimism that is complacently blind as well as a despondent pessimism that gives up the fight."

The letters of Paul contain passages that are brushed aside today as unworthy of serious study. Yet the primary letters of 1 and 2 Thessalonians take note of the idle, fainthearted and weak who need to be admonished so that they may be sound and blameless at the second coming (I Thess. 5:14, 23). Even before the great apostasy and the revelation of the man of lawlessness there was the danger that false teachers would lead them astray so that some would refuse to obey Paul (II Thess. 1:1–2; 3:14f.).

At one place he warns those who live on the level of knowledge, the Gnostic notion of knowledge that puffs up, that they can by their example destroy the faith of a weak brother who lives on the level of conscience (I Corinthians 8:11). Paul believed that even he, after preaching to others, could become disqualified, a castaway in the KJV, *adokimos* in Greek (I Cor. 9:27). A. T. Robertson has this observation: "Most writers take Paul to refer to the possibility of his rejection in his personal salvation at the end of the race. . . . It is a humbling thought for us all to see this wholesome fear instead of smug complacency in this greatest of all heralds of Christ" (cf. I Cor. 8:11; 10:12). This smug complacency continues among those who ignore the possibility that they may become castaways. The reference of Robertson to I Corinthians 10:12 has the warning: "Therefore let anyone who thinks he stands take heed lest he fall." Paul actually believed his readers could become reprobates, and "fail to meet the test" (II Cor. 13:5). Yet cheap preaching and compromise with sin have made such texts forbidden for serious study.

The Galatian letter of Paul has only one chapter without a serious warning about falling from grace, yet the phrase is forbidden language for some. What does Paul mean when he says: "I am astonished that you are so quickly deserting him who called you in the grace of Christ and turning to a different gospel" (1:6)? What does he mean by beginning in the Spirit and ending in the flesh (3:3)? Why does he fear that those who come out of slavery into sonship (4:1–7) will turn back to the weak, beggarly elemental spirits (4:8–11), if this is impossible? It is nonsense to say these passages have Peter and Barnabas in mind (cf. Gal. 2:12), but it is correct to see "the circumcision party" as the danger to believers.

Surely he would not warn the Galatians against putting on the "yoke of slavery" again, if that were not a real danger. All these questions are answered by the blunt statement: "You are severed from Christ, you who would be justified by the law; you have fallen away from grace" (5:4). A. T. Robertson translates the Greek to say "ye did fall out of grace." J. W. MacGorman rightly says: "To turn to the law as in any way necessary to effect the right standing with God is to turn one's back on Christ . . . nothing more, nothing less." They were running well until somebody hindered them (5:7).

The conclusion needs only to be read to be understood:

> Be not deceived;
>   God is not mocked.
> for whatever a man sows,
>   that he will also reap.
> For he who sows to his own flesh
>   will from the flesh reap corruption;
> but he who sows to the Spirit
>   will from the Spirit reap eternal life.
> And let us not grow weary in well-doing,
>   for in due season we shall reap,
>   if we do not lose heart (6:7–9).

Those who flee from these Pauline passages and look for shelter in Romans 8:39 do well provided they understand that nothing will separate us from the love of God if we are "in Christ Jesus our Lord." This does not apply to those who are severed from Christ. Before the precious promise in 8:39 is the warning and promise in 8:12f. which says: "So then, brethren, we are debtors, not to the flesh — for if you live according to the flesh you will die, but if by the Spirit you put to death the deeds of the body you will live." Brothers can keep on living according to flesh and die! Warnings noted in I Corinthians 8:11; 9:27; 10:12 are [repeated?] in Romans 14:13–23. A bad example can lead to the spiritual ruin of a brother for whom Christ died, even "destroy the work of God" (14:15, 20). Scripture should not be read with selective inattention. All of it is inspired and all of it is to be heard and heeded....

Some of the general letters and Hebrews seem to be from Hellenistic Jewish Christianity. James thought his brethren could wander from the truth and be in danger of spiritual death (5:19f.). I Peter teaches that even those "who by God's power are guarded through faith" need the admonition: "Be sober, be watchful. Your adversary the devil prowls around like a roaring lion, seeking some one to devour" (1:5; 5:8). II Peter teaches that those who do not grow in grace may forget they were cleansed from their old sins and that the last state can be worse than the first (1:9; 2:20–22). Jude wrote against those who "deny our only Master and Lord, Jesus Christ" and gave several examples of apostasy (3–16) before he concluded with a summary of apostolic Christianity and a benediction on God's ability to keep those who continue in faith, hope and love (17–25). It is unrealistic to ignore this distinction between apostate and apostolic Christianity.

If one follows the teachings of Hebrews all the other teachings on apostasy in the New Testament present no problems. It is when one tries to twist Hebrews to fit a traditional system based on false philosophy and dogma that difficulties arise. Few passages in the New Testament have been twisted with more violence than the five warnings on apostasy in Hebrews.

[Here Moody examines five passages, Hebrews 2:1–4, 3:7–4:13, 6:1–29, 10:19–39, and 12:1–29, concluding that all support his view.]

By the time that one has reached this point in the exposition of Hebrews three things stand out: (1) it is possible to press on to maturity and full assurance (6:1, 11; 10:22); (2) it is possible for believers who do not press on to maturity to commit apostasy; and (3) there is no remedy for the sin of apostasy. Many, like Martin Luther, would like to drop Hebrews out of the canon of Scripture, some for the second reason and others for the third, but this is out of the dogmatic bias that goes back to Augustine, not to other Scriptures.

Often those who reject the teachings on apostasy do so because they believe certain passages in the Johannine writings teach otherwise. They really misinterpret the Johannine passages by reading them through the colored glass of tradition. The Johannine writings do have a great emphasis on God's preservation of those who abide in Christ, but one may cease to abide in Christ. In their game of theological chess the trick question is often put: "can a person be unborn?" John 3:3–8 is usually in mind. They would never say that a friend who died "got unborn." The trick question grew up by ignoring the plain statement in I John 5:16 which teaches that it is possible for a Christian brother to die a spiritual death. This is not a case like I Corinthians 11:30. Death in I John 5:16 has the same meaning as in 3:14. It should be noted that John 3:16 speaks of those who do not perish as those who continue to believe. The Greek tense behind believeth is present linear, not past and punctiliar.

The next move is almost sure to be John 5:24, which speaks of those who believe as passing from spiritual death to eternal life so that they will not come into judgment, but again it must be pointed out that I John 5:16 says one can pass from eternal life back into death (cf. I Jn. 5:11–13). They work with the false assumption that the adjective "eternal" is an adverb, as if it says the brother eternally has life. It is the life that is eternal, not one's possession of it. Eternal life is the life of God in Christ the Son of God, and this life is lost when one departs from Christ (cf. Jn. 5:26). Eternal life is possible only in the Son of God.

The third move is to John 6:37 where it is said: "All that the Father gives me will come to me and him who comes to me I will not cast out." True! Those who come or keep on coming will not be cast out, but Judas was given to Jesus by the Father, yet he became the son of perdition (John 17:12). That is precisely the teaching of John 6. After the threefold promise that he will at the last day raise up those given by the Father (6:39, 40, 44), "many of his disciples drew back and no longer went about with him" (6:66). Simon Peter then speaks for those who did not go away, for to do so would forfeit eternal life, and Judas is singled out as one among the Twelve who was to go back into perdition (6:67–71). The whole of John 6 is built on the model of the Israelites who got all the way to Kadesh-Barnea and turned back to perish in the wilderness. That is why there is the frequent reference to murmuring against Christ (Jn. 6:41, 43, 61; cf. I Cor. 10:10 based on Exod. 16:7, 8, 9, 12; Num. 14:27; 17:5, 10).

Eternal life is the life of those who continue to follow Jesus. No one can retain eternal life who turns away from Jesus. John 10:28 is frequently used as a security blanket by those who ignore many of the New Testament warnings about going back or falling away, but a literal translation of John 10:27–28, all of the sentence, hardly needs explanation, for it is a promise to those who continue to follow Jesus. Not for one moment do I doubt this literal translation: "My sheep keep on hearing my voice, and I keep on knowing them, and they keep on following me: and I keep on giving them eternal life, and they shall never perish, and no one shall snatch them out of my hand." Some read the passage as if it says: "My sheep heard my voice, and I knew them, and they followed me, and I gave to them eternal life." The verbs are present linear, indicating continuous action by the sheep and by the Shepherd, not the punctiliar fallacy of the past tense.

Obviously, those who follow Jesus will not perish, but what about those disciples who "drew back and no longer went about with him?" The allegory on Jesus as the Vine and the Father as the Vinedresser in John 15:1–11 answers that question. "Every branch of mine that bears no fruit, he takes away.... If a man does not abide in me, he is cast forth as a branch and withers; and the branches are gathered, thrown into the fire and burned" (15:2, 6). Surely one will not appeal to some passage like I Corinthians 3:15 to prove that the words in the Gospel of John mean nothing more than the loss of reward by a saved person, yet that is just what is often done to defend the dogmatic theory of eternal security, which is never mentioned in the New Testament. It would hardly make sense for Jesus to say he taught his disciples to keep them from "falling away" (16:1) if it were not possible for them to fall away....

Apostasy in Tradition

Warnings against the danger of falling away from faith may be noted in every New Testament writing but Philemon, which has no doctrinal discussion at all! Why then has this teaching been excluded in much of the Christian theology of the West? The answer on examination comes home loud and clear: tradition has triumphed over Scripture. At least three distorted traditions and interpretations may be noted in Western theology.

The first was *Augustinianism.* In 429, Augustine, the Catholic Bishop of Hippo, wrote his last two books, *On the Predestination of the Saints* and *On the Gift of Perseverance.* These books, like the Vandal armies who at the time threatened the Christian world, were destined to cast a shadow over Christian life and theology down to this day.

In his battle with the Pelagians over the doctrines of original sin and God's grace, Augustine worked with a logic that later became a system in Calvinism. (1) To him the human race was a mass of perdition so depraved, as a result of Adam's Fall, that little unbaptized infants would be justly damned in limbo. (2) On no condition due to man, God had chosen to redeem a number of souls that would equal the number of the fallen angels. (3) For this elect group Jesus Christ came to earth to die, and (4) God would save them by his unmerited and irresistible grace. (5) By the gift of perseverance the elect were joined to God forever. He was indeed, as his biographer said, a man predestinate ([Possidius'] *Life,* Preface, 2). As the Vandals closed in on him and his flock in Hippo, he prayed that they would be able to persevere to the end (*Life,* XXIX. I).

The second tradition to distort the New Testament teaching on apostasy was *Calvinism.* The logic of Augustine was greatly modified in the history of Catholic theology, but his doctrines of predestination and perseverance were revived again by the French Reformer John Calvin. Calvin believed that God regenerated all elect infants before their baptism, so this softened some of the harshness on infant damnation, but Calvin hardened the doctrine of predestination into a double decree by which God was not only the author of salvation for the elect but of damnation for the non-elect (*Institutes,* III. xxi).

He also believed the elect are given assurance of their election, either at the time of repentance or before they die. This third point prepared the way for later debate on the doctrines of assurance and the second blessing, some holding that assurance came with faith and others that it came later.

As in Augustine, Calvin's doctrine of the perseverance of the saints is a part of his doctrine of predestination. "By predestination," said Calvin, "we mean the eternal decree of God, by which he has decided in his own mind what he wishes to happen in the case of each individual. For all men are not created on an equal footing, but for some eternal life is pre-ordained, for others eternal damnation" (*Institutes* [1539], III.xxi). Even the apostasy of those who experience all that the elect experience, is predestined for reprobates. Calvin followed Augustine in appealing to John 6:37; 17:6 to support his doctrine of perseverance. In his debate with the Roman Catholic scholar A. Pighe, d. 1542, Calvin erected a Johannine fortress using John 6:37; 10:28; 17:6–11 and other passages. A reading of the old Augustine and the old Calvin raises the question whether old men should discuss predestination, perseverance, and apostasy at all!

The crucial time for Calvinism was their condemnation of Arminianism at the Synod of Dort in Holland in 1618. Since the condemnation of the Remonstrants, as the disciples of James Arminius were called, their statements have been for the most part vindicated in the modified traditions of Calvinism. The five points that were condemned were:

[Here Moody quotes a summary of Dort's "five points" from Henry Bettenson, *Documents of the Christian Church*.]

About the only points that would now be questioned by evangelical Christians are the five quotations from Scripture raised as a question at the end of article V, yet the question is a composition from Hebrews 3:14; II Timothy 4:10; II Peter 2:22; I Timothy 1:19; Hebrews 12:15. A scholar as able as G. C. Berkouwer has exercised all his strength to bring Hebrews into line with Calvinism and to defend the Calvinistic doctrine of election and predestination. He really reduces the warnings to bluffing.

Despite the abundance of Scripture surveyed above, the strict Calvinists have defended the doctrines of predestination and perseverance imposed on Scripture by Augustine and Calvin. A study of the English Calvinist John Owen is an ordeal of verbosity in defense of the thesis that apostates were predestined to fall away by the decree of God.

Besides his books *The Doctrine of the Saints' Perseverance* and *The Nature of Apostasy,* John Owen wrote a commentary on Hebrews of 3,500 pages, and even then he was unable to bring the writing into line with his rigid Calvinistic system. Like so many since, he could discern the threat, but he was unable to twist the content. It is a strange spectacle to see so much energy expounded in the effort to make Scripture support a false tradition.

The third movement that found problems with the New Testament teachings on apostasy cherishes the name *evangelical.* By the nineteenth century, under the impact of evangelism and missions, the doctrine of the perseverance of the saints was falling into disrepute. In two branches of evangelical Christianity the terms that began to replace "the perseverance of the saints" were "the security of believers" and "eternal security." The biblical term predestination dropped into the background, the non-biblical terms "security of the believer" and "eternal security" took the place of the non-biblical terms "the gift of perseverance" and "the perseverance of the saints," and tradition continues to triumph over Scripture. All this was done by people who appealed to the Scriptures where their terms are never found....

Some Baptist thinkers in the twentieth century found it difficult to harmonize the Greek New Testament with the Augustinian-Calvinistic-Evangelical (Landmark Baptist-Dispensational) tradition. The roots of resistance go back to the renowned Baptist Greek scholar A. T. Robertson of Southern Baptist Theological Seminary in Louisville, Kentucky.

As early as 1909, Robertson was doing plain talk on falling from grace. The believers in Galatia, he said, "have fallen away from grace and gone back under the bondage of the law" (5:3f.). "They were Gentiles and had tasted the freedom of Christ...."

There are several other passages scattered throughout Robertson's many writings that indicate that he never thought within the confines of Calvinism on the question of apostasy, but his crowning work *Word Pictures in the New Testament,* from which frequent quotations were made in the first part of this chapter, brought all of these up to date before he died in 1934. Calvinism has no claim on him. If one thinks solely in the context of the New Testament, Robertson's views create no problem, but the effort to force the New Testament into the dogmatic straitjacket of Calvinism creates the dilemma that so many have faced.

According to official confessions of faith, Baptist theology really began its departure from strict Calvinism in The New Hampshire Confession of Faith of 1833 which said in Article XI (of the perseverance of saints):

[We believe] that such only are real believers as endure unto the end; that their persevering attachment to Christ is the grand mark which distinguishes them from mere professors; that a special Providence watches over their welfare; and [that] they are kept by the power of God through faith unto salvation.

Baptist Landmarkism alone, in 1955, rejected the term "perseverance of the saints" and adopted the term "eternal security of the believer." The Baptist Faith and Message of 1925 adopted the statement of The New Hampshire Confession of Faith with no significant change. The 1963 revision of the 1925 confession tried to harmonize statements from the older Calvinism that go back to The Westminster Confession of Faith of 1647 by Presbyterians and The Second London Confession of Faith of 1677 by Baptists, but there is no clarification on the question of apostasy. Nothing is said about those who do not "endure to the end." Cf. Mark 4:17.

It is indeed time to put the plain teachings of Scripture above all human traditions, for, as The Baptist Faith and Message of 1963 does rightly say, the Scriptures "will remain to the end of the world, the true center of Christian union, and the supreme standard by which all human conduct, creeds, and religious opinions should be tried." To this I fully subscribe.

[Dale Moody, *The Word of Truth: A Summary of Christian Doctrine Based on Biblical Revelation* (Grand Rapids: Eerdmans, 1981), 348–65.]

48

Orlando E. Costas

Orlando E. Costas (1942–87), a native of Puerto Rico, was ordained there to the Baptist ministry and served churches both in Puerto Rico and in the United States. Having completed his doctorate at the Free University, Amsterdam, he served as professor and then as dean of several theological institutions including the Latin American Biblical Seminary in San José, Costa Rica, and Eastern Baptist and Andover Newton seminaries in the United States. He was dean at the latter school at the time of his early death. Orlando Costas was the author of a number of books, including The Church and Its Mission, The Integrity of Mission *and* Liberating News: A Theology of Contextual Evangelism. *A practicing evangelist who continued right through his academic years to conduct revival meetings, his social convictions were strongly formed by his experience in what Westerners had called the "Third World," that part of the globe that was neither in their own West nor in the Communist bloc of nations (though this nomenclature seemed arbitrarily to relegate the poorer countries to last place). In this piece he contrasts the "formal" principle of evangelicals in the West, the authority of Scripture, with the "material" principle, what the Bible has to say, as the latter was understood outside the West. Although Costas here writes for a multidenominational journal, his article reflects the theological concerns of many of his fellow Baptists.*

Evangelical Theology in the Two Thirds World

Recognizing that many contemporary evangelical theologians in the Two Thirds World have been formed and informed (and sometimes even deformed!) by [United States'] New Evangelical theologians, they do not appear to be as concerned over the formal authority question as they are over the material principle. To be sure, one can find evangelical theological formulations in the Two Thirds World that reveal a similar concern over the authority of Scripture. However, such formulations are neither the most authentic expression of evangelical theology in the Two Thirds World nor the most numerous. To validate this assertion, I will turn to the concluding statements from three major theological conferences on Evangelical theology in the Two Thirds World held in Thailand (March 1982), Korea (August 1982) and Mexico (June 1984).

The Thailand and Mexico meetings had a missiological thrust and a theological content. They were sponsored by a loose fellowship of Evangelical mission theologians from the Two Thirds World. The Thailand conference revolved around "The Proclamation of Christ in the Two Thirds World." It produced a final document ("Towards a Missiological Christology in the Two Thirds World") and a book (*Sharing Jesus in the Two Thirds World,* ed. Vinay Samuel and Chris Sugden), published first in India and most recently (1983) in the United States. The Mexico meeting focused on the Holy Spirit and evangelical spirituality. It also produced a final statement ("Life in the Holy Spirit") which will be part of the book soon to be published with the conference papers. The Korean Third World Theologians Consultation was sponsored by the Theological Commission of the Association of Evangelicals in Africa and Madagascar, the Asia Theological Association, the Latin American Theological Fraternity and the Theological Commission of the World Evangelical Fellowship. Working with the theme "Theology and Bible in Context," it produced the Seoul Declaration ("Toward an Evangelical Theology for the Third World").

All three documents express a clear commitment to Scripture as the source and norm of theology. They express an unambiguous commitment to its authority, not only in terms of the content of the faith and the nature of its practice, but also in the approach to its interpretation. The Scriptures are normative in the understanding of the faith, the lifestyle of God's people, and the way Christians go about their theological reflection. Yet the Scriptures are not to be heard and obeyed unhistorically. Indeed, the normative and formative roles of Scripture are mediated by our respective contexts. These contexts are, generally speaking, characterized in these documents as a reality of poverty, powerlessness and oppression on the one hand, and on the other, as religiously and ideologically pluralistic spaces. Thus a contextual hermeneutic appears as a *sine qua non* of evangelical theology in the Two Thirds World....

Evangelicals North and South, East and West

So far, I have argued that though Evangelical theology emerges out of European and North American Protestant Christianity and has been carried to the Two Thirds World by the missionary movement, theological institutions, and publications, there is an identifiable difference between its most influential and visible contemporary expression (New Evangelical theology) and the emerging Evangelical theological discourse in the

Two Thirds World. This difference lies in the latter's concern with the [material] principle of Protestant theology. The emphasis on the content of the gospel and the teaching of the biblical text rather than on formal questions of authority and the philosophical presuppositions behind a particular doctrine of inspiration is freeing Evangelical theology in the Two Thirds World to employ a contextual hermeneutics patterned after the transpositional method witnessed throughout the New Testament. This also explains why Evangelicals in the Two Thirds World are more willing to deal with questions of religious pluralism and social, economic, and political oppression than most Evangelical theologians in the One Third World.

Without putting all mainstream Evangelicals in the One Third World in the same bag, it seems quite clear to me that mainstream Evangelical theologians are too obsessed with the Enlightenment and not enough with the explosive social, economic, political, cultural and religious reality of most people in the world. As Bernard Ramm has stated quite candidly in the opening pages of his book, *After Fundamentalism: The Future of Evangelical Theology,* "The Enlightenment sent shock waves through Christian theology as nothing did before or after. Theology has never been the same since the Enlightenment. And therefore each and every theology, evangelical included, must assess its relationship to the Enlightenment" (p. 4).

It should be pointed out that this obsession with the Enlightenment as an intellectual challenge to faith pertains basically to its seventeenth and eighteenth century phase, which revolved around the issue of freedom from authority through reason. This obsession is shared by practically all Euro-American theologies. Indeed it can be argued that all mainstream theologies in Western Europe and North America, from Immanuel Kant to Carl F. H. Henry, have been, by and large, discourses on the reasonableness of faith. Their primary concern has been the skeptic, atheist, materialist-heathen — the non-religious person. This is why the second phase of the Enlightenment, associated with the nineteenth century movement of freedom from political, cultural, economic, and social oppression has been in the main a peripheral issue in Euro-American theology, including Evangelical theology. Yet, this is one issue of fundamental importance in the theological agenda of the Two Thirds World. For all its missionary passion and experience, mainstream Evangelical theology in North America has yet to learn from its missionary heritage how to ask more central questions concerning the destiny of humankind, the future of the world, even the central concerns of the Scriptures. In airing this criticism I do not mean to belittle the fact that there are always two sides to the problem of unbelief: (1) the absence of faith, and (2) the denial (practical or theoretical) of faith. Theology in North America and Western Europe has been generally concerned with the absence of faith and its theoretical denial. But it must be acknowledged that from the Evangelical Awakening to the present there have been mainstream Euro-American theologies and theological movements that have sought to address the problem of the practical denial of faith in the unjust treatment of the weak and downtrodden. This is the case with the theology of the Wesley brothers, the Oberlin theology of Charles G. Finney, the theology of the Social Gospel, the practical theology of the early Reinhold Niebuhr, the political theology of Jürgen Moltmann and J. B. Metz, and the prophetic theologies of mainstream ecumenical theologians like Robert McAfee Brown and the Peace and Justice Evangelicals. These theologies have attempted, in varying degrees and in their own peculiar ways, to deal with the problem of social oppression and alienation. In so doing they have built a modest bridge toward a fundamental concern of any theology in the Two Thirds World, namely, the cry of the oppressed and its disclosure of the practical "unbelief" of professing Christians who oppress their neighbors.

My critique is, furthermore, not intended to obliterate the modest dialogue which has been taking place during the last several years around the question of poverty, powerlessness, oppression, and religious pluralism between some mainstream Evangelical theologians and their counterparts in the Two Thirds World. Indeed, during the Thailand meeting there were two theologians representing European and North American Evangelical thought, and while they came to the meeting with questions pertaining to traditional theological issues of the North Atlantic, they had to cope with other theological agendas (and did so positively and constructively). They realized that their particular agenda was pertinent to a rather small sector of humankind. They also acknowledged that their agenda was even different from that of the two "minority" participants from North America for whom North American Evangelical theology had dealt especially with the truth of God's justice. . . .

In November 1983, a consultation was held in Tlayacapan, Mexico, between several types of Evangelical theologians from North America and their counterparts in Latin America and the minority communities of the U.S. This consultation focused on "Context and Hermeneutics in the Americas" and established a methodology that permitted Evangelical scholars to wrestle with concrete biblical texts and debate such questions as whether our interlocutor is really the "atheist" (as Evangelical theologians who wrestle with the questions of the first phase of the Enlightenment argue) or the alienated (i.e., the non-person who may be religious but has been exploited, marginalized, and dehumanized by religious institutions, as many theologians in the Two Thirds World and North American minority communities would argue). The latter issue was not resolved, but the hermeneutical exercises were very fruitful.

Afterwards, Grant Osborne, from Trinity Evangelical Divinity School, wrote in *TSF Bulletin:*

> All in all, it was felt that North Americans need to enter a Latin American setting and do theological reflection in the context of poverty. Those from the North, before passing judgment, should be willing to enter a Nicaragua or an El Salvador and experience those realities from the inside. (March/April 1984, p. 22)

(One might add that this could apply just as well to the urban ghettos of North America.)

Lest I be misunderstood, let me conclude by saying that it has not been my intention to idealize Evangelical theology in the Two Thirds World nor endorse the tendency to generalize, avoid precision and even belittle the significance of Western theological debates. It is readily admitted that Evangelical theology in the Two Thirds World is represented by many voices with divergent views. Indeed, it has a long way to go, and in the process it will have a lot to learn from its counterpart in the One Third World. However, I submit that the ultimate test of any theological discourse is not erudite precision but transformative power. It is a question of whether or not theology can articulate the faith in a way that it is not only intellectually sound but spiritually energizing, and therefore, capable of leading the people of God to be transformed in their way of life and to commit themselves to God's mission in the world. As the Apostle Paul reminded the Corinthian church many years ago, "the kingdom of God is not talk but power" (I Cor. 4:20).

[Orlando E. Costas, "Evangelical Theology in the Two Thirds World," *TSF Bulletin,* September–October 1985, 7–12.]

49

Osadolor Imasogie

As the Christian missionary situation changed in this century with the end of colonialism, Baptist theology made exciting progress. Christians in many lands, especially in the two-thirds world of Africa and much of Asia and Latin America, found they could think for themselves with new freedom and creativity. Due to the heavy weight of past colonialism there, this change was particularly evident in Africa. Christian mission-ary theology, even when it tried not to do so, had inevitably been shaped by the Western context of the missionaries. Now this heritage might be recontextualized as African Christian theology. African customs, history, and culture generally were more clearly seen as theology's context. The African Independent Churches, beholden to no mission board (but often baptist in their ecclesiology) were now properly seen as communities of reference for local theology. The vitalism, communalism, and holism of traditional Africa were rediscovered (see Peter Kasanene's contribution to Charles Villa-Vicencio and John De Gruchy, eds., Doing Ethics in Context: South African Perspectives*). Osadolor Imasogie (1928–) em-bodied many of these strands in his life's work. A native of Nigeria, he studied in the United States at the Golden Gate Baptist Theological Seminary in Mill Valley, California (where he was McClendon's theology student), and earned a Ph.D. at Southern Baptist Seminary. Returning to Nigeria, he became the president of Nigerian Baptist Seminary in Ogbo-mosho, from which he is now retired. He served frequently in African and world positions of ecclesial leadership: he was the vice modera-tor of the Program for Theological Education of the World Council of Churches and was a vice president of the Baptist World Alliance. Notable among his writings is* Guidelines for Christian Theology in Africa; *some of its themes are reflected in the selection that follows. This paper was presented at the Silver Jubilee Annual Nigerian Religious Studies Conference of the University of Ibadan (Imasogie's birthplace) in 1991.*

African Theology

Prior to the late nineteen-fifties there was hardly any serious, documented attempt in non–North Atlantic countries to examine the theological methodologies underlying "received theological formulations" in order to unearth the subterranean factors that shaped these theologies. This blind spot in the development of theological thought was nurtured by a subtle theological imperialism of the North Atlantic church which was the "sending church," motivated by a legitimate missionary zeal to Christianize the world. North Atlantic church theologians came to the erroneous but dogmatic conclusion that their understanding of God as revealed in Christ had an identical universal application in all human situations and conditions, irrespective of different world views, self-understandings and consequent cultural expressions of religious experience.

In holding that view, North Atlantic church theologians inadvertently turned a blind eye to an historical, empirically verifiable truth, namely, that the Christian theology that came to them initially was hammered out in the encounter between the Jewish understanding of the Christ and the thought-patterns and views of the contemporary world. The testimony of church history is that, as Christianity spread to the gentile world, there was inevitably a conflict between the Jewish religious experience and expression and that of the Greek in the apprehension of the meaning of Christ and his gospel of salvation. This conflict resulted in several Church Councils convened to resolve the theological problems that were generated. The resultant theological formulations bear the marks of this symbiotic encounter which in turn was initially presented to the North Atlantic church.

Its failure to remember this history, however, made it unconscious of the fact that the theological formulation which it was presenting to the "receiving church" was not the formulation it received, but its own contextualization of that theology in its own response to the gospel in the light of its own philosophical, scientific and cultural self-understanding through the ages. The truth of this is substantiated by theological schools of thought, such as orthodox, neo-orthodox, liberal and liberation varieties....

The implication of this recaptured insight in theologizing is that for theology to be relevant and existentially satisfying, it must be attempting to answer the question which people are asking in the light of the gospel and their own self-understanding in their confrontation with the exigencies of life now and in wrestling with the ultimate meaning of such life. For Christian theology to be relevant, therefore, it must be incarnational in the sense that the Word must contemporaneously become Flesh in the culture, symbols and thought-patterns of a people. This is necessary for the Christ to be apprehended as God's answer to all human experiences as perceived by people in their own particular historical existence. Any failure to take full account of this fact in developing theological thought has serious negative consequences. It may lead to a wholesale adoption of theological answers formulated in a different culture with a different self-understanding. . . .

Theologizing as a spiritual reflection on the Bible as the inspired Word of God against the backdrop of a specific circumstance is a dynamic process in which the theologian listens intensely and reverently to the Holy Spirit. It is listening done in the light of the deepest human needs as perceived against the world view and self-understanding of the theologian. The theologian proceeds in this exercise from a basic faith commitment or presupposition. The faith commitment is that the living Word as mediated by the Holy Spirit stands ready behind the written word to grant to a spiritually sensitive and open searcher an insightful understanding of God's nature, his will and purpose in any human situation as perceived by the individual concerned. . . .

Theologizing, so understood, is a sacred venture and it must not be entered into with levity. It calls for the best in any one in terms of sensitivity to the presence of God as he seeks to interpret temporal reality in the light of God's self-disclosure which is never disclosed in black and white. Like a miner of any precious mineral embedded deep down in the rocks, the theologian, armed with a clear knowledge of the temporal situation and intently tuned into the divine wavelength, enters the quarry of God's Word with the understanding that the signals he receives come in and are interpreted through the antennae of his world view and thought patterns. That this is the model for theologizing is exemplified in the Bible itself, as demonstrated in the characteristics that distinguish one Bible writer from another. For instance, Pauline theology and his style of expression is quite different from Petrine theology and its thought form, yet they both encountered the same God in Christ.

It is clear from the above view of a theologian and the nature of this work that he cannot, as advocated by some, just select certain theological formulations of Christian doctrine as forged in the "crucible" of Western context, and either translate them into African concepts, or replace the identifiable Western cultural elements with equivalent African cultural elements. . . . The implication is that a theology that is simply passed from one cultural context to another, rather than being developed within that context, must always be irrelevant.

It is evident then that the task of developing African Christian theology, in addition to Christian commitment on the part of the theologian, calls for the possession of intellectual, biblical, and theological skills and a working knowledge of the principles of effective communication. Acquisition of skills in biblical and theological scholarship will enable him to analyze the historical and cultural circumstances in which the original message as enshrined in the Bible was revealed by God.

Assuming that the theologian has those skills, he is faced with the problem of how to communicate whatever revelation comes in that process. This is complicated for the African theologian by the sheer fact that he acquired his intellectual tools for biblical exegesis and theologizing within Western culture with all the implications that this connotes. That means that he has three different cultures to deal with: (i) the cultural setting in which the original biblical message was communicated; (ii) the Western culture in which he acquired his intellectual tools and the received theological formulations shaped by that culture; and (iii) the African culture through whose antennae he now must listen to apprehend God's message and to communicate it to his people.

If he is to be effective, he needs, beside his faith-commitment and intellectual tools, at least a basic knowledge of transcultural communication. The Westerner, indeed, needs this skill to communicate the original message within his own culture, but the problem is more complex for the African theologian, given the above analysis coupled with the truth that the current version of Christian theology in Africa is wrapped in Western culture. He is then faced with the subtle temptation to think that all that needs to be said is already contained in the package. This he must resist if he is to succeed in his attempt to develop theological thought.

Assuming that the budding theologian has surmounted these problems, he still has to wrestle with communication skills.... The bottom line is that the meaning an individual attaches to what I say is often more the product of his own extraction from what he "hears" me to be saying than the meaning I originally intended to convey. This being so, a wise communicator will strive to enter the frame of reference of his audience in order to know the types of symbols or stimuli that are derivable from the experiences which they both have in common. The attainment of this feat does not guarantee a one-to-one correspondence between the message and what is "heard" by the audience, because no two individuals ever have an identical experience of any reality. This effort does, however, help to narrow the difference between the message as presented and the meaning the hearer extracts from it. Paul definitely followed this principle when he decided to "be all things to all people in order to win some." To the Jews, Paul was a Jew, and to the Greeks he communicated as a Greek. He entered into the world of each audience so that he could participate in their "world" to be able to communicate with them from the vantage point of a "common world." Jesus Christ, as the Master Teacher, exemplified this principle because he taught deep spiritual truths, using the cultural symbols of the Jews in their everyday life which he and they shared in common.

Any African Christian theologian, taking appropriate note of what we have said above, is in a position to begin his theologizing, depending on his immediate need. For instance, (i) He may want to start with themes that are recurrent in African life and traditional religion as a springboard for presenting Christian theology as it relates to those themes; or (ii) He may want to write a systematic theology that is informed by African world views. From whichever angle he begins, he will discover that the overall frame of meaning of the African and his self-understanding, properly understood, will tilt the theological emphasis in the direction of certain themes, such as:

(a) *Emphasis on the meaning and efficacy of the sacrificial death of Christ and his present intercessory role.*

(b) *Apprehension of Christ, first and foremost, as the Victor and Liberator par excellence, who lives for ever to destroy the demonic forces wherever they are found.* This he does to liberate those committed to him from the stranglehold of evil forces as perceived by Africans.

(c) *Apprehension of Christ as the Cosmic Lord who supplies the total human needs within the context of each individual.* In this way, Christ's saving concern will be seen as transcending the narrow ambit of spiritual salvation to include liberation from human oppression and reconciliation not only with God but of each individual to his fellow human being and to nature.

(d) *A renewed emphasis on the role of the Holy Spirit in the day-to-day life of a Christian.* This has been neglected in the received theology imported from North Atlantic orthodox churches....

(e) *A new appreciation of the place of prayer in Christian life.* As a result of over-dependence on human technology, little more than lip-service has been paid to the importance of prayer in the received theologies. This has left the average Christian vulnerable to the attack of demonic forces for lack of a conscious sustained spiritual relationship with God. The contemporary attraction to new churches points to the void which this neglect has created in the spiritual life of most Christians.

In all these themes, it is quickly discovered that the African world view is very close to the one in which the original biblical revelation was mediated. Against that background, the following essential parameters emerge as sources for the development of Christian theology in Africa:

1. The living Christ
2. The inspired Word as mediated by the Spirit
3. A dynamic understanding of church tradition
4. The culture of the particular people
5. The life situation that calls forth the whole venture.

It is assumed throughout this paper that the theologian is a Christian who is sensitive to the presence of God as mediated by the Holy Spirit. With that faith-commitment he does his work, putting at the disposal of God all the intellectual skills discussed above. A faithful prosecution of this task will result in a Christian theology that bears the marks of African life, culture, and world view. Such an achievement will not only be spiritually satisfying to the Africans but will also enrich the whole corpus of Christian theology, since it will add freshness and new insights that have been ignored in other cultures because of the difference between such cultures and world views on the one hand and those of the Africans on the other. Above all, for the African Christian, Christianity will not be regarded as a foreign religion in which Christ is currently considered a foreign Savior who is not familiar with the perceived metaphysical forces in whose grips the African lives in fear and anxiety. A relevant theology that touches his whole life as he perceives it will lead to an existential apprehension of Christ and commitment to him as the incarnation of the one Creator God who created heaven and earth and all that are in them. The sufficiency of Christ may never be experienced by many African Christians until our theological formulations are thoroughly informed by the African cultural world view and perception within the context of the African situation, but when set in that context it is a bigger and more relevant Christ that they will discover.

[Osadolor Imasogie, "African Theology: The Development of Theological Thought in Nigeria," *The Baptist Quarterly* 34 (October 1993): 390–97. Used by permission.]

50

John Howard Yoder

This essay is here printed last, a bit out of chronological order, because the stature of baptist theologian John Howard Yoder (1927–97) makes his work a fit conclusion to this twentieth-century chapter. Thomas Kuhn, the historian of science, pointed out that while most scientific work is done by expanding and refining a particular scientific para-digm (Newtonian mechanics, for example), significant change in science comes only when a new paradigm (say, quantum mechanics) takes the place of the old. Applying this principle to theology, many have been skilled workers in the century just ending, but few have possessed the intellectual insight and spiritual power to develop a new theological paradigm. One of the few was John Yoder. His beginnings might not have predicted this. Yoder was born to Midwest Mennonite parents, at-tended public schools and denominational Goshen College, and took a Ph.D. in Basel while he was in Europe ministering to displaced and orphaned children after World War II. Subsequently, he served as a mis-sionary executive, taught at Goshen and in the Associated Mennonite Biblical Seminaries, Elkhart, Indiana, and from 1967 was professor at the University of Notre Dame in South Bend. His writing and speak-ing brought together three themes: One was the rebellion against liberal European (and American) theology — in this Yoder followed his teacher Karl Barth. A second theme grew from the work of Yoder's teacher at Goshen, influential Mennonite historian Harold S. Bender, who showed that the historic Anabaptists were not the horse-and-buggy tradition-alists contemporary Mennonites supposed, but had created a radical reformation. The third theme was the centrality of Scripture: this served to correct and expand the other two themes. Insisting on the congre-gational shape of the church, on believers baptism, and on Messianic pacifism (see his Nevertheless*), Yoder steadily maintained that we are the direct heirs of pre-Constantinian catholic Christianity. In this insis-tence he offended many current religious ethicists, whom he pointedly rebuked for ignoring Jesus (*The Politics of Jesus, *2d ed., 1994), and also offended many conservative evangelicals, who wanted him to sound more like Calvin. The present selection provides yet another side of Yoder: here we see the missionary strategist, aware of rising liberation* *theology, who believes that liberation theology's biblical basis is in need of correction and enlargement.*

Exodus and Exile: The Two Faces of Liberation

"Liberation" and "Revolution" are no longer the dominant slogans in the with-it culture that they were two years ago. If our concern were to join — or to resist — a fad, we would need to test in which churches and cultures the theme is still lively, and to develop a theological critique of faddism. That would not be an unworthy activity, especially since "peace" is also one of the words recently cheapened in the marketplace.

Yet for now my focus is more perennial. The fad may *formulate* our agenda and sensitize our ears, but the right answer will have to be as old as Israel. The fad may fade or it may bounce back — in Latin America in any case it is not waning — the question is perennial and so must the answer be.

In preparation for the Assembly of the Commission on World Missions and Evangelism of the World Council of Churches, which has since been held in Bangkok, a collection of documents was circulated in March 1972, under the heading *Salvation Today and Contemporary Experience.* In the Introduction to the collection, written by Thomas Wieser, we read:

> ... the contemporary quest for liberation, whether political, economic, cultural or personal, has for many Christians become the context for the Church's mission and its proclamation of salvation. The biblical story, too, especially in the Old Testament, is to a large extent a story of liberation. A number of interpreters see in this affinity a direct scriptural support for the present quest, contending that the biblical meaning of liberation must not be allowed to be "spiritualized." Others, however, warn that the Bible cannot be used to support what they believe to be a mere temporary political struggle.

The purpose of the following remarks is to foster critical thought in a context of ecumenical conversation where the statistical observation, "many Christians believe..." often takes the place of theological discourse about what Christians *ought* to believe. My good friend Tom Wieser is right; the dominant vogue of "with-it" theology since the late 1960s has been centered on liberation as the purpose of God. It seemed self-evident to many that the dominant biblical image is that of Exodus and that by taking off from the event of Exodus it would be possible in some broad sense to have a "biblical basis" for an especially committed Christian involvement in the political struggles of our age.

There have been a few thinkers asking careful questions about this very popular approach. José Míguez Bonino for instance has asked why it should be so obvious that out of the total biblical heritage it should be dominantly or even exclusively the picture of Exodus which becomes illuminating and motivating, without equal reference to exile, captivity, cross, the giving of the law, the taking of the land, the scattering of the faithful or other major themes of the biblical witness. To this observation our meditations shall return.

Another set of critics, thinking on the level of the methodology of proper theology, have expressed doubts about whether this approach was not a new and questionable form of natural theology, in the sense that the theologian tags after cultural styles trying to accredit his theology by proving that it can say what other people are saying anyway. Is not the relevance of a transcendent critique greater than the "search for relevance" of echoing contemporary styles?

Still another set of critics have been unconvinced about the clarity and solidity of liberation language when tested for its own sake. Do we really know what that liberating action is in which we should participate if we were to follow the mandate of Exodus? Are those particular guerrilla efforts which call themselves liberation fronts really liberated or liberating? Or are they a new form of cultural colonialism, imposing upon oppressed peoples yet another no less alien, no less self-righteous, no less violent form of minority rule in the name of a Marxist or a nationalist vision of independence? Have liberal democratic, or Marxist, or one-party nationalist movements demonstrated sufficient capacity to liberate that it should be the business of Christians to sanctify those programs by reverberating to them in theological idiom?

But all three of these criticisms — that on the level of biblical selectivity, that on the level of theological method, and the internal critique of the political ideology — have been expressed less sweepingly and less publicly than the liberation rhetoric, with the end result that it still seems useful to face that liberation language in its own right and to test the legitimacy of its claim to be echoing a biblical message.

Since that approach seems to get the most mileage by taking off homiletically from the story of Exodus, my invitation is to honesty in rhetoric. I am not doubting at all the propriety or the fruitfulness of leaping from the biblical language to the present; I am only asking that in that leap there be honesty and there not be unjustified selectivity.

We may take as expressive of the quintessence of the approach of which we speak a fragment of an address delivered by Mr. Poikail John George to the United States Conference for the World Council of Churches at Toledo, Ohio, in May 1972, on the theme, "Whence and

Whither World Council Studies?" This particular quotation is picked out not because it is unique or original but because it is representative, not only of a wide stream of thought and communication but also of an effort to encapsule that stream of thought in an interpretation of the work of the best known inter-church agency for thinking about these matters.

> The cries of God's people everywhere, the continents of Africa and Asia particularly, as well as those around us here at home, have reached the ears of the Lord when he tells us first of all to go and tell the Pharaohs of this world "Let my people go." Exodus must come before Mt. Sinai, liberation of God's people must come before communion with God.

The same centering upon the paradigm of Exodus is typical of the "Liberation Theology" of Latin America; Rubem Alves or Gustavo Gutiérrez show the same selectivity. The following sample from Alves will suffice:

> The Exodus was the generating experience of the conscience of the people of Israel. It constituted the structural center which determined their way of organizing their time and space. Observation: note that I am not simply saying that the Exodus is part of the content and conscience of the people of Israel. If it were that, the Exodus would be some information among much other. More than information it is the structural center because it determines the integrating logic, the basis of organization and the interpretation of the facts of the historical experience. Thus the Exodus does not go down as a past experience which took place at some well-defined time and space. It really becomes a paradigm for the interpretation of all of space and all of time.

Our respectfully critical response shall lead us in two directions: First, by staying with the Mosaic model itself, we shall test the appropriateness of its application by extension to the revolutionary rhetoric of our day; and secondly, we shall return to the question of Dr. Míguez Bonino: what of the other models?

Our first concern then is with the story itself. Assuming Exodus to be the valid model our authorities say it is, what does it say? What kind of "Revolution" does it represent?

First Observation: The Exodus Was Not a Program but a Miracle

The exodus experience is of a piece with the ancient Hebrew vision of Holy War. The wars of JHWH were certainly lethal, but they were not rationally planned and pragmatically executed military operations; they were miracles. In some of them (and the Red Sea is such a case), the Israelites, according to the record, did not even use arms. The combatant was not a liberation front or terrorist commando but JHWH himself.

The legitimate lesson of the wars of JHWH for contemporary ethics is not that "war must not be sin because God commanded it," but rather that because God declared and won it, entering a war was not a matter of human strategizing, and winning it was not an effect of preponderant human power. The Red Sea event is for the whole Old Testament the symbol of the confession that the Israelites do not lift a hand to save themselves. They only trust, and venture out. What the wars of JHWH point to in their fulfillment in Christ is not righteous bloodshed but non-violent non-conformity.

Second Observation: The Exodus Was Not a Takeover but a Withdrawal

The model of revolution most currently called "liberation" in our time is for subject peoples (or more accurately for a minority group acting in their name) to seize sovereignty within the land within which they are oppressed, taking that sovereignty away from a foreign power or from a feudal minority in their own society. This is very strikingly not what the Exodus did. Even though the princely figure of Moses would not have made unthinkable an effort to rise up and take over Egypt, as minority groups of invaders and infiltrators did many times in the history of the ancient Near East, this never is suggested as the story is told. Liberation means literally Exodus: going out. The only reason there must be plagues and ultimately death is that the hardness of Pharaoh's heart would not permit the Exodus to be peaceful.

It thus appears that if the appeal to the model of Exodus were to be taken seriously as a model rather than whimsically as a slogan, it would point far more clearly to the creative construction of relatively independent counter communities, and less to a seizure of power in the existing society. This counter community would be built with the sober expectation that it would call forth a violent reaction by the powers in control, and that in this violent reaction the powers might expose themselves to their own destruction. But the way it is done is very different. Moses was no Bonhoeffer. The old tyranny is destroyed not by beating it at its own game of intrigue and assassination, but by the way the presence of the independent counter community (and its withdrawal) provokes Pharaoh to overreach himself.

Third Observation: The Exodus Was Not a Beginning but a Culmination

There would never have been a Red Sea experience if there had not previously been the willingness to follow Moses out of Goshen. This was a leap of faith, made in common by the Hebrew people, not on the basis of any calculation of their capacity to destroy the Egyptians, but fully trusting in the transcendent intervention of Yahweh.

Before that there was the fostering of a sense of communal solidarity and vocation as the Israelites had survived through the plagues as an experience of their distinct identity as objects of God's care. There had already been a series of smaller experiences of liberation as a minority people.

Before the experience of preservation through the plagues, there had to be proclamation: preaching of the liberating purpose of God, addressed to both the oppressed and the oppressor, by the preacher Moses who had come from outside the situation with a message from God. That preaching involved a need to accredit (by signs) the status of the prophet; it did not involve planning processes to engineer liberation, or predicting either a possible or a utopian design for the liberated state. Its insistence was upon the identity and the saving purpose of JHWH.

Even before there could be a Moses and a people to hear him, there had to be an oppressed community affirming its identity by talking about the Fathers and the God of the Fathers. Moses would not have recognized his mandate, and his brethren would not have heard him, if there had not been a prior common history of recital amidst and despite the bondage. Goshen is prior to Exodus. The identity of the people, and even in a serious sense the identity of the liberating God himself were dependent upon the confessing community. The God of their Fathers could not have called them to the Red Sea if they had not already been a people under the whips. Peoplehood is the presupposition, not the product of Exodus.

The tragedy of many "liberation fronts" in our time is that the minority which claims to have the right to establish the new order leaps to righteous violence without passing through the experience of creating a supportive people that gives them the right of spokesmanship, or creating a coherent ethos that will permit their own leadership team to work together without recurrent new divisions. To say it another way, to be oppressed together is not sufficient to constitute a people. Nor being a people yet sufficient to be the people of God. Exodus is not a paradigm for all kinds of groups with all kinds of values to attain all kinds of salvation. Exodus is a particular form of withdrawal into insecurity.

Before there could be that preaching there was the overwhelming and solitary experience of the calling of the prophet at Horeb, which in the tradition merges with Sinai.

Before that there was the unique cultural experience that produced the man Moses, in his own personality an amalgam of three cultures, that of the Israelite slaves, the Egyptian court and the desert. As in the New Testament story the bi-cultural identity of the Hellenists and of Paul was the key to the missionary opening of the church, so in this case the tricultural identity of Moses is the prerequisite for the idea and the implementation of the Exodus.

Recent experience demonstrates equally well the dependence of valid freedom movements upon distinctive personal charisma or vocations. In fact such experiences are so tied to the personality of a Gandhi, a King, a Dolci, a Chavez, that mainstream churchmen and ethicists are prone to interpret that personal quality as an argument against either the ethics or the objectives of the movements. Yet both such current experiences and the model of Moses would lead us to affirm that dimension of distinct personal creativity and focus. To take it seriously would mean that both ecumenical administrators and academic ethicists should put their discussion of decision-making processes and their intellectual competence into a framework with more room for the distinct contemporary divine intervention which brings into the scene a man with a catalytic message.

The cultural uniqueness of a Moses reminds us of one dimension where the interpreters of current social change are conscious of the issue but the advocates of legitimate revolutionary violence are usually not. Gandhi was not a Hindu alone but also had a British and South African education and experience. Martin Luther King was not only a representative southern Black Baptist, he also had a doctorate from a liberal Methodist New England school. Whereas liberation movements, especially after the loss of a leader, may gladly appeal to national or tribal or racial identities to provide an audience or even a rationale for revolution, the possibility of true liberation would seem to be dependent upon a leader who is not simply the incarnation of distinct tribal cultural drive but who at the same time has been beyond that culture, can project a vision of liberation which includes the wider world, and can communicate the legitimacy of that liberation in a way that the power centers of the wider world cannot permanently close their ears to it. If we are, then, interested in fostering genuine liberation of oppressed peoples, our concern should be less to reiterate the classic moral legitimations of seditious violence, and more to facilitate transcultural educational experiences for leaders who at the same time would remain identified with their people and become mature and confident participants in the wider world.

Even before Moses, before his vocation could be conceivable and its implementation feasible, there was the memory of the slaves who knew that they were the children of Abraham and Isaac and Jacob and Joseph, who in their time had been in conversation with their own God, so that "the God of the Fathers" was known to them as a living memory in their past.

At this point we must note that Mr. George, in the quotation above, seems to equate indiscriminately the phrase "people of God" with any and all subject peoples. This is certainly counter to the meaning of Exodus, which is the experience of one oppressed and wandering minority, not of any and all suffering peoples. "The people of God" is not everybody.

Not only is "the people of God" not to be equated with any or every nation or any oppressed portion of any nation; it is equally illegitimate in Jewish or Christian theology to talk about "the people of God" at all outside the context of historical relationship to the calling of Abraham. The people of God is an elect people chosen by sovereign divine initiative from among many nations not because of any particular merit (not even because of any particular suffering), only because it pleased the Lord to demonstrate His goodness in that visible way. To transpose the motif of liberation out of that distinct historical framework and thereby also away from the distinct historical identity of the God of Abraham, Isaac, and Jacob, into some kind of general theistic affirmation of liberation, is to separate the biblical message from its foundation. There exists a liberation message only because of the particularity of the God of the fathers; Jews and Christians cannot talk confidently about liberation except in that connection.

Thus peoplehood is not the product of liberation; peoplehood with a history and a trust in the God who has led the fathers is prior to liberation. This has implications for contemporary thinking.

A. One is the awareness that what really makes liberation possible is the cultural fruit of generations prior to liberation which developed in the fiber of their cultural personalities a sense of those values which could then lead them together into new liberating engagement. Several generations of ex-slaves singing Black spirituals are the presupposition of a Martin Luther King. If you want to help liberate the people, it is not a service to tell them that violence is justified; it is a service to help them develop their spirituals.

B. A more negative conclusion to draw from the above observation is that there are times and places where no liberation is possible because no peoplehood has been formed. There are slums and *favelas*, there are perhaps whole racial groups and especially there are refugee cultures who have no songs, no historical self-understanding even as oppressed peoples. In such a context there is no base for liberating change either violent or non-violent. But in such cases the argument for violence is even less fitting. There is no possibility of constructing a new people on the other side of the Sea if peoplehood does not exist in Goshen.

Fourth Observation: Exodus Is Only the Beginning

The slogan "Exodus before Sinai" presupposes that "liberation" is a single and final event; that is the claim that justifies treating its violence as a legitimate ethical exception. Yet Sinai was to become the place of a new bondage. Exodus leads not to the promised land but to the desert, and in that desert Sinai is the place of a new enslavement motivated partly by loyalty to the values of Egypt.

What happened at Sinai was thus first the fall of Israel, unwilling despite the liberation just experienced to be patient in awaiting the Word of God from the mountain, preferring under Aaron's leading to take things into their own hands. If this has any relation to the question how we take the initiative in the combat against injustice it would hardly be in the direction of fostering the authority of any human community to define autonomously and implement violently its own liberation.

Let this reminder of the golden calf point us to the awareness that after slavery was left behind everything was yet to be done.

Mr. George in the text I quoted referred to Sinai as the symbol of the "communion with God" that can come only after liberation. Yet what happened at Sinai was not "communion with God" in any such "religious" sense, but rather the formal constitution of Israel as a community under the law. This consolidation of the community is part of the meaning of liberation. Not only the divinely chiseled tablets of Torah, but also the commonsensical borrowing from Moses' father-in-law of a model of grassroots government was needed for the mixed multitude to become a people. Exodus was the leap of faith but Sinai was its landing. Historically Exodus was the prerequisite of Sinai, but morally it is the other way 'round. Liberation is *from* bondage and *for* covenant, and *what for* matters more than *what from*.

If Exodus was the prerequisite of Sinai, in terms of movement, Sinai was the prerequisite of Exodus in terms of motive. It was the reason given to the Egyptians (Ex. 8:2, 20, 26f, etc.). Even before the arrival at Sinai, the column of fiery cloud was a symbol of Sinai leading them. Liberation after the model of Exodus issues in the reconstitution of community around the liberator. This is then another point at which to take the contemporary rhetoric seriously. Can the various "fronts" and "movements" which today call themselves "liberation" point us with any confidence, on the basis of experiences elsewhere or of the inherent quality of their vision, to a constitutive event *following* the "exodus" that will give substance to their separate existence? Or is not what is today called "liberation" sparked and justified only by the wrongness of the oppression it denounces, while sharing with the oppressor many of his ethical assumptions about how to deal with dissent, about the use of violence, about the political vocation of a liberating elite?

So liberation has its post-requisites as well as its prerequisites. It is not a revolution but only a threshold linking two phases of pilgrim peoplehood.

In giving this degree of attention to the fuller dimensions of the Exodus story I am not merely pressing a parable beyond its limits into allegory; I am unfolding the meaning of "story," as illumination of how we understand a God who works among men for their salvation. The primary resources for the Exodus are not located in the money or the weapons or the stratagems brought to bear at a particular point to destroy some tyrant. They are rather the prior developments of an identity, a common story, a sense of community and purpose and a set of expectations as to the shape of the divine initiative, without which the story of the Red Sea would have no frame and no point. It is not too much to suggest that as Christians talk about Exodus and liberation there is still need for the awareness of similar prerequisite dimensions. Clarifying the identity and mission of minorities might then be a better guide even today than efforts to take over the pagan society from above and make it a good.

Parallel to the alternative Exodus/Sinai Mr. George placed the pair liberation/communion. This is to suggest, as we noted, a distinct (and secondary) place for "communion with God," and thereby a replay of the polemic, frequent in World Council circles, against "pietism." But since Sinai is the formation of a community, the polarization in the phrase of Mr. George does not serve for the argumentative purpose which he intends. In order to speak to the present polarity represented by "pietism" on one hand and "social action relevance" on the other, Mr. George has made Sinai something it never was, namely "communion with God" in a "religious" sense. Or to reverse the parable, he has also made piety something it never was. It is a misreading of history to see in the worship patterns of pietism, or of any other group of real cultic concern, an idea of distance from the world that seeks authenticity through heightened separateness. Pietism — and valid sacramental worship for that matter too — celebrates the working of God within history in the creation of community; it is not a self-contemplating mystical exercise.

Fifth Observation: Exodus Is an Exception

I noted before in an introductory way that the preference of modern preachers for the model of Exodus can be challenged as an unexplained and arbitrary selectivity. Why is there not some broader review of all the great events which Scripture puts in the light of the Word of God at work: the taking of Canaan, the pluralism of the age of the judges, the rise and fall of the Kingdom, the dividing of the Kingdom, exile...(to stay with the Old Testament)? But the point here to be made is much more than that by concentrating on Exodus something or other is omitted; it is that the elements omitted are relevant. Israel's experience with trying Kingship and even empire, and ultimately abandoning them, is part of the lesson of the biblical witness; exile and the abandoning of nationhood as the form of peoplehood are prophetically interpreted as the way of JHWH. Ezra and Nehemiah reestablish the community precisely without national sovereignty.

Most relevant to the "oppressed people" theme, and most in tension with the juxtaposition of exodus language with modern guerrilla theology, is the fact that over against the paradigm of leaving Egypt and destroying Pharaoh on the way we find in the Old Testament, more often, another model of how to live under a pagan oppressor. It is the way of Diaspora. This is the model taken over by the New Testament Church, and the model as well of two millennia of rabbinic Judaism.

> These are the words of the letter which Jeremiah the prophet sent from Jerusalem to the elders of the exiles, and to the priests, the prophets, and all the people whom Nebuchadnezzar had taken into exile from Jerusalem to Babylon....Build houses and live in them; plant gardens and eat their produce. Take wives and have sons, and give your daughters in marriage, that they may bear sons and daughters; multiply there, and do not decrease. But seek the welfare of the city where I have sent you into exile, and pray to the LORD on its behalf, for in its welfare you will find your welfare. For thus says the LORD of hosts, the God of Israel: Do not let your prophets and your diviners who are among you deceive you, and do not listen to the dreams which they dream, for it is a lie which they are prophesying to you in my name; I did not send them, says the LORD. (Jeremiah 29:1, 5–9)

The exile of Judah had begun with the move to Babylon of the King, the Queen mother, the temple treasurer, the artisans, and the priests and prophets.

But young Zedekiah, left in Jerusalem to rule the rest, got ideas of liberation. Prophets like Shemaiah encouraged him to believe that Judah was still where the action was. "Don't settle down in Babylon, you'll soon be back." "Jerusalem will again be free." These are the deceiving diviners Jeremiah denounces; these are the lying dreams.

"You'll be in Babylon a long time. Seek the peace of *that* city. Identify your welfare with theirs. Abandon the vision of statehood."

There is only one Exodus in the history of Israel; but on the other hand there are several samples of the way a moral minority can "seek the welfare of the city." This advice of Jeremiah was given in the age of the exile after the defeat of Josiah: but we have the same stance taken by Joseph in Egypt, by Daniel under Nebuchadnezzar, and by Mordecai in Persia and even in a sense by Jonah in Nineveh. Far from destroying the pagan oppressor, the function of the insightful Hebrew is to improve that pagan order so as to make it a resource of protection for the people and viable as a government. He does this in ways which force the pagan power to renounce its self-mythologizing religious claims and to recognize the higher sovereignty that is proclaimed by the Hebrew Monotheist. This Joseph/Daniel/Mordecai model is so characteristic in the Hebrew Bible that we have to claim that this kind of elite contribution to the reforming of the existing order is more often the fitting contribution to the pagan community than any theocratic takeover. The complement to the Exodus of the counter community is not a *coup d'etat* by the righteous oppressed, but rather the saving message of the resident minority.

Closing the Circle

Let us return to the last words of our opening quotation from Thomas Wieser. Some want to identify "the contemporary quest for liberation" with biblically understood "salvation in contemporary experience," to ward off "spiritualization." Others don't want the Bible to be used to support a "mere temporary political struggle." We have not been testing the latter position, though it may be pointed out on the basis of our parable that to object that salvation should not be "temporary" is not an argument. According to most other definitions salvation in the form which can be experienced today is also temporary. It would be a more serious reproach that it is "temporal"; i.e., lacking in or denying transcendent depth which goes beyond the present power struggle. This is what Mr. George was trying to safeguard by retaining "Sinai" as symbol of "communion with God" subsequent to "Exodus" as liberation. I personally doubt that either way of safeguarding transcendence above the temporal is adequate or Biblical; either Mr. George's two-step dialectic or Wieser's critique of the "merely temporal."

More important in our present concern, however, is that Wieser's phrasing misframes the criticism of the "liberation" focus as "spiritualizing" or as avoidance of the "political." It will be visible from the above that that is not my criticism at all. It is rather that the "many Christians" in question have borrowed from the Bible an imagery or language of liberation, but have avoided learning from the biblical story anything about the meaning of liberation. (Elsewhere Wieser, like Rubem

Alves, shows sympathetic insight into the "people-in-exile" alternative. The "typical" quotations used here should not be seen as representative of their authors' best wisdom.)

The form of liberation in the biblical witness is not the guerrilla campaign against an oppressor culminating in his assassination and military defeat, but the creation of a confessing community which is viable without or against the force of the state, and does not glorify that power structure even by the effort to topple it.

The content of liberation in the biblical witness is not the "nation-state" brotherhood engineered after the take-over but the covenant-peoplehood already existing because God has given it, and sure of its future because of the Name ("identity") of God, not because of a coming campaign.

The means of liberation in the biblical witness is not prudentially justified violence but "mighty Acts" which may come through the destruction at the Red Sea — but may also come when the King is moved to be gracious to Esther, or to Daniel, or to Nehemiah.

From the "Believers Church" perspective, the "neo-constantinian" approach that blesses a going political movement, and the "spiritualist" approach that downgrades the "temporal" are mirror images. Both use biblical imagery more for window dressing than for content, both avoid seriously dealing with the way in which pilgrim peoplehood is projected by the Bible as the shape of salvation in any age.

So let us abandon the spiritual/secular polarity and ask what kind of spiritual historicity reflects the shape of liberating grace.

We will be farthest along if instead of following only the pattern of going out into the wilderness — which the Exodus taken alone really was — and instead of dreaming of a theocratic takeover of the land of bondage by the brick makers — which ideological exegesis has sought to do with the Exodus imagery — we seek more creatively to describe what can best be done by creative minorities in a society they don't control. Let us observe:

- Jesus and his movement;
- Christians in the second century Roman Empire;
- the Jews in medieval Europe;
- the Pennsylvania Dutch in colonial America;
- the Indians in East Africa;
- the Chinese in South Asia;
- the unmeltable ethnics in contemporary America.

The line runs from the ten good men who could have saved Sodom through Paul in his boat saving his captors on the way to Rome.

You know the famous description in the (second century?) *Letter to Diognetus:*

They reside in their respective countries, but only as aliens. They take part in everything as citizens and put up with everything as foreigners. Every foreign land is their home, and every home a foreign land.... They spend their days on earth, but hold citizenship in heaven. They obey the established laws, but in their private lives they rise above the laws. They love all men, but are persecuted by all.... They are reviled, and they bless; they are insulted and render honor. Doing good, they are penalized as evildoers;... and those who hate them are at a loss to explain their hatred.

In a word: what the soul is in the body, that the Christians are in the world.

We need not bother debating the questionable metaphysics of body/soul dualism to confirm the writer's point about the church/society dualism. What the world most needs is not a new Caesar but a new style. A style is created, updated, projected, not by a nation or a government, but by a people. This is what moral minorities can do — what they have done time and again.

Liberation is not a new King; we've tried that. Liberation is the presence of a new option, and only a non-conformed, covenanted people of God can offer that. Liberation is the pressure of the presence of a new alternative so valid, so coherent, that it can live without the props of power and against the stream of statesmanship. To be that option is to be free indeed.

[John Yoder, "Exodus and Exile: The Two Faces of Liberation," *Cross Currents* 23 (Fall 1973–74): 297–309.]

God of Grace and God of Glory

God of grace and God of glory, on thy people pour thy power;
Crown thine ancient church's story; bring her bud to glorious flower.
Grant us wisdom, grant us courage, for the facing of this hour,
For the facing of this hour.

Lo! the hosts of evil round us scorn thy Christ, assail his ways!
Fears and doubts too long have bound us; free our hearts to work
    and praise.
Grant us wisdom, grant us courage, for the living of these days,
For the living of these days.

Cure thy children's warring madness, bend our pride to thy control;
Shame our wanton, selfish gladness, rich in things and poor in soul.
Grant us wisdom, grant us courage, lest we miss thy kingdom's goal,
Lest we miss thy kingdom's goal.

Set our feet on lofty places; gird our lives that they may be
Armored with all Christ-like graces in the fight to set men free.
Grant us wisdom, grant us courage, that we fail not man nor thee,
That we fail not man nor thee.

Save us from weak resignation to the evils we deplore;
Let the search for thy salvation be our glory evermore.
Grant us wisdom, grant us courage, serving thee whom we adore,
Serving thee whom we adore.

Harry Emerson Fosdick (1930)

Selected Baptist Voices

(A Wider List)

Theologian	Dates	Dominant Context
Petr Chelčický	c. 1390–c. 1460	Late medieval Bohemia and the Holy Roman Empire; Czech Brethren
Balthasar Hubmaier	c. 1480–1528	Medieval sacramental and magisterial reformation theology; South German Anabaptism
Michael Sattler	c. 1490–1527	Swiss and South German Anabaptism; Schleitheim Confession; persecution and martyrdom
Menno Simons	c. 1496–1561	Reaction to Münster; Dutch and North German Anabaptism (*Doopsgesinden*)
Conrad Grebel	c. 1498–1526	Erasmian humanism; early Swiss Anabaptism
Claesken Gaeledochter	?–1559	Dutch Anabaptism; persecution and martyrdom
Dirk Philips	1504–68	Dutch and North German Anabaptism (*Doopsgesinden*); moderate use of ban
Peter Riedemann	1506–56	East German Anabaptism (Hutterites); communal life
Thomas Helwys	c. 1550–c. 1615	Separatism; Arminianism and millenarianism; General Baptists in England
John Smyth	c. 1570–1612	Separatism; General Baptists and Waterlander Mennonites
Anne Hutchinson	1591–1643	New England Puritanism; antinomian controversy; expanding role of women
Hanserd Knollys	c. 1599–1691	First and Second London Confessions of Particular Baptists; Puritanism; millenarianism
Roger Williams	1603–83	New England Puritanism; religious freedom in Rhode Island; typology
John Milton	1608–74	European and English literary tradition; Puritanism and Independent religion

Theologian	*Dates*	*Dominant Context*
William Kiffin	1616–1701	First and Second London Confessions of Particular Baptists; closed communion
John Bunyan	1628–88	Puritanism and Congregationalism; Civil War; English popular prose; jail experience; open communion
Thomas Grantham	1634–92	English General Baptists; catholic and primitive Christianity; Arminianism and Calvinism
Benjamin Keach	1640–1704	Westminster theology; Second London Confession of Particular Baptists; pro-hymn singing
Robert Barclay	1648–90	George Fox and English Quakerism; the Inner Light and Arminianism
Alexander Mack	1679–1735	Palatinate Reformed Christianity; Anabaptists; Church of the Brethren
John Gill	1696–1771	Hyper-Calvinism; deist and anti-trinitarian controversies in Great Britain
Johannes Stinstra	1708–90	Socinianism and English rationalism; Dutch Mennonite culture
Isaac Backus	1724–1806	Great Awakening; New Light Congregationalism and Separate Baptists; struggle for religious liberty
Hannah Lee Corbin	1728–83	Great Awakening; American Revolution; Separate Baptists; human rights and women's suffrage
Andrew Fuller	1754–1815	Evangelical Calvinism and Baptist Missionary Society in England
John Leland	1754–1841	Revolutionary era struggle for religious liberty; Jefferson and Madison; natural rights
William Carey	1761–1834	Baptist Missionary Society; British colonial India
Robert Hall Jr.	1764–1831	Industrial Revolution; Arminianized Calvinism v. Enlightenment skepticism
William Miller	1782–1849	New England revivalism and Adventism; "the Great Disappointment"
Lucretia Mott	1793–1880	Hicksite Quakerism; abolitionism and women's suffrage
Alexander Campbell	1788–1866	Second Awakening; denominationalism and restorationism; common sense philosophy

Theologian	Dates	Dominant Context
John Leadley Dagg	1794–1884	Common sense philosophy and the Princeton theology; Southern culture
Francis Wayland	1796–1865	American democracy and populism; Baptist higher education; the Triennial Convention
Nat Turner	1800–31	Slavery and abolitionism; mysticism and apocalypticism
John Nelson Darby	1800–82	Dispensationalism; Plymouth Brethren
Noah Davis	1804–66	Unsegregated black-and-white Southern revivalism
James Robinson Graves	1820–93	Strict denominationalism; Landmarkism
Alvah Hovey	1820–1903	Conservative Calvinism and the Princeton theology
Sytse Hoekstra	1822–98	Kant and Protestant liberalism; Dutch Mennonite culture
James Petigru Boyce	1827–88	Common sense philosophy and the Princeton theology; Southern culture
Ellen G. White	1827–1915	Millerism; Seventh-Day Adventism
Charles Haddon Spurgeon	1834–92	Victorian England; British evangelicalism; Down-Grade controversy
Rufus Perry	1834–95	Persisting African models of religion and culture; emancipation experience; consolidation of black Baptists
Augustus Hopkins Strong	1836–1921	Conservative Calvinism; modern science and Scripture scholarship; German idealism
Alice Armstrong	1846–1928	Southern Baptist Convention; Woman's Missionary Union
James Milton Carroll	1852–1931	Baptist colleges; Landmarkism
William Bishop Johnson	1858–?	Jim Crow Southern culture; formation of the National Baptist Convention
William Newton Clarke	1841–1911	American modernism; Schleiermacher's liberalism
Edgar Young Mullins	1860–1928	Post Civil War South; Christian experience; James and Schleiermacher; fundamentalism v. modernism
William Bell Riley	1861–1947	Fundamentalism, dispensationalism and anti-Semitism

Theologian	*Dates*	*Dominant Context*
Walter Rauschenbusch	1861–1918	German-American education; urban industrialization and poverty; the Social Gospel and democracy
Helen Barrett Montgomery	1861–1934	Northern Baptist Convention; foreign missions; women's suffrage
Shailer Matthews	1863–1941	Chicago modernism; the Social Gospel; ecumenism
Curtis Lee Laws	1868–1946	Fundamentalism; Northern Baptist Convention; religious liberty
Douglas Clyde Macintosh	1877–1948	Canadian evangelicalism; Chicago modernism and empiricism; pacifism
Walter Thomas Conner	1877–1952	Southwestern revivalism; Strong, Rauschenbusch, and Mullins; neo-orthodoxy and biblical theology
Harry Emerson Fosdick	1878–1969	Modernism and popular American culture; social gospel; pacifism
Eberhard Arnold	1883–1935	Radical biblicism and discipleship; Johann and Christoph Blumhardt; new Hutterian Brethren in Germany
Muriel Lester	1883–1968	Britain in World Wars I and II; peace movement and Gandhi; urban poverty
Benjamin Elijah Mays	1894–1984	Post-Reconstruction and pre-civil rights South; all-black higher education
Howard Thurman	1900–81	Black Baptist churches South and North; still-segregated American higher education and civil rights movement; radical biblicism
Robert C. Walton	1905–85	Waning industrialism and growing secularism in Britain; seventeenth-century Baptist heritage; ecumenism; sacramentalism
John Christian Wenger	1910–95	Mennonite culture in America; biblical theology
Clarence Leonard Jordan	1912–69	Southern (segregated) culture; literary biblicism; radical communitarianism
Carl F. H. Henry	1913–	Fundamentalism; philosophical idealism; emerging evangelicalism
Dale Moody	1915–92	Evangelicalism; European neo-orthodoxy; biblical theology
Bernard Ramm	1916–92	Abraham Kuyper, Karl Barth, and emerging evangelicalism

Theologian	Dates	Dominant Context
Edward John Carnell	1919–67	Fundamentalism v. modernism; evangelical "orthodoxy"
C. Norman Kraus	1924–	Cross-cultural experience in America, Asia, and Africa; disciples perspective
James Wm. McClendon Jr.	1924–	Linguistic philosophy and speech-act theory; baptist ecumenism and systematics
Gordon Kaufman	1925–	Kant; American liberalism; historicism; science and technology
James Leo Garrett	1925–	Evangelical and Reformed theology; cumulative Baptist tradition
Takashi Yamada	1926–	World War II; Mennonite missions; Japanese pastorates
John Howard Yoder	1927–97	Harold Bender and the radical reformation renaissance; Karl Barth; catholic biblicism
James Deotis Roberts	1927–	Liberation and reconciliation in the African-American experience
Osadolor Imasogie	1928–	Baptist foreign missions; Nigerian independence; African spirituality
Martin Luther King Jr.	1929–68	Black Baptist Southern churches and colleges; civil rights movement; Vietnam War
Harvey Cox	1929–	Secularity; liberation theology; Baptist pluralism
Millard Erickson	1932–	New evangelicalism; moderate Calvinism
C. René Padilla	1932–	Latin American evangelical and liberation theology; two-thirds world social concerns
Clark H. Pinnock	1937–	Canadian and British evangelicalism; inerrancy; Arminianism
Thomas Finger	1942–	Reformed theology; Mennonite tradition
Orlando Costas	1942–87	Caribbean and Middle-American evangelical and liberation theology; two-thirds world social concerns
Luis N. Rivera	1942–	Latin American evangelical and liberation theology; violence and colonialism; missions and evangelism

For Further Study

Fifteenth and Sixteenth Centuries

Primary and Biographical Sources

Petr Chelčický

Vojta, Vaclav. *Czechoslovak Baptists.* Minneapolis: Czechoslovak Baptist Convention in America and Canada, 1941.

Wagner, Murray L. *Petr Chelčický.* Scottdale, Pa.: Herald, 1983.

Conrad Grebel

Bender, Harold S. *Conrad Grebel c. 1498–1526: The Founder of the Swiss Brethren, Sometimes Called the Anabaptists.* Scottdale, Pa.: Herald, 1950.

Grebel, Conrad. "Letter to Thomas Münzer by Conrad Grebel," trans. Walter Rauschenbusch, *American Journal of Theology* 9 (1905): 91–99.

Harder, Leland, ed. *The Sources of Swiss Anabaptism: The Grebel Letters and Related Documents.* Scottdale, Pa.: Herald, 1985.

Balthasar Hubmaier

Bergsten, Törsten. *Balthasar Hubmaier: Anabaptist Theologian and Martyr.* Trans. I. Barnes and W. Estep. Valley Forge, Pa.: Judson, 1978.

Pipkin, H. Wayne, and John H. Yoder, eds. and trans. *Balthasar Hubmaier: Theologian of Anabaptism.* Scottdale, Pa.: Herald, 1989.

Michael Sattler

Sattler, Michael. "The Schleitheim Confession." *Baptist Confessions of Faith.* Ed. William L. Lumpkin. Valley Forge, Pa.: Judson, 1969, 22–31.

Snyder, C. Arnold. *The Life and Thought of Michael Sattler.* Scottdale, Pa.: Herald, 1984.

Yoder, John H., ed. and trans. *The Legacy of Michael Sattler.* Scottdale, Pa.: Herald, 1973.

Menno Simons

Klaassen, Walter. *No Other Foundation: Commemorative Essays on Menno Simons.* Bethel, Kans.: Bethel College Press, 1962.

Littell, Franklin H. *A Tribute to Menno Simons.* Scottdale, Pa.: Herald, 1961.
Simons, Menno. *The Complete Writings of Menno Simons.* Scottdale, Pa.: Herald, 1956.
———. *The Complete Works of Menno Simon* [*sic*]. Leonard Verduin and J. C. Wenger, eds. and trans. Elkhart, Ind.: John F. Funk and Brother, 1871.
———. *Confession of My Enlightenment, Conversion, and Calling: The New Birth and Who They Are Who Have the Promise.* Lancaster, Pa.: Lancaster Mennonite Historical Society, 1996.

Claesken Gaeledochter

van Braght, Thieleman J., ed. *The Bloody Theater or Martyrs Mirror of the Defenseless Christians.* Scottdale, Pa.: Herald, 1990.

Dirk (Dietrich) Philips

Philips, Dietrich. *Enchiridion or Handbook of the Christian Doctrine and Religion.* Trans. A. B. Kolb. Elkhart, Ind.: Mennonite Publishing Co., 1910.
———. *The Writings of Dirk Philips, 1504–1568.* Scottdale, Pa.: Herald, 1992.

Secondary Sources

Bender, Harold. *The Anabaptist Vision.* Scottdale, Pa.: Herald, 1944.
Estep, William R. *The Anabaptist Story: An Introduction to Sixteenth-Century Anabaptism.* 3d ed. Grand Rapids: Eerdmans, 1996.
Klaassen, Walter. "Anabaptism." In *Mennonite Encyclopedia.* Scottdale, Pa.: Herald, 1990, 5:23–26
The Mennonite Encyclopedia: A Comprehensive Reference Work on the Anabaptist-Mennonite Movement. 5 vols. Vols. 1–4: Hillsboro, Kans.: Mennonite Brethren Publishing House, 1955; vol. 5: Scottdale, Pa.: Herald, 1990.
Pipkin, H. Wayne, ed. *Essays in Anabaptist Theology.* Elkhart, Ind.: Institute of Mennonite Studies, 1994.
Snyder, C. Arnold. *Anabaptist History and Theology.* Scottdale, Pa.: Herald, 1995.
Snyder, C. Arnold, and Linda A. Hecht, eds. *Profiles of Anabaptist Women: Sixteenth Century Reforming Pioneers.* Waterloo, Ont.: Wilfrid Laurier University Press, 1996.
van Braght, Thieleman J., ed. *The Bloody Theater or Martyrs Mirror of the Defenseless Christians.* Scottdale, Pa.: Herald, 1990.
Williams, George H. *The Radical Reformation.* 3d ed. Kirksville, Mo. Sixteenth Century Journal Publishers, 1992.

Seventeenth Century

Primary and Biographical Sources

John Smyth

Coggins, James R. *John Smyth's Congregation: English Separatism, Mennonite Influence, and the Elect Nation*. Scottdale, Pa.: Herald, 1991.

Whitley, W. T., ed. *The Complete Works of John Smyth*. Cambridge: Cambridge University Press, 1915.

Thomas Helwys

Helwys, Thomas. *A Short Declaration of the Mystery of Iniquity*. London: n.p., 1612. Reprint Macon, Ga.: Mercer University Press, 1998.

Payne, Ernest A. *Thomas Helwys and the First Baptist Church in England*. London and Dublin: Baptist Union of Great Britain and Ireland, 1966.

Thomas Grantham

Grantham, Thomas. *Christianismus Primitivus: Or The Ancient Christian Religion*. London: Francis Smith, 1678.

John Bunyan

Bunyan, John. *The Pilgrim's Progress*. Puritan Edition. New York: Revell, 1903.

Hill, Christopher. *A Turbulent, Seditious, and Factious People*. New York: Random House, 1988.

Sharrock, Roger, ed. *The Miscellaneous Works of John Bunyan*. 12 vols. London: Oxford University Press, 1976–89.

Wakefield, Gordon. *Bunyan the Christian*. Glasgow: HarperCollins Religious, 1992.

John Milton

Hill, Christopher. *Milton and the English Revolution*. New York: Viking, 1977.

Milton, John. *John Milton: Complete Poems and Major Prose*. Ed. Merrit Y. Hughes. New York: Macmillan, 1957.

———. *Paradise Lost*. London: B. White and Son, 1793. Reprint New York: Heritage Press, 1940.

Parker, William R. *Milton: A Biography*. Oxford: Clarendon, 1968.

Roger Williams

Gaustad, Edwin S. *Liberty of Conscience: Roger Williams in America*. Grand Rapids: Eerdmans, 1991.

Williams, Roger. *The Complete Works of Roger Williams*. 7 vols. New York: Russell and Russell, 1963.

Anne Hutchinson

Adams, Charles F., ed. *Antinomianism in the Colony of Massachusetts Bay.* Boston: The Prince Society of Massachusetts, 1894.

Hall, David D., ed. *The Antinomian Controversy, 1636–1638: A Documentary History.* Durham, N.C.: Duke University Press, 1990.

Williams, Selma R. *Divine Rebel: The Life of Anne Marbury Hutchinson.* New York: Holt, Rinehart, and Winston, 1981.

Secondary Sources

Crosby, Thomas. *A History of the English Baptists.* 4 vols. London: n.p., 1740.

Hill, Christopher. *Milton and the English Revolution.* New York: Viking, 1977.

Holifield, Brooks E. *The Covenant Sealed: The Development of Puritan Sacramental Theology in Old and New England, 1570–1720.* New Haven, Conn.: Yale University Press, 1974.

Juster, Susan. *Disorderly Women: Sexual Politics and Evangelicalism in Revolutionary New England.* Ithaca, N.Y.: Cornell University Press, 1994.

Miller, Perry. *The New England Mind: The Seventeenth Century.* New York: Macmillan, 1939.

Thompson, Philip E. "A New Question in Baptist History: Seeking a Catholic Spirit Among Early Baptists." *Pro Ecclesia* 8 (Winter 1999): 51–72.

Eighteenth Century

Primary and Biographical Sources

John Gill

Gill, John. *A Body of Doctrinal Divinity.* 3 vols. London: n.p., 1769–70. Reprint Atlanta: Turner Lasseter, 1950.

Haykin, Michael A. G., ed. *The Life and Thought of John Gill, 1697–1771: A Tercentennial Appreciation.* New York: Brill, 1997.

Andrew Fuller

Clipsam, Ernest. "Andrew Fuller: A Study in Evangelical Calvinism." *Baptist Quarterly* 20 (1963): 214–25.

Fuller, Andrew. *The Works of the Rev. Andrew Fuller.* 8 vols. Ed. John Ryland. London: B. J. Holdsworth, 1824.

Kirby, Arthur. "Andrew Fuller: Evangelical Calvinism." *Baptist Quarterly* 15 (1954): 195–202.

Ryland, John. *The Work of Faith, the Labour of Love, and the Patience of Hope, Illustrated: In the Life and Death of the Rev. Andrew Fuller.* Charlestown, Mass.: Samuel Etheridge, 1818.

William Carey

Beck, James R. *Dorothy Carey: The Tragic and Untold Story of Mrs. William Carey.* Grand Rapids: Baker, 1992.
Carey, William. *An Enquiry into the Obligations of Christians to Use Means for the Conversion of the Heathens.* Leicester: n.p., 1792.
George, Timothy. *Faithful Witness: The Life and Mission of William Carey.* Nashville: Broadman, 1995.

Isaac Backus

Backus, Isaac. *Church History of New England from 1620 to 1804.* Philadelphia: American Baptist Publication Society, 1844.
————. *Isaac Backus on Church, State, and Calvinism.* Ed. William G. McLoughlin. Cambridge: Belknap Press, 1968.
Grenz, Stanley. *Isaac Backus, Puritan and Baptist.* Macon, Ga.: Mercer University Press, 1983.

Hannah Lee Corbin

Armes, Ethel, ed. *Stratford Hall: The Great House of the Lees.* Richmond: Garrett and Massie, 1936.
Lumpkin, William L. "The Role of Women in 18th Century Baptist Life." *Baptist History and Heritage* 8 (July 1973): 158–67.
Roberts, Carey, and Rebecca Seely. *Tidewater Dynasty: The Lees of Stratford Hall.* New York: Harcourt Brace Jovanovich, 1981.

John Leland

Broadway, Mikael N. "The Ways of Zion Mourned." Ph.D. diss., Duke University, 1993, chapter 5.
Leland, John. *Discourses on Various Subjects.* London: Johnson and Dodsley, 1768–69.
————. *The Writings of the Late Elder John Leland.* Ed. L. F. Green. New York: G. W. Wood, 1845. Reprint New York: Arno, 1969.

Secondary Sources

Faust, Clarence H., and Thomas H. Johnson, eds. *Jonathan Edwards, Representative Selections.* Rev. ed. New York: Hill and Wang, 1962.
Gaustad, Edwin S. *The Great Awakening in New England.* New York: Harper and Brothers, 1957.
Haykin, Michael A. G. *One Heart and One Soul: John Sutcliff of Olney, His Friends, and His Times.* Darlington, Durham, U.K.: Evangelical Press, 1994.
Outler, Albert, ed. *John Wesley.* New York: Oxford University Press, 1964.

Smith, John E., et al., eds. *A Jonathan Edwards Reader*. New Haven, Conn.: Yale University Press, 1995.

Underwood, A. C. *A History of the English Baptists*. London: Carey Kingsgate, 1947.

Whaling, Frank, ed. *John and Charles Wesley*. New York: Paulist, 1981.

Nineteenth Century

Primary and Biographical Sources

Robert Hall

Hall, Robert, Jr. *The Works of Robert Hall*. 6 vols. London: Henry G. Bohn, 1851.

John Leadley Dagg

Dagg, John L. *Manual of Church Order*. Charleston: Southern Baptist Publication Society, 1858.

———. *Manual of Theology*. Charleston, S.C.: Southern Baptist Publication Society, 1858.

Alice Armstrong

Armstrong, Alice. *Special Obligation of Woman to Spread the Gospel*. Baltimore: Maryland Baptist Mission Room, 1888.

Sorrill, Bobbie. *Annie Armstrong, Dreamer in Action*. Nashville: Broadman, 1984.

Charles Haddon Spurgeon

Day, Richard Ellsworth. *The Shadow of the Broad Brim*. Philadelphia: Judson, 1955.

Spurgeon, Charles H. *The Autobiography of Charles H. Spurgeon*. Chicago: Revell, 1900.

———. *Spurgeon's Sermons*. 20 vols. New York: Sheldon, Gould, and Lincoln, 1857–60. Reprint Grand Rapids: Zondervan, n.d.

Noah Davis

Davis, Noah. *A Narrative of the Life of Rev. Noah Davis, A Colored Man*. Baltimore: John F. Weishampel Jr., 1859.

Francis Wayland

Crane, Theodore R. *Francis Wayland: Political Economist as Educator*. Providence: Brown University Press, 1962.

Wayland, Francis. *The Elements of Moral Science*. New York: Sheldon and Co., 1834.

———. *A Memoir of the Life and Labors of Francis Wayland, Late President of Brown University*. New York: Sheldon and Co., 1867.

———. *Notes on the Principles and Practices of Baptist Churches*. New York: Sheldon and Co., 1856.

Alexander Campbell

Campbell, Alexander. *The Christian System*. Cincinnati: H. S. Bosworth, 1866.

Garrison, Winfred E. *An American Religious Movement*. St. Louis: Christian Board of Publication, 1945.

Wrather, Eva J. *Creative Freedom in Action: Alexander Campbell on the Structure of the Church*. St. Louis: Bethany House, 1968.

James Milton Carroll

Carroll, James M. *The Trail of Blood*. Lexington: Ashland Baptist Church, 1931.

Nat Turner

Gray, Thomas R. *The Confessions of Nat Turner*. Baltimore: Lucas and Deaver, 1831. Reprint Boston and New York: St. Martin's Press, 1996.

Oates, Stephen B. *The Fires of Jubilee: Nat Turner's Fierce Rebellion*. New York: Harper and Row, 1975.

Rufus L. Perry

Perry, Rufus L. *The Cushite: The Descendents of Ham from Noah to the Christian Era*. Springfield, Mass.: Willey and Co., 1893.

William Bishop Johnson

Johnson, William Bishop. *The Scourging of a Race*. 7th ed. Washington: Beresford, 1904.

Washington, James M. *Frustrated Fellowship: The Black Baptist Quest for Social Power*. Macon, Ga.: Mercer University Press, 1986.

Curtis Lee Laws

Bradbury, John W. "Curtis Lee Laws and the Fundamentalist Movement." *Foundations* 5 (January 1962): 52–58.

———. "Curtis Lee Laws, DD, LLD: An Appreciation." *The Watchman Examiner* 34 (18 July 1946): 29.

Laws, Curtis Lee. *The Fiery Furnace and Soul Liberty*. Baltimore: First Baptist Church of Baltimore, 1904.

Secondary Sources

Harnack, Adolf. *What Is Christianity?* New York: Harper and Row, 1957.

Hatch, Nathan. *The Democratization of American Religion.* New Haven, Conn.: Yale University Press, 1989.

Holifield, E. Brooks. *The Gentlemen Theologians.* Durham, N.C.: Duke University Press, 1978.

Leonard, Bill J. "Getting Saved in America: Conversion Event in a Pluralistic Society," *Review and Expositor* 82 (Winter 1985): 111–27.

————. *God's Last and Only Hope: The Fragmentation of the Southern Baptist Convention.* Grand Rapids: Eerdmans, 1990.

Mathews, Donald G. *Religion in the Old South.* Chicago: University of Chicago Press, 1977.

Shenk, Wilbert. *Anabaptism and Mission.* Scottdale, Pa.: Herald, 1984.

Welch, Claude. *Protestant Thought in the Nineteenth Century.* 2 vols. New Haven, Conn.: Yale University Press, 1972, 1985.

Twentieth Century

Primary and Biographical Sources

Augustus Hopkins Strong

Strong, Augustus H. *Systematic Theology.* 3 vols. Philadelphia: Judson, 1907.

Wacker, Grant. *Augustus H. Strong and the Dilemma of Historical Consciousness.* Macon, Ga.: Mercer University Press, 1985.

Edgar Young Mullins

Ellis, William E. *A Man of Books and a Man of the People.* Macon, Ga.: Mercer University Press, 1985.

Mullins, Edgar Y. *The Axioms of Religion.* Philadelphia: Baptist Publication Society, 1908.

————. *The Christian Religion in Its Doctrinal Expression.* Philadelphia: Judson, 1917.

Helen Barrett Montgomery

Cattan, Louise A. *Lamps Are for Lighting: The Story of Helen Barrett Montgomery and Lucy Waterbury Peabody.* Grand Rapids: Eerdmans, 1972.

Montgomery, Helen B. *The King's Highway: A Study of the Present Conditions on the Foreign Field.* West Medford: Central Committee on the Study of Foreign Missions, 1915.

————. *Women in Eastern Lands.* New York: Macmillan, 1910. Reprint New York: Garland, 1987.

Walter Rauschenbusch

Handy, Robert T., ed. *The Social Gospel in America, 1870–1920.* New York: Oxford University Press, 1966.
Minus, Paul. *Walter Rauschenbusch: American Reformer.* New York: Macmillan, 1988.
Rauschenbusch, Walter. *Christianity and the Social Crisis.* New York: Macmillan, 1907. Reissued Louisville: Westminster/John Knox, 1992.
———. *A Theology for the Social Gospel.* New York: Macmillan, 1917. Reissued Nashville: Abingdon, 1945.

Douglas Clyde Macintosh

Macintosh, Douglas C. *Theology as an Empirical Science.* New York: Macmillan, 1919. Reprint New York: Arno, 1980.
Warren, Preston. *Out of the Wilderness: Douglas Clyde Macintosh's Journeys through the Grounds and Claims of Modern Thought.* New York: Peter Lang, 1989.

Harry Emerson Fosdick

Fosdick, Harry E. *Christianity and Progress.* London: Nisbet and Co., 1922.
———. *The Living of These Days: An Autobiography.* New York: Harper, 1956.

Muriel Lester

Deats, Richard. *Ambassador of Reconciliation.* Philadelphia: New Society Publishers, 1991.
Dekar, Paul. *For the Healing of the Nations.* Macon, Ga.: Smyth and Helwys, 1993.
Lester, Muriel. *It Occurred to Me.* New York: Harper, 1937.
———. *A Way of Life.* New York: National Preaching Mission Committee, FCC in America, 1930.
———. *Ways of Praying.* Nashville: Publication House M.E.C.S., n.d.

Walter Thomas Conner

Conner, Walter T. *The Cross in the New Testament.* Nashville: Broadman, 1954.
———. *The Gospel of Redemption.* Nashville: Broadman, 1945.
———. *Revelation and God.* Nashville: Broadman, 1936.
Newman, Stewart A. *W. T. Conner: Theologian of the Southwest.* Nashville: Broadman, 1964.

Robert C. Walton

Walton, Robert C. *The Gathered Community.* London: Carey Press, 1946.

———. *Jesus Christ: History, Interpretation, and Faith*. London: National Society, 1956.

Carl F. H. Henry

Henry, Carl F. H. *Confessions of a Theologian: An Autobiography*. Waco: Word, 1986.
———. *God, Revelation, and Authority*. 6 vols. Waco: Word, 1976–83.
———. *The Uneasy Conscience of Modern Fundamentalism*. Grand Rapids: Eerdmans, 1947.

Howard Thurman

Johnson, Alonzo. *Good News for the Disinherited: Howard Thurman on Jesus of Nazareth and Human Liberation*. Lanham, Md.: University Press of America, 1997.
Smith, Theophus. "Howard Thurman," in *A New Handbook of Christian Theologians*, ed. Donald W. Musser and Joseph L. Price. Nashville: Abingdon, 1996, pp. 440–48.
Thurman, Howard. *Jesus and the Disinherited*. Nashville: Abingdon Press, 1949.
———. *With Head and Heart: The Autobiography of Howard Thurman*. New York: Harcourt Brace Jovanovich, 1979.

Benjamin Elijah Mays

Mays, Benjamin E. *Born to Rebel: An Autobiography*. New York: Scribner, 1971.
———. *The Negro's God, as Reflected in His Literature*. New York: Negro Universities Press, 1969.
Mays, Benjamin E., and Joseph W. Nicholson. *The Negro's Church*. New York: Russell and Russell, 1969.

Martin Luther King Jr.

King, Martin L., Jr. *Why We Can't Wait*. New York: Harper and Row, 1963.
McClendon, James Wm., Jr. *Biography as Theology: How Life Stories Can Remake Today's Theology*. 2d ed. Philadelphia: Trinity Press International, 1990.
Oates, Stephen B. *Let the Trumpet Sound: A Life of Martin Luther King, Jr.* New York: HarperCollins, 1982.
Washington, James M., ed. *A Testament of Hope: The Essential Writings and Speeches of Martin Luther King, Jr.* San Francisco: HarperSanFrancisco, 1991.

Takashi Yamada

Yamada, Takashi. "Reconciliation in the Church." *Proceedings of the 9th Mennonite World Conference,* Curitiba, Brazil, 1972.
Yoshinobu, Kumazawa, and David L. Swain, eds. *Christianity in Japan, 1971–1990.* Tokyo: Kyo Bun Kwan, 1991.

Dale Moody

Moody, Dale. *Spirit of the Living God: What the Bible Says about the Spirit.* Nashville: Broadman, 1976.
———. *The Word of Truth: A Summary of Christian Doctrine Based on Biblical Revelation.* Grand Rapids: Eerdmans, 1981.

Orlando E. Costas

Costas, Orlando E. *Christ Outside the Gate: Mission Beyond Christendom.* Maryknoll, N.Y.: Orbis, 1982.
———. *The Church and Its Mission: A Shattering Critique from the Third World.* Wheaton, Ill.: Tyndale House, 1974.
———. "Evangelical Theology in the Two Thirds World." *TSF Bulletin* 9 (September-October 1985): 7–12.
———. *Liberating News: A Theology of Contextual Evangelization.* Grand Rapids: Eerdmans, 1989.

Osadolor Imasogie

Imasogie, Osadolor. "African Theology." *The Baptist Quarterly* 34 (October 1993): 390–97.
———. *Guidelines for Christian Theology in Africa.* Achimota, Ghana: Africa Christian Press, 1983; Ibadan: Oxford University Press, 1986.
Saunders, Davis L. *A History of the Baptists in East and Central Africa.* Th.D. Dissertation. Southern Baptist Theological Seminary, 1973.

John Howard Yoder

Nation, Mark Thiessen. *A Comprehensive Bibliography of the Writings of John Howard Yoder.* Goshen, Ind.: Mennonite Historical Society, Goshen College, 1997.
Yoder, John H. *For the Nations: Essays Public and Evangelical.* Grand Rapids: Eerdmans, 1997.
———. *He Came Preaching Peace.* Scottdale, Pa.: Herald, 1985.
———. *Nevertheless.* 2d ed. Scottdale, Pa.: Herald, 1992.
———. *The Politics of Jesus: Behold the Man! Our Victorious Lamb.* Grand Rapids: Eerdmans, 1972, rev. 1994.
———. *The Priestly Kingdom.* Notre Dame, Ind.: University of Notre Dame Press, 1984.
———. *The Royal Priesthood: Essays Ecclesiological and Ecumenical.* Ed. Michael G. Cartwright. Grand Rapids: Eerdmans, 1994.

Secondary Sources

Chopp, Rebecca. *The Power to Speak*. New York: Crossroad, 1989.

Dorrien, Gary J. *Soul in Society: The Making and Renewal of Social Christianity*. Minneapolis: Fortress, 1995.

Ford, David F., ed. *The Modern Theologians: An Introduction to Christian Theology in the Twentieth Century*. 2d ed. Oxford: Blackwell, 1997.

Gilligan, Carol. *In a Different Voice*. Cambridge: Harvard University Press, 1982.

Grenz, Stanley J., and Roger E. Olson. *Twentieth-Century Theology: God and the World in a Transitional Age*. Downers Grove, Ill.: InterVarsity Press, 1992.

Hudson, Winthrop. *Baptist Concepts of the Church*. Chicago: Judson, 1959.

McClendon, James Wm., Jr. *Biography as Theology: How Life Stories Can Remake Today's Theology*. 2d ed. Philadelphia: Trinity Press International, 1990.

Murphy, Nancey, and James Wm. McClendon Jr. "Distinguishing Modern and Postmodern Theologies," *Modern Theology* 5:3 (April 1989).

Scarry, Elaine. *The Body in Pain*. New York: Oxford, 1985.

Torbet, Robert G. *Venture of Faith*. Philadelphia: Judson, 1955.

Villa-Vicencio, Charles, and John De Gruchy, eds. *Doing Ethics in Context: South African Perspectives*. Maryknoll, N.Y.: Orbis, 1994.

Washington, Joseph R., Jr. *Black Religion: The Negro and Christianity in the United States*. Boston: Beacon, 1964.

Some Additional Resources: All Periods

Adams, John Quincy. *Baptists, The Only Thorough Reformers*. New York: Sheldon and Co., 1876.

Basden, Paul, ed. *Has Our Theology Changed?* Nashville: Broadman and Holman, 1994.

Bebbington, David W. "Baptist Thought" in *The Blackwell Encyclopedia of Modern Christian Thought*, ed. Alister E. McGrath. Cambridge: Basil Blackwell, 1993, 28–30.

———. *Evangelicalism in Modern Britain*. London: Unwin Hyman, 1989.

Brackney, William H., ed. *Baptist Life and Thought: 1600–1980*. Valley Forge, Pa.: Judson, 1983.

Conyers, A. J. "The Changing Face of Baptist Theology." *Review and Expositor* 95 (1998): 21–38.

Durnbaugh, Donald F. *The Believers' Church: The History and Character of Radical Protestantism*. Scottdale, Pa.: Herald, 1985.

Freeman, Curtis W. "Can Baptist Theology Be Revisioned?" *Perspectives in Religious Studies* (Fall 1997): 273–310.

Furr, Garry, and Curtis W. Freeman, eds. *Ties that Bind: Life Together in the Baptist Vision*. Macon, Ga.: Smith and Helwys, 1994.

George, Timothy. "New Dimensions in Baptist Theology" in *New Dimensions in Evangelical Thought*, ed. David S. Dockery. Downers Grove, Ill.: InterVarsity Press, 1998, 137–47.

George, Timothy, and David S. Dockery, eds. *Baptist Theologians*. Nashville: Broadman, 1990.

Hudson, Winthrop, ed. *Baptist Concepts of the Church*. Chicago: Judson, 1959.

Jeter, Jeremiah B. *Baptist Principles Reset*. Richmond, Va.: The Religious Herald, 1901.

Latourette, Kenneth Scott. *A History of Christianity*. New York: Harper and Brothers, 1953.

Leonard, Bill J. "Getting Saved in America: Conversion Event in a Pluralistic Society." *Review and Expositor* 82 (Winter 1985): 111–27.

———. *God's Last and Only Hope: The Fragmentation of the Southern Baptist Convention*. Grand Rapids: Eerdmans, 1990.

Loewen, Howard John. *One Lord, One Church, One Hope, and One God: Mennonite Confessions of Faith in North America, An Introduction*. Elkhart, Ind.: Institute of Mennonite Studies, 1985.

Lumpkin, William L. *Baptist Confessions of Faith*. Valley Forge, Pa.: Judson, 1969.

Marsden, George. *Fundamentalism and American Culture*. New York: Oxford University Press, 1980.

McBeth, H. Leon. *The Baptist Heritage: Four Centuries of Baptist Witness*. Nashville: Broadman, 1987.

———. *Women in Baptist Life*. Nashville: Broadman, 1979.

McClendon, James Wm., Jr. *Ethics: Systematic Theology, Volume I*. Nashville: Abingdon, 1986.

———. *Doctrine: Systematic Theology, Volume II*. Nashville: Abingdon, 1994.

Moody, Dwight A. "Contemporary Theologians Within the Believers' Church" in *The People of God*, eds. Paul Basden and David S. Dockery. Nashville: Broadman, 1991, 333–54.

Noll, Mark A., et al. *Evangelicalism*. New York: Oxford University Press, 1994.

Shenk, Wilbert R., ed. *Anabaptism and Mission*. Scottdale, Pa.: Herald, 1984.

Stanley, Brian. *A History of the Baptist Missionary Society, 1792–1992*. Edinburgh: T. & T. Clark, 1992.

Stealey, Sydnor L., ed. *A Baptist Treasury*. New York: Thomas Y. Crowell Co., 1958.

Sykes, Stephen. *The Identity of Christianity*. Philadelphia: Fortress, 1984.

Tull, James E., *Shapers of Baptist Thought*. Valley Forge, Pa.: Judson Press, 1972.

Underwood, A. C. *A History of the English Baptists*. London: Carey Kingsgate, 1947.

Wardin, Albert R., ed. *Baptists Around the World: A Comprehensive Handbook*. Nashville: Broadman and Holman, 1995.

Weber, Timothy P. *Living in the Shadow of the Second Coming: American Premillennialism (1875–1925)*. New York: Oxford University Press, 1979.

Yoder, John Howard, and James Wm. McClendon, Jr. "Christian Identity in Ecumenical Perspective," *Journal of Ecumenical Studies* 27:3 (Summer 1990).

INDEX